Praise for *Deep Living*

"This is a book that makes possible deeper intimacy with yourself, by bringing together the practical and the profound. *Deep Living* offers many pathways for the active practice of presence in the exploration of what it means to be fully human. Using the Enneagram to radically and compassionately shift the reader's understanding of him or herself, Roxanne Howe-Murphy offers wise guidance to an inside-out process that teaches readers how to refocus their attention and build upon their innate capacity for living with more joy, aliveness, and fulfillment. We recommend this book as an important source of spiritual guidance to support and accelerate your own awakening."

> – DON RICHARD RISO AND RUSS HUDSON,
> Authors, *The Wisdom of the Enneagram and Personality Types*

"*Deep Living* is profound transformational inner-directed therapy…"

> – NANCY LORRAINE,
> Senior Reviewer, *The Midwest Book Review*

"The malaise of our time is shallow-mindedness, superficiality, and abbreviated awareness. *Deep Living* by Dr. Roxanne Howe-Murphy offers a compelling antidote."

> – MICHAEL J. GELB,
> Author, *How to Think Like Leonardo da Vinci*

"*Deep Living* does, indeed, transform your relationship to everything that matters, starting with that most important relationship—the one between you and YOU. Read this book to understand yourself more fully and appreciate yourself more deeply. Read it to move beyond your current, outworn, habitual patterns to the freshness of being authentically present in the moment. Read it to better understand the other relationships in your life. Read this book. You'll be so glad you did!"

– MARCIA CANNON, PhD, MFT,
Author, *The Gift of Anger*

"SHE is a modern mystic!!!! Roxanne Howe-Murphy captures the deepest beat of life and translates it for the ears, eyes, and hearts of all who claim readiness to what life can be about. To live deeply may not be for the faint of heart, but there is much Light and Liberation in the pilgrimage to our very essence. The Enneagram, as Roxanne sees it and utilizes it, is a sacred path, an expedition in love of Self and of others. To know one's inherent nature is to be realized and truly free."

– HARRIETT SIMON SALINGER, MCC, LCSW,
Executive and Personal Coach, Spiritual Director, and Certified Seeker,
Los Angeles, CA

"If you are ready to witness yourself with both eyes wide open, to understand why you act the way you do (even when it is ineffective), and to learn how to live in alignment with your true essence, this is the book for which you have been waiting. Roxanne shares her wisdom, compassion, and deep coaching expertise, leaving you with the gift of deep living. A must read for anyone ready to begin or continue their personal life journey!"

– SUZANNE GLAZER,
Assistant Director, Executive CoachingLeadership Initiative,
Harvard Business School

"Soul excavation is hard work—but the Enneagram is a powerful tool and Roxanne Howe-Murphy a very able guide to this process. For spiritual directors—or anyone who is ready to pay attention to the call of authenticity in their lives, and allow themselves to be truly present—*Deep Living* provides a map to interior freedom and more genuine relationships with God, Self, and others. This book challenges the reader to move to new levels of self awareness and healing, providing concrete steps and real help for true transformation."

SUZANNE BUCKLEY,
Director, Mercy Center,
Editor, *Sacred Is the Call—The Transformational Work of Spiritual Direction Programs for Personal and Professional Growth*

"In *Deep Living*, Roxanne Howe-Murphy combines her wisdom and experience as a coach with the profound wisdom of the Enneagram. She lays down a multi-perspective frame for each of the nine personality types, enabling us to see ourselves through many lenses—from our most disabling patterns to our greatest gifts. She also provides accessible, type-specific practices that support movement out of those patterns and into a more integrated way of being. Those who truly take this work to heart, however, learn to create the conditions for an inner shift that can peel away the need for self-limiting personal stories and judgments and open to a life lived with greater possibility and presence. A very worthwhile read!"

– LAUREN VANETT,
Founder and Director, Core Strengths Coaching Program,
San Francisco State University

"Roxanne Howe-Murphy's book is truly one of the greatest gifts to come forth from the Enneagram world! In *Deep Living*, Roxanne provides one of THE most accessible (simple and understandable) descriptions of the spiritual journey yet published. She has made understandable and simple what generally defies language—the experience of the soul. I'm finding myself wanting to give this book to almost everyone I know and care about. What a gift!"

– LYNDA ROBERTS,
Faculty, The Enneagram Institute,
Treasurer, The Board of the International Enneagram Association,
Project Management Professional

"*Deep Living* clearly and concisely describes the fundamentals of personal growth and spiritual awareness. This could easily be a textbook for a college class focused on the emotional and social intelligence required to excel personally and professionally. It will transform your life."

– DOUG MOORE, PhD,
Psychologist and Life Coach

"Finally, here is a book that reveals how to achieve inner peace by first tuning into your body's brilliance. Roxanne Howe-Murphy's *Deep Living* is a book that you will reference again and again. Using the ancient wisdom of the Enneagram, Roxanne skillfully navigates a life path of happiness and fulfillment. You will find veil after veil lifting to reveal your true and beautiful self."

– VICKY CRUZ, DC,
Speaker, Facilitator, and Instructor,
NET Certified Practitioner,
Cofounder, Full Moon Healing Center

"Roxanne Howe-Murphy's latest book, *Deep Living*, is an absolute treasure! Based on the ancient wisdom of the Enneagram, this book provides us with a detailed map of our personality, our frequently occurring behavioral patterns, and the deep living transformation process. Roxanne gifts us with the necessary tools to become 'pattern detectives'; thereby enabling us to shift from seeing our patterns in life's rearview mirror, to noticing and catching ourselves in the midst of enacting our patterns, to seeing them just before we engage in them. Roxanne's book is a rich resource that I will turn to time and again to access wisdom and understandings about personality and behavioral patterns, and to move towards greater awareness and presence."

– JANET SMITH, PhD,
Director, The Education Institute,
University of Canberra, Australia

"*Deep Living* is a valuable resource to unlock our personality structure and to transform into our evolutionary nature."

– PATT LIND-KYLE,
Author, *Heal Your Mind, Rewire Your Brain*

"The Enneagram is a powerful resource for gaining a unique doorway into self-knowledge, an essential benefit for people in the midst of career change and other life transitions. As you dive into *Deep Living*, you'll uncover nuances about your own innate capacities, gifts, and beliefs that will help you discover ways you can deepen the way you live your life."

– CAROL MCCLELLAND, PhD,
Author, *The Seasons of Change: Using Nature's Wisdom to Grow through Life's Inevitable Ups and Downs*

Deep Living

TRANSFORMING YOUR RELATIONSHIP
TO EVERYTHING THAT MATTERS
THROUGH THE ENNEAGRAM

Roxanne Howe-Murphy, EdD

Deep Living

Transforming Your Relationship to Everything that Matters through the Enneagram

By Roxanne Howe-Murphy, EdD

Published by Enneagram Press, Santa Fe, NM
Copyright ©2013 Roxanne Howe-Murphy, EdD
All rights reserved.

Library of Congress Control Number: 2012951591

Publisher's Cataloging-in-Publication Data

Howe-Murphy, Roxanne, 1949-

    Deep living : transforming your relationship to everything that matters through the Enneagram.

    p. cm.

Includes bibliographical references and index.

ISBN 9780979384714 (paper)

    1. Self-actualization (Psychology)   2. Spiritual life.   3. Peace of mind.
4. Enneagram. I. Howe-Murphy, Roxanne, 1949— II. Title.

BF637.S4 2013

158.1

Dedicated to
Jim Murphy, PhD
*for his kind and loving spirit, for being a
teacher of and advocate for human dignity,
and for being the love of my life.*

And dedicated to the memory of
Don Richard Riso
*Enneagram pioneer, teacher, mentor,
colleague, and friend for his profound
contributions to awakening consciousness.*

Table of Contents

Foreword

When *Chicken Soup for the Woman's Soul* was first published in 1996, my co-authors and I saw how deeply people craved nourishment for their souls. Almost two decades later, it's clear that deep longing hasn't diminished. Wherever I speak around the world, the #1 complaint I hear from audiences is that even though they have much to be grateful for, they often feel a profound and perplexing emptiness inside.

Despite years of personal development, reading self-help books, attending workshops, or even taking "happy drugs," so many people still feel disconnected from themselves. Our modern society has trained us to look outside of ourselves for our meaning and fulfillment. We *know* there is something more—a peace within—and it beckons us.

In *Deep Living*, Roxanne Howe-Murphy identifies that urge for inner-connectedness as *our soul's call to what is real within*—the truth that lies beneath our stories about ourselves. Thankfully, she also shows us how we can navigate the journey back to our essence.

A brilliant and soulful guide, Roxanne is a master of the ancient wisdom of the Enneagram—a tool that sheds light on how we unknowingly tend to move away from our deepest nature, while also showing us what our greatest latent gifts are. With crystal clarity, Roxanne helps us recognize the patterns we've come to rely upon that no longer serve us. With her guidance, we discover a whole new realm of gifts that come out of greater self-understanding and self-embracing.

In 1998, I first heard of the Enneagram from an old friend, therapist Chris Wright, who raved about the insights he'd gained from it. Having been a seeker as long as I can remember, I was intrigued. The Enneagram explained my behavior and my life in a much deeper way than any of the other personality "typing" tools I'd learned and taught in my workshops and corporate trainings. Since then, the Enneagram has been invaluable in helping me understand my own fears, motivations, and longings, as well as those of my family, friends, and colleagues. In recent years, I've been delighted to see the Enneagram gain more widespread recognition in the corporate world, as well as in the field of personal development. *Deep Living* now takes the use of the Enneagram to a whole new level.

In *Deep Living*, Roxanne introduces the radical idea that personal change and evolution is not about fixing something that's broken in you— rather, it's about *being with yourself in an entirely new way*. I personally know how vital that is. During one particularly challenging time in my marriage years ago, I went to Hawaii by myself for a few weeks to work on a book project. I started seeing how every complaint and criticism that I had in my marriage was a reflection of the way I treated myself. If I was hard on my husband, it was because that's how I treated myself. Something internally shifted, and I discovered how to treat myself differently, with self-compassion. It wasn't about fixing something in me, but about embracing all parts of me. As I've come to love myself more, everything in my world has changed. *Deep Living* builds on this paradigm and provides stunning insights that will challenge your concept of what personal development means.

Roxanne encourages us to look at the issues that keep coming up in our life. Do you ever think, "Oh no, not *this* again!" *Deep Living* will help you see why you revisit the same old patterns and more importantly, how you can resolve them at long last. This profound message is delivered in an easy-to-digest manner so that you can incorporate it into your life right away.

Based on my own research in the field of positive psychology for my book *Happy for No Reason,* I've seen how happiness is, in fact, a physiological state of being. Neuroscience confirms this. In *Deep Living,* Roxanne shows us how to use the Enneagram as a powerful tool to shift our neural pathways to support our greater happiness and fulfillment.

A great paradox is revealed in this book. Ironically, our automatic patterns unconsciously drive us to a false sense of what will feed or nourish us. They move us in the opposite direction of what will create lasting happiness for us. We think, "if I just get enough of this," then I'll be happy. Each of the Enneagram archetypes has a different "this" that we think will make us happy—but it will NEVER satisfy our deeper longing. In *Deep Living,* we discover our false pursuits, and we're given understanding and a strategy to experience real satisfaction. This remarkable approach to fulfillment is nothing short of a revelation!

Roxanne has dedicated her life to helping others transform. I am moved by her commitment and passion for guiding people on their journey of healing and awakening.

May this book guide you to experience greater unconditional happiness and the deep nourishment your soul has been yearning for.

— Marci Shimoff

Preface

What is DEEP LIVING?

You've just been given the invitation to Deep Living. Perhaps this sounds intriguing, but what does it actually mean? How's deeply living different from everyday life?

My Thread

We all have a thread that runs through our lives. It shows itself when we pay attention to our inner voice.

I grew up on a farm just outside a small midwestern town of twenty-five hundred people. On some levels, it was a simple life. Although I haven't lived on a farm since I was eighteen, to this day I relish my deep connection to the land and the sky.

For as long as I can remember, I've been drawn to the big spiritual questions of life. I have vivid memories of sitting on the well-worn steps of an old farm building as a child, gazing into the night sky, filled with awe. As I wondered about my place as a human being in the vast and mysterious universe, feeling both inspired and scared about my own life, I intuitively knew that this experience of being part of a bigger universe was core to life.

Not knowing who to talk with about this wondrousness and the adventure ahead, this innate knowing eventually receded. As happens for so many of us, over time, I lost track of the sacred and majestic nature of life, and I got on with what I thought life must be about.

I was fortunate, for, along the way, I've had many teachers, some of whom I sought and others who seemingly just appeared. I unexpectedly came to know one during my early professional years working at the United Cerebral Palsy Association. There, a young woman about my age named Terri gave me a lesson in the power of the human spirit. She was a wheelchair user who lived in a nursing home due to the extent of her physical care needs. With no speech or control of any of her limbs, she enthusiastically became the subject of a documentary which she wrote over months and months, pointing to one letter at a time using a headstick. She named the video "Don't Just Look." The subtitle could have been, "See Deeply at What's Inside; Recognize Who Is Here." I feel her influence still.

For over twenty years, I had the great pleasure of serving on the faculty at three different universities where I taught dozens of undergraduate and graduate courses in leisure theory, recreation therapy, leadership, wellness, and research. With a diverse student body, my most important challenge was to discover ways to deeply connect with students so that they might have a meaningful and real learning and growth experience. I co-authored what turned out to be a leading-edge textbook, *Therapeutic Recreation: An Ecological Perspective*; contributed sometimes controversial articles in professional, juried literature; served as an editor for professional journals; gave numerous keynote speeches; and presented hundreds of workshops and conference sessions to professional groups.

But after a period of time, something began gnawing at me and it wouldn't quit. I was in my late thirties when my inquiry into the not-so-visible aspects of life—the deep terrain of the human soul—was reignited. I still have a clear image of a particular longtime professor walking on campus with slumped shoulders, his head down. I sensed the waning of his life energy and decided I would not let my own life force be diminished in this way.

I had told my students at the beginning of every semester that I was in the classroom because I loved it, stating that if and when I felt that the fit was no longer right, I would leave. There, I claimed my intention to live from the inside out.

While life was really pretty good, I eventually felt an inner pull toward something else. The source of my inner discomfort could not be resolved even by the love of my husband, my passion for teaching, and my wonderful friendships. It was time to act. But what did that mean?

The first step was to resign from the university.

It was a painful but necessary separation, and I didn't expect what happened next. On this mighty mission to live from the inside out, I discovered that what I found inside lacked direction and purpose. I was filled with self-doubt and fear and was almost paralyzed by depression. If this is what my inside had to offer me, it could only mean big trouble. At some level I trusted my choice to resign, and at another level, serious questions remained. I had read a lot about overcoming limiting ideas, feelings, and other distortions of the small self. And now here they were in blazing glory; obstacles that I just couldn't get over. These experiences held a great deal of energy, and magnified something that I had long held as a secret—there was something innately wrong with me.

So, I did everything I could to fix myself—not knowing that this would automatically take me in the wrong direction, as "fixing" isn't a useful strategy. (But more on this topic in the book!) While this was an important time in my development, one experience nearly left me unraveled. I attended a workshop with a well-known self-help speaker and author. With some desperation, I told her about my insistent lack of direction, and she recommended that I not sleep until I got clarity! Had I followed her recommendation, I certainly would be dead.

With more self-exploration and research in various opportunities, I discovered work that deeply resonated with my heart, education, professional and life experience, and belief in the human capacity: coaching. I created my coaching and education company in 1997 and had the great fortune to work with wonderful people, most of whom were leaders in their own fields and in the midst of some kind of life transition.

Still, I sensed that something core was waiting to be uncovered.

Shock Waves

About the same time, I was reintroduced to a body of work that I had learned about a decade before, but hadn't pursued. This reintroduction sent shock waves through what I had taken to be "me."

I learned that my whole inner experience was largely the result of an interrelated web of psychological, emotional, physical, spiritual, and neuro-biological systems which were wired in a specific, unique way. I could hardly believe that what felt like my very private, personal experience was shared with about one-ninth of the world's population, and there were eight other seemingly private interpretations of life that were quite different from mine. What I felt had been missing in my life really wasn't, and was—shockingly—right in front of my nose...a part of the fabric of my life that I hadn't had the lens to see. I came to realize that external influences certainly interacted with and influenced each of our lives in unique ways, but they did not cause my state of being. And they certainly did not need to determine my future.

It was the first half hour on the first night of a weeklong training on the Enneagram with Don Riso and Russ Hudson. In advance, I had decided to attend just this one training to give me further insights for myself and perhaps my clients. As one not prone to having sudden alternative reality experiences, I was again shocked when I felt the touch of invisible hands on my shoulders, gently shaking me, and heard the emphatic words, "This is your work. ...This is your work!" With tears rolling down my face, I had no idea what that meant, but I said yes.

Over time, it became crystal clear that I had long mistaken what it meant to live from the inside out. In fact, I had significantly misinterpreted what the inside actually was.

I began to see that I had interpreted each of my inner feelings, thoughts, and ideas as a truth of my inner experience. They weren't. How stunning to discover that it was the conditioned reactions of my personality that I was taking so seriously, taking as the truth. They weren't. It turned out that I had been missing a vast and hidden dimension of life that exists beyond and below the experience of the personality. I was on the journey of a lifetime. Bit by bit, more depth was revealed. I was experientially learning about deep living.

Life is full of interpretation. My dad was a farmer and an amateur historian. We always had copies of a magazine in our home called *Palimpsest, A History Magazine of Iowa*. It wasn't until cleaning out my parents' home in their final years that I rediscovered copies of the *Palimpsest* and was fascinated to learn the meaning of the term. A palimpsest is a parchment or other writing material from which one or more records had been erased to give room for later writings. But the erasures were generally not complete and researchers were given the task of deciphering and translating the fragments of earlier texts.

It occurred to me that each of our lives has an element of the palimpsest. There are layers in our lives: some have been pushed away, some have been held onto, and some have been completely hidden. The parallel between a palimpsest and our individual lives continued with more questions: Just what is this material that the layers of our lives have been written on? And who has done the writing? What wants to be revealed? What part wants to remain hidden? I found that continuing to ask the questions and using them as guides kept leading me into more sacred territory.

Deep Living Is Revealed

Having the great privilege of writing *Deep Coaching: Using the Enneagram as a Catalyst for Profound Change* and teaching professionals in the Deep Coaching Institute, I surely have learned as much as I have taught. I'd been encouraged to write a companion book to *Deep Coaching* after it was published. That's how this book started out—as a small guidebook. But apparently that's not what this book wanted to be!

Through my studies and after hundreds of honest conversations with students, clients, colleagues, and people I met seemingly at random, I know that my experience of not having the inner and outer life aligned is a universal experience. Our lives may differ in terms of the outward appearances, but this internal experience is part of the larger human journey.

With years of studying with some of the world's leading presence and transformational teachers and the transmissions they shared, along with discoveries that came from my own inner exploration, the real meaning of living in alignment became clear, and what I came to call the deep living approach™ made sense. Basically, it means:

- going below the historic storyline of our life to heal and to discover the deeper truth
- having enough awareness to get unhooked time and time again from a profoundly addictive substance—which is the idea of who we take ourselves to be
- experiencing what is beyond our self-image
- building our innate capacity for accessing our deeper intelligence
- being profoundly compassionate and accepting of our life's journey
- being open to rare perspectives and the paradoxes of our life which are sure to astound us
- discovering our true nature

Why I wrote *DEEP LIVING*

I have always been in awe of the human spirit and this journey that we are all on. I sometimes weep over the suffering that is part of the human condition, and I rejoice in the magnificence of true nature. And I know that every person is part of this magnificence.

Everyone on the planet is here to heal, to fulfill their soul's calling, and to express their most authentic and exquisite qualities. Yours is your birthright.

From my perspective, the Enneagram is the most profound system for transformation. Whether you are a longtime meditator, have studied a great system of spiritual wisdom, have done years of therapy, or are newer to the realm of self-knowledge and transformation, the Enneagram can offer you precise insights not easily arrived at through other means. Wherever you are in your soul's journey and whatever traditions or tools that you currently follow in your psychological and spiritual work, the Enneagram can fill in many missing pieces and help accelerate your evolution.

The Enneagram as presented here is heavily influenced by the pioneering, robust and expansive teachings of the late Don Richard Riso and his colleague Russ Hudson. I have deep roots as a Riso-Hudson Enneagram lover, friend, practitioner, and teacher, and their work is one of the treasured threads in my life. It helped me discover the multitude of layers in my life's palimpsest. In many ways, *Deep Living* is an outgrowth of the Riso-Hudson tradition as this book translates, expands on, and integrates the Enneagram throughout the journey of development, awakening, and evolving.

Along the way we encounter what some call our demons, which we begin to redefine and experience differently in light of our new understandings and changing relationship to ourselves. We encounter more frequent glimpses and experiences of our expanded nature.

What I've learned along the way is that all of life is an invitation to drop into our depths, open into our hearts, and see clearly what is really here.

I wrote this book to be a shepherd and companion as you walk your own path. It is offered with the deepest reverence for your soul's journey, along with an invitation to meet yourself with compassion beyond anything you have ever known. At its heart, the book and I welcome you to the whole of who you are, held in the arms of loving compassion so that how you know yourself becomes transformed into a knowing of the precious being that you are.

—Roxanne Howe-Murphy
Santa Fe, New Mexico

Introduction

Who was really honest with you about what was happening inside of their own skin? Who shared with you that they were anxious or scared, even if they looked confident on the surface? Who confided that they didn't have the slightest inkling of what steps to take next, even as they went about their daily lives, seemingly in control?

Who let you know that it was safe to acknowledge, accept, and be compassionate with your own inner experiences, and that doing so—quite paradoxically—would widen the path to a deeper connection with yourself?

Most of us did not grow up in families, communities, and cultures that support awareness and acknowledgement of the inner life, whether that included moments of emotional or spiritual pain or deep joy. It's rare to learn of environments where exploring and developing one's spiritual path was just as important as the content—the plans, the activities, the relationships, the accomplishments, the challenges—that make up the more visible part of daily life. As a result, we learned best how to live at the surface of life, either denying the existence of the inner world, or trying to manage it.

Unfortunately, that division between the inner and outer world leaves us feeling separate and alone.

From the perspective of adult development, focusing on the external aspects of life plays an important role as we build careers, explore relationships and find partners, and perhaps raise families. In effect, we are making our way in the world, trying to find our place, and be as happy and fulfilled as possible. It's a daunting job!

But at some point, the time comes to turn our attention to what's been kept in the recesses—our inner life, our soul. The timing of this shift often occurs with the approach of midlife, though it's no longer unusual for people in their 20s and 30s and even younger to be drawn to this inner exploration. When unexpected crises or life-threatening illnesses come into their lives, some people find themselves searching for something more real than the temporary fixes offered by society.

Yet, Western culture doesn't do much to prepare us for or to support this turn in attention from an external focus to one that incorporates our inner life. Richard Rohr, a widely-respected Franciscan priest, wisely calls this a "first-half-of-life culture."[1] A significant mismatch exists between what is needed by people who are pulled to discover their deeper nature and develop as whole human beings, and society's outward priorities.

It's not surprising, then, that *most people* feel alone in their interior worlds, not realizing that the vast majority of human beings share this common experience. The degree to which our hearts hurt and our souls are famished show up in the statistics: 23 percent of women aged 40–59, right in the midst of midlife, take antidepressants, more than in any other age-sex group.[2]

One of every eight Americans has a significant problem with alcohol or drugs.[3] Behaviors such as excessive working, running, shopping, TV-watching, gambling, eating, or keeping up with the neighbors can all take the form of behavioral addiction and are considered commonplace and even expected in some environments. They can and frequently do exact a heavy toll. Feeling alone and separate is a potent contributing factor to stress, and it's widely known that there's a strong relationship between stress and physical, emotional, and mental illness. More significant than these statistics, however, is the degree to which these *dis-eases* affect real people's lives, the lives of those around them, and the planet.

What's clear is that the division between our interior lives and what we focus on in the external world is leading us further from any sense of true connection to ourselves and to others. This leads to what I call the *depleted soul*.

At the same time, we have many hundreds—maybe thousands—of books, programs, and professional speakers giving advice on how people can make things better for themselves. Clearly, the deep urge for spiritual awakening will not be denied. So what's going on? What's missing in our understanding about the path from a depleted soul to a deep sense of inner peace?

We've Reached the Right Time in History for a New Conversation

Almost everyone wants to know more about who they are, and to feel whole and completely at home within themselves. They, and we, want to be loving and to be loved. And it's the nature of our personalities to strive to make the best of these deep yearnings. Our personalities work mightily to lead us to the land of happiness, fulfillment and well-being. But there's a problem: The personality can't grasp how that process actually works, and, further, the personality doesn't have the power to create fulfillment on any sustainable, real basis.

It's time to revisit our understanding of the personality—what it is, how it works, how it expresses itself, how we can be fooled by it, where it helps or hinders the experience of deep inner peace, and, perhaps most importantly, our relationship to the personality itself. From my perspective, one of the significant failings of the self-help field in addressing the hunger of the soul at a core level is that much of what has been produced in this field has largely been based on unconscious and false notions of the personality. In many cases, the personality has been misinterpreted as something to get rid of, to fix, or to transcend. Self-help strategies based on this misconception have created substantial and unintentional suffering for many seekers.

Experiencing a meaningful, real, and affirmative relationship with yourself *hinges on* having an accurate understanding of the nature of the personality itself. Within this fascinating and often surprising exploration lies a key to addressing your soul's deep yearnings.

It's difficult to know what it means to "understand the personality and our relationship to it." First, as I've inferred, there are many ideas about what it means to have a personality. I found my own learning around the nearly revolutionary perspective that is offered in *Deep Living* to be riveting, and I suspect you, too, will have previous concepts turned upside down!

Second, with such a wide range in how personalities are expressed, and without a precise map that names and illuminates predictable patterns in the personality, it's hard to distinguish the personality from those experiences that feel simply and unquestionably like *who you are*. In *Deep Living*, you're invited to reflect on a markedly different perspective of what it means to have a personality, what stories it creates, and how your relationship to your personality affects your sense of inner peace and wholeness.

A unique, precise map of the psychological and spiritual journeys of human beings has been given to us in the form of the profound system of wisdom known as the Enneagram. With this remarkable system, you'll recognize that which you have taken yourself to be (which is actually a very narrow slice of your true nature) and gain insights into what is real about you.

You'll see that there are nine versions of the human condition—nine personality types or archetypes—each encompassing a specific range of characteristics, including the precious gifts *and* specific sources of difficulties that individuals dominant in a particular type experience.

Each of the nine versions of the human condition has its own core belief, fears, avoidances, fixed idea, and "flavor" of an inner critic, along with an unquestioned perspective on exactly how reality operates. Thus, you'll discover those precise habits of the mind and emotions that create a sense of aloneness and separateness. All these dynamics lead to a particular, distorted, and limiting self-image, and they result in a specific form of human *un-ease*. These experiences feel so normal that we don't recognize how much energy we put into avoiding feeling the pain of this un-ease.

We also explore the spectrum of our experience through the Enneagram— and discover the profound, essential qualities that are part of our deepest and truest nature. For every one of the nine psycho-spiritual journeys, the unique and expansive qualities that reflect each soul's greatest gifts and blessings are revealed. And it's through these qualities that we have access to our fundamental connectedness to our divine, loving, and exquisite nature, and to the All that exists. Surprisingly, we find that the whole spectrum of human experience offers unexpected doorways to the Divine.

The real value of coming into a deeper self-recognition and self-understanding through the Enneagram is that your journey into this new territory only *begins* with identifying which of the types or archetypes you most relate to. **A fundamental brilliance inherent in the Enneagram system is that it then invites each of us to enter a particular path of healing and integration.** With nine different dimensions of life which are expressed in such different ways, there could not possibly be just one path to wholeness and fulfillment. Rather, each of the nine types requires a unique response to acknowledging and embracing the inner life, so there are, correspondingly, nine paths.

Deep Living is designed to help you see yourself in a way that is sure to feel strange, yet exciting. You will likely feel deeply "met" by what you read, as if your inner life—that is so intimately familiar, but seldom if ever named—is reflected back to you with a great deal of understanding and love.

I believe that it is when we feel deeply seen *without judgment* that we can dare to utter the truth as we've experienced it. Not until we can recognize and give voice to our inner experience, with all of the challenges and vulnerabilities—our pain, doubt, fears—and our dearest hopes and dreams, that we see that we are not alone. We realize that where we are now is not where we'll always be. There's a profound freedom that results from coming face to face with yourself with honesty and compassion. We find that all of our experiences offer an invitation to drop into our depths, experience whatever is there, and, subsequently, to embrace the astonishing intelligence of our inner life.

It is my great prayer that *Deep Living* will inspire you to be kinder and more compassionate to yourself and, as a result, to others. Kindness and compassion are profoundly needed in the world, and each of us holds an essential and unique element for this global healing and transformation to occur.

The Deep Living Approach™

The Deep Living Approach™ integrates four key elements to help you experience a deeper connection to yourself:

1. The Enneagram as a body of wisdom:

The Enneagram is an ancient and profound body of wisdom and a vehicle for compassionate and accurate self-understanding, self-recognition, and self-embracing.

It reveals major patterns that exist in life—some of which are fundamental expressions of a creative universe, and some of which become troublesome in our lives. For its use to have maximum benefit, it's important to identify your dominant Enneagram type or to at least narrow the types that have most familiarity in your own experience to two or three possibilities.

2. The Deep Living Orientation:

Deep Living offers an orientation that is beyond self-help or self-improvement. In truth, the perspective embraced here leads toward less self as we have come to know it and instead leans more toward an expanded sense of being and into the mystery of life. Yet, it's not "woo-woo" but very grounded in the here and now, and in your direct experience of life.

Fundamental to this *Deep Living* orientation is that there is nothing wrong with you. This principle begins to take root and feel real with an understanding of how the personality works and its relationship to your true nature. We look to the Enneagram for its wisdom here, as it beautifully illuminates the relationship between the personality and true nature, and it leaves you with a better grasp of the fullness of your nature. **Deep Living is a voice, a vehicle, for practical and radical compassion for the full spectrum of the human experience.**

This principle—that there is nothing wrong with you—affects how we think about the change process.

It's a foreign, if not radical, idea: That, if there's nothing fundamentally wrong with you, you do not need to do something to fix yourself. The Western way of thinking generally favors the active perspective, that is, taking action to make things different.

In *Deep Living*, rather than identifying with what we think is wrong with us, we're guided to create a new orientation. **When our approach to ourselves changes, and we gain a new perspective on the change process itself, something important happens in our consciousness— and this becomes the basis for a new relationship to ourselves and everything that matters to us.**

3. A set of practical tools that can be used in everyday life:

Deep Living offers a number of tools for supporting the new orientation to yourself, which ultimately will impact your orientation to others, and to life itself.

These tools might initially seem simple or easy. Well, while they're not simple, there is a simplicity to them. It can be easy to dismiss tools that, on the surface, may seem simple. There's always that part of us that may try to distract us, saying, "Oh, I already know how to do that." But see for yourself what happens as you work with even the basic tools presented here— developing the capacity for self-observation, curiosity, radical compassion, truth-telling, and trust of the process. No doubt, life will not remain the same for you.

4. Processes for advanced healing and awakening:

Deep Living is founded on developing the capacity for presence, that is, for being in contact with the moment-to-moment experience happening in reality. We generally are unaware that we're not present, for when we see the world through the lens of our personality, that perception often gets mistaken for being present. Throughout the book, we gradually build on your innate capacity for being present. In essence, you are guided to notice where you habitually focus your attention and then to re-orient that attention toward experiences that yield contact with what is real and true. This creates a change in your neurophysiology that accompanies an experience of feeling more liberated from the usual way you have perceived life.

These four elements, when woven together in life, act to redefine your relationships to most everything that has meaning in your life and, subsequently, to transform those relationships. You'll see this addressed and emphasized throughout the book.

In response to requests from some of my readers, this book began as a companion to my earlier book, *Deep Coaching: Using the Enneagram as a catalyst for profound change*, which was written primarily for coaches and other growth-oriented practitioners who work directly with individual clients and groups. Thus, *Deep Living* has a similar structure to the earlier text. Some of the material presented here can be found in *Deep Coaching*, but this book expands on the former writing and presents new material, reflecting my own further development, understanding, and personal and professional experience.

I've worked with the material in the book extensively with my coaching clients, professionals in the Deep Coaching Certification Program, and participants in my courses and workshops. There are many examples of people's experiences included throughout the book. For most of these examples, I have combined the work of several individuals who have shared very similar profiles and processes. In all cases, I have used a different name for the purpose of protecting confidentiality.

How Deep Living Is Presented

The book is presented in three parts, Sections I, II, and III.

I encourage you to read Section I, *Orienting to Your New World*, before getting into the later Section that focuses on the specific Enneagram types. This first section presents the basic principles and orientation that are vital to the applications of the remainder of the book. Here you'll encounter important perspectives on both the nature of the personality and on the change process itself that set the stage for understanding how the personality takes you in the opposite direction of what you most deeply desire. Some of the important tools for this work are presented in chapter 4.

In Section II, you'll encounter the Enneagram Iceberg Model™, which is used to illustrate and provide a shorthand overview of the personality structure. Subsequently, each of nine chapters presents a discussion and insights on the nature of the human condition and the consciousness of individuals dominant in a specific Enneagram type. I invite you to try on the descriptions of each type to reflect on what aspects of that type are familiar to you. Case studies, observations, and practices unique to each type will be useful to understanding and working with these experiences within yourself as you learn about the nine variations on *how to "do" life*.

Section III, *Change for Life*, offers more tools and practical applications to support your spiritual journey. Chapter 15 describes the many ways we *turn away from* ourselves, and it provides strategies for *turning toward* yourself. In chapter 16, we explore the three Centers of Intelligence that are vital to experiencing presence and learning how to develop the innate capacity of each center to support your well-being. Chapter 17 focuses on the inner critic—something everyone has and which is the basis of incredible suffering. This chapter will help you recognize your inner critic's voice and learn specific strategies for changing your relationship to its negative consequences. The final chapter invites you to shift your attention to your more expansive nature, synthesizing and expanding on some of the main themes of the book. In it, you'll also find more beneficial strategies.

Whether you're finding this book on your own, or perhaps through a recommendation by a coach or other growth-oriented professional, my intention is that *Deep Living* will offer you relief, a breadth of understanding, and a real and uplifting sense of what is possible for you. I hope you will come back to it time and time again, always finding something new to remind you of your true nature. It's my hope that this writing will help stoke your curiosity, affirm your courage as you walk this spiritual path, fuel your compassion for yourself and others, and deeply nourish your soul.

Section I

ORIENTING TO YOUR NEW WORLD

1

Following the Urge to Be Real

Anne expressed a mixture of hope and resignation. She had wanted to build her own business for years but found that she often got distracted by other responsibilities or interests. "I'm so tired of getting excited but then floundering again. I've tried so many times. What's wrong?"

Upbeat Joshua is known as an optimistic guy who pays attention to other people. His friends, coworkers, and family know that he can be counted on to get things done, and generally he does so with a smile. But in a private conversation, he shared, "For as long as I can remember, I have felt hurt when others don't respond to me with the same concern I have for them. So, I just try harder to please them. Why do I feel that there is something inside that I want to avoid?"

Since her early forties, Emma frequently attended spiritual retreats. Her bookshelves are overflowing with self-help books. At age fifty-three, she wondered if she would ever truly feel more at ease in her life. Dealing with bouts of mild depression and big doses of self-criticism, she confided, "Maybe I can't expect anymore than this. Is this all there is?"

Cecile had a list of accomplishments that included multiple master's degrees, a doctorate, and several advanced professional certifications. She held an executive position in the workplace, which afforded her and her family an elegant lifestyle. But behind the public image, she had long experienced a nagging sense that something was missing. She hated slowing down because her sense of inner emptiness increased, yet she knew she must. "I feel the urge to make a change. I just don't know what it is, and I'm scared to death."

3

Expressions of the Human Experience

From even these brief glimpses into four individuals' lives, we recognize a few of the familiar dilemmas, puzzles, emotions, and questions about the unknown that are part of being human.

For a society that offers daily technological advances, a doubling of the knowledge base every fifteen to eighteen months, hundreds of new products to choose from in the marketplace every week, and the launch of civilians into outer space, we know very little about being human. While the majority of our collective attention has gone into feeding the desire to discover, understand, create, build, and control the external world, the internal world has been left famished.

With this imbalance, life comes to feel automatic, mechanical, and overwhelmed. There's a sense of running from something. But from what? The fluidity and joy of our inner aliveness thickens and coagulates. We feel denser, heavier, contracted, and fatigued. When the lack of attention to and awareness of the inner world continues, we harden and grow even more fearful of what we might find within.

This distortion has consequences in every part of life, in every part of the human family. People hurt and do not understanding why.

The good news is that this continued imbalance of life is not inevitable. It need not be prolonged.

The Call to Being an Awakened Human

I talk to people all the time who want to feel good about what they are doing with their precious time on earth, and make a positive contribution. They are asking big questions about their lives and are trying to find resolutions to pressing and sometimes stubborn dilemmas that seem to elude any sense of real satisfaction. With or without using these specific words, they want to feel at home inside themselves.

While some have discovered how to live with a great sense of ease, most, like the individuals above, feel that their lives are not working as well as they would like. There is something about who they are that feels off or missing. Others reveal that they feel lost, and that the inside and outside of their lives don't match. And others intuitively know that there is more to life than having more of the same. They are looking to experience a deeper fulfillment.

Most people feel the tug of two opposing energies within. On one hand, they are drawn to authentically express their soul's higher qualities, such as inner strength, compassion, joy, gratitude, courage, or inner peace. On the other hand, they find themselves repeating familiar experiences that seem to pull them downward in the opposite direction. They act in ways that sometimes disappoint or embarrass them. How is it possible that we can experience such inner polarities?

One of the many paradoxes is that at some crucial turning point in life, everyone feels alone and as though they're trying to shield a secret sense of self that they think few others would understand or accept…yet everyone else feels the same way! Like new lovers wanting to show to each other only what they consider their best side, we create an inner division between what we believe is acceptable and not acceptable. And because the true experience of inner life is not customarily discussed in public, it is easy to think that others do not or have not had similar experiences. It is easy to think that you are on your own.

But you are not.

Historical and contemporary spiritual teachings, along with psychological understanding, speak to the inevitable sense of pain and estrangement that result from turning away from unwanted aspects of ourselves. This inner division between what we perceive to be either acceptable or unacceptable in our own nature leads to a deeply embedded and universal experience of being disconnected from something essential within. Paradoxically, it is this very experience of disconnect—that we have tried with all our might to avoid—that puts us directly on a path to healing and wholeness.

As personal as it feels, setting foot on this healing path is not simply an individual journey, but is embedded in the shared evolutionary unfolding of the human community. The continued development of

One of the many paradoxes is that at some crucial turning point in life, everyone feels alone and as though they're trying to shield a secret sense of self that they think few others would understand or accept…yet everyone else feels the same way!

human consciousness is reflected in every dimension of life—in new mathematics, physics, biological and neuro research and technology, to name just a few areas that affirm the ancient spiritual teachings that speak to the deep interconnections that exist among us all. And frankly, people who experience the compelling urge to discover their truer nature, and are curious about what lies below the surface of their lives, need each other and benefit from one another's honest questioning and ongoing learning.

Not recognizing and accepting the full range of the human experience that exists within us severely hampers the realization of the deeper qualities that most of us seek. Coming to accept that we have the full range of light and dark dimensions within ourselves is at the crux of becoming a whole and fully human *being*.

Where You Focus Your Attention Matters

So where do you start? What is the next step on your own quest?

Some of my clients have asked, "Even when I look inside, exactly *what* do I look for and just *where* do I look?" These questions often are coupled with doubts and fears that when looking within for this indescribable "it," absolutely nothing will be found. The great fear is that there will be nothing there.

I have long loved this old teaching story, as it so exemplifies this common human dilemma.

A man was walking home late one night when he saw Nasrudin searching under a streetlight on hands and knees for something on the ground. "Mulla, what have you lost?" the man asked.

"The key to my house," Nasrudin said.

"I'll help you look," the man said.

Soon, both men were down on their knees, looking for the key.

After a number of minutes, the man asked, "Where exactly did you drop it?"

Nasrudin waved his arm back toward the darkness. "Over there, in my house."

The first man jumped up. "Then why are you looking for it here?"

"Because there is more light here than inside my house."

Much like Nasrudin, most people don't find what they are looking for because they put their attention on areas that do not lead to desired states. This results in feeling alone and vulnerable.

Learning to focus your attention on what yields real contact with your inner self is what this book is about. Using the profound system of awareness known as the Enneagram, we will travel together into territory that allows you to feel safe about knowing yourself, and yields new understandings and revelations.

As a condition of being born into the human community, each of us has a particular way we unconsciously move away from our deepest nature, away from that which is rich and precious beyond measure. It is in this movement away from our true nature where the inner polarity gets established.

One reason I love working with the Enneagram is that it brilliantly illuminates this movement. Through gaining more understanding and awareness of the reasons behind what many consider to be the fundamental inner dilemma, you will learn more about the way you have historically turned away from your most exalted nature. This helps you grow your capacity for having a more intimate relationship with yourself, and here you'll discover more of your own innate and wondrous capacities.

Developing a Presence-Based Orientation

We live in such an exciting and challenging time because we are all called to be more consciously aware. We are supported now more than ever before in rising to a new level of awareness and of psychological and spiritual maturity through access to a repertoire of strategies, tools, attitudes, and an orientation that can be applied and integrated into daily living.

This is why the Enneagram is such a gift. It offers a body of wisdom that, when used wisely, reveals a rare way to see yourself. It helps you understand yourself through a surprisingly precise and wise lens, and it allows you to know that you are not alone. By seeing where you have habitually placed the majority of your energy, the unseen internal dynamics that have shaped your orientation to life will become clearer. This will help you make sense of much of your life up to now. Going forward, new and more effective choices become available.

I find that it works best to meet the sacred knowledge of the Enneagram with three intentional behaviors that create an attitude toward learning and development.

One behavior is that of grounding. This includes becoming aware of your breathing, and giving your breath the space to find its own natural rhythm. This simple but deliberate action can lead to feeling more settled within. Grounding also involves making felt the contact between your body and whatever it is in physical contact with. For example, paying attention to the contact of your feet on the floor, and your hips and back physically held by a chair can further lead to being where you are at the moment. Grounding is a process that enables us to gradually *take up residence* in our physical nature, offering us a source of vital intelligence.

A second behavior brings our attention to our heart. With a kind attitude oriented toward your heart, you may feel a slight softening and opening here. The heart responds at a different rhythm and pace than does the head, so taking sufficient time to simply be *with* whatever you are experiencing in your heart supports the development of a new relationship with yourself. In essence, this practice invites you to be kinder and more receptive to yourself.

A third behavior is that of being curious. It's useful to bring a willingness to question your ideas about who you are, and how life works. We humans carry so many stories about life and we have believed those stories to be true. Learning about ourselves through the Enneagram is filled with surprises, including those where we discover that a particular story we've long held as unquestionable simply isn't true. The qualities of curiosity and open-mindedness help us to use those surprises for our growth.

Together, these three behaviors increase your capacity to be present. When you orient yourself to being present with this material, you may discover that you are moved, and something within begins to change. Approaching this material with presence, you and I are actually communicating at a more intimate level than just writing and reading the words on the page. This engages your soul, which naturally leads to having more contact with your deeper self.

This call to being human, then, is an invitation to the truth and experience of our real nature. *Deep Living* offers an orientation, tools, and practices for applying the insights that you develop.

This call to being human, then, is an invitation to the truth and experience of our real nature.

The Enneagram:
A Map of the Human Experience

Let's start with a few basics about the Enneagram. While no system takes every aspect of human nature into account, nor is it a panacea to address all of life's challenges and opportunities, the Enneagram is a profound field of knowledge and guidance that supports remarkable life-shifts and transformation.

The questions asked by seekers over the eons regarding the nature of the human experience and its relationship to the spiritual realm—or, in religious terms, to knowing God—are as relevant today as ever. The Enneagram integrates knowledge about human behavior and motivation with the quest for psychological and spiritual redemption that has come to us from the ancient wisdoms that are nearly universally shared. We find the basic tenets of awakening are common to the major spiritual traditions—including Christianity, mystical Judaism, Buddhism, and Sufism.

The Enneagram symbol was originally introduced to the West before World War I by Georges Gurdjieff as a system for awakening—for waking up to the trouble that we humans experience when we are asleep to our true nature. Although many people think of the Enneagram as a personality-typing system, originally, it was not taught from that perspective.[1]

In the mid-1900s, Oscar Ichazo recognized that there were specific correspondences between the nine points that we find on the Enneagram symbol and the nine specific psychological and spiritual themes or questions found in the human experience. Today, contemporary psychological understanding, spiritual wisdom, and research in the field of neuroscience continue to converge and be reflected in the Enneagram. Many who have worked with this body of wisdom for years, and even decades, find that the Enneagram continues to teach and deepen our awareness.

As we will explore in this book, identifying your dominant personality type is simply a first step in the process of becoming more aware, of getting to know yourself at a deeper level, and of having real experiences that reflect your truer, more expansive nature.

This ancient system illuminates the polarity of our human condition, which we discussed earlier. Between the two polar ends of life, we have experiences that range from healthy and effective to that which are ineffective and troublesome, or even to behavior that, for some, is a violation of themselves and/or others. The Enneagram also gives guidance on the important questions often asked by those who are seeking freedom from their suffering, such as, "How is it possible to have such high ideals about how I want to live my life (as more loving or courageous, for example, or with more integrity or gratitude) and to know that I often fall completely short of my ideals?"

The Patterns of Life

Through the Enneagram, we learn that there are nine major dimensions, or archetypes, or spheres of consciousness that exist in the world. On a human scale, this translates to the existence of nine dramatically different orientations to life.

Each of us specializes in one of these dimensions. In the Enneagram, these are called personality types and are identified as Types Ones through Nine.

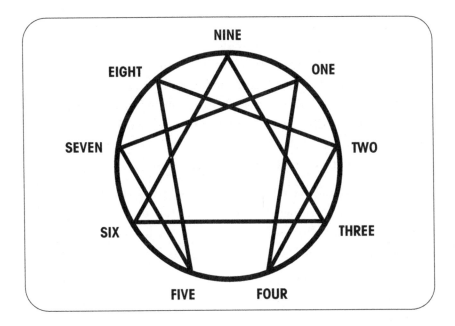

Figure 1-1: The Enneagram

Each of these nine orientations has specific and repeating patterns of thought, emotion, attention, and behavior. Repeating patterns are a part of nature and all of life. While many naturally occurring patterns are beautiful, unfortunately, when we humans unconsciously repeat behaviors, thoughts, or emotional experiences, they often lead to a degree of dissatisfaction without us being able to point to the source of our discomfort.

A Repeating Pattern in Nature

The Enneagram shines the light of awareness on the specific thought, emotional, and behavioral patterns associated with each of the types. Most of us have a story about who we are, how we behave, or how we imagine others see us. But our self-concept is likely clouded. As we learn about ourselves through the Enneagram, it is not unusual to discover a discrepancy between how we want to be seen and how we actually function in life. One of the hardest things for most people to do is to peer through the clouds and see themselves accurately.

You will then have the remarkable ability to see yourself clearly, perhaps for the first time.

Underneath our repeating patterns, there are important psychological and spiritual themes that run through our life experiences. If you have ever wondered why you experience recurring difficulties that have some similarities, but that occur under different circumstances and with different people, you can look to these underlying dynamics to gain important understandings. Many of those who have studied this system say that they start connecting the dots among their various life experiences, and that their life makes more sense.

It is these underlying dynamics that most precisely distinguish each type from the others. Learning about yourself at this deeper level can offer remarkable insights about where you tend to overdo and what you avoid in life—often to your own detriment.

Here's a great example of this. An executive arrived for her coaching session with me and was obviously quite relieved as she shared a shift in a pattern.

> *"I stopped taking on so much responsibility for my staff's projects. I can see how I have been overdoing my 'helper instinct' and how I have believed that I need to take care of my staff at my own expense. Ouch! Rather than trying to provide all the solutions as I always have, I instead practiced asking team leaders clear questions and giving some guidance so that they could focus on completing the projects themselves. It is working! I'm less stressed, and I think they feel better too. I know I will be practicing this for a long time, but I definitely recognize that I'm on the right track."*

You, too, can recognize when you have historically relied on a narrow range of automatic responses, which led to overdoing one particular strategy and feeling dissatisfied. These habitual behaviors have put a very precious part of you on the back burner of your life.

Recognizing the predominant patterns in your life gives you a window into the nature of your personality structure. You will then have the remarkable ability to see yourself clearly, perhaps for the first time.

Why Awareness Matters

Why is that awareness so important?

Because it is a key that unlocks the door to your hidden self. Without that awareness, most people stay stuck. With awareness, however, comes a sense of melting the places that have felt frozen. Fluidity is accompanied by natural, healthy change.

Awareness of the patterns of personality structure leads to another profound outcome. We begin to identify the false stories that we have carried internally and that create great struggles and suffering. The release of these stories results in inner healing and more expansive energy we can instead put into the service of that which we most love.

And awareness points to the specific and unique gifts of your Enneagram type. It reveals a map with a unique path to those gifts that is completely counterintuitive to our ordinary way of thinking. Many people have found that by being more present and embracing the authentic gifts shown to them through the Enneagram, they were able to more deeply accept themselves and find joy in expressing these innate gifts, and thus experience their real purpose.

This lights up the soul.

One Size Does Not Fit All

You may have read books that offered a specific set of strategies for getting more satisfaction or success in life, and yet were disappointed, frustrated, or even hopeless that the suggestions did not work effectively for you. Over the decades, I have collected a library of these books. I used to try to follow the author's suggestions for an authentic life but ended up feeling even worse when the suggestions didn't work for me.

Well, no wonder. One size does not fit all.

In this book, you'll find nine different sizes, nine different pathways. Each offers specific suggestions for individuals who most relate to a particular way of experiencing life, of treading that particular pathway. As you identify your own orientation on the Enneagram, I encourage you to

It may completely surprise you that the ideas, actions, feelings, and reactions that are familiar to you are actually reflective of a particular Enneagram personality type.

focus on the suggestions associated with it. What will best support you might be very different than what would support a good friend or your significant other, because you and your brain are designed differently than most of the people around you.

It may completely surprise you that the ideas, actions, feelings, and reactions that are familiar to you are actually reflective of a particular Enneagram personality type. With just this awareness, and when you accompany it with a non-judgmental attitude, change begins to occur. With ongoing and committed practice, your innate qualities will be stirred awake, and you will move toward inner peace. Over time, you'll increase your psychological, emotional, and spiritual liberation, and gain more effectiveness in life.

But the Enneagram is much more than a system for understanding personality types—its roots are deeper and more profound than that. Instead, it is an ancient tool of sacred psychology that supports our transformation so that each of us may live from our specific facet of essential, true nature.

Understanding *Personality* and What It Means for You

The term *personality* has many usages and connotations in daily life. Because our desire in this book is to explore, understand, and illuminate the dynamics that lead to feeling more whole, integrated, and fully human, we also need to understand what causes the inner split we discussed earlier. The Enneagram offers a riveting and profoundly different explanation of the personality and its relationship to our true nature than you may have been introduced to previously.

We all have a particular personality, and will have it until our last breath. But that personality is a part of—not all of—who we are.

Before reading further, take a moment to jot down your answer to the following question: How would you describe yourself? Write whatever comes to mind and not what you think you are supposed to write.

Did you do it? Good. Let's keep going.

Many of us are tempted to describe ourselves in certain ways, often by our:

- physical characteristics
- roles in life (our marital or occupational status, for example, or relationship to another person, such as a spouse, parent, sibling, or child)
- preferences, interests, or activities
- qualities we think we display, such as being creative, bold, fun, emotionally sensitive, stoic, responsible, quiet, caring, calm, or smart, to name a few

Look at your responses to my earlier question regarding your self-description. See if any of your descriptions fall into one or more of the categories in the above list.

All of these are ways that we might describe our personality— that dimension of ourselves that is most apparent to us. It feels completely natural to think of ourselves *as* the personality, that is, to be identified with it. We may not realize that there is an alternative.

The experience of "being identified with" means that your self-concepts, thoughts, feelings, behaviors, qualities, reactions, discomforts—any experiences that you might have—are so intricately tied into your day-to-day experience, that they are unquestioned. These make up the stories of your life, and you believe them. They feel like who you really are, they're a reflection of the authentic self.

Have you ever heard yourself say something like this: "Of course, I worry (or get mad, or look for a new adventure, or demand perfection of myself, or want total control, for example). **That's just who I am. I can't help it.**"

This is a common way of relating to the personality. You might think that there's not much that can be done about it, but you'll see later that there is. Meanwhile, let's examine what happens when we think about personality in this way.

Being identified with the personality—mistaking your personality for who you are—is where the internal split has its roots. To the degree

Being identified with the personality— mistaking your personality for who you are— is where the internal split has its roots.

that you are identified with the personality, the experience takes center stage, and there is no "I" outside of that experience. The less often that the nature of these experiences and why they occur are examined, the stronger the identification becomes.

Further, it seems that only certain personal characteristics are acceptable while many are not. Thus the inner split widens.

Being identified becomes quite tricky in daily living because having a certain kind of identifiable personality is considered an admirable trait in different environments. For example, being visionary is a respected leadership trait, while being caring is a desirable characteristic for capable health professionals. Children who are shy sometimes discover that outgoing children receive more favorable feedback. Motivational speakers are expected to be energetic, upbeat, and, well, motivating. In some religious communities, expressing humility and piety is a prized social norm. In most cultures, it is the personality that receives attention and even adulation, so this is further reinforcement of the idea that personality is the basis for who we think we are.

At different times in your life, your own personality characteristics have been encouraged, critiqued, and commented on by family members, friends, and co-workers, which has given even more credence to the idea that you are your personality.

So, who are you, if you are not your personality?

It can be shocking to consider the notion that we are not primarily a personality.

Yet it is that identification with the personality that creates so many of life's struggles and challenges. Developing a more expansive understanding of what it means to be human creates a welcome shift in how you relate to yourself, those you interact with, and your whole environment.

Considering the vast array of possibilities that exist within the human experience, our typical self-descriptions are inherently limiting. Whatever you take yourself to be results in cutting off other parts of yourself. Your personality becomes troublesome when you live inside its narrow walls.

The Key to Real Choice

At the heart of healing the inner split is the recognition that you have choice—real choice that comes from an inner knowing. The faulty sense that "there's nothing I can do about my personality" limits the experience of this choice.

One of the fundamental teachings of the Enneagram is that the personality itself is not one solid, static entity that coalesces around just a few characteristics that do not change. Instead, the personality has the potential to be fluid, which means we can respond in new, fresh, and creative ways to the circumstances and opportunities in our lives.

For example, sometimes we realize we need to try out a completely new attitude or behavior toward a recurring and troubling situation in life because our usual approach isn't working. While that new approach may feel foreign and scary, your inner guidance tells you that it is necessary for your own peace of mind, and perhaps it will lead to an improved outcome. Experimenting with that new approach is an example of moving beyond the repetitive nature of the personality's patterns and entering new territory.

The key to this fluidity is consciousness. The more we bring compassion and awareness to the design of our personality and where and why we get stuck, new approaches begin appearing as interesting and possible choices. Research in neuroscience, or brain plasticity, has shown that the brain never stops changing, so your whole body contains the wiring to grow, develop, and evolve. On a practical level, you fundamentally have the capacity to create and enjoy a more fulfilled and purposeful life at home and work.

The Enneagram provides a remarkable framework for understanding what the personality actually is and how it acts, thereby opening a whole new world to us.

Three Perspectives on the Personality

Below are three particular perspectives on the personality. Each one provides insights into why the personality has developed, a purpose it

It can be shocking to consider the notion that we are not primarily a personality.

is fulfilling, and how it operates. I hope it will also invite compassion as you recognize how completely natural it is to think of yourself as your personality, and the challenge of building the capacity to recognize it as simply a part of the wholeness that is you.

I want to emphasize that the personality is not bad. It has and continues to serve important purposes, including bringing you to this exploration. It is just not *all* of who you are.

Perspective #1:
The Personality as a Structure of Identity
("I Am...")

Your personality comes equipped with an internal blueprint that serves as the foundation for how you express yourself. Just as a building's architectural blueprint comprises many different elements of that structure—including dimensions, relationships between rooms, and points of egress that provide the foundation for the form and function of the building—the blueprint of the personality provides the hidden structure for the functioning of the personality. This blueprint comprises various elements, such as your preferences, behaviors, attitudes, desires, fears, defense mechanisms, primary Focus of Attention, and other factors, many of which typically are hidden to awareness.

Each of the nine Enneagram types has its own characteristic version of the architectural blueprint. Our experience of ourselves is based on this internal structure, which shapes our inner story—our self-perception, how we perceive others, and our relationship to the larger world. In effect, the specific personality structure gives rise to a person's sense of identity and leads to his or her experience of *this is just who I am.*

Each of the nine blueprints (which will be examined individually in upcoming chapters) forms a unique agenda and context that have a pervasive influence on an individual's entire life experience—at least, until the system is exposed and new options become visible.

The Enneagram Iceberg Model™, described in detail in Chapter 5, provides a template for illustrating the architecture of the personality. Briefly, the Iceberg Model captures the behavioral (i.e., observable) characteristics of the Enneagram type in the section extending above the waterline in the illustration below. By contrast, the type-specific motivational factors, which give shape to the behavior, are shown below the waterline.

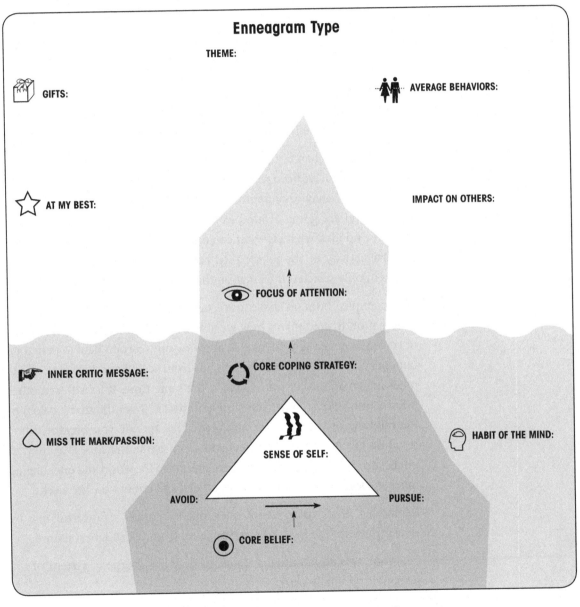

Figure 1-2 The Enneagram Iceberg Model®

In the early 2000s, an Enneagram colleague and I selected the analogy of an iceberg to make the concept of personality more transparent and, thus, less mysterious and more accessible.[2] As I continue to use newer iterations of the original Iceberg Model, I think of it as a way to take ourselves out of our psychic fishbowl so we can see how we have habitually oriented toward life and to gain a more expansive and healthful perspective.

Perspective #2:
The Personality as an Energetic System
("I believe...")

The personality is also an *energetic system* that, like any unexamined or uninterrupted system, continues to build on itself.

The experience of an uninterrupted system, for example, is felt when you realize that you have been repeating—over and over again—a troublesome or ineffective behavior or approach to different situations in your life. You feel like you are going around in a circle or that you are in a rut, and you have no idea what else you could do. When a system, including the familiar activity of the personality, remains uninterrupted, that system allows in only selected information that reinforces its existing patterns.

For example, humans have a certain filter that allows in selective information that confirms how we already think of ourselves. This filter, or screen, is amazingly talented at allowing only certain data to penetrate our consciousness, and at preventing us from seeing and receiving all the other information that is available at the same time. It is as if that other information doesn't exist; you simply don't see it, so the many colors of the rainbow of your life are obscured. Like the air you breathe, these resulting assumptions and beliefs you carry are so invisible that they go unquestioned. They lead to a fixed orientation to the world and unchanging inner stories about ourselves, about others, and about how life works.

Remember, that which is not questioned assumes a powerful role by leveraging your life force to turn you away from your highest nature.

Let's look at a streamlined account of how the energetic system of the personality actually works.

For starters, each of the nine personality types has a specific core belief.

- The core belief can be thought of as a central operating principle that helps shape the developing personality.
- The core belief actively filters and selects data that reinforces itself from the vast field of information that bombards an individual each moment. Data which does not fit into the core belief patterns are unconsciously dismissed.
- Therefore, data that could provide another perspective are ignored. The individual likely doesn't realize that other information is present. When a person looks at his or her own recurring experiences over time, it's easy to become convinced that this experience is the truth.
- When responses are predictable, they are actually automatic reactions. Since a person's reaction/behavior is based on a belief, it generates feedback that reinforces the original belief. Thus, the feedback mirrors the message of the internal voice. The core belief is again affirmed.
- The seeming truth of this core belief often leads to re-experiencing such early emotional reactions as anger, frustration, fear, emotional dependency, shame, or even a sense of being rejected. Most often this emotional response is not fully in the consciousness, and the experience again feels like "who I am," or is attributed to early-life situations.
- These patterns feel so real that we come to think of ourselves as actually *being* these habitual patterns. But we need to remember that patterns are not bad; they are just limiting. They are like the air we breathe—so natural that it never occurs to us to question them. We don't suspect that a belief even exists—it is just—what is.

Let's examine a real-life example of an inner story that is an outgrowth of a belief system in which the core belief is "I am flawed."

- This powerful core belief acts as a filter and finds or perceives data that reinforces the belief from the vast field of information available.

- The individual's experience becomes: "I think of myself as always messing up. In fact, I see how I make a multitude of errors. I am either constantly apologizing to others or cutting off communication because, underneath it all, I am embarrassed."
- This person's internal critic says, "See, I told you that you are messed up. You just can't get your act together. Face it, you're flawed. And, of course, that just isn't okay. You're more flawed than anyone else."
- Now, the person acts as if she is exceptionally flawed. She may find herself in constant trouble or conflict with others.
- The consequences are damaging. The individual is likely very hard on herself. She feels both victimized and ashamed. And her relationships may be in tatters.
- The personality hardens. The person falls into the trap of feeling stuck in this sense of who she thinks she is. All of the evidence supports the "I am flawed" belief.

The uninterrupted personality is a closed system with little active awareness or curiosity operating. Information incongruent with existing beliefs are filtered out, and it is easy to fall prey to the automatic responses that are familiar—sometimes painfully familiar. In effect, this is when we lose ourselves to the hypnotic effects of both the personality's patterns and the cultural conditioning. Both the personality and our cultural experiences habitually reinforce placing attention toward the past or the future, or toward other people—anything but to the present.

Yet, it is in the present that you have more access to your lighter, more expansive nature, to your inner strength and inner authority.

The great news is that these personality systems can be interrupted and opened to receive new input. But this only happens with awareness and with the quality of presence.

Perspective #3:
The Personality as a Coping Mechanism and Protection ("I guard.../I protect...")

There are important and valid reasons that you identified with certain personality qualities throughout life. Some of these reasons may now feel outdated or less relevant as you focus on your growth, yet they're still contributing to unsatisfying behavior or inner discomfort. That's why we explore the personality as a coping or protective mechanism: so we recognize and bring more attention to healing the emotional pain that lies under the surface of the human experience.

It is through a kind, compassionate attitude toward ourselves that healing can occur and that new forms of inner freedom and choice can exist.

Let's go back to the beginning: Everyone on the planet experienced pain when they came into the world. Every one of us was an intrinsically sensitive little being who picked up the spoken and unspoken, the seen and unseen elements of our environments. For some, there were objective forms of abuse in early years. For most, our unique and sensitive perspectives, especially as young children, resulted in interpreting the actions or attitudes of others as meaning something that was not actually intended. Either way, we learned how to cover our fears, anger, shame, disappointments, sense of being rejected, and feelings of being lost and all alone.

You learned to cope and how to hide a lot of those hurts. The accumulation of your hurts resulted in emotional energy that you neither had the words for (many of these experiences took place before you could talk) nor the neurological or biological capacity to tolerate. You needed to suppress and mask these early experiences to survive as an intact person.

That was the role that your personality took on. It protected you from experiences which were unacceptable or simply too much for you at that moment.

Over time, your coping mechanism crystallized. Growing into adolescence, then adulthood, those coping strategies predominated, so your inherent capacity to handle those old hurts didn't have a chance to develop.

But now, having arrived at a new phase in life, your capacity as a psychological and spiritual being is maturing and you are outdistancing your need for all that protection. Now you might ask, "What is more important to me than relying on my familiar coping strategies?"

For most, our unique and sensitive perspectives, especially as young children, resulted in interpreting the actions or attitudes of others as meaning something that was not actually intended.

So why do you have the personality that you do? From what we know at this time, you came into life with a particular *spiritual template*, as it's called, that results in you being attuned to a particular grouping of higher spiritual qualities. Very early in life, perhaps even before you were born, you felt the *great loss* of connection with those spiritual qualities. Your particular personality feels so real to you because, in some ways, it is trying to mimic those qualities, yet at the same time, still trying to protect you from the experience of your early wounds.

In Section II's description of each personality type, we'll explore this loss, the resulting ways in which a person dominant in the particular type coped, a path to healing, and the inherent spiritual qualities associated with the type.

Parallel Living

The personality structure is designed to keep repeating a particular version of life, but it is not the real thing. It's a padded version, a faux replica of what you really want.

However, if that which is essential and real, and that which is the personality, were both visible entities, then we might see that they actually live side by side. In effect, when we are fully embedded in the personality, we live parallel to our true nature, not in it.[3] Naturally, when you continuously experience your personality's version of life, it is easy to feel both a sense of inevitability—"this is just how I am"—and, at the same time, to feel stuck.

When you were younger, you really could not have tolerated dealing with life in any other way than how you did. It worked at the time, and it's important to respect and honor that.

But in the midst of vast changes just about everywhere we look, you might also notice that you, too, are changing. I'm guessing that you feel ready for a more vibrant, alive, real, and full-hearted experience. If you feel that something has been missing, perhaps you can approach that sense of something missing as a gift, because it has already brought you to a new awareness.

The truth, however, is that there is nothing missing in you. What is lacking is a direct, unfiltered, real experience of inhabiting your own life.

Years ago, I moved to an area of Northern California that was very smoggy at the time. I was working on my master's degree and had to drive back and forth from home to the university on a large, ten-lane freeway. During my first semester, I remember seeing only various shades of gray in the sky, and the vague shapes of distant hills. Then, one rare and clear evening, I looked to the east and gasped. The smog had lifted and I saw the hills in the background clearly for the first time! I was stunned. They had been so filtered from sight by the smog that I hadn't realized they were so close.

Our inner journey parallels this revelation! The smog created by an individual's personality also obscures reality. Our view can be so filtered that we don't experience what or who is here. We only have an idea of it, and that idea is often distorted or even wrong. When the personality has an exaggerated role and is running the show, it filters out contact with your own realness.

The Personality as *It*

Rather than perceive the personality as exactly who you are, it is helpful to see the personality as an *it* or as *that*. It is not right or wrong, good or bad. It has its uses, and you need some degree of it to function in the world.

However, your personality is not you. When you believe that it has the answer or when you allow it to completely define you, then it will continue to cause you suffering—and it will suffocate the deepest yearnings of your soul.

A Few Principles to Apply

- The Enneagram provides a system for you to see the characteristics and qualities you have historically identified with and how you have coped with life. Based on your particular Enneagram orientation, you'll gain insight into how you make decisions, handle stress, and interact with others.

- Seeing how your particular Enneagram structure, or type, is expressed through you can be an astonishing experience.
- As you learn more about yourself, you may experience a range of emotions that might include embarrassment or even substantial relief.
- Be kind to yourself during this exploration! It is not unusual for that inner voice, often called the inner critic, to make itself heard, bringing with it all of its reasons for why this undertaking of increasing self-knowledge is completely wrong. So it is vital to bring as much tenderness and compassion to your journey as possible.
- Be curious. I have found that one of the greatest gifts we can give ourselves is to approach this self-study from a perspective of being less certain about ourselves. This is not the same as doubting ourselves, but more of an orientation toward, "Hmmm…I wonder what this is about and what it could offer me?" With this perspective, you will discover that this curiosity is actually more connected to a sense of wonder!
- The Enneagram sheds light on the hidden motivations underlying the choices you've made in the past. With kind awareness into these insights, you may naturally notice that something in you begins to shift. It can be quite a relief to realize that those habits which no longer serve you can be relaxed over time and that other creative responses will be more available to you.
- You'll have to take this one on faith: There is nothing in you that needs fixing! This is one of the most challenging of all the principles, because most of us live in cultures that focus on fixing or doing something to make us better.
- But it is that very act of trying to do something to ourselves that works against the real you being able to emerge. And there is nothing wrong with what is real in you. There is no fixing our way through this. But there are ways to work with what you discover.

A primary benefit of using the Enneagram is that it helps you see that you are so much more than you have taken yourself to be. As you continue to work with this body of wisdom, you will recognize that the Enneagram is a powerful orientation that helps you become present and to recognize that you are more precious, real, lovable, and courageous than you know.

A Map of Love

That's why I call the Enneagram a **Map of Love.**

It speaks to the river that runs deep in the shared human experience with truth that is seldom spoken. It lets us know that we are not alone. It illuminates the places where we hurt and the exalted qualities where we shine. It explains and normalizes the inner polarities and allows us to knit our lives back together with real meaning.

It shows that every human being, regardless of their outward image, is on his or her own unique, but similar journey.

It invites us to awaken to a greater reality. And love is the nature of this reality.

Creating Choice

Feeling stuck: Being in a hole. No way out. Trying to achieve new results, but getting the same outcomes over and over. Alternatives are not identifiable. Having no choice.

Choice: Abundance of variety. Selection. Knowing and acting on options. Increased freedom.

Most people seem to enter into personal development because they feel unsatisfied or have a longing in some part of life. An abundant supply of books, Internet sites, motivational speakers, self-help programs, and professionals provide guidance on special techniques, tools, or approaches that are designed to create new results in life. Even in the midst of these abundant resources, what I find informative is that the sense of being stuck, even with outwardly very successful people, prevails.

What does it look like to experience freedom of choice internally?

In this chapter, we will penetrate deeper to explore the nature of choice, what distinguishes real choice from the usual exercise of making decisions, and how the personality structure affects one's relationship to choice.

Real and False Choice

There are hundreds of TV channels to choose from, more kinds of beverages than you can count, and a dizzying array of products to buy, but the choices of how to conduct one's life are clouded.

Let's look at the experience of choice on a continuum.

Scenario One: You may know those times when you are open, curious, responsive, alive, and feeling more at ease. Life works well, even when things are not perfect. These are the times when you feel lighter, more expansive, and able to respond to life's situations. When you are free to move with the flow of life and accept what is happening, it is easier to see that many of life's challenges turn out to be opportunities. You likely feel enormous gratitude for the many gifts and blessings in life, regardless of your current circumstances.

Both internal and interpersonal struggles are minimal and your natural strengths, openness, and clarity are more easily expressed. Life seems to work, and even when things do not go as planned, you adjust and go with it. You feel "at choice."

Scenario Two: Then, there are times when you find yourself stuck, non-productive, and reacting to situations and people that do not go your way. Life seems complicated, messy, and frustrating. You might think that life is working against you. As much as you might desire to, it's difficult to see any other way of responding to the situations that occur. You might engage in behavior that you know is not healthy, or not even what you want, but something drives you to do it anyway.

With the benefit of reflection, many people in this state find that they repeat the same experiences over and over, and get the same outcomes. Having little idea about what their alternatives could be, they feel very alone and perhaps ashamed of their inner discomforts. This feels like how life actually works. It wouldn't be unusual to hear an internalized or even an external voice saying, "Just get real. This is how life is."

Can you feel how a basic sense of internal choice is far more limited here? There are hundreds of TV channels to choose from, more kinds of beverages than you can count, and a dizzying array of products to buy, but the choices of how to conduct one's life are clouded. Yet, in the midst of this discomfort, the quiet inner voice that urges you to explore your options is still faintly audible.

But we can be even more cut off from real choice.

Scenario Three: Have you ever had times in your life when you were not going to budge? You were determined to have it your way, no matter what? Everyone else had it wrong, was impossible to deal with, or was a jerk? Or you just couldn't deal with life, and walled everything out except a familiar activity that consumed your attention? Nothing could get through to you. This experience is generally accompanied with a significant amount of internal tension and stress. With little room for reflection and a broader perspective, real choice is hidden from sight. Decisions are not choices, but re-enactments of a personality structure without serious reflection or insight.

Do you recognize any of these experiences in your own life? While we would rather not admit it, most of us have experienced many degrees of freedom and non-freedom along this continuum.

How is it possible that one person can have such a wide range of states?

The truth is, we are not nearly as free as we think, as long as the personality is driving our thoughts, emotions, and behaviors, because that is what keeps us coming back to the same experiences, over and over. Real choice increases every time some part of the personality is relaxed. You can feel the difference when this happens.

In this chapter we will look at three important keys that shape how much real choice you actually have, factors that create a more constricted view of life, and how you can turn your attention toward your more expansive, freer nature.

Key #1: Attributing Dissatisfaction to the Actions of Others

It is not only tempting, but culturally encouraged, to see the *cause* of the difficult or stuck times in life as coming from the external world. If you follow the news at all, it is not uncommon to see references to "who is to blame" for almost any difficult situation. And that easily gets transferred to our personal lives. For example, it may seem as if an unplanned change

The truth is, we are not nearly as free as we think, as long as the personality is driving our thoughts, emotions, and behaviors, because that is what keeps us coming back to the same experiences, over and over. Real choice increases every time some part of the personality is relaxed.

in your workplace, a new company policy, a decision made by your significant other, a difficult conversation, or someone else's behavior is the cause of your unhappiness. It can feel like something is happening *to* you or even as if someone is intentionally pushing your buttons.

Here is an example from Sandra, a talented woman in the midst of an important life transition. She revealed:

> *"It's so easy for me to immediately say yes to friends or people in my community when they ask me to lead a program or be in charge of a new project. Everybody knows I'll agree to do it. They know I will do a good job, and I know it, too. But I see how resentful I feel after I've said yes. It seems that those people who ask for my help know exactly which button to push so that I will do what they want me to."*

It's not uncommon to believe that others are responsible for our frustrations and disappointments. To get a sense of this in your own life, consider the amount of time and energy that is consumed by thinking about or talking about what other people have done or not done that has affected or seemingly offended you. It might seem that others can read your mind and know just what to do to intimidate, intrude upon, anger, withdraw from, or demand something of you.

One of the reasons for this is that, even though we may know intellectually that people see things from different perspectives and process situations in different ways, there is a deep and mostly unconscious belief that everyone looks at life in basically the same way. They approach life basically the same way you do. Check this out for yourself.

> *When other people do things that you don't understand or that upset you, have you ever thought, "If I was doing that, I'd approach it THIS WAY"? That might be followed with another inner objection: "If they don't do it the way I would, they should!" That objection might well be followed with some judgment about that person or, perhaps, that inner judgment gets turned against you. Or you might try to persuade or teach the other to approach the situation the way that is natural for you.*

Does this feel familiar? I certainly know these experiences well.

What we discover through the Enneagram is that people have wildly different internal worlds and vastly different ways of processing. Our inner experience of life seems so normal, so natural, so right. Why wouldn't everyone see it this way? How can I help them to do so?

But others don't experience life in the same way, unless you are both dominant in the same type, and there still could be significant differences. Your inner world could be very unfamiliar, even completely foreign, to a person who has a different personality type, as theirs could be to you. It is stunning to realize the substantial contrasts that exist between these inner landscapes.

What this means is that in the majority of situations, other people are not trying to create unhappiness for you. They are simply living inside their own inner landscapes that make perfect sense to them, if not to you. Getting a predetermined reaction from you is not what is most important in other people's lives. Thus, it is easy to misinterpret the intentions and behaviors of others.

And the reverse is also true. Your own perspective can seem perfectly normal to you, but not to those you interact with. I would guess that most of the time you do not intentionally try to create discord with others. Yet, when others are not deeply familiar with the dynamics that influence your typical behavior, they may well misunderstand you and your intentions, too. Since every part of life is impacted by our relationships—personal and intimate, at work, in our families and communities, this awareness of differing inner landscapes requires that we place into question our interpretations of the behaviors of others. We cannot expect most others to deeply understand us, at least until we are in the process of deeply understanding ourselves.

Learning more about the characteristics and inner experiences of people dominant in each of the Enneagram types and seeing specific examples will help this understanding land for you. Deepening into a recognition that each person is doing his or her best to live in concert with what makes internal sense can help you step out of the dance with others where you have unconsciously given them the responsibility for your well-being and satisfaction, and reclaim that as a personal responsibility.

In the majority of situations, other people are not trying to create unhappiness for you. They are simply living inside their own inner landscapes that make perfect sense to them, if not to you.

Letting others off the hook for our disappointments paradoxically expands the experience of inner choice. Most people have a sense of relief and increased freedom when they use their interactions with others as a basis for their own insight and development, rather than trying to change the other person. We psychologically and spiritually mature when we accept responsibility for our reactions and choices.

I want to be clear that we are not talking about self-blame here. Sometimes the word *responsibility* gets confused with *blame*, even in dictionaries! But there is an important difference. Blame incorporates some degree of accusation, condemnation, and finger-pointing. Most people do not feel safe when being the recipient of those charges. This is just as true if we are pointing the finger at ourselves with an accusatory voice. Then, it's hard to feel safe inside.

From my perspective, responsibility and, more specifically, self-responsibility convey an attitude of accountability to oneself. It is accompanied by a belief in one's capacity to fulfill a commitment or a promise. Even if we haven't fully developed that capacity, we work on it until it becomes a part of us.

We recall Sandra from earlier in this chapter. She shared her inner dilemma as she practiced letting others off the hook for her discomforts:

> *"As I'm learning how hard it is for me to say no, I see it's not really the other person's fault that I have such difficulty. Something is going on for me. I have come to recognize that if I say no, I feel guilty, and that's so painful that I'd rather just do the project, even if I'm resentful. I'd like to learn how to get beyond this."*

Key #2: Seeing Beyond the Either/Or Conundrum

Another dynamic that impacts the degree of inner freedom that you experience involves the seemingly dual choice between "*either* this option *or* that option."

Return once more to Sandra, as her inner sense of self shifted when she said no to the usual requests for her time and energy:

"But I'm now seeing that it's not just an either/or choice—either I say no and feel guilty, or say yes and feel resentful. There is another way. I am discovering that as I'm paying more attention to what brings me deeper satisfaction and even joy, I have less time for taking on things I don't love. And I'm realizing that the guilt is easing up. It's not quite as powerful or even real to me though there are still vestiges of it. I'm much more relaxed about this whole issue."

As she explored her typical responses to requests and allowed herself to experience the internal impact they had on her, Sandra saw two opposing dynamics at work: *yes was paired with resentment* and **no** *was paired with guilt*. She learned that she was caught in a conundrum between two undesirable states, and only from that recognition did she identify and practice what we could call a "middle way." For the first time in her life, she took a step back from this previously unseen dynamic and had enough perspective to recognize that other options were available to her. Experimenting with a new approach led to valuable results over time. She chose to identify and spend more time on things that brought her joy, and she experienced a palpable sense of relief and more real freedom.

Most of us have experienced either/or dilemmas. They keep us returning time and time again to familiar struggles. But without looking inwardly, it is nearly impossible to recognize that options exist. So it is to our internal experience that we need to draw our attention. During those times when you regularly feel frustrated, upset, resentful, irritated, guilty, judgmental, or burdened, you don't feel good about yourself or others. Inherent in these experiences lies a big clue that the personality is having its way with you. This is a red flag that your kindness and curiosity can be put to good use.

Key #3: The Role of Awareness

As we discuss the third dynamic, the role of awareness in contributing to greater choice and freedom, the *personality structure* again comes under the microscope. As a reminder, the personality structure refers to the way that the personality is designed and how it functions. The structure is not who you really are. Because this is a radically different approach to

You had what we call an awakening: the idea you had believed about yourself was not actually true.

understanding personality, it is hard for the mind to grasp. I encourage you to lessen the need for a full intellectual understanding at this time. This material is meant to communicate to a deeper part of you.

Let's look at another example, which I think of as Peter's shock-and-aha! moment:

Peter was a student in one of my workshops. He returned on day two with a big smile that had not been apparent on day one. I asked him about it.

"Oh," he said with an even bigger smile, "I saw 'it!' I saw a part of the structure of my personality that we talked about yesterday. I had never seen it before, and there it was."

He continued, "I laughed, because I do this all the time—I start fantasizing about what I'd rather be experiencing—and NOW, for the first time, I realize that I have a choice here. I can't even tell you what a difference it has already made for me."

His enthusiasm for this new self-awareness was evident. He saw clearly a frequently recurring behavior, a pattern—fantasizing—for the first time. Imagine the impact that could have.

You, too, may have had the experience of suddenly seeing a habitual and not particularly beneficial behavior that you use. This may have been accompanied by your own shock-and-aha! moment. Through consciously choosing to practice a different attitude or behavior, you may have felt some relief and hope. You had what we call an awakening: the idea you had believed about yourself was not actually true. This is an astonishing experience to have, and it opens the doors to more freedom.

The Enneagram delineates many specific, automatic patterns associated with each of the nine dominant Enneagram types. When unconscious, these patterns can stir up quite a bit of trouble for us. As you learn about the specific, automatic patterns that are part of the particular Enneagram type that is most dominant for you, you may experience moments of recognition—your own shock-and-aha! moments.

With your new awareness, you will begin to see how to soften your grasp of one automatic pattern at a time. You discover yourself as a more dynamic, fluid person. You have more real choice.

The Impact of the Personality's Constriction and Expansion

Try this exercise, taking your time with it:

EXERCISE: Tense your hand into a hard fist. Hold it for ten seconds, and notice how it affects you. What happens to your breath? Are other parts of your body tensing as well? Notice the sensations that you feel. Now, begin to release ever so gradually…Stay with your sensations as every tiny muscle, every cell, releases slowly, slowly… until your hand is fully open and relaxed.

When you tightened your hand, it became restricted in what it could do. It was more prepared for battle than for holding a gift. This is similar to what happens when you tense. You are more prepared for battle than for sharing your talents, recognizing opportunities, or receiving a gift.

Tension is a normal response to the daily stresses of life and is associated with the fight-or-flight response. From an evolutionary perspective, this response was necessary for survival when our ancestors' physical safety was threatened. The fight-or-flight response is still active in today's life, and most people live with an elevated stress-response as part of *normal*, daily life. If you are closely attuned to yourself, you may recognize tension physically, mentally, and emotionally. For example, even as you sit and read these words, you might notice tightness in certain parts of your body. It feels normal. *Is this tension necessary in this moment?* As you scan your body, what areas are ready to release the tension? You might notice that your breath is shallow, or even that you have quit breathing. You might notice the areas around your heart or head. For example, you might experience heaviness in your chest cavity or a tight band of tension around your head.

What most people are less familiar with is that the personality itself is made up of constrictions and tensions.

Stress is an internal response to external circumstances. Sometimes we recognize that these circumstances are cause for alarm, as when a natural or human-made disaster strikes, or when a high-speed car cuts in front of us unexpectedly on a busy highway.

We might also recognize that the stress response is ignited under so-called ordinary circumstances, for example, seeing a person at a party around whom we feel uncomfortable. Someone else seeing that same person might not experience a stress response. This indicates that it is our personal history that automatically triggers the majority of our stress-generating events.

What most people are less familiar with is that the personality itself is made up of constrictions and tensions. Contained within the system of the personality is a mechanism for generating stress and reinforcing tension. Thus, our varying degrees of tension during the day are a function of the personality's constriction or relaxation.

Consider times when you notice that you are tense for seemingly no reason at all. You might experience yourself as irritable, angry, jealous, anxious, resentful, suspicious, or controlling, or having other emotional responses that do not particularly make sense to you in the moment. Or there might be a specific trigger, such as being unhappy with a friend, colleague, or work situation, that appears to be the source of these same emotions. On reflection, you might see this as familiar. This is your personality's way of coping with your personal history.

As you identify and learn more about the personality structure that most closely reflects your life experience, you will also learn some tools for what we can call *relaxing the personality*. In everyday use, the word relaxation often is associated with vegging out on the couch, going to sleep, or going into some kind of visionary experience that takes you out of your body. For our purposes, it is something quite different. It entails an active awareness that supports the recognition and release of habitual patterns that are no longer serving your higher good. These patterns, surprisingly, are held together with internal tension. It is astonishing to see how much tension exists within. You can learn to pay close attention to the sensations associated with your body's inner tensions and, over time, gradually relax many of these constrictions. Later in the book, we'll identify some practices you can use to notice and let your body's tensions subside in order to release some of the personality's energy so that it doesn't have as much power to shape your life and limit your freedom.

The personality exists along a continuum. Each person's experience can range from highly constricted to highly expansive. We can say that the personality is *engaged* or *activated* when you feel compelled to act in a certain way, and when the characteristic signs of constriction are present. The patterns of the engaged personality generate the highest percentage of stress and constriction in people's lives. When we are more expansive and are not getting in our own way, we are open to enjoying the many blessings of life. Who wouldn't love more of that?

Table 2-1 (page 40) lists a number of attributes that characterize the polar opposites of the personality. These are shown on a continuum of constriction to expansion.

The vast majority of people in the world do not spend most of their life at either the pole of expansiveness or at the pole of constriction. In truth, there are many shades of expansiveness and constriction in between. In 1977, the late Don Riso, Enneagram pioneer, began exploring the varying dimensions of personality, which resulted in his discovery that there are nine levels of expansiveness and constriction within each type. Together Riso and Russ Hudson, another pioneering Enneagram teacher and author, and their team at the Enneagram Institute, have comprehensively defined the behaviors, attitudes, fears, and desires that describe each of the nine levels, which they call the *Levels of Development*, within each personality type.[1]

These levels are divided into three major categories: the three healthy or more liberated levels, the three average levels, and the three unhealthy or highly constricted levels. In other words, not only are there nine different Enneagram types, but there are also nine different levels of health, well-being, and freedom based upon this vertical dimension of the personality.

The patterns of the engaged personality generate the highest percentage of stress and constriction in people's lives.

Healthy Attributes: Expansive	Unhealthy Attributes: Constricted
Expansive	Highly constricted
I have my personality	Personality has me
Observant of patterns and non-attached	Highly attached to my patterns
High level of inner freedom and choice	Imprisoned/ no true choice
Curiosity about what I'm experiencing	Certainty that *how I am is who I am*
Broad range of perspectives	Narrowing of perspective
Receptive, transparent	Closed off/ closed to input
Most available to possibility	Most unaware of alternatives
Flexible, responsive	Inflexible, reactive
High degree of ease	High degree of tension
Energetic lightness	Energetic denseness
Most positive impact on others	Most negative impact on others
High level of emotional intelligence	Low emotional intelligence

Table 2-1: The Dynamic Nature of the Personality Along the Continuum of Constriction and Expansiveness

The differences in levels, say between the highly constricted and average levels, or the average and most liberated levels, translate to profound differences in our individual lives. Remember the three different scenarios that I included at the beginning of this chapter, under the subtitle, "Real and False Choice"? The first experience I described is a representation of the healthy levels. The second experience is more reflective of the average levels. And the third scenario is more representational of highly constricted levels.

Even within any one of the above categories, a difference in level has a substantial impact on our relationship to ourselves and to others, and to our capacity to live our highest purpose.

According to Riso and Hudson, the factor that determines the developmental level of a person dominant in any particular type is the degree to which the person is *present*.[2]

We are exploring and deepening our understanding and practice of *presence* throughout this book. For now, we can say that the more we are freed up from the automatic activity of our personality, the more present we are. It is the incessant, repetitive workings of the personality structure that blind us to our true nature and imprison us. To reiterate a teaching of Georges Gurdjieff,[3] the influential spiritual teacher who in the early twentieth century introduced the Enneagram as a system of awakening, it is these same patterns that, once recognized and relaxed, help us to take the journey toward awakening and inner freedom.

There are several additional benefits to understanding the vertical dynamism within types.

First, it describes the experience of many people who have a deep desire to continuously express their highest nature, and then are disappointed or resigned when faced with their own ineffectual or troubling behavior, feelings, or doubts. We see that this inner polarity is part of the human condition that is shared across humanity. No one is alone with this experience. However, on this journey, we each are invited to heal and resolve the polarities within ourselves.

It is these same patterns that, once recognized and relaxed, help us to take the journey toward awakening and inner freedom.

Second, even when the personality has a strong grip on our behavior, the Enneagram provides a specific map to our freer state of being. The map shows us that these higher qualities are part of the fabric of our real nature, and not something foreign to our existence. The levels illustrate the relationship between the less healthy characteristics and more healthy qualities—they are all connected along the continuum--and they point us to what our highest potential is.

Third, this continuum illustrates how, even within one day, you might experience moments of more or less expansiveness. For example, in one situation, you might express genuine gratitude, receptivity to others, and a deep sense of trust; moments later, after receiving an unwelcome phone call, for example, you might feel an internal tension and be compelled to react with distrust and cynicism.

Fourth, even when two people are dominant in the same type, they might express quite opposite characteristics because they are functioning at different levels. In Section II of this book, you'll see specific examples of the differences in the characteristics at the healthy and average levels for each Enneagram type.

Between the Polarities

So, what is happening in the average or mid section of the continuum, between its two ends? This mid section, after all, is where the broad majority of us spend most of our lives. It feels normal.

Below are just a few of the common characteristics experienced in this mid area of the continuum. Some of these will likely be quite familiar to you; other characteristics will not. Whatever you recognize in yourself, I invite you to meet this awareness with kindness and curiosity.

> *Limiting beliefs—holding onto diminished ideas about your possibilities, abilities, worth*

> *Being certain about how things are—not being open-minded or curious about options*

> *Grasping at something—continually striving to obtain, achieve, or make something happen*

Resisting what is—not accepting current realities

Keeping busy—not allowing for moments of inner quiet or reflection

Holding one's breath—forgetting to consciously breathe

Denial—refusing to acknowledge a troubling situation

Blaming—pointing the finger to outside causes of your dissatisfaction

Worrying—continual mental activity over worst-case, future scenarios

Not telling the truth to yourself or to others—holding back on what needs to be acknowledged and/or communicated

Judging—a focus on what is perceived as flaws in yourself or in others

Feeling victimized—making other people or situations responsible for one's unsatisfactory experience

Trying to control other people and situations—demanding that others do things a particular way

Trying to change others—putting relentless effort into causing another person to think or do as you think or do

Over-obligating yourself—scattering and depleting your energies

Trying too hard—keeping in the mode of "struggle"

Having an overly-busy mind—overthinking, analyzing, projecting, over-anticipating

"See me"—putting energy into having others see you and respond to you in a certain way

Withdrawing—leaving a situation physically, mentally, or energetically

These are typical characteristics of trying too hard or overusing a particular strategy to get a particular outcome in order to feel better internally. The characteristics are not bad and they don't make us bad, but when they are used habitually, they neither work nor serve in the long run.

Paradoxically, while they are used to achieve a particular positive outcome, they almost always create more stress, fatigue, and dissatisfaction in the long run, and they use a great deal of our life's energy. For example, a person might physically withdraw from a challenging conversation if he doesn't have confidence that he can be an effective participant or if the conversation is overwhelming for him. Solitary time may be much more comfortable, and withdrawing seems to resolve (at least, temporarily) the discomfort of the conversation. At best, the anxiety associated with the conversation may be temporarily interrupted, but it is not resolved. Another individual, for example, could spend an enormous amount of time worrying about one situation after another. To this person, worrying is necessary for ensuring that nothing bad happens, and that she and her family are secure. The act of worrying itself builds the level of tension and anxiety and often results in perceiving more threats than actually exist. In both of these examples, we get a glimpse into a pattern that returns again and again to re-create familiar results.

One of the difficulties posed by the habitual use of a particular strategy is that individuals are trying hard to create outcomes that make sense to them while other people are simultaneously trying to create very different outcomes that make sense in their inner world. When these two different efforts interfere with each other, they create conflict, much of which might be avoided with more awareness.

These strategies also point to the individual's desire to create certain outcomes that will lead to a greater sense of satisfaction, happiness, or fulfillment, as these are defined by the individual. Translated, it goes like this: "When THIS _____ (fill in the blank) changes, then I'll be happy."

EXERCISE: This is a good time to reflect on the conditions that you have felt need to be met in order for you to feel complete, fulfilled, happy, or present. To support you in exploring these generally hidden conditions of life, here are some guiding questions:

- What have you been trying to make different?
- What or who needs to change?
- What do you hear yourself saying regularly (loudly or almost imperceptibly) to yourself that needs to happen for you or for life to be okay?
- What haven't you been able to do that you really would love because of where you have been putting your energy?

Some of the characteristics on the above continuum may be familiar, but they are not inevitable for the rest of your life. Regardless of where you are on the continuum, what matters is that you meet yourself where you are now with **nonjudgment** and kindness and that you pay attention to the direction you are facing—toward health and expansiveness or toward constriction.

As we continue in this exploration, you will gain more insight and tools for detecting the more constricted aspects of yourself and creating conditions that support the unfolding of your soul.

Direct Experience Leads to Change

With growing awareness, you will not only notice your automatic patterns more frequently, but you can learn to have a **direct experience** of them. Direct experiences happen when you feel the sensations in your body that are associated with an interaction or situation that has impacted you.[4]

Generally, we have an idea about our experiences, or try to analyze them. We can tell whole stories about who did what to whom, complete with our opinions and judgments, however, this approach seldom contributes to any positive change. It keeps us hooked into our personality's version of life, and denies us the benefit of a more expanded perspective.

A direct experience is radically different. It is not filtered through our mental processing or emotional upsets, but instead is sensed in the body. Having a direct experience takes our attention below the level of ideas and *below* the circumstances surrounding a situation. We shift our focus from the obvious entanglements of the situation and focus on what we might consider very unusual territory—what is happening within our bodies. Here, in the sensations conveyed through the body, we discover a whole new source of information about ourselves, and about what contributes to our personality's usual strategies.

John, the director of a graphics department in a large firm, offers a great example of shifting his attention from his ideas about what was going on in the workplace to his direct experience:

In a coaching session, John shared a challenge he was having with his staff not getting their work done to his expectations. He was frustrated by feeling he needed to step in and improve on their work, which he had done many times. He now felt considerable resentment about having to take on this additional work.

He also indicated he felt this same, familiar frustration on a daily basis in other situations. He felt his frustration was justified due to other people's inability to perform to his standards, and wondered why others weren't upset by these irresponsible behaviors. Then John started to recognize that this frustration was a repeating pattern of his personality.

I asked him to check in with himself and see what he noticed going on in his body, below the idea of his frustration with his staff. What he found was that his whole chest, shoulder, and heart area were tight and tense. As we took the time he needed to breathe into the tightness, tears came as he realized that he felt totally cut off from his staff, as well as from himself. He recognized that he focused almost exclusively on the tasks to be done, to the exclusion of the human beings working in the same environment.

He also came to see that most of his interactions included some degree of criticism and negative feedback, even though his intentions were usually to be helpful.

Over time, he practiced looking at the faces of people he was interacting with, rather than focusing solely on the project. He learned to slow down and to be more curious about these individuals. He experimented with communicating with them differently, so that the focus was more about the work challenges that they were having rather than simply pointing out what was wrong. That led to more shared problem-solving and the implementation of new strategies.

Over time, his frustration and resentment decreased remarkably. Not only did he change, but his change allowed for his staff to respond to him differently, too. He became more approachable.

His recognition and subsequent direct experience of his frustration pattern that was creating obstacles to a healthier work environment gave way to new insights about himself and, eventually, about his impact as a leader. Refocusing his attention from the inadequacies of his staff to his felt, internal experience was an important step in healing an inner pain that he had not addressed and in discovering new possibilities both for himself and for his team. He learned how he could reach out to his staff and still have high standards.

Can you imagine the freedom and relief that he experienced? You, too, have the capacity for this release. You are part of the great human experiment in releasing patterns!

A Stunning Perspective on Change for Your Personal Journey

We're not in a search to rid ourselves of our personalities. Rather, a question worth asking is, "Do I have a personality, or does it have me?"

Used with awareness, your personality can serve you well. You can use it when you need to reconcile your bank account, and approach that task with clarity and serenity, for example.

But if the personality has you in its grip, it is in charge. It is making the decisions. It is your master. It is running your life. You have far less choice than you realize.

Our purpose here is to explore the process in which you discover how to become more aware of and have the capacity to relax the personality structure. An essential key to this process is being as nonjudgmental as possible about your self-discoveries.

Every time you recognize a familiar, unsatisfying experience, and meet that experience with nonjudgment, it counts. You soon start to inquire about the hidden motivations behind a pattern, and it begins to relax. Every time you can realize that the pattern is simply that—a protective and familiar pattern associated with an Enneagram type—it allows the pattern to soften. Every time a pattern is softened, it no longer has such power or control in your life. Over time, your natural strengths arise, and you feel more at ease and at peace within yourself, and the behavior of others which caused an emotional reaction in the past has much less of an impact on you.

The *real you* is naturally open, responsive, alive, generative, and present. At this more expansive end of your personality's health and flexibility,

But if the personality has you in its grip, it is in charge. It is making the decisions. It is your master. It is running your life. You have far less choice than you realize.

47

you naturally express what is best within you. You have more contact with your eternal and essential nature.

With every level of relaxing the protective layers of the personality, there is movement toward higher levels of your emotional and spiritual health. Your perspective becomes more neutral (as opposed to the energetic charge associated with certain situations that have pushed your buttons in the past); objective (that is, you see things for what they are, rather than interpreted through the layers of personal biases); and fluid. Your natural gifts and authentic generosity of spirit are more available to you and to others.

As a metaphor for the difference, I invite you to consider this exercise:

EXERCISE: Imagine that you're swimming in a pool. The pool is all you know. It is life itself. The pool has sides which provide limits to where you can go. You don't know that there is anything but the pool.

Now, imagine that you've risen above the pool and see that it is contained within an expanse of water that is so vast that you cannot see any end to it. There are no edges.

The pool is like the personality. When you're in it, there's nothing more. The pool is all there is.

The vast expanse of water is like your higher, healthier nature. You're aware of the pool and can dip into as you need. When it's time to take laps, the pool will do. But you recognize its limitations. The ocean holds far more possibility.

Like being in the pool, being caught in personality narrows and limits perspective. It is easy to get caught up in the drama of life and to get emotionally charged around various circumstances.

As you become more observant of how you interact with the specific circumstances in your life and are in deeper touch with the actual internal sensations that are growing in your awareness, you gain a more expanded perspective. If you can be aware without acting on your inner urges, you release a percentage of the hold that the personality has on you at that time. You are more present to what is really happening, rather than reacting from an idea of what's happening or from an emotional trigger to that situation. You have a broader viewpoint from which to observe the personality in action. With more presence, you gain a sense of choice about how to respond, a gift of incomparable worth.

Your work with the Enneagram helps you recognize what happens when your personality structure is operating on automatic. At the same time, it gives you a template for moving out of total reliance on your personality and into a deeper relationship with your more expansive and truer dimension of self. In that vein, I have found it useful to distinguish between *having* a type rather than *being* a type. For example, there is a difference between saying, "I have a Type _____ personality" and "I am a Type _____." Recognizing that you have a type connotes that there is far more to you than the patterns of the personality and that you are becoming more aware of both the patterns and your innate expansive nature.

Learning How You "Do" Life:
Decoding the Ego's Inner Logic

Simply going along with how we naturally approach day-to-day living is the easiest and most natural thing in life. We are heavily conditioned to think that how we do life is life itself.

As we grew up, we naturally identified with our particular approach to life and took it to be the real thing—reality. Most people find it quite stunning to realize that their automatic way of living, thinking, behaving, and doing is actually a core strategy for managing life. As discussed in Chapter 1, it is a strategy for managing the pain and challenges of life. However, this core strategy often creates more unhappiness and dissatisfaction.

Each of the nine personality styles has a way of organizing life around core ideas about self and life that feels necessary, right, and real. What you organize your life around is related to where you naturally put your attention. Figure 3-1 reveals where people who are dominant in different types focus their attention when the personality is most active or engaged. This is a snapshot of what a person dominant in each type automatically thinks about, acts on, or unconsciously focuses a lot of energy on when their personality is in charge.

The Focus of Attention creates a narrowing of the field of possibilities.

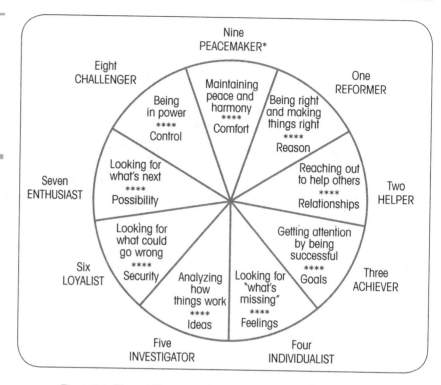

Figure 3-1: "Engaged" Focus of Attention in the Nine Enneagram Types
* The names of the Enneagram types are those of Riso and Hudson.

Let's take a look at how the Focus of Attention (FOA) functions. First, consider all the areas of life that could capture a person's attention. The field of possibility is stunningly vast—our minds cannot take it all in at once. We might say that our personality, supported by our neurobiological wiring, creates a set of blinders that manages where our attention is placed so that we are overwhelmingly interested in a particular slice of life. The Focus of Attention creates a narrowing of the field of possibilities.

As a by-product, this narrowing creates a set of expectations. We naturally expect that others will have the same Focus of Attention as we do, and these expectations inform how we interpret what is happening in the environment, as well as shape what we listen and look for. When we are emotionally charged, the FOA becomes more pronounced, defined, and fixed. Of course, the difference in the Focus of Attention affects how we relate to others.

Here is an example:

Chelsea and Nolan, a professional couple in their mid-forties, often had disagreements about how to use their weekends. Chelsea loved being on the go and created lists that she shared with her partner of what she considered exciting activities or places where they could enjoy their weekends. She naturally wanted him to be enthusiastic about the possibilities that they could explore. When Nolan saw a list, he paid attention to possible difficulties. Before agreeing to go anywhere, he carefully reviewed any potential problems that they might encounter. He naturally wanted her to understand the possible consequences of their travels. Truthfully, he preferred to stay close to home. When they could not reach an agreement, their emotions often intensified as their personal approaches to the weekend hardened. Chelsea pushed more to get away; Nolan was more insistent about telling her all the things that could go wrong if they were away. Their perspectives narrowed so that they could only see the situation from their own particular lens.

As you review figure 3-1, some of these different ways to focus attention may seem surprising or even silly to you, but they won't feel silly to those who have that particular focus. You may recognize one of the areas of attention, and think, "Well, yes, of course I do that. Doesn't everyone? But that's not a type. That's just how life is."

While teaching a workshop, I briefly discussed how people dominant in Type Three focus on goals. Once one goal is achieved, another immediately takes it place. Individuals who have this type experience a strong drive to achieve each goal successfully. Goals are viewed as a vehicle to achievement and recognition.

One of the participants said, "I don't understand. Everyone focuses on goals. That's just part of life. I don't see how doing that is part of a particular type." She added that she was frustrated with some of her staff who didn't seem as goal-oriented as they "should be."

Over the course of the workshop she recognized that, because she was dominant in Three, the goal orientation was natural for her. That's where she put a great deal of attention.

For those dominant in other types, goals might be important or not, but goals will not be the focus of their attention. In fact, they might have to work really hard on identifying worthwhile goals.

The FOA points to how dramatically different the internal world of the nine types actually are. The less aware we are that these differences exist, the more potential there is for inner struggle and interpersonal conflict. With awareness, we create the possibility for greater understanding and less insistence that our way is really the best, if not the only, way.

How the FOA defines the scope of attention for each type will be addressed in Section II.

> **TIP**: Should you have a response similar to the woman in the story to any of the descriptions of the personality types as you read, allow that to serve as a clue that this could actually point you to your dominant type. If a description leads you to respond, "Well, of course I do that! That's what people do, or are supposed to do," you want to pay particular attention to the description of that type.

Nine Approaches to "Doing" Life

Not only does each type have a specific Focus of Attention, it is also organized around a particular logic that creates a sense of internal coherence. We don't have a choice about this, as the template for our particular internal logic lies within us from our earliest moments of life.

Let's see how this works.

The Great Loss

As mentioned in Chapter 1, very early in your human journey, before you could think or talk, you had prelingual and preconceptual experiences of being separated from qualities that your soul loved. This loss of connection left you feeling hurt, separate, and alone. The egoic structure began developing as a protection from the pain of this loss, trying to mimic the qualities of your true nature. Of course, it can never be successful in doing so.

Within the context of this inevitable pain of your early life, you came to know yourself in relationship to the world in a very defined way.

As an adult, the ego's attempt at replicating any essential quality often creates internal confusion because it can be difficult to discern between the faux version and the real experience of that quality. For example, if you're dominant in Type Nine, the egoic structure tries to recreate the experience of "All is One." Indeed, at the level of Essence, this is true. But the Nine personality structure holds onto this belief as a sacred cow and puts substantial energy into demanding it. Then, any experience that challenges the inner sense of oneness is dismissed. With the mimicked experience comes much efforting and reactivity. The authentic experience arises naturally, with no energetic grip, when we are present to the deeper truth.

But often, we are not aware that an effortless experience of our true nature is possible. The ego structure or personality type is so powerful that we forget that this deep and intimate connection with our higher nature actually exists. As part of the psychological and spiritual journey, the loss represents the shift from the original experience of unity to one of duality. We feel divided. In Christian traditions, for example, this is referred to as the fall from grace. This shift delivers a devastating blow to the soul of the sensitive little being, and has been referred to as the primal catastrophe[1] and primal terror.[2]

Here, we refer to it as *the great loss.*

The Basic Inner Logic and the Triangle of Identity

Remember the description of the core belief from Chapter 1? A core belief forms our basic assumptions about life. Only when we're working at deeper levels of self-understanding do we begin to recognize that this belief actually exists. Nevertheless, a core belief is potent and a major factor in shaping how we respond to life.

> *Within the context of this inevitable pain of your early life, you came to know yourself in relationship to the world in a very defined way.*

Though it's very hard to admit, we humans continue to filter our life through the experience of a very young child unless we achieve awareness and healing around our primary core beliefs.

Fundamentally, as a person's core belief arises unconsciously at a very early stage in life, it creates in that person a sense of inner inadequacy or weakness in relationship to others and to the larger environment. Of course, this sense of "not being enough" is too painful for the little child that we once were to tolerate. So, the ego's strategies take on the job of protecting that little child from this experience. Eventually, the little child grows into an older child, an adolescent, and then an adult. Unless that person becomes conscious of this core belief and questions its veracity over and over, the core belief continues to shape daily life with the inner logic subsequently falling in line. Though it's very hard to admit, we humans continue to filter our life through the experience of a very young child unless we achieve awareness and healing around our primary core beliefs. To mature emotionally and spiritually requires that we delve into this deeper self-understanding.

The general description of how this inner logic works goes like this:

Each Enneagram type comes with a core belief, or the ego's basic assumption of how life works. Thus, your dominant Enneagram type comes equipped with a particular core belief.

Each of the nine core beliefs leads the individual dominant in that type to want to have a particular experience repeat itself over and over. For example, those individuals dominant in Type Two likely want to have a warm connection to the various people in their life, and they have a habit of reaching out and doing a lot for these people. Those dominant in Type Five want to understand how things work and need a lot of private time to focus on increasing their understanding. In other words, each of us wants what, at some level, we think will make life satisfying, or at least make it work the best it can.

This supposedly satisfying experience is *what you pursue* and will go to great lengths to satisfy. For example, if feeling safe is what you want, you will do what you can to create this sense of safety wherever you go and with whatever you are working on. You will likely check for any existing problems and be alert to what could go wrong. You may take note on how to exit a building quickly in case of a threat, or you may want to know exactly what is expected of you in various situations.

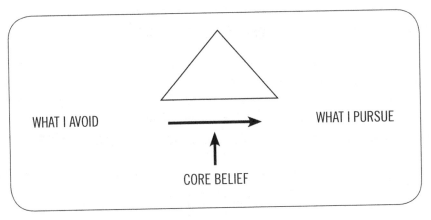

Figure 3.2 Foundation of Triangle of Identity

You may not know why it's so important to pursue this activity; you just know that you must. You feel authentic when you are doing so. What is hard to see is that there is a belief operating underneath this behavior. Referring to the above example, a core belief is that you are not safe, that there is nothing you can really trust. Even if you are as safe as any of us could be, the necessity of " just making sure" that all the possible kinks have been worked out in a given situation is compelling.

Simultaneously, running in the opposite direction to that compelling experience is another experience that *we try mightily to avoid*. The experience that we avoid, again depending upon the dominant Enneagram style, is the opposite of the experience we pursue. For example, if experiencing your strength, power, and being in control is of utmost importance, then you would go to great lengths to avoid what your ego considers the opposite: any sense of weakness, limitation, or vulnerability.

In fact, even the *idea* of experiencing this opposite quality can lead to a great anxiety, fear, and resistance. This opposite quality feels like one to be avoided at all costs because it threatens our very sense of self. But what it is actually threatening is the ego's idea of itself.

The inner logic continues. In order to satisfy this inner polarity of what the personality pursues and what it tries to avoid at all costs, we use a seemingly perfect and obvious—at least to the personality—coping strategy which keeps us in the loop of trying to get a certain need met, and avoid the opposite, undesirable situation. We don't think about the coping strategy much. It is our default approach to meeting the demands of life.

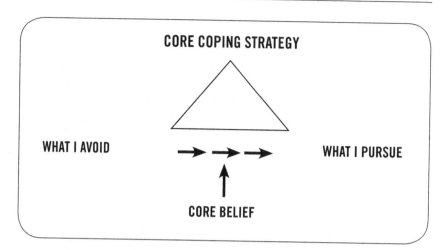

Figure 3.3 Development of Triangle of Identity

Arising from the core belief, these three elements, interacting together—what you pursue, what you avoid, and your default core-coping strategy—lead to a particular sense of self. Depending on the type that you most identified with, this sense of self is how you come to know yourself.

Depending on one's dominant Enneagram style, these elements create an internal program, which I call the Triangle of Identity, that reflects the general themes of how a person does life. Illuminating this program helps each of us to see our automatic, repetitive response to life with more clarity. Becoming familiar and conscious of this default program is a valuable step in lessening reliance on the automatic patterns and experiencing new possibilities in life. All of this is in support of you experiencing positive changes in how you relate to yourself, to others and the environment, and, ultimately, to your higher nature.

A diagram and example of the Triangle of Identity for people dominant in Type Three is on the next page. Let's see how to apply the concepts within the Triangle of Identity to this particular type.

A woman dominant in this type, for example, has the core (unconscious) beliefs that life is a contest and she has to be the best, and that she doesn't have value beyond her accomplishments.

She believes the way to **pursue** having value is to set goals that are perceived as having a high value in the eyes of those whose recognition she desires. It seems that there is no end to her having goals. Once one goal is attained, another immediately takes its place.

She wants to **avoid** the experience of being seen as a failure. To her, failing would reinforce her great fear that she lacks inherent value. She avoids putting herself in situations where there's a good chance that she won't succeed, whether that be participating in auditions for a school performance, engaging in an athletic competition, or applying for a position that she would truly enjoy.

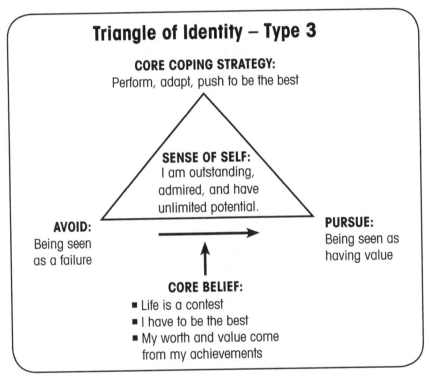

Triangle of Identity – Type 3

CORE COPING STRATEGY:
Perform, adapt, push to be the best

SENSE OF SELF:
I am outstanding, admired, and have unlimited potential.

AVOID:
Being seen as a failure

PURSUE:
Being seen as having value

CORE BELIEF:
- Life is a contest
- I have to be the best
- My worth and value come from my achievements

Figure 3.4 Triangle of Identity for Type 3

So she **copes** by adapting or re-inventing herself to be successful in whatever environment she is in. She can change quickly from being a high-producing member of a team, to being the most flexible and accomplished yoga student, to being a gracious and inspiring hostess.

When we get to the more expanded discussion of Type Three in Chapter 9, we'll see how this dynamic reinforces her **sense of self** as "outstanding, admired by others, and having unlimited potential," and how the

When any of us get attached to being a certain way, then we cut ourselves off from the rest of what is possible in life.

combination of a core belief, a powerful emotional force, a mental habit, and the inner critic keep her locked in this closed system of pursuing/avoiding/coping. In other words, this inner logic continues until it is brought into the open and explored with curiosity, compassion, and honesty. As is true for all types, the inner logic becomes the basis for her inner stories and how she relates to life.

The inner logic also sets up an internal, either/or polarity. For this woman, it is easy for her to believe that either she must perform to meet or exceed the standards of success that she feels are expected of her to win admiration, even when she has reached her limits and is exhausted or she shows her vulnerability and fatigue, and feels like a loser.

Neither of these options is fulfilling, but it is difficult to recognize that other options are available when someone is entangled in this Triangle of Identity.

Just to note, being outstanding and admirable are both beautiful traits to have. The problem is not that the woman in this example has these qualities, but that this is who she believes herself to be. When any of us get attached to *being* a certain way, then we cut ourselves off from the rest of what is possible in life. We limit our growth and deny ourselves access to what is real, true, and ultimately, most soul-satisfying. When we are too attached to being a certain way, we color our perception of life.

Let's see how the inner logic continues in this example: The Type Three woman now has a fixed idea about who she is and what is acceptable and not acceptable. She is too strongly adhered to her Triangle of Identity, and she feels habitually caught between her public persona and her inner feeling of inadequacy.

Doesn't it make perfect sense that you would feel stuck if you are repeating the same cycle over and over again, but without being able to see it? And doesn't it make sense that you would feel lost because this recurring cycle keeps you out of contact with what is real, authentic, and nourishing to your soul?

Under these circumstances, we feel lost because, at some level, we really do know that we have lost an essential connection with that which is real—with our soul.

The more we forget about our expansive, freer self, the more we lose contact with a precious, innate capacity that is available when we are most aware and present. As this innate capacity becomes hidden to your view, a specific energetic drive, called the *passion* in Enneagram language, kicks into gear.

This **energetic drive**, or **passion**, is part of the inner logic. It acts like an engine, fueling and driving the logic. The less aware or present a person is, the more this engine gains momentum. Its impact is to take you away from what your heart and soul most love, and away from your highest nature. In effect, the greater momentum the passion has, the more you go off course from your soul's desire. Off you go, moving in the exact opposite direction of what would bring you the most joy, peace, love, aliveness, and satisfaction.

Let's go back to our example from above: The energetic drive for personality Type Three is called vanity. It can be understood as wanting to be seen as the sole reason for one's success. The energy of vanity centers around "my accomplishments." So, this wonderful, talented, and inspiring woman, when caught in the grip of her personality, wants her successes, or those of her children or husband, for example, to be the center of attention. She works so hard at being productive and achieving at the highest level that she has lost sight of the bigger picture, and of herself. She has forgotten that many factors have contributed to her success, and that there is a life outside of accomplishing something.

This is an astonishing discovery for most of us. This inner logic truly makes sense to the personality, or, in other language, to the egoic self. From its own tightly contained perspective, the personality can't see that the inner logic moves us in the wrong direction.

> **NOTE**: *This is an example of the closed personality system at work, as we explored in chapter 1.*

It feels exactly right, until you begin to see it from a larger perspective.

When we have more breathing room and awareness, this inner logic shows us one of the most remarkable of all paradoxes in life: *The direction that our personality is designed to take us actually creates more wanting, more frustration, and more dissatisfaction.* The personality, following its own dictates, seems to work up to a point, but, uncontested, eventually leads to suffering. As Thomas Moore wrote, "The odyssey of soul runs in counterpoint to the odyssey of life."[3] No wonder we can feel at odds within ourselves.

The absolute irony of discovering the inner logic of the personality is that, without having it illuminated, it is generally the last place you would even think of examining.

Recognizing the inner logic that most resonates with you from the type descriptions in Section II is a powerful way to tap into the mechanisms of your personality and how you have previously thought of yourself. You also might find it valuable for self-typing or for validating your type.

The more you become aware as to how this inner logic operates, and the less power you give it, the freer you become. Without this awareness, life can easily remain unsatisfying and disappointing, and positive change can be difficult to sustain.

Identifying Your Dominant Type

Identifying the type that you most recognize in yourself will support you in seeing how you have lived. You already may have an inkling of what your dominant type is, based on the short descriptions we've discussed so far. Keep in mind that discovering your dominant type is a process. While some readers readily recognize their dominant type, for many people, accurately identifying their type comes with time and reflection.

Strategies for identifying your dominant type include taking paper and pencil or online tests, reading more about the Enneagram, scheduling a typing interview with a Deep Coaching or other Enneagram practitioner, and taking classes on this topic. But before you do any of those, finish reading this book, with special emphasis on Section II chapters on the nine types. By the time you've done that, chances are you'll have either figured out your type or have it narrowed down to a few choices.

For more help with deciding your type after reading this book, check out the Resources (page 403) for typing support from our website.

Tips on Finding Your Type

None of us want to be in a box. Finding your dominant type is an important first step in starting to move out of the box that the patterns of your type have already created. Ultimately, we are supported in becoming freer of the box as we expand our capacity for being present and disengaging from our historical sense of self. We call this process *dis-identifying* from our personality's patterns.

We all have some aspect of each of the nine types within us, so it is likely that you'll relate to some qualities of most types in yourself. What most distinguish one type from another are the underlying motivating factors. By focusing on those factors, you are more apt to identify your type.

We are the only ones who can actually type ourselves. While others may comment, "Oh, you are a Type ____," please do not take them too seriously. The reason that we are the only ones who can determine our actual type is that the motivating factors underlying our behaviors are hidden to others. You are the one who is having your experience, and, ultimately, it will be you who says, "Oh, yes, this is the type that I most recognize in myself."

I would also discourage you from telling others what you think their types are, as even seasoned Enneagram professionals can be wrong about another person's type. Instead, you can point your friends and loved ones to resources such as this book and invite them to explore for themselves.

Sometimes individuals want to have a different dominant type than they have. That's called *type envy*! We don't get to choose our type. Every sphere of consciousness, every Enneagram style, has its own gifts and challenges, and no type can be measured against another in terms of better or worse. Each one offers a unique journey that is profound and sacred.

Remember that finding your type is a process. Try keeping an open mind about what you discover. As you learn more about the Enneagram and continue to be more observant of yourself, you eventually will land in the territory that most deeply resonates with your internal experience and your history.

The Social Style Clusters

Trying to find your type through learning about all nine inner worlds at once can feel overwhelming. One way to get a handle on this knowledge is to cluster the nine types into groups of three. While there are several approaches to grouping the types, I have found the Social Style Clusters to be very beneficial and this is the approach I use in this book. These clusters are based on the pioneering work of Karen Horney.

Horney was a psychotherapist who recognized that people experience significant amounts of stress in many social situations. While this kind of stress is often swept under the carpet, it is a very real source of inner discomfort. Horney identified three kinds of strategies[4] that individuals use to reduce the anxiety that is triggered by the demands of unfamiliar social interactions.

Since we live in a changing world and are frequently in new, unfamiliar, or uncomfortable social contexts, the opportunity to recognize your interactions from this perspective offers another window into how you do life, and it may help point you to your dominant type.

Dealing with Social Discomfort

Horney noted that we develop and tend to use one of three basic strategies or solutions for dealing with social discomfort in childhood: resignation, expansiveness, or compliance. We can continue to unconsciously use these through adulthood.

EXERCISE: Take a moment to consider the scenario described below:

You are about to walk into a civic or professional meeting, a party, or other social gathering comprised of individuals who are acquaintances and others whom you do not know at all. You do not have any special role to fulfill in this group.

NOTE: *Your inner responses are probably going to be quite different if you are meeting with people you like or know well. So for this exercise, please imagine walking into a room of acquaintances and strangers.*

See if you can tune into the following information about how you respond to this experience:

- What do you notice about your body's responses?
- What are your thoughts?
- What is your emotional state?
- What do you notice about your behavior that you would likely exhibit (not that which you think you should be exhibiting)? How much does your outer behavior reflect your inner experience?
- Do you feel a sense of discomfort, for example, but mask that with friendly chatter? Do you quietly say hello and look for a place to sit? Do you confidently approach the host or facilitator and introduce yourself?

Your honest reflection about this scenario may give you a window into your customary approach to dealing with the stress of unfamiliar interpersonal relationships.

If you pay close attention, you may even notice that you have a heightened level of stress or anxiety. This is common. Settings which involve interpersonal communication often are accompanied by some underlying, if hidden, discomfort.

Have you ever noticed how important food is at these kinds of events? Yes, people may be hungry, but food serves as a potent social lubricant—a way to provide a source of comfort or even distraction from social discomforts.

Keep in mind that some of us cover over the discomfort so quickly that we don't even notice it's there.

Enneagram pioneers Don Riso and Russ Hudson found a connection between their work and that of Horney's. They discovered that three Enneagram types corresponded to each of Horney's interpersonal coping solutions.[5]

Here are the three Social Style Clusters comprised of three Enneagram types each:

1. The first cluster, called the Private, or Solo, style (Riso and Hudson label these as the Withdrawn types), is comprised of Types Nine, Four, and Five. These coincide with Horney's *resigned* solution, in which the individual *moves away from* or withdraws from others. This cluster is the first to be presented in Section II, in Chapters 6–8.

2. The second grouping is called the Assured/Confident Cluster. Riso and Hudson, using the term Assertive types, identified that Types Three, Seven, and Eight belong here. This cluster reflects Horney's *expansive*, or aggressive, solution, in which the individual *moves against* others. This cluster will be presented second in Section II, in Chapters 9–11.

3. The third cluster, the Service-Oriented/Responsible grouping, includes Types One, Two, and Six, and is called the Dutiful group by Riso and Hudson. These respond to Horney's *compliant* solution, in which the individual *moves toward* others. We will discuss this final cluster in Chapters 12–14 in Section II.

Also in Section II, at the beginning of the discussion on each cluster, you will find a brief description of the coping strategy, or solution, that binds the three types together in that particular cluster.

The Case of Mistaken Cause and Effect

If it's difficult to identify your dominant Enneagram patterns, it may be because you are explaining your life experience based on your personal history, such as your early emotional or living environment or the impact that someone in particular had on you. It's true that our early experiences have contributed to shaping our life story, however, they are not the sole cause of how you have approached or interpreted your life.

Here are a few examples to show you how people often attribute their behaviors exclusively to their childhood experiences, rather than taking into account the patterns of their Enneagram type:

A man who is dominant in Type Six connects his continual propensity to think about and do everything possible to ensure that he and his family are safe and supported to the fact that he grew up in an environment that lacked safety, stability, and protection. Over the decades, he accumulated a large amount of data to reinforce his need to be vigilant against potential threats to his family. Those threats seem to exist everywhere. He has not yet recognized that being on the outlook for threats is part of the Type Six personality structure.

A woman dominant in Type Two continually looks for approval and affirmation from important people around her. She does extra little things for others that she hopes will be well-received, acknowledged, and greatly appreciated. If the appreciation isn't forthcoming in the way that she would like, she feels unappreciated or rejected. She remembers her mom not having enough time for her, and feeling rejected by her early on. And over the decades, she accumulated a lot of experiences where she felt that others turned away from her, which all confirm her need to continually give to others as a way to receive loving acceptance. She has not yet recognized that the propensity to give too much reflects the Type Two personality.

A woman dominant in Type Four desires to have the best in life. She grew up with wealth and with an assumption that there would always be enough wealth to live the life she wanted without having to work. Facing unexpected and considerable financial loss in her mid-forties, she felt unprepared to support herself. She did not have the confidence in her abilities to develop skills, nor did she have a particular interest in doing so. She pointed to her parents for not better preparing her for life. She has not yet recognized that her experience reflects the patterns of Type Four personality.

In these examples, it would be easy for the individual to believe that his or her life experience was based solely on early life experiences. Perhaps you too have thought, "I am the way I am because of my previous life experiences." However, the personality structure plays a dramatic role in shaping how we respond to our life experiences.

It's impossible to change the past, but it is possible to change consciousness.

In identifying your dominant Enneagram orientation, it's important to remember that, as part of being human, the filter of your personality has always been functioning. It magnetically draws to you certain information that resonates with your personality's structure, and it keeps competing information off the radar screen.

For example, it is likely that the woman who has felt a lot of rejection has a soul that is very sensitive to the experience of rejection. From an objective perspective, she may not have received a higher degree of rejection than most other people. She is just more sensitive to how others have interacted with her. Simultaneously, she probably is not attuned to the amount of acceptance and love that comes her way, or perhaps the experience of actual acceptance doesn't stick with her easily.

One of the great benefits of discovering your type is that, eventually, your personal history can begin to lose its power in present-day life. Realizing how much of your life experience is filtered through the lens of your dominant type leads to letting other people, especially from your childhood, off the hook for at least some of your experience. And that release frees you to make desired change. It's impossible to change the past, but it is possible to change consciousness.

As you become more aware of the narrow range of information allowed on your radar screen by virtue of your type, then you are on the road to enlarging your vision, expanding your life, and growing your capacity to make life-affirming changes.

I am excited to be with you on this journey of discovering or confirming your dominant type. It contains an amazing range of experiences—from recognizing the internal sources of your lifelong suffering to experiencing your most elevated nature. I can think of no other journey so worth your time, awareness, and love.

Creating a New Relationship with Yourself

Gaining deeper insight into how you do life can feel like a journey. Whenever we take a new journey, it's important to prepare for it. This chapter provides guidance on how to do that.

I have a bumper sticker on the door to my office that reads, EXPECT SOMETHING WONDERFUL TO HAPPEN. That is true with this work. When you agree to go beyond your customary way of knowing yourself, it is useful to remember that you wouldn't even be reading this if you weren't ready. Something inside of you is urging you on.

Most people who have gained more profound self-knowledge through the Enneagram report that they have experienced times of great surprise, sadness, relief, embarrassment, grief, hope, and a kind of spiritual humor. You are likely to have an array of emotions yourself, which can be signs of coming into a more intimate relationship with yourself. Developing a deeper, authentic relationship with yourself is necessary for healing and for fully participating in the continual, evolutionary nature of life. While letting go of dated notions about our identity, it is natural to experience ourselves in the flow of life.

With that in mind, it's important to orient to and call upon qualities that will support you. Here are four qualities that I've found helpful in this soulful journey. These qualities are already available to you. Naming them is a way to remember to open to and access them.

Developing a deeper, authentic relationship with yourself is necessary for healing and for fully participating in the continual, evolutionary nature of life.

Four Vital Qualities

*Curiosity comes
with a willingness
to not know
an answer in
advance.*

1. Being Curious

The quality of curiosity allows us to see things from a new perspective, to engage our inquisitiveness, and to be open to discoveries. This is quite different than feeling an internal pressure to already have an answer figured out. Curiosity comes with a willingness to not know an answer in advance. Many people reach a certain age in life (what is that for you: 27? 36? 54? 63? 72?) with an assumption that they are supposed to know about life and already have it figured out. But that assumption, like so many others, turns out to be a mind game.

Mostly, we *don't* already know: We don't really know the true reasons behind another person's behavior; we often don't really know what is underneath our own decisions; and we don't know what's going to happen tomorrow. Our busy minds do not like not knowing.

But if it's true that we don't really know, then we are just making stuff up. We fill our minds with conjectures, assumptions, and imaginings that suddenly seem real to us, then proceed as if the illusions are true. The illusions become solidified and serve as the basis for predicting the future. A consequence is that we put ourselves in the position of having to defend those assumptions and predictions when they are questioned or challenged.

I find it a relief to recognize that I don't need to know most things in advance. It's both humbling and freeing to realize that what I often have been certain about has been wrong. How easily a mere thought or opinion can be mistaken as reality.

Being curious supports an open-minded attitude of inquiry. It helps lighten the experience of self-discovery and allows us to not take ourselves too seriously. With curiosity, there's less room for having an opinion or judgment about what we find. Experimenting with curiosity often leads to feeling more playful and being more open to possibility. You create room for a more expansive experience of life and of yourself.

What does curiosity look like? It might start with, "I wonder..."

- "I wonder what it would be like to pay attention to this inner inkling that has been nudging me?"
- "I wonder what new outcomes I might have if I experimented with a different approach to the situation?"
- "What would happen if I let myself feel this sadness, rather than trying to make it immediately go away, like I usually do?"

Being curious also leads to a lack of attachment to the specific outcomes of our discoveries, which is conducive to expanding our awareness. I invite you to be curious about your experience. This is an important factor in developing a new relationship with yourself.

2. Practicing Compassion and Seeing Your Patterns as Normal

When people learn about the idea of a personality, and specifically about the unconscious ways that their own personality has shown up, they often feel as if they have been "found out." Many people say that they feel like someone has read their diary when they learn about their own personality type. This is often followed by embarrassment or grief.

There are two factors that help cushion these feelings.

First, every person on the planet has personality patterns of which they are unaware. This is completely normal. However, the vast majority of the population is not aware that *personality patterns* can be changed. What makes you unusual, then, is not that you have these patterns, but that you are taking steps to see the personality more objectively, and you are moving toward having more choice in how you live. Learning that there are more options available than your personality's familiar and automatic ways of reacting is a rare experience.

In this process of becoming more aware, most people discover that their personality patterns do not fit with their customary self-images. This can be disconcerting to see and acknowledge. Recognizing the disconnect between your self-image and how your personality actually expresses itself is an important step in increasing awareness and developing a more honest, healthy relationship with yourself.

A second factor to keep in mind is that an emotional response of sadness, grief, embarrassment, shame, or relief that you might have when you see something new about yourself is also completely normal. There is nothing wrong with you. The real issue is that, in the past, these patterns are who you have taken yourself to be.

Most people experience deep heartbreak upon recognizing that these patterns have had so much power in defining their lives. How can our hearts not be broken when our long-held illusions that have caused so much struggle and pain are revealed? Life itself breaks our hearts whenever we move away from our most precious nature. In truth, our broken hearts allow us to open to deeper truth and more intimate contact with ourselves and with one another.

So being compassionate with yourself is vital in this process. Having compassion means that you do your best to meet yourself with non-judgment and kindness where you are right now, even if there is pain, even if there are aspects of yourself that you would rather not acknowledge. Remember: Anything that is difficult for you to acknowledge or sit with right now is there because it is associated with an inner wound that has not yet been resolved. There is no true healing without compassion.

A beautiful by-product is that you will experience more compassion for others, as well. Imagine how different the world would be if compassion was openly shared and expressed.

Judging yourself will do absolutely nothing to alleviate any uncomfortable experience you might have. Truly, it will only exacerbate it. You undoubtedly learned over the decades to be hard on yourself. It is second nature for most people, and is so much a part of life that it is seldom in our awareness. Yet, this inner judgment is one of the greatest sources of individual and collective suffering because we give it so much authority over our lives. In Chapter 17, we explore how to work with the inner judgment. There, you'll learn strategies for decreasing its negative impact and for strengthening your authentic sense of inner authority.

For now, it is my great wish that you will remember to be kind to yourself. Understand that the patterns of the personality have a life of their own—

one that you have not been privy to before. Today, they are becoming more transparent to you. This is a great gift.

3. Embracing Radical Honesty

It's rare to meet people who are willing to be honest with themselves. The vast majority of individuals are naturally invested in seeing themselves in a certain way and in having you fully concur with their self-assessment. This investment is demonstrated through the many ways that individuals defend themselves and point a finger at others when there's a disagreement or conflict. And it's easy to see why.

When we discussed in earlier chapters the way the personality develops, we saw that the ego structure is designed to protect us and help us cope with the hurts we experienced early in life. It has a mission, in a sense, to protect us from coming into contact with an earlier experience, because it is convinced—and had us convinced, too—that we could not tolerate seeing what is true or not true about how we have done life.

In an example from my own life, before I knew about my dominant Enneagram type, I had thought of myself as a generous, giving, and people-oriented person. I thought of myself in this way to the extent, that, when I began to explore the Enneagram, I originally mistyped myself as a Two, known as the Helper.

But as I looked deeper, I saw that my personal inner description did not fully match my external behavior or even my life attitude. It's not to say that I don't have a quality of generosity—I do, and there are many ways that it gets expressed. But I discovered that I was not focusing on others in the way that people dominant in Type Two do, where the lives of others are prominent on the radar screens of Type Twos. The nature of my personality structure is to be more inward-focused and private, rather than heavily involved in the lives of others. Initially, it was difficult to see this about my personality. Having already done a significant amount of psychological and spiritual work, I was deeply embarrassed that I had been so off the mark about myself.

But, soon, I came to recognize the behaviors and life orientation that absolutely fit the qualities and descriptions of my dominant type. And

Our personality structure takes us in exactly the opposite direction of what will nourish and satisfy us at the deepest level.

what relief! Ahhh...I was no longer so alone. The particular way I energetically held myself got a little looser, and my life force actually felt freed up more than I had ever experienced. This was a major turning point in my life. Of course, my journey continues to unfold, as does everyone's.

You probably have heard the maxim, "The truth will set you free." One of the greatest of the paradoxes that we encounter in our dedication to know the truth— with a small *t* pointing to the truth of the moment, or with a capital *T* to a Universal Truth—is that our personality structure takes us in exactly the opposite direction of what will nourish and satisfy us at the deepest level. The ego has lived a parallel, mimicked life to our deeper nature. Ripe with its own story, focused on its own mission, it takes us away from deeper truth. Your honest inquiry will help uncover the falsehoods and lead you to deepening layers of truth that will fill your heart, nurture your spirit, and liberate you. That's the quest.

4. Trusting the Process

I have long referred to the process of exploring our true nature as a *trust walk*. This journey invites you to fundamentally trust that you are being guided in the right direction and supported as you move into new territory, even when evidence is missing in that moment.

This is different than taking big risks just for the sake of the risk. The trust walk means that you are listening to something from within—your soul. Even if it's scary, it feels more honest and real. The size of the step that you are being guided to take could be quite small or seemingly insignificant to others, but feels substantial to you. For example, a person whose habit it is to retreat into his private world behind closed doors may feel awkward, embarrassed, and hesitant to check in on a neighbor in poor health. Despite his discomfort, he does so and learns something about himself in the process.

Small steps matter, and they matter to your soul. It counts every time you take even a small action that feels foreign but right for you. These small steps accumulate, and as they do, you gain confidence in this guidance, and trust in yourself.

Trust also has to do with how we meet life. Depending on your life experience, and, yes, on your dominant Enneagram type, you might lean toward cynicism and doubt, or you may tend toward the positive in everything and jump in headfirst without discernment. From this perspective, the idea of trust does not have to do with whether another person or an organization, for example, is trustworthy. Rather, it's a deeper sense that whatever happens will ultimately be for the good.[1] Thus, when things don't turn out as planned, you have an inner experience that there's something else that needs to happen instead, even though you cannot see the alternative. Rather than trying to make or force something to happen, you take a deep breath and work with what is actually happening. Distinct from a Pollyanna-type concept, this is grounded in an internally-felt knowing.

I've heard many stories from my clients and students about the great surprises and the synchronicities that come into their lives once they released a long-held belief or life strategy, or took a specific action despite experiencing great fear. Whether that individual described the resulting experience of increased inner freedom as Grace, or God's hand, a Divine Presence arising, or Creative Intelligence moving through him or her, each individual discovered that a new window or door opened and served as tangible confirmation of being on the right track. I've found that it is actually far rarer when something surprising or profound doesn't occur when one releases some aspect of the personality's certainty.

EXERCISE: Before responding to these questions, take a few moments to breathe and ground yourself. Then, practice letting yourself be surprised by what you learn from responding to the questions.

BEING CURIOUS:

- Remember a time when you were truly curious about a situation or about an aspect of yourself that had some significance for you.
- What was it that allowed you to be curious?
- What did you discover?
- What was the impact of this discovery on you?

PRACTICING COMPASSION:

- Remember a time when you felt real compassion, preferably toward yourself. If you can't remember that, then the compassion could have been around something or someone that you cared about.
- How did it affect you to experience this compassion? What was different for or about you?

EMBRACING RADICAL HONESTY:

- Remember a time when you came to a totally new realization about yourself that felt deeply true. Perhaps you saw yourself in a completely different light. Maybe you received feedback from a caring person that dissolved some old idea you had about yourself.
- Write about that experience.
- What old idea or illusion about yourself did you release? How did that affect you?

TRUSTING THE PROCESS:

- Recall a time when you surrendered something you were trying to make happen in the way you wanted it to happen, and instead let it unfold in its own way.
- What happened?
- What was that experience like for you?
- What did you learn from this?

Relinquishing Certainty

These four qualities share an underlying dynamic. In every case, they contribute to a slight release of internal certainty about how life works and how things should be. With the diminishment of certainty comes a softening of attitude, a relaxing of the protective tension that encases parts of the body, and a heartfelt gentleness. People who practice these qualities say that they feel more open and receptive to the flow of life and experience less internal struggle.

The designers of skyscrapers in earthquake-prone geographies know that they need to create enough flexibility in the structure of tall buildings to diminish the possibility of the buildings' collapse. The more flexible the structure is, the less energy is required to keep the building upright. If you have stood while riding on a public bus or rail system, you know this same phenomenon. When you stay flexible, it is easier to stand upright than if you stiffen against the starts and stops. The same experience shows up while flying: the more relaxed you are during momentary turbulence, the easier it is to tolerate the bumpiness.

Certainty creates rigidity. Life feels harder when we insist that we know, and that our way is the right way. Holding onto certainty is a way of defying the intelligence of the creative universe in which we live.

With the release of certainty, we are more expansive. Our capacity for moving with life and thriving is increased. We relate to ourselves from a new stance.

Deeply Living Requires Self-Observation

Deeply living is noticeably different than simply doing life. When we are doing what we do, day in and day out, without much self-reflection, our lives are repetitious, habitual, and automated. There are profound limits and grave consequences of letting the patterns be the primary expression of our lives. If they are, we are removed from the realness, the aliveness, the innate flow of the life force which is always available.

To take the next step in developing a new, more intimate relationship with oneself requires being able to see oneself clearly through the capacity of self-observation.

There are profound limits and grave consequences of letting the patterns be the primary expression of our lives. If they are, we are removed from the realness, the aliveness, the innate flow of the life force which is always available.

> *One of the reasons that people often feel so disconnected from themselves is that a large part of their life experience is occurring outside their field of awareness.*

Self-observation is a powerful ally in developing this new relationship with yourself. Introduced to the Western world by Gurdjieff, this concept illustrates how self-observation is vital to moving beyond the habitual patterns and identifications that form the historic basis for knowing ourselves.

Self-observation is a life-changing and uniquely human capacity for recognizing how we do life and for making real contact with ourselves. It invites the direct contact with ourselves as part of the whole of experience that is actually taking place within, often below our level of awareness. One of the reasons that people often feel so disconnected from themselves is that a large part of their life experience is occurring outside their field of awareness. One of the great benefits of incorporating self-observation as part of everyday living is the greater sense of intimacy we develop with ourselves.

Self-observation is sometimes referred to as the inner *observer* or the *fair witness* that is void of judgment and evaluation. This capacity exists outside of the activities of our ego. Rather, it is a presence-based capacity that witnesses whatever is occurring at the moment with neutrality and non-attachment. Recent research in neuroscience indicates that the practice of self-observation changes certain parts of the brain itself, supporting its evolution into a higher level of functioning.

Like many of the capabilities we desire and which enhance our growth, this one develops and matures with intentional practice over time. Self-observation is not a habit, so it requires that we remember to practice it.

Three Areas for Observation

So much is going on in any one moment that it can be puzzling to know what to pay attention to. Let's look at three levels of experience that can be observed: the *What* of Experience, the *How* of Experience and the *Inner Experience* of Experience.

The *What* of Experience

The *what* refers to the content of your experience. It includes you, other people, specific tasks or activities, places, and things. Examples of the content of your life might include your daily routine of getting the kids ready for school; having a conversation with a company's customer service agent when trying to resolve a problem with their product; exercising; preparing to host friends at your home; having a difficult interaction with a colleague; making Sunday night dinner; trying to find a life partner; managing a move across the country; or negotiating a raise at work. The *what* is made up of the mostly obvious big and little details that can easily fill daily life. The list of *whats* is endless.

Putting most of our attention on the *what* keeps our minds busy and can also be a distraction from the deeper experiences that we long for. Yet it is the most obvious material for us to notice, and it really gets interesting when we notice that very similar content pops up in life over and over again. For example, you might realize that people are always coming to you for help, and that you oblige. Or you might notice that you powerfully express your anger and, all of a sudden, the person on the receiving end of your anger backs further away or even vanishes from your life. Or maybe you notice that you end up taking on more responsibilities because others are just not doing things the way you think they should.

Recurring experiences are familiar and feel normal, though seldom are they satisfying. In fact, you can become rather tired of having very similar experiences show up time after time. However, recurring experiences can be a sign to look deeper. "Why am I having this experience again?"

The *How* of Experience

What is harder to notice is *how* you are approaching or interacting with the content of your life. What are you actually doing? What are your behaviors? As we noted earlier, our ideas about our behavior often do not line up with the actual behavior.

Through the Enneagram, we are offered a powerful lens that challenges long-held ideas and illuminates our actual behaviors. Putting more attention on the how of your experience opens doors to deeper self-awareness, understanding, and healing. Recognizing that you frequently behave in a certain way offers you a new perspective on yourself and brings you a few degrees closer to what is true. You are getting to know yourself at a new level of awareness.

There are emotions, memories, feelings, and attitudes toward life that lie underneath the content.

The *Inner Experience* of Experience

But the *what* and *how* are not the whole of your experience. There are emotions, memories, feelings, and attitudes toward life that lie underneath the content.

The Enneagram will help you identify and name some of the feelings that you experience underneath the content of your experience. What had seemed like a very personal experience is shown as part of the attributes of a particular Enneagram type.

So noticing what is emotionally happening for you underneath the content provides you with more information about your experience, about what is really going on for you, and about why you react to a situation in the way that you do.

The second area of the inner experience focuses on the internal motivations or dynamics that fuel the how of your life. (Some of these inner dynamics were discussed in Chapter 3 and specific motivations are named for each of the Enneagram types and are described in the Iceberg Model for each of the types.) When brought into awareness, these dynamics help answer the question, "Why am I expressing myself this way?" The less awareness you have of these dynamics, the more power they have in your life. Developing your capacity to notice and observe these lifelong internal dynamics supports the process of making new choices.

The third inner experience, and the most important from my perspective, focuses on your body. For most people in Western culture, there is not a lot of attention paid to the body's experience unless there is illness or pain. Then, an array of sensations ranging from physical tensions, physical fatigue and pain, and digestive tract problems to everyday aches and pains demand attention when they become severe. But there are much more subtle bodily (also called *somatic*) sensations that exist. They typically live below the level of day-to-day awareness. We benefit from bringing the capacity of self-observation to these sensations, as they carry useful information and serve as a path to deeper healing. We'll come back to the topic of tapping into your body's sensations later in this book.

Even without the benefit of the Enneagram, you may have already made some changes in your life after spotting a repetitious behavior that was no longer working and only added to your unhappiness. The Enneagram heightens and quickens the ability to discern what supports and what no longer serves you.

An Example of Self-Observation

A high percentage of internal conversations center around individuals reiterating their version of the particular content of a situation. The individual's perspective of the situation is, of course, filtered through their personality. In other words, an inner story is being told about an incident, and that inner story often becomes the individual's truth.

In practical terms, to develop self-observation, you experiment with shifting your awareness from your version of the situation to your own behavior in the situation. Here's an example:

Your idea of the situation:
You think that you are being more than fair when you make a decision to deny your staff member a day off because she has already taken so many days off. "She's always taking time off. I'm drawing the line here."

Observing your behavior:
But when you shift your attention to your behavior, you see that you are talking down to her and even scolding. You may see that you are acting a bit icy while making a surprisingly biting remark. Observe your feelings and motivation:

From a place of self-observation, you recognize that your interaction feels cumbersome and emotionally charged. In fact, you notice that you are feeling resentful. The time she has already taken off has impacted you, even though you haven't told her that. You took on more work to cover her absence, and you haven't told her that either. Yes, you are feeling resentful. And that resentment is fueling your scolding response.

Observing your body's sensations:
You notice that your shoulders are tight and that you are hardly breathing.

You begin to distinguish between the habitual conditioning that has taken up so much space and has defined much of your life, and you tune in to deeper channels of your internal experience and see what is really there. This is what is meant by becoming present.

The result is that, although you feel justified, you are not really feeling good about this interaction. And it has done nothing to create a better working relationship.

Self-observation can lead to examining how you would like to handle this kind of situation in the future, so that your behavior is not based on resentment. While still drawing the line about her time off, you may see that another choice is to be more honest with the staff member about the impact of her absence. You may decide not to take on her workload and let it be there when she returns. Or this may be part of a series of conversations that lead to a work termination.

Ultimately, this interchange could lead to recognizing an ongoing, familiar experience of resentment. Here it is—a personality pattern that is no longer serving you. Experiencing this resentment may not feel good, but the truth is, it is there.

Breathing helps! When you take a breath and make a seemingly subtle yet potent decision to pay attention to exactly how you are behaving or what you are sensing or feeling in the moment of the experience, your whole experience undergoes a subtle change. You create an in-the-moment, direct experience of your behavior as well as an awareness that there is something going on for you internally, below the surface. You are, in effect, more present to yourself.

In other words, the content or the story becomes secondary, and your direct experience is primary. With practice, your capacity for using this very simple—but not necessarily easy—process grows. An expanded capacity for observation of your direct experience leads to healing and resolving familiar, if unconscious, struggles.

Through the use of this process, you begin to distinguish between the habitual conditioning that has taken up so much space and has defined much of your life, and you tune in to deeper channels of your internal experience and see what is really there. This is what is meant by becoming *present*.

The Enneagram names the patterns and points your awareness toward the conditioning so that you might recognize it more easily. However, it is your quiet, neutral observer that helps you dissolve your identification with the ego's inner conversations and stories.

As you continue your exploration here, invite in your observer to support your inquiry. You might notice where there is an inner, and often, evaluative commentary about what you are discovering. This noisy self-criticism is also part of the habitual conditioning. Whenever you see that operating, take a few slow breaths to experience a bit more space between you and the conditioning.

In other words, the content or the story becomes secondary, and your direct experience is primary.

Meeting Paradox

Janice was used to being in control. She knew what she wanted, and she went after it. It was easy for her to directly state what she wanted to have done, then expect the task to be done by the deadline she had imposed. She didn't have time for people who didn't get to the all-important bottom line, who were unsure of what they wanted, or who were touchy-feely. Who needs all those emotions? What a waste of time, she thought.

Yet, underneath the air of confidence she exuded, she experienced unease. Not that she would ever admit it, but she felt bad about herself. And at the soul level, she felt great sadness and grief.

After working with the Enneagram, she realized how much she incessantly pushed others and herself away—away from her heart. The very thing that she had tried so hard to do—keep others from hurting her by getting close to her heart—had actually created her own suffering.

She consciously focused on softening her energy so that she could actually feel her heart. Even though she was more deeply aware of her internal pain, she gradually started letting other people in. Rather than feeling the movement of people away from her, she noticed that people were drawn to her. They truly cared for her. And this contributed to important healing in her heart.

As we delve into the formerly hidden aspects of our personalities, we encounter paradoxes. As discussed in Chapter 3, we find that what we have thought to be true—perhaps for a very long time—is at complete odds with what is actually so. Entering our deeper experience means that we are deepening our contact with our inner life force, our soul, and this experience contrasts and often contradicts our ego's orientation. The pull of the external forces in life runs in the opposite direction of our soul's yearning.

The paradoxes that we come across have the potential for challenging personal and societal myths, for increasing our capacity to hold the creative tension of apparent incongruity, and for lessening the judgement and shame that we can hold for years. Since our Enneagram types are filled with their own paradoxical nature, if you're not encountering paradoxes in your learning experience with the Enneagram, it might mean that you haven't landed on your dominant type.

Two Core Purposes of Deep Living— What We're Up to Here

Over time, you will practice the four elements we've discussed of this healing/awakening orientation to the transformational and evolutionary journey:

- Being curious
- Practicing compassion
- Embracing radical honesty
- Trusting the process

As you do this, you'll develop and expand your capacity for self-observation, and something important will happen. *Your attention begins to shift.*

Why is this shift in your attention important?

Because it begins to change who you think you are!

One of the underlying purposes of working with Deep Living processes is to unhook from the strong identification with the small self. In other words, becoming free, step by step, of the unrelenting demands of the egoic structure leads to experiencing and embracing your higher nature. When you recognize that "your way" is simply that—just *a* way which exists as a tiny fraction of the whole of life—then your perspective and experience radically change.

In concert with your change in perspective, your kinder attitude toward yourself contributes to resolving early emotional pain. Supported by this awareness and compassion, there is a less ardent ego to defend and to judge in yourself and in others. Since an enormous amount of energy gets put into doing something your way, there is a massive sense of relief when you can let go.

If we consider the ultimate costs of judging (and mostly *mis*judging) in our personal lives, our relationships, our work, our families and communities, and in the world, we see that we are dealing with a force that has the power to do great damage. It's stunning.

Simultaneously, as the process of becoming unhooked from the demands of the ego takes place, it is possible to tap into your greater potential and into the greater intelligence that is available to you. I often hear clients say that they feel they grow up when they release old patterns and experience their inherent capacities. This is an integral dimension in recognizing and claiming your more expansive nature.

A second core purpose of Deep Living is to enhance the experience of our inherent sense of interconnectedness.

I've long loved this quote from John Muir that is etched at the beginning of a trail in Yosemite National Park: "When we try to pick out anything by itself, we find it hitched to everything else in the universe." Another, perhaps less eloquent way to say this: *to feel separate is a delusion of the small self.*

You've read about *interconnectedness* before, and if you've ever had a direct experience when you felt at one with everything, then you know how life-changing it is. When we are wrapped up in the inner world of our Enneagram type, we feel separate. That's the nature of the ego-state. This sense of separateness is consciously and unconsciously experienced at many different levels. The more deeply we relax our identification with the limiting nature of the personality and come into contact with what is real, the more we perceive everything more accurately. With this perception comes a compassion for the challenges of the conditioned human experience that we all share.

On a very practical level, with a depth of self-understanding, you naturally begin to recognize your existing and potential impact on others and on the environment. Moving beyond the "inner fishbowl," you can swim more freely in an oceanic environment.

Deep Living, then, is an approach to awakening that is founded on building your capacity for living with presence in everyday life. The Enneagram provides a natural and precise framework for illuminating the predicable, paradoxical patterns that keep you out of the present moment, and an equally robust system for experiencing expansive qualities that are available only in the present. With increased awareness, self-observation, and an open spirit, the movement into unfamiliar terrain yields to contact with your deeper, real capacities which support you in realizing outcomes that are aligned with your inherent strengths and true priorities. Your purpose becomes clearer. Your own journey is experienced as part of the shared spiritual journey of awakening to the greater intelligence that is always available. You are an integral part of the evolutionary unfolding that is calling each of us.

Section II

NINE VARIATIONS ON HOW TO "DO" LIFE

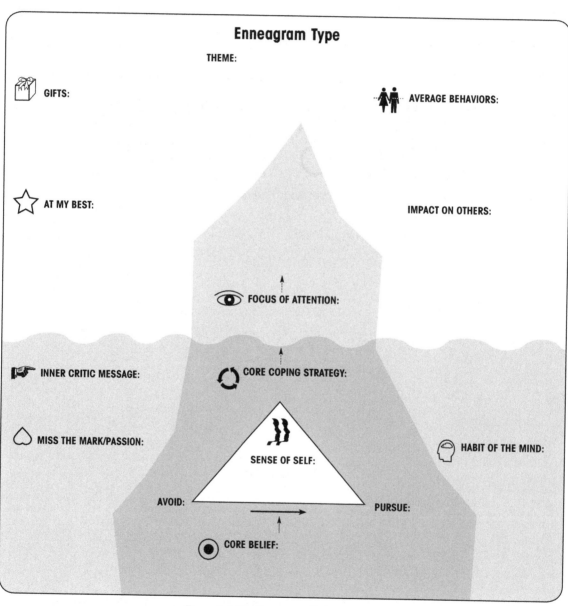

Figure 5-1: The Enneagram Iceberg Model

5

The Iceberg: The Architectural Blueprint of the Personality

The personality can be understood as an interrelated configuration of *elements* that, together, form a cohesive framework that reflects both an individual's inner experience, as well as the way that person expresses him or herself. Each element or aspect of the personality reinforces and builds on the others. When this configuration is allowed to operate within itself, it exists as a closed or uninterrupted system.

Jung referred to the architecture of an iceberg as a metaphor for the human experience. What's visible above the water are those aspects of ourselves that are available to the conscious. And it's this part of us *above the waterline* that others see. What we know about an iceberg is that the vast majority of it lies *below the waterline*. So it's with the human personality.

Thus, the model using the iceberg metaphor helps make sense of the different elements that make up the architecture of the personality's structure. What lies above is what's visible or what's most apt to be *felt* if unnamed in relationships; what lies below is what informs and drives the personality. The elements that lie below the waterline are motivations that shape the behaviors.

To more deeply understand what motivates our behaviors and to make sustainable shifts, it's important to acknowledge and work with what's both above and below the waterline. This combination of elements give us insight into the human experience or condition of individuals who are dominant in any particular type.

The description of each of the nine Enneagram types in this section of the book focuses on various levels of the personality that was discussed in chapter 2. Perusing the material on each type's Iceberg for each type will help you identify—or at least narrow your options—as to which type is most dominant for you.

A Description of the Enneagram Iceberg Model

This visual depiction of an Iceberg shows behavioral and attitudinal descriptors located *above* the wavy waterline for each Enneagram type. *Below* the waterline, you will see identified and described the dynamics that shape and motivate a person's behaviors when he or she is at the average level of health and functioning, that is, when a person is in the grip of the personality.

Refer to the visual as you read the description for each of the elements of the personality. This generic framework will be used to present the specific information on each of the nine personality types in chapters 6 through 14 to help you either begin to recognize the types that have the most resonance for you, or if you already know your type, to give you some additional perspectives.

Theme

In the upper left corner of the model is this descriptive thread, or theme. It captures the flavor of the particular Enneagram type. As a metaphor, the theme reflects an underlying way of orienting toward life that is unique to people dominant in that type. For example, the theme for Type Nine is, "Can't we all just get along?" This is drastically different than the themes for each of the other types. Some people find that the themes help them recognize their type.

As you read each type's theme, ask yourself if it resonates with you, and if it does, how it reflects your relationship to yourself and with others. If you resonate with "Can't we all just get along?," for example, you might see that you tend to downplay or even avoid conversations in which there's a potential for conflict.

Above the Waterline

The Gifts, Daily Habits, and Challenges

GIFTS and AT MY BEST
(When I'm expansive and at my healthiest)

This left section above the waterline includes behavioral and attitudinal descriptors that characterize an individual at a healthy level of the particular type. They show us what gifts people who are dominant in this type experience in themselves and offer in an unconscious way to others.

At the higher levels of health, there's *no efforting or trying to make something happen* to create these behaviors. They are naturally available and easily expressed. You are more apt to experience that you have a personality, but it's not in charge of you.

You will probably find that the gifts at the healthiest levels of your dominant type will most resonate as ones that you deeply appreciate, desire, or cherish, even if they are not yet apparent in your daily life. While the characteristics of all nine types at the healthiest and most liberated level of the personality are desirable, the ones associated with your dominant type will be the qualities that you most love.

The elements of the personality located under the waterline are not as powerful in shaping your experience as they are in the average or unhealthy levels of type, when you are less present. There's been considerable healing and releasing of the compulsive energy and suffering that is expressed at the average and lower levels.

AVERAGE BEHAVIORS *(Distinguishing characteristics when my personality has its grip on me)*

We notice that there's tremendous variation of behaviors, emotional expression, and orientation to life within each type, depending on one's degree of attachment to the familiar personality structure. This section in the upper right corner describes an individual when his personality has its grip on him.

When the personality has you in its grip, the personality is taking up more space and leaving you less present. Here, you are more likely to react than to respond, and operate from an automatic, habitual way rather than from a fresh, open perspective. Life is more troublesome, especially as attachment to the ego's version of life becomes increasingly dominant.

Here, the dynamics identified under the water line are more activated, shaping and limiting your behaviors, thoughts, emotions, and experiences in mostly unconscious ways.

The characteristics at the average level—when your personality has its grip on you—may be quite familiar, as *this is where most people operate from most of the time.*

To note, there are characteristics associated with **the least healthy and lowest functioning levels** within each type as well, however, they are not the focus of this book. *The unhealthy characteristics look almost the opposite of the healthy qualities.* For example, a person at the healthy levels of Enneagram One is highly ethical, fair, and has a capacity for joy and gratitude. A person at the unhealthy levels of One harshly judges themselves and others, behaves unethically, and is extremely rigid emotionally, physically, and mentally. These and other behaviors cause great suffering for themselves and others around them.

FOCUS OF ATTENTION, or FOA *(Where I put my attention when I'm attached to my personality)*

The Focus of Attention (FOA) was introduced in chapter 3. It appears in the center of the Iceberg Model, just above the waterline. Let's take another look at it.

Energy follows attention. Habitually focusing on a particular object of attention narrows one's field of awareness and interest. It can be astonishing to see how much energy is channeled through one's thoughts, feelings, behaviors, and all the efforts that go into making something *come true* around that object.

Let's return to the example of the person dominant in Enneagram Type One and try on this example for yourself. The habitual Focus of Attention for a person with this type is *doing things right*. If you have a Type One personality, or at least an active Type One dynamic in your life, you will probably recognize this Focus of Attention quite easily. If not, it may be more challenging to have an inner experience of how this narrowing of attention plays out in daily life. It entails monitoring your verbal and written communication to make sure that you are responding *correctly— the way it should be done*. It entails scanning for cues in conversations to determine if you need to take on another responsibility. It may mean always being on the alert, ready to defend what you are doing, or offering rationales for your behavior. Being criticized for *not doing things right* can feel like a major threat to your sense of self and, thus, your well-being.

You have a particular sensitivity to these issues, consequently, it's easy to become reactive if you hear or see something that threatens your sense of being right. You want it to be true that you are right and that things around you are right.

In each type's Iceberg Model, there's a brief description of what happens as the FOA becomes narrower and narrower. It's important to note that the degree to which our FOA is activated is shaped by our degree of presence. With more presence, what we pay attention to expands, rather than narrows.

The arrows pointing upward:

Above the Focus of Attention, or FOA, are arrows pointing upward, toward the tip of the iceberg. These arrows (and the descriptive statements above and below them) indicate a core cognitive-emotional thread of the type that is shaped by the FOA and further driven by the hidden dynamics located below the waterline. For each type, we will see how the cognitive-emotional qualities become more pronounced and ineffective as the grip of the personality is strengthened.

This thread raises our awareness of type-specific patterns that play out, generally, unconsciously. This information may help you find your dominant type by describing a pattern shared by others with this type.

+
—
The personality's IMPACT ON OTHERS (+ and –)

Our behaviors, attitudes, and general energetic orientation have consequences in relationships with others. This section briefly identifies the impact on others when a person dominant in the type under consideration is having *a positive impact* (typically, this relates to being at a high or high-average level of health) and when that individual is having *a negative impact* (typically, this relates to being at an average or low-average level of effectiveness and health). The less psychologically and emotionally healthy we are, the greater our negative impact. When we operate from an average level of health and attachment to our personality, we typically are unaware of our impact on others and are surprised to learn that our impact does not reflect our intention. In fact, **our unintended negative impact often creates results just opposite of what our souls are seeking.**

When our personality has its grip on us, we discover that we are trying to get others to do as we want. We want others to support our ego's agenda.

This awareness can lead to great sadness that we have unintentionally caused hardship for others.

Below the Waterline

You will see that there are many different dimensions of the personality taking place below the waterline. Again, we seldom are consciously aware of these aspects of our inner world. However, as we learn about them, it's possible to begin to recognize them. As a reminder, it's valuable to use the *tools for the journey* discussed in chapter 4 as you discover how the dimensions of the personality structure are expressed through you.

First, here's a brief description of what each of these elements means when used in the context of understanding ourselves better through the Enneagram. We begin our understanding of what's happening under the water by starting at the bottom of the Iceberg graphic.

The CORE BELIEF

Each type carries with it a core belief about itself in relationship to others and to the world. The core belief creates the basis for how the individual sees his or her place in the world, and it acts as a core operating principle that silently filters through the many layers of life.

This belief most often exists at an unconscious level and was most likely formed very early in a child's life. It becomes a part of the child's life pre-verbally and precognitively, and it may have been reinforced by early life experiences, as well as by the individual's subsequent history. It's so central to the individual's ego structure that it seems to be beyond questioning. It's important to realize, however, that the core belief is not accurate, though it has held so much power in the past that it has felt beyond questioning.

The TRIANGLE OF IDENTITY

You've seen this triangle before. Here, it's located under the waterline to illustrate an interaction that takes place among the different elements of the personality's structure. We can see how all of the elements interact in a way that creates a coherent inner experience of self.

What I PURSUE

Look on the lower right corner of the Triangle of Identity. The ego structure is designed to pursue that which it assumes will bring your greatest happiness. The personality tries to recapture a precious and essential quality of your soul that felt cut off in your earlier years. This experience occurred pre-conceptually and pre-lingually, so generally it's not in immediate awareness. The ego can never satisfy what it's trying to achieve, but since it doesn't know that, it can go to greater and greater lengths to try and re-create the true quality that your soul loves. The best it can do is replicate what you truly want, by using the ego's unsatisfactory version of that state. Failing to achieve that, it tries harder and harder, only to create more pain in your life.

Here is one of the paradoxes that you will meet.

What I AVOID

Based upon your dominant Enneagram type, there's some experience that you try to avoid at all costs. This experience is diametrically opposite of what the ego is pursuing. To move in this direction makes no sense to the mind, to the ego, and in fact, can feel very scary. *In truth, what you avoid is of central importance to what will make you whole.* This is depicted in the lower left corner of the Triangle.

My CORE COPING STRATEGY

Each Enneagram type is a specialist in certain behavioral and attitudinal strategies. These strategies, depicted at the top of the Triangle, keep the personality intact and congruent. The usual strategies that become the language of your type appear to be exactly what's needed and that will help you find the greatest satisfaction. The core coping strategies of your type make perfect sense and represent a practical interpretation of what's avoided and what's pursued by the personality. However, since they primarily operate on automatic, they are used unconsciously, whether or not they are effective and appropriate for the situation. They reinforce the personality and move you in just the opposite direction of your highest levels of health and flexibility.

SENSE OF SELF *("I am...")*

Within each type's Triangle of Identity is the Sense of Self, which depicts the particular way each type has of seeing itself and leaves little room for us to see ourselves as we actually are. Most of us have a distorted and either an overinflated or deflated view of ourselves that likely does not match what's real. These fixed perceptions are reaffirmed by a narrowing of our Focus of Attention and the resulting data that supports our self view, and disregard other experiences that would provide much different information.

The particular view that is listed for each type is based on a description that Don Riso and Russ Hudson identified for each type at a high level of health. Interestingly, many people see themselves at a high level of health for their own type, whether or not they are actually operating at that level of health.

Paradoxically, what the ego is set up to pursue and avoid—and which is reflected in the core coping strategy and sense of self associated with the type—is what leads to increased suffering, unrest, and inner and outer struggle.

WHERE I MISS THE MARK
(The energetic drive of the passion)

This is a powerful element of the personality structure that creates an energetic drive *away from* the higher aspects of life; in a sense, it's an energy that moves a person in the opposite direction from their more expansive and open-hearted nature. In Enneagram language, this is called the *Passion* of the type, not to be confused with the colloquial use of this word as being passionate about something or someone you love. In lay language, "Where I MISS THE MARK" refers to a distorted, hidden emotional drive that plays a significant role in self-identity. It's such an innate element of the internal structure that it acts like psychic wallpaper. Thus, it cannot be easily identified from the inside. Learning about this element of the personality offers information that often feels very personal, and perhaps somewhat intrusive. Upon learning about this personality element, sometimes individuals remark that they've been *found out.*

One way of understanding this element is that it covers up a wound deep within one's heart[1] and, as a result of its protective function, drives you away from what your soul most loves. The more activated it gets, the further you move away from your soul's true home base. It can be helpful to remember that everyone has some experience with the Passion associated with the nine types, and that about one-ninth of the population shares a particular resonance with the same one that you will come to most recognize in your own life.

HABIT OF THE MIND *(Fixation of the personality)*

Each type has a particular habitual pattern of the mind that is called the *fixation* of the type, and it's shown on the far right of the Iceberg Model. This mental habit is the ego's automatic, unquestioned way of solving the problems of one's life. This is a pattern that was developed in early childhood to compensate for the loss of connection with one's true Essence. Reliance on the fixation as the strategy for dealing with much of life is limiting to adults who are committed to their continuing evolution. The recognition of how pervasive the fixation is and how it functions in one's life is vitally important in transformational work.

 ## INNER CRITIC MESSAGE
(*What my Inner Critic insists upon*)

One way of understanding the inner critic, or the *superego* in Enneagram terms, is that it functions as the internalized voice of authority, embracing the rules, standards, and expectations that have been with you from your earliest moments in life. We'll explore the inner critic more in a later chapter. For now, look at the left side of the Iceberg Model, just under the waterline. You can see that the inner critic's message is a potent force in the personality structure and is set up to keep the rest of the personality in check. It tells the personality what it okay and what's not okay to do, say, feel, or experience, and it can give harsh feedback if its dictates are not followed.

The specific inner critic messages that are included in this book for each type were identified in Riso and Hudson's early work with the Enneagram.[2]

Each of the elements described above contributes to the whole experience of what we have come to think of as ourselves. The core belief, the emotional force of the passion, the mental habit (fixation), and the inner critic all unconsciously conspire to reinforce the Triangle of Identity.

Additional Information on Enneagram Types

The information in this section is not referred to on the visual of the Enneagram Iceberg Models, but it does provide other approaches and access points for determining and working with your personality type.

What causes me *stress*

Each type experiences particular sources of stress that can be non-issues for people who are of a different Enneagram type. Thus, it's when the personality has a grip on the individual that a particular event or situation is perceived as threatening. The source of stress is seen as the cause for discomfort, and it ignites a predictable reaction. When the personality relaxes, the particular source of stress (unless it's truly a rare, life-threatening situation) is seen in more neutral terms.

When I'm most constricted and inflexible

Severely limiting behavioral, emotional, and mental patterns are evident when the individual feels as if there are no options available, and life looks bleak and hopeless. There's so little access to presence that harm can be done to the self or to others. People who are living at these highly constricted levels of health can and often do function in society, but sometimes they cannot. Most individuals experience times when they drop into these unhealthy patterns for a limited length of time. If an individual consistently stays in this range of the human condition, there will be considerable acting out. Therapeutic intervention is usually necessary to support this person and perhaps others who may be affected.

The dynamic movement between types—a direct connection to *Stress Points, Integration Points,* and the *Hidden Dimension of Self*

Here we expand our awareness of how we "do" life.

Each of the nine chapters on Enneagram types concludes with a referral to two other Enneagram types. Remember that the Enneagram is a dynamic system. Not only is there a dynamic movement within each type, **but there's a predictable and dynamic movement that takes place *between* types.** And it's clearly visible within the Enneagram symbol itself.

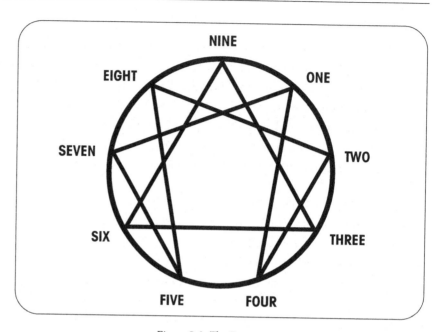

Figure 5-2: The Enneagram

Each Enneagram point is connected to two other types' points by an internal line. Thus, the internal lines connect all the points around the Enneagram. One of the remarkable aspects of the Enneagram is that the symbol itself and the types that the numbers refer to are not random, but represent the natural movement of the personality as it actually occurs in people's lives. This movement is an outgrowth of our nature as multi-dimensional beings, so we generally are not thinking about making a move to another type. It's not something we *make* happen. Whether we're responding on autopilot to the demands and opportunities in daily life, or we're engaged in substantial change (evolving or devolving), an interior dynamism is operating. This does not mean that our dominant type changes, but that the qualities or behaviors associated with one of these points are expressed.

For example, Types Three, Six, and Nine are connected by an inner triangle. When stressed, a person with a Type Three personality will move toward his Stress Point, which is Type Nine, and may experience the inner states and demonstrate the outer behaviors associated with that Type Nine personality.

Likewise, a person with a Type Three personality will experience the inner states and demonstrate the outer behaviors associated with a Type Six personality, because that is where the Three's Integration Point is. (See below for more information on Integration Points and the Hidden Dimension of Self.)

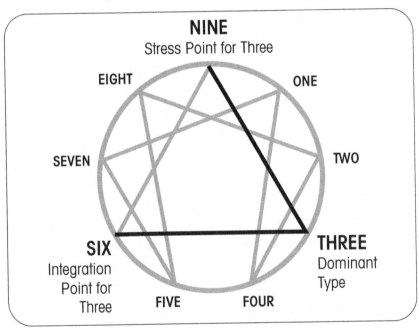

Figure 5-3: The Stress and Integration Points for Type Three

Here's another way of saying it, using a different type as the example. Under specific circumstances, a Type One personality will experience the inner states and demonstrate the outer behaviors associated with either Type Four (the Stress Point) or Type Seven (the Integration Point).

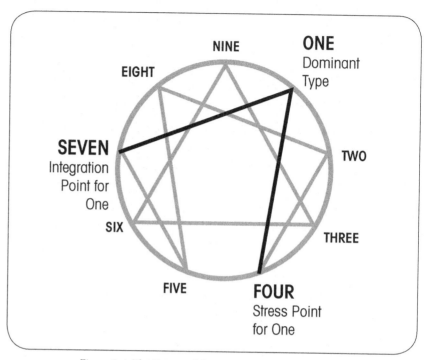

Figure 5-4: The Stress and Integration Points for Type One

So, when does this movement occur? Good question.

We typically access, experience, and express some of the qualities of our Stress Point when we've been under considerable pressure. **Under extended periods of stress, it can be easy to misidentify your Stress Point as your dominant type.**

The Integration Point, on the other hand, that is associated with any dominant type includes characteristics and qualities that support the movement of the individual to *a greater sense of wholeness.* Many of the qualities of the Integration Point can feel quite alien, and it's possible to have an adverse reaction to those qualities. For example, a person dominant in Eight who relies heavily on his or her sense of strength and power may deny the softer, loving qualities of the Type Two, which are part of the Eight's Integration Point.

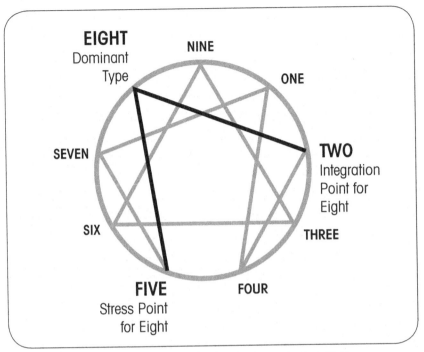

Figure 5-5: The Stress and Integration Points for Type Eight

When the personality has its grip on us (when we're at the average levels of health), there's a term, the *Hidden Dimension of Self*, for the behaviors and attitudes we exhibit that are found in the Integration Point. The Enneagram predicts those behaviors and attitudes if we look in the direction of the Integration Point from where our dominant type's point is. Different names have been given to this hidden dimension of the personality, including Security Point[3] and the Soul Child.[4]

This Hidden Dimension of Self is a difficult and often painful dimension to recognize in ourselves. We tend to have a lot of judgment about these qualities, and we tend to deny them in ourselves because they feel barely tolerable within the context of the self-image. We might say, "There's no way that I do this. I can't stand people when they do this." So, these characteristics stay in the shadow, that part of ourselves to which we are blind. But it doesn't mean that they don't exist—we just don't see them.

As an example, a person dominant in Type Three might have a can-do personality and show a lot of confidence and drive in getting things done at an average level of health. However, this same person may secretly or unconsciously experience insecurity, a lack of self-confidence, and anxiety. These are not the attitudes and behaviors seen at the average levels of a Type Three. Instead, these are behaviors that are seen in the average levels of personality Type Six. Not surprisingly, Type Six is the Integration Point for Type Three. These characteristics, however, seem so foreign to the Type Three that it's natural to deny their existence. Yet with an expanded awareness, a Type Three individual will gain awareness of these experiences that show up at their Integration Point (i.e., at Type Six). Expanding this awareness requires much kindness and, often, some outside professional support to help an individual recognize, heal, and embrace the fuller range of human experience that exists within him or her.

The Integration Point, then, offers many qualities to challenge us and to help us psychologically and spiritually mature. Kindly asking yourself how you experience the formerly verboten characteristics of the average level at your type's Integration Point is important to your soul's journey toward wholeness.

The Enneagram does not guide which direction we go and when; it simply illustrates the natural movements to the Stress Point and the Integration Point, the latter of which includes the Hidden Dimension of Self. If you think you have figured out which type you are dominant in (or even if you haven't), review the descriptions of the two associated types, which may help you more firmly identify your dominant type.

As a reminder, we have the potentiality to experience the characteristic energy for all nine types, but the impact of the *structure* of these three types—of our dominant type, and the stress and the integration points—will be the most familiar and potent in daily living.

Exploring Self-Knowledge with Care

The Enneagram is a powerful source for gaining rare self-knowledge, self-recognition, and self-deepening.

As you read more, you will see that there's a vast range, or continuum, of qualities and characteristics that can be experienced by every individual, no matter which type is dominant for that person. I find it forever humbling that each of us has the potential for operating anywhere on the continuum, from healthy to unhealthy. This awareness helps me remember that this is no us and them. That is, when we note another person operating at a less than effective level, we can recognize the possibility that this state also exists within us.

Keep in mind that the one factor that is most influential in where we most often find ourselves on the continuum is *the quality of our presence*. We will talk about this more in upcoming chapters.

It's important to note that the descriptions of the types need to be approached with sensitivity, open curiosity, and self-care. To see, for the first time, the nature of your inner psychological structure can be quite unsettling. It's not unusual to feel that your *conscious or unconscious secrets* have been exposed, and to feel some embarrassment around this. It's okay. And it's part of the experience of becoming more conscious.

To reiterate from an earlier chapter, it's important not to use the Enneagram to label other people, that is, to *not* tell other people what you think their type is. The Enneagram's highest benefit is for our own individual exploration, personal inquiry, and transformation.

Let's begin our exploration of the human condition and consciousness described by the nine Enneagram types.

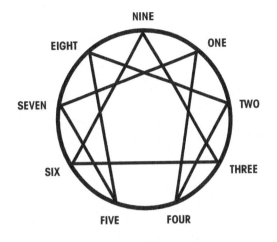

INTRODUCING THE NINE ENNEAGRAM TYPES

The next chapter begins our focus on the types, and their inner and some external characteristics. The types are organized in groups of three, around the Social Style Clusters mentioned in an earlier chapter.

At the start of each cluster of types, I include a brief overview of some of the major characteristics that are shared by the three types. We start with the Private/Introspective Types, move to the Assured/Confident Types, and finish with the Service-Oriented/Responsible Types.

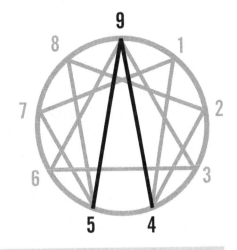

Social Style Cluster One

The Private, Introspective Group—
Types Nine, Four, and Five

Shared Themes

Energetically withdrawing from active social, physical, emotional, spiritual, or intellectual engagement is one strategy that can be used to cope with the stress that accompanies interpersonal relationships.

When in the grip of the personality, people dominant in these three Enneagram types share the common personality structure of removing themselves from active engagement with external reality. Individuals dominant in Types Nine, Four, and Five often need private downtime to reconnect with their inner sanctuary or inner world, which provides what feels like safe space in order to avoid external demands that may feel too overwhelming.

If your dominant type is in this cluster, you may prefer to work solo, have a private office, or sufficient alone time to prepare before interacting with others.

The personality structure for each of these types leads to a particular way in which the individual *disappears into an interior world. For example, you might have* difficulty staying connected with your body or getting out of fantasy or mental abstractions. You may find it hard to move your ideals or visions into reality through sustained and purposeful action.

People dominant in these types often secretly feel that they *don't belong* or *don't fit in* with other people or with groups. They may feel emotionally, spiritually, or mentally superior to others, and simultaneously, sense that there is no place for them in a group. Thus, if Type Nine, Four, or Five is your dominant type, you could experience feeling outside of the norm of society. Feeling *left out,* you stay on the periphery of engagements, and end up *losing the voting rights* to your life.

Being able to reflect on and enjoy one's own company is a healthy attribute to be celebrated. When the *withdrawing strategy* is the automatic and habitual pattern, however, the result is that life is not lived in the objective, real world. Life goes on without your involvement.

Energetically, these type structures often are experienced as being *pulled back* and away from the action. These individuals may literally or figuratively sit on the sidelines, occasionally experimenting with the edges of participation, only to pull back if the world feels like it is demanding too much of their attention. There may be a sense of mental or emotional vacancy, or a sense of being detached from their bodies. They may be physically clumsy or awkward.

People dominant in these three types are not necessarily quiet. In their own realm of comfort, they can be expressive and talkative. However, there is some element within these individuals that can seem untouchable, unreachable.

An important part of the inner journey for you, if you recognize something of yourself here, is moving *from* being "a step removed" *to* "stepping into your body and the world."

The Human Condition and Consciousness of Type Nine: The Peacemaker

It was a big decision for Jessica to decide to work with a coach. The significance of this step was magnified because she was not used to taking action that reflected her own needs and interests. In fact, she historically had found it difficult to know what she truly wanted. Rather, she would go with the flow of whatever life brought her.

Having experienced a layoff as a project manager several months prior, she thought it was a good time for her to change her career path. With this transition, she knew that she wanted her next career move to be based upon a clearer sense of personal priorities and professional direction. And she wanted to develop the confidence and internal power that would fuel her motivation to follow-up on her priorities.

During the coaching relationship, she came to recognize with both sadness and relief some patterns associated with the Type Nine personality that were prevalent in her life:

- *the frequency with which she would go along with others in an effort to accommodate their interests and viewpoints*
- *how she erased herself from her own life; and that she seldom took seriously any ideas she might have, quickly dismissing them as irrelevant*

- *how much she disliked conflict; and she came to see some of the consequences of having avoided it all together*
- *how much she waited for something to happen, rather than initiate action that could lead to a desired outcome*

One important theme throughout the coaching relationship was the development of a conscious relationship to her body. She found that she barely recognized any sensations in her body outside of pain, and that walking or moving with a direct experience of being *in* her body and of actually inhabiting her body was absolutely foreign. With committed practice over time, she started developing a whole new relationship to it, and thus, to herself. It gave her ground to stand on, increased her ability to know what she wanted, and expanded her confidence in her ability to follow-through.

The Internal Coherence of the Type Nine Experience

Your True Nature

If this is your dominant Enneagram point, you are naturally drawn to the experience of "All is One." While this might seem rather "woo-woo" to some people, your soul knows the truth of this, regardless of what's happening around you. Life can be noisy and unpredictable, there can be environmental and human disasters and tumultuous changes taking place, and yet at the deepest level, you experience the interconnectedness of all, while being engaged and present.

When not in touch with your true nature, what you might not recognize *yet* is that you are an indomitable force, meant to *be here*. Your presence contributes to the whole and is needed.

The Story of Your Life:
Relating to Your Inner and Outer World

Your inner sense of self and your place in the world were set in place early in life. How you internalized your experiences contributed to the characteristic way you relate to yourself and others, and to your very way of being. If this is your dominant type, the following brief story of your childhood inner experience will likely sound very familiar.

From your earliest years, you were a well-behaved child. You were easy to get along with and didn't cause trouble. Somehow, you learned that you were expected to be an undemanding, low-maintenance child. By being obedient, you maintained a feeling of harmony and connection to the important people in your life. To disobey meant that you could lose this connection.

As a child, you were not often asked what you wanted to do. Decisions were made by others, and you went along, conforming to and shaping yourself around these decisions. If you attempted to assert yourself, you may have heard a message similar to "little girls are made to be seen and not heard."

You might also have heard an adult say to you, "Don't say that. You didn't really mean it." And you came to experience that your emotional connections with your family depended on you accommodating their wishes and priorities. You might have heard a message similar to this: if you follow your own dreams, something terrible could happen, perhaps to another person.

Soon, you couldn't really remember what it was that you wanted. It was easier to say, "Oh, whatever you want is fine." It was far more comfortable to have neither an opinion nor your own priorities.

Even your expression of excitement or other big emotions felt unsafe. It wasn't acceptable to show anger, and you couldn't tolerate having someone angry with you. Since you couldn't express yourself externally, you found safety in a safe space inside yourself. No one ever really knew what you thought or felt. You began to feel invisible. You kept a low profile.

Since expressing your natural anger didn't feel safe, you had times when you felt depressed, even though you didn't know why you were down. It didn't feel like your presence mattered much.

You came to organize your life around it not being okay to assert yourself, not being okay to show your strength or will. Your life became shaped around saying no to and erasing big parts of yourself.

What you didn't see is that your presence actually does matter very much, and that your voice, your ideas, and your engagement in the world make a big difference. What you couldn't see is that when you show up for your life, you help people's lives change and you experience your own exuberance for life.

Your Great Loss

As a little being, even before your conscious thought and language skills developed, you had experiences that left you feeling separated from the essential qualities that your soul loved—that it was in tune with. This pain was too much to bear, so the ego structure began to form, taking on the role of protecting you from the severity of this early loss.

We remember that the ego attempts to mimic our true nature, though it can never be successful in doing so. Thus, the Type Nine personality structure has tried to recreate the experience of All is One. Indeed, at the level of Essence, this is true. But the personality distorts what All is One actually means, and holds on to it as as a sacred cow, or an unquestioned requirement. As the ego grows stronger, it demands that certain conditions exist for peacefulness, such as, "everyone plays nice or I will go away." It's natural to feel that it's appropriate to interact with others and manage situations that support a sense of inner and outer peacefulness, and it's also natural to pull away from discordant or troubling situations that could potentially lead to a sense of separateness or a severing of relationship. Both energies, however, when overused, pull you away from your true nature and create the feeling of being in a familiar rut.

Before you can be "one with all that is," your unique individuality needs to be developed and expressed. Your ideas, talents, and particular experience of life need to come out of hiding. As uncomfortable as it may feel, learning to invite, honor, and assert your own perspectives, opinions, and insights are a necessary part of your development.

Here is the great loss—the pain—for Type Nine: Not recognizing the significance of your presence nor your capacity for engaging in the world in whatever you are called upon to do, you fade into the background. Who you are as a unique human being disappears. When your light isn't allowed to shine, your sense of insignificance is further magnified.

The Inner Logic and the Triangle of Identity for Type Nine

Type Nine's CORE BELIEF

We see that a core belief is set into place, providing an unconscious filter that accepts only information that supports the ego's belief. This filter, unfortunately, misses and dismisses data that would otherwise provide alternate perspectives. This belief acts as a core operating principle that shapes a person's relationship to life.

Each core belief is false but feels real until we can compassionately bring it into the light of awareness. It's particularly important to approach this with great kindness and truthfulness.

For the Nine, the core belief is that you have to erase yourself in order to maintain a sense of oneness with—and keep yourself from being cut off from—what brings you connection and comfort.

How might this belief show up in your life? Here are some examples of what you might hear yourself think, say, or do/not do:

- I just didn't get around to it.
- It doesn't really matter that I didn't do it. It's not that important anyway.
- It would be too disturbing to get involved in that conversation. It's just more comfortable here, and I don't really have enough energy anyway.
- Look, we're all in this together. Let's not make a fuss over this.

This core belief leads us to the **Triangle of Identity,** *which provides a shorthand illustration of how you "do" life.* I invite you to try on the following description to see how it fits with your experience.

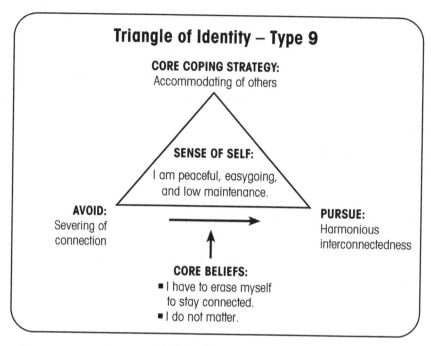

Figure 6-1: The Triangle of Identity for Type Nine

Here is how a person with the Type Nine personality structure might recognize this inner logic that is illustrated by the Triangle of Identity:

I *pursue* a sense of harmonious interconnectedness within myself and in my world. Sensitive to the energies of others, I pull back my own energy to insure that those in my environment are feeling comfortable and at peace. When they show that they are at ease, I can feel at peace.

I do what I can to *avoid* the experience of having my relationships severed from other people important to me. It feels that they might disregard, leave, or even "disown" me if I disagree or get in arguments or have differences of opinion. Expressing anger toward another person or being in conflict are definitely the hardest things in life to do.

So I *cope* by accommodating to the wishes, opinions, and directives of others. I express my own wishes indirectly. I think others should be able to take into account what I want without me speaking up, and if they don't, I can deliver a stinging, if indirect, message. I can be passive-aggressive.

As an extension of my coping, I can see that my life is or has been organized around keeping things emotionally comfortable, peaceful, and harmonious. If only I can keep negative emotions at a distance and keep a calm environment, then I'll feel inwardly peaceful, at least for the moment.

All of this leads me to see myself as a calm, peaceful, easygoing person. This self-definition—this *sense of self*—ends up imposing limits. It keeps me from recognizing and appreciating the fuller range of my human experience.

An Awakened Capacity of Type Nine: Showing Up, and Being Present and Here

Being present and here and in contact with your body's energy (your life force), with your body's substance (your particular physical nature, or the matter making up your body), with your body's groundedness (your contact with the sensations of your physicality, especially with your physical center—the belly), and with your body's dimensionality (the space you physically take up with the three dimensions of your body)... all these things allow you to engage, interact with, and show up for life, regardless of what's going on. Basically, *showing up* helps you to open your heart.

It's when you have forgotten and lost contact with your innate capacity for being in direct contact with your physical nature that you internally remove and erase yourself from experiences that would take you out of your comfort zone. Uncomfortable with disagreements and conflict, you focus on ideals and commonalities, and you try to minimize any factors that would lead to anger or other so-called negative emotions.

Paradoxically, it's staying with situations and becoming engaged, even when they are uncomfortable, that provide a key to unlocking the door to a freer life.

The Iceberg Model for Type Nine reiterates some of this material in a visual format.

The model starts with some of the expansive qualities that are innate gifts of individuals dominant in this type. These qualities are naturally and increasingly experienced as we recognize and gradually release our attachment to our more limited definition of self. It also increases our understanding of the observable expressions found above the waterline in Type Nine individuals, and fills out more of what goes on below the waterline, i.e., those inner dynamics that shape and motivate the behaviors that occur when the personality has its grip on us. (Refer to chapter 5 for more discussion on the Iceberg Model.)

Decoding the Personality Structure of Type Nine

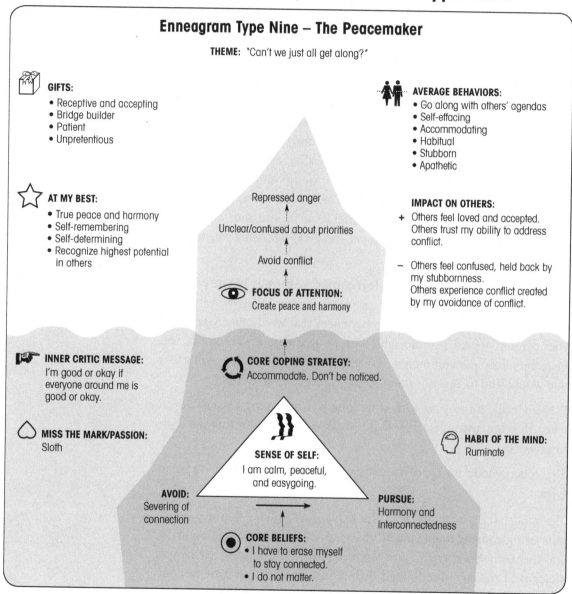

Figure 6-2: The Iceberg Model for Type Nine

Type Nine's Theme

"Can't we all just get along?" is the theme of this personality structure.

Above the Waterline

The Gifts, Daily Habits, and Challenges of Type Nine

GIFTS and AT MY BEST
(When I'm expansive and at my healthiest)

I am receptive and open to the wishes and the well-being of others. I am able to accept others as they are and where they are.

I am a bridge builder. I am good at listening to and understanding the differences in viewpoints, and at finding elements of commonality to bring people together.

I am patient. I recognize and trust the natural rhythm inherent in achieving certain outcomes, and I tend not to push to reach a goal *before its time.*

I am unpretentious. What you see is what you get. I'm genuine.

I bring a sense of authentic peace and harmony to wherever I am. Others can be at ease with me.

I am self-remembering. I naturally take into account my own priorities and include those in my day-to-day life.

I am self-determining. I take the initiative on actions that reflect what has the deepest meaning and purpose for me and I stay the course, even when that involves working through disagreements. I realize that this does not diminish my true inner sense of peace.

I recognize the potential in others and can see what's possible for them. I see the commonalities among and between people.

AVERAGE BEHAVIORS *(Distinguishing characteristics when my personality has its grip on me)*

I *go along with* others and their agendas so that I don't create a scene. It's just so much easier to do it that way.

I am self-effacing, downplaying my contribution. I keep a low profile so as not to bring undue attention to myself.

I accommodate the wishes of others, thereby avoiding the potential for emotional discomfort.

I have lots of habits and use repetitive sayings. Operating on auto-pilot, I stay busy with whatever is getting my attention in the moment and have trouble accomplishing what's important to me.

I am stubborn. I appear to agree with others, but sometimes don't follow up with action. In fact, I can balk at suggestions and refuse to let others have their way.

I have a semi-sweet exterior disposition, but *don't allow others to get too close to my private, inner world.*

I am apathetic, indifferent, and numb. Basically, I'm *missing in action.*

FOCUS OF ATTENTION, or FOA *(Where I put my attention when I'm attached to my personality)*

NOTE: *This is a brief description of what happens as the FOA becomes narrower and narrower. It's important to note that the degree to which our FOA is activated is shaped by our degree of presence. With more presence, what we pay attention to expands, rather than narrows.*

I focus on creating peace and harmony, even if only on the surface, when I'm in the grip of the personality. This entails looking for the positives in the situation in order to highlight them, and to downplay or ignore situations with potential for creating conflict or other difficulties.

I try to create conditions that will bring about a sense of comfort and peace. If that fails, and anger, disagreements, or arguments flair, then I withdraw from the situation. I may become quiet, emotionally unavailable, or may physically leave. I easily forget about what's important to me. I experience confusion and cloudy thinking and lose touch with my energy and vitality.

To be drawn into difficult situations or to express my own emotional discord can feel deathly. When the anger can't be contained, I can have a momentary explosion, surprising everyone around me.

My IMPACT ON OTHERS

+
−

+ *Positive:*
- Others feel loved, accepted, valued.
- Others experience my groundedness and sense of presence.

− *Negative:*
- Others feel confused and frustrated by my outward *niceness* and inner resistance/stubbornness.
- Others experience a lot of conflict that is created by me trying to avoid it.

Below the Waterline

To understand the inner dynamics for Type Nine, we turn our attention to what lies under the surface of the water, starting at the bottom and working up.

Type Nine's CORE BELIEFS

These core operating principles filter through many layers of life, in both seen and unseen ways.

I believe that I have to erase myself in order to stay connected to others. I believe that if I do voice my perspective, I will lose my psychic and emotional connections to other people—which feels deadly. Therefore, I need to forget myself, my agenda, and my ideas.

I believe that my presence is unimportant. And because I believe that I'm no one special, my perspective or my active engagement does not matter. My contribution is not going to make a difference.

The TRIANGLE OF IDENTITY

What I PURSUE

I *pursue* harmonious interconnectedness.

I try to keep an even and low level of energy within me and around me.

I don't want to upset the apple cart. Peacefulness, as I've defined it, requires that I stay calm, unaffected, and nice.

What I AVOID

I *avoid* anything that could potentially sever my connections with others.

I have a belief that if I give voice to what I really want, that I will be "disowned" or left. Simply expressing myself in an honest way can feel like a big gamble, and anything that I fear will disturb another's peace of mind feels like it could be cause for being separated from a source of comfort. I so seldom put forward what's important to me that I actually forget my priorities.

My CORE COPING STRATEGY

My *core coping strategy* is to accommodate, especially in situations where there's conflict. I'm careful not to *rock the boat,* so if I engage at all, it's in looking for points of agreement. Basically, I avoid asserting myself and using my energy for my life's priorities, and this perpetuates my feeling of being unseen or unheard.

SENSE OF SELF *("I am...")*

I see myself as being calm, peaceful, and easygoing. I see myself as being a *nice* person. I want others to see me as peaceful and low maintenance, which I have come to believe helps me stay connected to them.

WHERE I MISS THE MARK
(The energetic drive of the passion)

I don't fully engage in the matters that shape my life. I tend to stay on the edge of activities, groups, and events rather than getting fully involved. Rather than living inside the picture, *I live along the picture's frame.* I take pride in being *detached* from situations that involve conflict and opinions. I may be very busy in relatively unimportant activities, but lazy when it comes to taking a stand, making a decision, and moving into action. This energetic drive, or passion, is called *sloth.*

> **REMINDER**: No matter what type you are dominant in, the passion is a part of the personality and is a motivator that drives your emotional life. The passion covers up a wound in your heart[1] and creates an emotional reaction to how you relate to life, which takes you away from what your soul loves. This is true for all personality types.

HABIT OF THE MIND (*Fixation of the personality*)

This mental habit is the ego's automatic, unquestioned way of solving the problems of one's life. For Type Nines, this habit is to ruminate.[2] Rumination is the process of soothing one's self through repetitiously reviewing an idea or thought. Ruminating leaves the Type Nine experiencing a clouded, blurry version of *peace,* as it replaces the need for taking responsibility for expressing oneself and taking purposeful action.

Here's what it might look like:

I mostly think about the same things, over and over, rehashing them in my mind. This obstructs me from remembering what my priorities in life are. A state of mental fog or slushiness is common.

> **REMINDER**: No matter what type you are dominant in, the fixation is a part of the personality. It's a motivator in your fixed behaviors and thoughts about yourself and the world. It bolsters a false sense of reality, and as the ego's automatic, unquestioned way of solving one's problems with life, it takes you away from your true self. This is true for all personality types.

INNER CRITIC MESSAGE
(*What my Inner Critic insists upon*)

My inner critic insists that other people must feel good *in order for me to be okay.*[3] It insists that it's *not okay* for me to feel good, happy, and comfortable if others are in pain or uncomfortable. As long as I'm caught in the web of my inner critic, I will try to maintain the impossible task of making things comfortable for everyone else at the expense of my own life's priorities.

Each of the elements described above contributes to the whole experience of what we have come to think of as ourselves. The core belief, the emotional force of the passion, the mental habit (fixation), and the inner critic all unconsciously conspire to reinforce the Triangle of Identity.

Additional Information on the Enneagram Type Nine

What causes me *stress*

Conflict causes me to feel stressed. I just don't feel capable of handling conflict; my mind gets fuzzy, and I can't remember what I wanted to say.

This is so painful that I want to avoid it at all costs.

Making decisions causes stress. When I don't know what I want and yet I need to make a choice, I can see all sides of the issue. I prefer others to make the decision, though I'm often not happy with their decision either.

When I'm most constricted and inflexible

I tune out and deny anything that might cause discomfort. I don't even recognize when a problem is getting out of hand.

I become immovable. I will not budge.

I am confused and disoriented.

I feel powerless and unimportant.

I disappear.

Other Personality Types Related to Type Nine

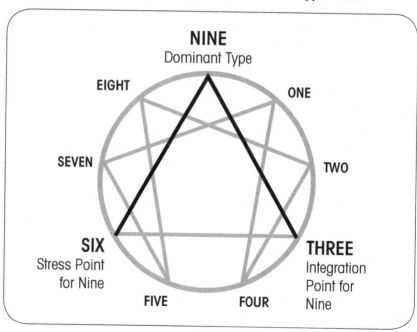

Figure 6-3: The Stress and Integration Points for Type Nine

People dominant in Type Nine experience characteristics of Type Six under stress. Type Six is the *Stress Point* for Type Nine. For more information on this, see chapter 14. Pay particular attention to the sections on average-level behaviors and to the "Notice and Observe Patterns" section of that chapter.

Type Nine's *Integration Point*, including the *Hidden Dimension of Self,* is found in Type Three. See chapter 9 for more information on Type Three. For Type Nine's Integration Point, pay particular attention to the "Gifts" and "At My Best" sections in chapter 9. For Type Nine's Hidden Dimension of Self, review the sections on average levels of behavior in that same chapter.

The Enneagram also works in reverse, which yields helpful information to everyone discovering their dominant type: Type Nine is the Stress Point for Type Three, and it's the Integration Point for Type Six.

Recognizing Patterns That Pull You Off-Course

Notice and Observe Patterns

In this section you'll find some of the patterns that are associated with the Type Nine personality structure. These patterns provide useful information. Rather than making you bad or wrong in some way, these patterns can be used as signposts on your path of awakening. They help you notice and get to the heart of your experience in a tangible, direct way. Eventually, you can relax the particular, habitual—and often troublesome—strategies, which will allow you to be more present, open, and free.

The pattern of discounting yourself

Individuals dominant in Nine who are in the grip of the personality tend to discount themselves.

The act of discounting can take on a number of different behaviors.

- For example, have you noticed instances in which you *go along with others?* Not wanting to anger or disappoint them, you find it easier to acquiesce rather than voice a different opinion. You may actually think that you don't have an opinion, and if you do, you think you should be above having one. More likely, you really don't know what you want for yourself.

- You *forget your own agenda*. For example, after a meeting with another person, you realize that he or she did most of the talking. You listened. You learned something about them. They learned very little about you. What value do you receive from the conversation? You may notice that it feels *rude* to be the first to initiate your contribution in the conversation, so you nicely wait to be asked.
- You have something to say in a group but *feel awkward in speaking up*. Doing so would focus a lot of attention on you, and you tell yourself that what you have to say may not really be very important. You feel upset when someone says what you were thinking and their comments are positively received.
- You simply *forget what's important to you* and what your priorities are. They get shoved to the side. And you numb out.

The pattern of withdrawing from real-time engagement

Individuals prominent in Nine who are in the grip of the personality tend to withdraw from engagement and participation.

If this is a predominant pattern for you, you may also notice your tendency to:

- Avoid situations that might produce conflicting ideas, strong emotions, and/or even mild dissent among people.
- Disengage from being present with what's actually occurring in the moment in order to create an idealized relationship with the other person or situation. Idealizing is experienced as an internal reverie, where you are in a fictitious relationship with what's going on. This may result in ignoring actual problems that need to be resolved.

The pattern of denying anger

You might at first think, "Anger? What anger?" but if you are dominant in Type Nine, I encourage you to:

- Become familiar with your experience of anger.
  Notice your evaluation of what it means to be angry. Nines typically think that *anger is a negative expression*, and one to be avoided at all costs—either in themselves or hearing it from others. Anger can feel very scary.

- Notice your ego's attempt to *make anger wrong* in some way. Perhaps it's difficult to notice how much of your emotional and physical energy you use to repress your anger, but the truth is that anger is a natural human emotion to experience. Overexpressed or underexpressed anger can both have a negative impact, but healthy anger clarifies and activates energy. Healthy anger offers a surprising and empowering boost that counterbalances fuzziness and confusion.

- Notice your tendency to *make nice on the outside*, but put the brakes on when interacting with others. Notice the resistance that is in your body. When you get curious about the resistance, you may find anger lurking not far below the surface.

Surprising and Effective Practices for Building Your Capacity

The following capacity-building practices will help you turn toward your true nature.

1. Ask yourself what you need and want.

It may take time to discover what's really important to you. Your priorities have taken a backseat to making certain that those around you are okay first. Try making a list of things you really loved doing as a child. Be conscious about paying attention to things that speak to your heart.

2. Develop a relationship with your body.

Because it so challenging for Nines to remain in touch with their physicality or *their place in space*, it's important to incorporate useful, body-oriented strategies to keep reminding you to pay attention to your body. Here are some possibilities:

- If you like walking, practice being very aware of your body's movement and feeling your feet contact the ground while you are in movement.

- Practice *belly breathing, or deep breathing,* several times throughout the day.

- Get frequent massages or other kinds of body work that help you experience your body.
- Find a form of yoga that quickens your energy.
- Study aikido to strengthen your groundedness and your presence while being physically engaged with another person.

3. Take intentional, focused action on your priorities.

Take strong, purposeful action. Perhaps that means enrolling in classes or workshops or going to a retreat that focuses on your interests and needs. Notice the temptation to back down at the first inkling of resistance on the part of a significant person in your life. Remember, this is for you.

At the beginning of each day, ask yourself what your most important priority is to focus on. Focus on completing some aspect of your priority daily.

4. Learn about your anger.

Anger feels very threatening to a Nine, so it may be useful to work with someone who can create a safe space for you to practice experiencing your anger.

Having anger doesn't mean that you go around yelling at people. But it does mean that you allow yourself to feel the energy of anger moving through your body. And it does mean that you get in touch with an instinctual energy that can fuel your movement toward greater health, creativity, and liberation.

5. Speak up.

Practice saying what's on your mind, either in one-on-one relationships or in groups.

Forging Your Healing and Evolutionary Path

A major theme of this book is that the primary reason for working with the Enneagram is to help us awaken to our true nature. It puts us on a path of healing and real transformation that, for most of us, takes place over time—with patience, trust, faith in our awakening journey—and by being as present as possible. Section III takes us into processes that support and are beneficial for everyone, regardless of type.

Not surprisingly, there are specific processes that are vital for individuals dominant in each type.

If you are dominant in Type Nine, your healing and evolutionary path includes the following:

Fully embrace your physical, human experience. Reconnect with your physical existence and consciously be in your body as you move through the world and claim your individuality.

Notice your hidden desire for attention. That's right. You may have dismissed that basic human need in the past, but acknowledging and embracing it will support your development. It's hard to celebrate this revelation—this discovery of the Hidden Dimension of Self—but as you do, it will help you recognize your inner strength. From this source of strength, you can experience that your participation in the world is important. Your soul longs for this.

> **REMINDER**: The Hidden Dimension of Self is found at the average and lower levels of health in the Integration Point.

Allow your natural feelings of anger. This does not mean acting it out. There may be times that it's important to share your experience with another person honestly. Sometimes, all you need to do is experience the energy of anger in your body. You may be surprised to realize that it gives you more access to your life energy and leads to the incredible feeling of being truly alive.

Allow yourself to be affected by life. Let your inner world be disrupted, let your heart be broken, and take in life. You will recognize that great inner peace arises from being engaged and being present.

The Human Condition and Consciousness of Type Four: The Individualist

A deep desire to use her unique gifts of insight, intuition, emotional sensitivity, and creative expression for healing the pain and challenges of others brought Denise to coaching. She held high hopes of being able to make a positive impact in the lives of others, yet found it difficult to take specific, steady steps into the pragmatics of making a living.

A talented and highly skilled woman, she felt blocked when trying to create a regular structure or take the practical steps of following through on the sometimes mundane activities involved with building her own business. But now, she felt more drawn than ever to making her dreams become a reality, and she expressed a desire to experience results.

Initially, Denise wasn't sure what the Enneagram could do for her. Her big concern was that she would be put in a box. However, as she worked with the material, she became aware that many of her feelings and ideas weren't unique just to her, but were common to individuals dominant in Type Four and served as a basis for her growth.

For example:
- *She recognized that frequent fantasies about what her business would look like didn't have a chance to be tested in the day-to-day world as long as they stayed in the realm of imagination. Her plans for setting up her business were stymied because the step-by-step tasks seemed too mundane to interest her.*

- *She noticed how frequently she felt depressed or negative about herself, which was in contrast to what she wanted to offer others.*
- *She saw that there was fairly consistent emotional drama around events in life that preoccupied her.*
- *She saw that without regular attention and sensitive feedback from others, she spent time feeling bad about herself.*

An initial focus of Denise's work was to help her find her way back into her body.

As a woman used to living in a heady and emotional world, she found that her body was a source of some surprise. She survived a life-threatening illness some years earlier and found that she hadn't really trusted her body since then.

Conscious walking, dancing, and other forms of intentional movement to become aware of sensations helped her to feel grounded and eventually more able to focus on the day-to-day activities of building her new business. With more connection to her body, she relied less on a rich imagination and focused more on activities such as making necessary phone calls and addressing legal matters even when she didn't feel like it. *Actions she previously had considered mundane now brought her closer to manifesting her dream of developing a successful practice as a healing professional. Most importantly, she discovered her capacity for accomplishing something which she held as deeply significant.*

Her work now speaks for itself. Denise's creative approach and capacity to enter into the depth of the human experience is a beautiful expression of her life's purpose.

The Internal Coherence of the Type Four Experience

Your True Nature

If this is your dominant Enneagram point, you are naturally drawn to the experience of penetrating the depth and the meaning of life. You love the inherent beauty that exists everywhere and recognize yourself as an integral expression of the creative force that reveals itself in unique and deeply layered ways.

When not in touch with your true nature, what you might not recognize *yet* is that there's nothing missing in your life. You have everything you need to be an original expression of life. Even the so-called mundane experiences are aspects of a life intricately laced with beauty and meaning.

The Story of Your Life:
Relating to Your Inner and Outer World

Your inner sense of self and your place in the world were set in place early in life. How you internalized your experiences contributed to the characteristic way you relate to yourself and others, and to your very way of being. If this is your dominant type, the following brief story of your childhood inner experience will likely sound very familiar.

Even as a small child, you felt so very different from your parents. You wondered how you came to be in this family. Almost from the beginning, you felt unseen and misunderstood. You felt emotionally abandoned or lost.

Having the feeling of being very different from others in your family led you to have a sense that there was something wrong with you— perhaps something profoundly wrong. You felt as if you were missing some special ingredient that everyone else had. You may have spent much of your energy envying and comparing yourself to others. You often felt frustrated.

Almost as long as you can remember, you were searching for a deeper sense of yourself—trying to figure out who you were and how you fit into life. You tried to create your personal environment to reflect your unique internal experience.

Thus, you were drawn to others who you felt had sufficient emotional depth. You yearned for others to see into your depths, but at the same time, were scared that they would leave you. Eventually you would become disappointed or even angry at others for not fully seeing you or for not seeing your degree of suffering and struggle. How could they not see?

Torn between being abandoned and the desire to have other people know what you are feeling, you would go back and forth between withdrawing from others and concealing yourself AND revealing your feelings. Either way, when you were emotionally intense, it felt that you were being the most you, the most authentic.

You came to organize your life around the sense that you were missing something important. While the ever-changing experience of intense feelings became the basis of your sense of self, the feeling of happiness didn't feel as real.

What you did not see is that you are okay just as you are, that there's no missing ingredient in your life. You did not see that you have all that you need, and that your natural love of depth and beauty is a deep blessing. You could not see that your gifts and authentic nature shine through you as you come to accept yourself as a regular and beautiful human being that is inherently connected with the Divine.

Your Great Loss

As a little being, even before your conscious thought and language skills developed, you had experiences that left you feeling separated from the essential qualities that your soul loved—that it was in tune with. This pain was too much to bear, so the ego structure began to form, taking on the role of protecting you from the severity of this early loss.

We remember that the ego attempts to mimic our true nature, though it can never be successful in doing so. So, the Type Four personality structure has tried to recreate the experience of having an identity of meaning and depth. Indeed, at the level of Essence, this is true. But the personality distorts what having an identity of meaning and depth actually is, and holds onto it as a sacred cow, or an unquestioned requirement. As the ego grows stronger, it demands that certain conditions exist for having a unique identity, such as, "Show me that you recognize the depth of my soul, or I will be disappointed and frustrated." Intense emotions that are easy and natural to access become a basis for your sensitive and deep nature, which you then look to other people to affirm. It's natural to feel misunderstood when others don't respond to you in the desired way, and then to sink into feelings of disappointment, frustration, and even despair that no one will ever "get" you.

Before you can experience your true depth and original nature, your capacity for living in the day-to-day, seemingly ordinary world needs to be acted on. As inauthentic as it may initially feel, taking purposeful action—even when you don't feel like doing so—will lead you to make the unique contributions that only you can make.

Here is the great loss—the pain—for Type Four: With a sense that something in you is inherently wrong, you feel unrecognizable and misunderstood. It seems that nobody really sees you, not even God. You are caught between trying to prove your depth and uniqueness to others, while feeling as if you don't have what it takes to get on with life.

The Inner Logic and the Triangle of Identity for Type Four

Type Four's CORE BELIEF

We see that a core belief is set into place, providing an unconscious filter that accepts only information that supports the ego's belief. This filter, unfortunately, misses and dismisses data that would otherwise provide alternate perspectives. This belief acts as a core operating principle that shapes a person's relationship to life.

Each core belief is false but feels real. The more it can be brought into the light of awareness with great compassion and truthfulness over time, the less hold it will have.

For the Type Four, the core belief is a deep sense that something vital in you is missing. Whatever this mysterious element is, it would allow you to be seen for the unique expression of life that you are. Without this element, you feel intrinsically flawed, and this becomes the basis for your sense of self.

How might this belief show up in your life? Here are some examples of what you might hear yourself think, say, or do/not do:

- I am invisible. I don't even see myself.
- Will no one ever really understand me?
- I don't have to do the mundane or follow-through on action steps. Those are for other people, not me.
- Why don't I get to have the wonderful things that others have? But, really, I wouldn't want their lives.

This core belief leads us to the **Triangle of Identity,** *which provides a shorthand illustration of how you "do" life.* I invite you to try on the following description to see how it fits with your experience.

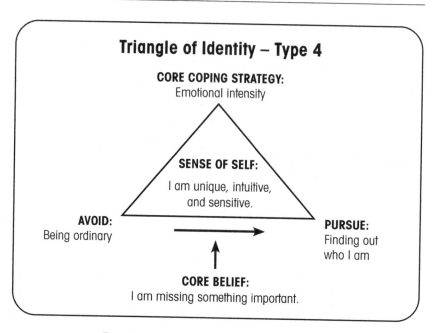

Figure 7-1: *The Triangle of Identity for Type Four*

Here is how a person with the Type Four personality structure might recognize this inner logic that is illustrated by the Triangle of Identity:

*I **pursue** wanting to know and express my distinctive sense of self. I'm constantly comparing my life to what I think the lives of others are like, and seeing myself as simply different. For example, I might have more difficulty than others in finding work that feels sufficiently meaningful, or I might have a physical condition that sets me apart, or I might customarily dress in a one-of-a-kind way that helps me stand out.*

*I **avoid** ordinary experiences. They feel like death. While I may envy what others have, the other side of the coin is that the daily lives of others seem superficial and lacking meaning. Living a life that others might think is normal but that requires me to follow conventional standards is one of the hardest things to do. This is an ongoing inner conflict.*

*I **cope** by paying close attention to, and magnifying, my emotional experience. This gives me a sense of depth and realness. The bigger and more dramatic these emotions, the more I have a sense of identity. In other words, my emotional state at any given time, which often has the flavor of inadequacy, depression or other so-called negative emotions, is the basis for my identity. These darker states are no stranger to me.*

As an extension of my coping, I can see that my life is or has been organized around being sensitive to the depth, suffering, and exquisiteness of life, and that I hope others will recognize my originality. Then I would feel that my life meets my expectations. I create imaginative and rich scenarios in my mind's eye, minimizing my need to deal with ordinary life. If only others would reflect back to me my individuality, then I would inwardly experience a sense of identity, at least for the moment.

*All of this leads me to see myself as a unique, intuitive, sensitive person. This self-definition—this **sense of self**—ends up imposing limits. It keeps me from recognizing and appreciating the fuller range of my human experience.*

An Awakened Capacity of Type Four: Emotional Balance, or Equanimity

Being in real contact with your heart allows you to open to the beauty, the magnificent depth, and the mystery of life. Being in contact with your heart is different than being identified with your emotional state. Emotions come and go, but contact with the actual sensations in your heart helps you experience yourself from a new perspective and leads to an unexpected experience of knowing self.

It's when you have forgotten and lost contact with your innate capacity for experiencing the real depth and beauty that is part of all of life, that your self-comparison to others get magnified, and you envy others for what they seem to have.

You have forgotten that there's a richness and depth in ordinary experiences, which is a key to unlocking the door to a freer life. When you live this freer life, you can experience your life's beauty, meaning, and truly unique expression.

The Type Four Iceberg Model reiterates some of this material in a visual format.

The model starts with some of the expansive qualities that are innate gifts of individuals dominant in this type. These qualities are naturally and increasingly experienced as we recognize and gradually release our attachment to our more limited definition of self. It also increases our understanding of the observable expressions found above the waterline

137

in Type Four individuals, and fills out more of what goes on below the waterline, i.e., those inner dynamics that shape and motivate the behaviors that occur when the personality has its grip on us. (Refer to chapter 5 for more discussion on the Iceberg Model.)

Decoding the Personality Structure of Type Four

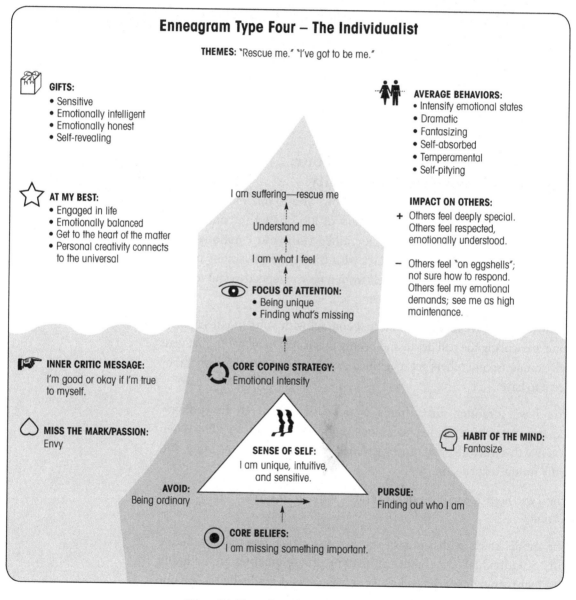

Enneagram Type Four – The Individualist

THEMES: "Rescue me." "I've got to be me."

GIFTS:
- Sensitive
- Emotionally intelligent
- Emotionally honest
- Self-revealing

AT MY BEST:
- Engaged in life
- Emotionally balanced
- Get to the heart of the matter
- Personal creativity connects to the universal

I am suffering—rescue me

Understand me

I am what I feel

FOCUS OF ATTENTION:
- Being unique
- Finding what's missing

AVERAGE BEHAVIORS:
- Intensify emotional states
- Dramatic
- Fantasizing
- Self-absorbed
- Temperamental
- Self-pitying

IMPACT ON OTHERS:

+ Others feel deeply special. Others feel respected, emotionally understood.

– Others feel "on eggshells"; not sure how to respond. Others feel my emotional demands; see me as high maintenance.

INNER CRITIC MESSAGE:
I'm good or okay if I'm true to myself.

CORE COPING STRATEGY:
Emotional intensity

MISS THE MARK/PASSION:
Envy

HABIT OF THE MIND:
Fantasize

SENSE OF SELF:
I am unique, intuitive, and sensitive.

AVOID:
Being ordinary

PURSUE:
Finding out who I am

CORE BELIEFS:
I am missing something important.

Figure 7-2: The Iceberg Model for Type Four

Type Four's THEMES

"Rescue me" and/or "I've got to be me" are the themes of this personality structure.

Above the Waterline

The Gifts, Daily Habits, and Challenges of Type Four

GIFTS and AT MY BEST
(When I'm expansive and at my healthiest)

I am sensitive to the emotional environment and experiences of others, and I am able to reach out to others with understanding and care.

I am emotionally intelligent. I am aware of my emotions and those of others, and I work with the emotional experiences and interactions to increase healing for myself and others.

I am emotionally honest. I take time to understand the motivations behind my emotions and neither deny nor magnify them. I look for the insights that I gain from understanding my emotions.

I can reveal my emotional depths in original, creative ways.

I am engaged in life and feel solidly connected and present with others.

My emotions are even and balanced. I recognize and appreciate the changes in my emotional state but don't get overly attached to any of these emotions.

I can dive into the heart of the matter and get to the underlying emotional thoughts and reactions of a situation. I can ask emotionally difficult questions and have the deep capacity to be with others who are in painful situations. Dark places don't scare me.

My personal creativity taps into universal themes. This can help others learn more about the depths of life for themselves.

AVERAGE BEHAVIORS *(Distinguishing characteristics when my personality has its grip on me)*

I generate intense feelings through my imagination.

I can be dramatic, experiencing and expressing overly charged emotions related to even the most mundane event.

I have an expansive fantasy life, which feels more interesting than day-to-day life. Ordinary life can feel *beneath me* and too superficial or mundane.

I am absorbed in my emotions and myself. I don't distinguish between life and emotions. Emotions are the basis for life. My emotions are me.

I can be temperamental with dramatic mood swings. People never quite know what to expect from me. My highs are high and my lows are low (and there are more lows than highs).

In self-pitying, I feel sorry for myself and am looking for the sympathetic understanding of others. Not receiving that, I feel alone and misunderstood once again.

FOCUS OF ATTENTION, or FOA *(Where I put my attention when I'm attached to my personality)*

NOTE: *This is a brief description of what happens as the FOA becomes narrower and narrower. It's important to note that the degree to which our FOA is activated is shaped by our degree of presence. With more presence, what we pay attention to expands, rather than narrows.*

I focus on feeling special and unique. The basis for my uniqueness lies in my inherently flawed state, which sets me apart from others. I'm missing something that others have.

I (unconsciously) try to create conditions that point to my unique depth and sensitivity to a broad range of emotions. I identify closely with my feelings. They are my truth.

Simultaneously, I monitor how others respond. While I want others to really understand me and my innate sense that something is missing from my life, I have a hidden sense that this is impossible.

If I fail to get the understanding I'm specifically looking for, I can become touchy, and my moods take precedence over what's actually happening—the tasks at hand or the interaction that is taking place, for example. My emotions, especially painful ones from the past, play out powerfully in my life, and I use them to re-experience my past and to define who I am now.

When that happens, my feeling of uniqueness is saturated with suffering. I look for someone or something that can rescue me from my pain.

My IMPACT ON OTHERS

+ *Positive:*
- Others feel deeply understood and seen.
- Others are inspired by the depth of my authentic expression and originality.

– *Negative:*
- Others walk on eggshells, unsure of what mood I will be in.
- Others may be exhausted by my emotional demands and need for attention. They are likely to back away, seeing me as high maintenance.

Below the Waterline

To understand the inner dynamics for Type Four, we turn our attention to what lies under the surface of the water, starting at the bottom and working up.

Type Four's CORE BELIEF

This core operating principle filters through many layers of life, in both seen and unseen ways.

I believe that I'm missing something important that would make me whole. I'm convinced that because I'm missing an important *something*, I'm so different that no one else can understand or help me. My uniqueness also exempts me from the expectations of others. The usual rules of life don't apply to me.

The TRIANGLE OF IDENTITY
What I PURSUE

I *pursue* wanting to know who I am, and having a special, deep identity.

I'm constantly comparing my life to what I think the lives of others are like. I don't understand why others should have things or people in their lives that I don't. This reinforces my sense of distinctness. Identity, as I've defined it, requires deeply felt emotional states.

What I AVOID

I *avoid* being ordinary.

Everyday experiences that others engage in don't meet my standards. While I may envy what others have, the other side of the coin is that the daily lives of others seem so superficial and lacking meaning. To have ordinary experiences or to be ordinary makes me indistinguishable and feels like a death sentence.

My CORE COPING STRATEGY

My emotions shape my experience. The more pronounced they are, the more sensitively and deeply I feel. I search for the ideal situation or person that will compensate for what I feel is missing internally, and I seek attention and understanding from the other. This creates distance and tension in my relationships, which, conversely, feels like I'm being true to myself.

SENSE OF SELF *("I am...")*

I see myself as being unique, intuitive, and sensitive. I want others to see and reflect back these qualities in me, which will reinforce my identity.

WHERE I MISS THE MARK
(The energetic drive of the passion)

I miss the mark when I become envious of others. I'm constantly comparing my life to what I think the lives of others are like, and I usually determine that their lives are easier than mine. I believe that others fit in better than I do, and that I'm basically an outsider.

REMINDER: No matter what type you are dominant in, the passion is a part of the personality and is a motivator that drives your emotional life. The passion covers up a wound in your heart[1] and creates an emotional reaction to how you relate to life, which takes you away from what your soul loves. This is true for all personality types.

HABIT OF THE MIND *(Fixation of the personality)*

I fantasize about what could be and what could have been. My fantasies take on a life of their own and become more real than external reality. I spend a lot of time and energy on the way I want my life to look. My rich fantasies become magnified and can easily become the focus of my life. The more extensive the fantasy, the less possibility that I can take any action that would result in the fantasy coming to fruition. The result is that I can have a very difficult time taking any action at all that moves my life forward.

REMINDER: No matter what type you are dominant in, the fixation is a part of the personality. It's a motivator in your fixed behaviors and thoughts about yourself and the world. It bolsters a false sense of reality, and as the ego's automatic, unquestioned way of solving problems with life, it takes you away from your true self. This is true for all personality types.

INNER CRITIC MESSAGE
(What my Inner Critic insists upon)

In order for me to feel good or *okay*, I have to be true to myself.[2] That means that I have to follow my feelings, because to me, they are truth. If I'm feeling sad, then I must act sad, even dramatically sad, as that means I'm being true to myself, and I will get rewarded by my inner critic. As long as I'm caught in the web of my inner critic, I will continue to be trapped in emotional turmoil as a substitute for the equanimity of living fully in the world.

Each of the elements described above contributes to the whole experience of what we have come to think of as ourselves. The core belief, the emotional force of the passion, the mental habit (fixation), and the inner critic all unconsciously conspire to reinforce the Triangle of Identity.

Additional Information on the Enneagram Type Four

What causes me *stress*

My stress level increases when I feel that others undervalue or misunderstand me. My stress is dramatically increased when others don't meet my emotional expectations, and disappoint or even abandon me. Feelings of abandonment reinforce my innate sense that something important is missing within me.

When I'm most *constricted and inflexible*

I become emotionally paralyzed and depressed.

I feel totally alienated from others and from myself.

I'm self-loathing and tormented by delusions.

I feel hopeless and become self-destructive.

Other Personality Types Related to Type Four

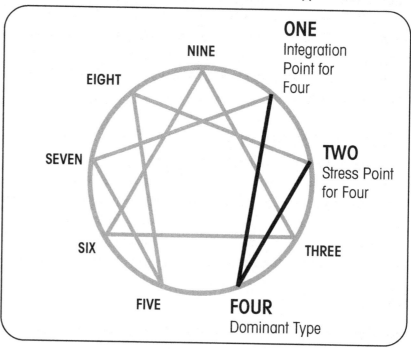

Figure 7-3: The Stress and Integration Points for Type Four

People dominant in Type Four experience characteristics of Type Two under stress. Type Two is the *Stress Point* for Type Four. For more information on this, see chapter 13. Pay particular attention to the sections on average-level behaviors and to the "Notice and Observe Patterns" section of that chapter.

Type Four's *Integration Point*, including the *Hidden Dimension of Self*, is found in Type One. See chapter 12 for more information on Type One. For Type Four's Integration Point, pay particular attention to the "Gifts" and "At My Best" sections in chapter 12. For Type Four's Hidden Dimension of Self, review the sections on average levels of behavior in that same chapter.

The Enneagram also works in reverse, which yields helpful information to everyone discovering their dominant type: Type Four is the Stress Point for Type One, and it's the Integration Point for Type Two.

Recognizing Patterns That Pull You Off-Course

Notice and Observe Patterns

In this section you'll find some of the patterns that are associated with the Type Four personality structure. These patterns provide useful information. Rather than making you bad or wrong in some way, these patterns can be used as signposts on your path of awakening. They help you notice and get to the heart of your experience in a tangible, direct way. Eventually, you can relax the particular, habitual—and often troublesome—strategies, which will allow you to be more present, open, and free.

The pattern of letting your emotions control your experience

- Notice the tendency to let your emotional state *color your entire experience* of the moment or even the day. This especially tends to happen when you become absorbed with feeling down or depressed.

- Has anyone referred to you as *moody?* When you are feeling a particular way, do you express that emotion outwardly so that other people will know you are feeling the way that you do?
- Notice when you exaggerate your emotional state. You might see this happen when you retell your *story* to others repeatedly, or when you continually focus on re-experiencing the feeling. This may take the form of *longing* or *yearning* for things to be different.

The pattern of creating environments that support or help you sustain your moods

- This might mean that you *have to have just the right kind of day* to tackle a task, or that just the right chair in just the right color is necessary. You might be drawn to the exotic or unusual to reinforce your mood.
- You might notice the tendency to overindulge yourself with too much of something—which can include food or sex or drugs—as a way to further reinforce your moods. Notice if you feel that you are somehow *exempt* from the so-called rules that apply to other people's behavior.

The pattern of fantasies taking you away from reality

- Type Fours can spend a great deal of time fantasizing about their desired life, their desired partner, their ideal situation. For example, you might fantasize about having a more ideal body shape, or a more sensitive partner, or having a better-paying job, or being more talented in a particular skill. You might notice that you tend to reject anything that doesn't match your fantasized ideal.

Do you sometimes think that what's available to you is beneath you?

The pattern of having drama in relationships

- Notice the expectations you have of your relationships. If you think other people have it better than you, you may tend to act with jealousy. Or you may tend to *dump* your miseries on your friends and expect them to rescue you from your unhappiness. Do you expect that others will take care of you and your problems?

- Drama can be created by withdrawing or withholding information or affection from your partner. Fours often notice a tendency to create crises in a relationship, then have an emotional reconciliation.

The patterns of comparison and envy

- Do you think that other people have it easier than you or that your life just pales in comparison to others? Fours tend to negatively compare themselves to others and generalize those negative comparisons to all dimensions of life.
- Do you find yourself feeling frustrated or irritated? These emotions often result from comparing your current circumstances against a fantasized or idealized situation. Notice how the process of evaluating your circumstances against these fantasies affects your energy and your willingness to take purposeful action.

Surprising and Effective Practices for Building Your Capacity

The following capacity-building practices will help you turn toward your true nature.

1. Develop a relationship with your body.

Type Four individuals are normally disengaged from their bodies, so it's very useful to have a regular practice of mindful body movement, such as yoga or other forms of conscious physical activity where you are supported in embodying your experience.

Horseback riding, dance, aikido, and other interactive forms of exercise can also support you in getting into your body and experiencing sensations, balance, and relating to other living beings from a place of physicality.

2. Acknowledge your actual gifts and talents.

Individuals dominant in Type Four are challenged with identifying and claiming their actual talents.

Focus on relaxing the self-talk that diminishes what you have. Instead, take meaningful action to use your talents in the world.

147

3. Find the extraordinary in the ordinary.

Fours tend to be attracted to the exotic, and overlook the amazing nature of what they may have thought of as *ordinary*. Appreciate the small things—the gift of being here in this moment—and enjoy what you already have.

4. Become interested in and engaged with others.

Look for ways that you can help others and take meaningful action. This helps shift your attention from one of self-absorption to a balanced way of interacting. Many people dominant in Type Four have found that volunteering for an organization that has meaning for them has had beneficial outcomes.

5. Recognize feelings for what they are.

Feelings come and go, unless we consciously or unconsciously hold onto them. While feelings offer us useful information, they don't define who we are, nor are they a reflection of reality.

Remember that other people may respond to situations very differently than you do.

Forging Your Healing and Evolutionary Path

A major theme of this book is that the primary reason for working with the Enneagram is to help us awaken to our true nature. It puts us on a path of healing and real transformation that, for most of us, takes place over time—with patience, trust, faith in our awakening journey—and by being as present as possible. Section III takes us into processes that support and are beneficial for everyone, regardless of type.

Not surprisingly, there are specific processes that are vital for individuals dominant in each type.

If you are dominant in Type Four, your healing and evolutionary path includes the following:

Practice not acting out emotional dramas and recognize your capacity to successfully cope with life's experiences. As you release your need to have others see you as flawed, you will recognize that you don't need to be rescued.

Notice that you can be judgmental and perfectionistic (a part of the average levels of Type One). That's right. You may think that others are the ones that beat up on you, but recognize when you are hard on others. It's difficult to embrace this revelation—this discovery of the *Hidden Dimension of Self*—but as you acknowledge these qualities, they will help you move *from* the feeling of being a victim *to* owning the healthier side of your inner authority. These qualities will allow you to experience more of the mystery of life, which you love.

> **REMINDER**: The Hidden Dimension of Self is found at the average and lower levels of health in the Integration Point.

Recognize that there's beauty even in the most ordinary. While all humans beings are unique, they also all have commonalities which are part of normal living.

Claim your essential qualities of equanimity and forgiveness.

Allow your heart to be deeply touched by all of life. You will discover that a true experience of identity will be far more expansive than anything you could have imagined.

The Human Condition and Consciousness of Type Five: The Investigator

Daniel is an engineer with a strong entrepreneurial orientation who was hired in the start-up phase of a high-tech company. He sought coaching after he realized that he was being expected to take on a leadership role with new hires as the company entered a period of substantial growth. While he'd been working intensely to help the company break ground with its technology, he'd not put much thought into what this organizational expansion would require of him outside of his ability to design new product strategies. A role that required working more closely with people felt daunting.

He stated that he wanted to quickly figure out how to work with people without getting involved in the drama that is often a part of an office environment, so that he could concentrate on what was most important—the design of the company's leading-edge products for success in the marketplace.

He had been introduced to the Enneagram through a mentor. His intellectual curiosity was aroused by the strong knowledge base that is inherent in the Enneagram, but he was also intrigued by its deeper spiritual roots. He wanted to know more.

During the coaching relationship, Daniel experienced deep insights and awakenings around the patterns of the Type Five personality structure. He saw:

- *how hard it was for him to stay in conversations, especially those that involved process. He recognized how he physically withdrew from interactions in order to get privacy and personal space. Most often, he felt overwhelmed by the emotional energy of others.*
- *the increasing amount of time he spent in preparation for meetings or meeting an agreed-upon target. He wanted to cover all the bases and not be caught off-guard by a coworker asking a question.*
- *the excitement he felt surrounding a new idea; and then he came to see how much of his life centered around his thinking about ideas that intrigued him, to the detriment of other aspects of life.*
- *his high level of irritability and anxiety when someone interrupted his private thinking time or wanted his involvement in a task that seemed unimportant or beneath him.*

He began to see the many ways he removed himself from situations requiring emotional and social contact. Clearly, this was not going to be effective in the changing workplace, and not in other aspects of his life, either.

One major theme of coaching centered around supporting Daniel as he reconnected with his body. He seldom exercised and simply had little awareness of his body. He found that massage helped him to actually feel his body in ways he couldn't ever remember. He also experimented with body-based meditation. These strategies helped him feel more grounded as he experimented with new ways of interacting with others. He practiced having a well-defined, open-cubicle time during the day when colleagues and direct reports could have easier access to him. Over time, his social awkwardness decreased and his heart opened more to himself and others. He started to realize that his contributions as a tech expert and as a colleague and person were of value, and that one did not exclude the other.

The Internal Coherence of the Type Five Experience

Your True Nature

If this is your dominant Enneagram type, you are naturally drawn to a love of clarity and a deep, inner *knowing* that comes with a spacious, quiet mind. The fundamental structures or operating dynamics which exist behind the surface of life and are not usually visible to the unaware eye are illuminated, providing you with new insights. The astonishing stillness of your mind allows you to see clearly and understand what's available for discovery in the moment.

When not in touch with your true nature, what you might not recognize *yet* is that beyond your inner knowing, it's the tenderness of your heart that invites you into deeper contact with others. Here you experience that you have a place in life, and that your valued contributions both include and transcend your mental knowing. You have a tender, lovable heart with the capacity to be deeply touched and to deeply touch others.

The Story of Your Life:
Relating to Your Inner and Outer World

Your inner sense of self and your place in the world were set in place early in life. How you internalized your experiences contributed to the characteristic way you relate to yourself and others, and to your very way of being. If this is your dominant type, the following brief story of your childhood inner experience will likely sound very familiar.

> As a little child, you were exceptionally curious. Intrigued by specific things, you could spend hours by yourself, trying to understand how these things worked. You were also very sensitive to the energy of others, and could feel overwhelmed by the high level of activity, the talking, and the emotional energy in your home environment. It was hard to know how you fit into your family and to feel safe in a sometimes confusing environment.
>
> The only place that felt safe was your mind. There was so much to figure out, so much to understand, that it felt you would never have

enough time to do so. Thus, it felt natural to retreat into your mind as a safe and interesting haven. Here, you could not be rejected.

Even as a small child, you may have felt that there was no space for you in your family, as if all the places at the table were taken—so you continued to seek safety and solace in your mind. The more emotionally intense your environment, the more you retreated from experiencing your own emotions and personal needs.

Perhaps you sensed that your parents wanted more from you. You may have heard, "Come on, let's make sure you meet some new friends," or "I want you to be more outgoing, more active and involved with others." Although you yearned for your parents' love, you really wanted to be left alone to figure things out. And that didn't seem acceptable.

You felt you didn't have enough energy to do everything that seemed expected of you, so you conserved whatever energy you had. Rather than participate, you observed.

Your strong imagination created intense anxieties about yourself and about the world, with dark scenarios about what could happen in the future.

You did not expect much from others, except to be left alone. It was as if you said, "I won't expect much of you if you don't expect much of me." This helped you keep your distance from emotional closeness and nurturing.

You came to organize your life around the idea that the only way to be safe was by being in your head and being smart. Your mind was the basis of your self-confidence.

What you did not see is that you have the capacity to live in the world, to take action that helps you reach your goals, and to make the contribution that only you can make. What you could not see is that you have enough energy and resources to be engaged and experience the fullness of life and the amazing sweetness of your heart.

Your Great Loss

As a little being, even before your conscious thought and language skills developed, you had experiences that left you feeling separated from the essential qualities that your soul loved—that it was in tune with. This pain was too much to bear, so the ego structure began to form, taking on the role of protecting you from the severity of this early loss.

We remember that the ego attempts to mimic our true nature, though it can never be successful in doing so. Thus, the Type Five personality structure has tried to recreate the experience of clarity and deep understanding. Indeed, at the level of Essence, this is true. But the personality distorts what *clarity and deep understanding* actually means, and holds onto it as a sacred cow or an unquestioned requirement. As the ego grows stronger, it demands that the mind make sense of the world by tackling, analyzing, memorizing, and storing information. It's also natural to disappear from situations that could take you away from the safety of your mind, which now has a quality of grasping. Both energies—over-analyzing and disappearing from active engagement—however, when overused, pull you away from your true nature.

Your body is the source of intelligence which, in turn, gives you a sense of being grounded and having substance. But with so much energy swirling around the mind, it's easy to lose contact with your body. You also lose contact with your heart, which is the source of your genuine tenderness.

Here is the great loss—the pain—for Type Five: When you lose contact with the source of your true knowing, you have a sense of being dumped off into a big, unknowable world. There are no recognizable signposts to find your place, and it feels as if the world will overwhelm you. Terror looms large with this experience of being lost in the dark chaos of life.

The Inner Logic and the
Triangle of Identity for Type Five

Type Five's CORE BELIEF

We see that a core belief is set into place, providing an unconscious filter that accepts only information that supports the ego's belief. This filter, unfortunately, misses and dismisses data that would otherwise provide alternate perspectives. This belief acts as a core operating principle that shapes a person's relationship to life.

Each core belief is false but feels real until we can compassionately bring it into the light of awareness. It's particularly important to approach this with great kindness and truthfulness.

For the person dominant in the Five structure, the core belief is that there's no place for you in an unwelcoming, strange world, and that you are on your own. You cannot rely on anyone else to explain what's going on; your experience has been that any understanding you receive will have to come through you. You feel an intense fear because everything around you feels so chaotic.

How might this show up in your life? Here are some examples of what you might hear yourself think, say, or do/not do:

- I've got to work out these solutions on my own. No one else is going to be able to figure it out.
- I wish people didn't expect so much from me. Why's it so important to share my feelings or have meetings where people talk about such unimportant issues? These conversations feel so foreign to me. Maybe I really am an alien.
- Interacting with people is scary. I don't know how to connect with them. I don't mind watching them from afar, but I'd rather be left alone.
- I'm terrified that I won't be able to figure out how to do this. Just give me more time to work it out.

This core belief leads us to the **Triangle of Identity**, *which provides a shorthand illustration of how you "do" life.* I invite you to try on the following description to see how it fits with your experience.

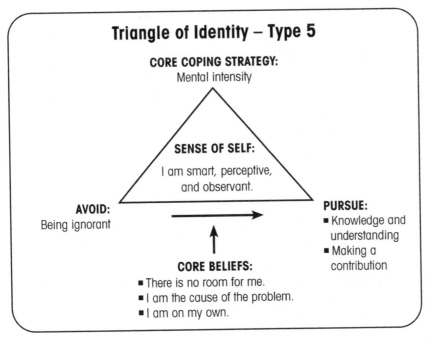

Figure 8-1: The Triangle of Identity for Type Five

This is how a person with the Type Five personality structure might recognize this inner logic that is illustrated by the Triangle of Identity:

*I **pursue** knowing more and being more knowledgeable in certain topics than anyone else. I'm drawn to studying and understanding rarefied topics which escape the attention of most people. Seeking knowledge of the many details and intricacies of a topic is a way to feel masterful and competent. This knowledge becomes my contribution to others.*

*I **avoid** experiences where I don't understand what's going on and feel ignorant. Why would I participate in activities or interactions that make no sense to me? They will only deplete my energy and leave me feeling small and shaky.*

*I **cope** by going into my head to learn, to analyze, to understand, and to recite. I handle interactions by telling others what I know about a topic. I minimize my emotional needs, and I don't ask others for anything, because they may want something back from me. I don't feel that I can give much energy to others, because I would become depleted. I cope by putting all of my attention on my thinking.*

As an extension of my coping, I can see that my life is or has been organized around figuring things out, and analyzing and becoming engrossed in ideas. If I can be an expert at understanding how specific things work, then life will feel manageable. I don't want to put my ideas into action until I'm sure of the outcome, so I often don't get around to implementation. If only I can keep a distance from those human activities that make no sense to me, and if I can keep filling myself up with knowledge, then I'll feel safe, at least for the moment.

*All of this leads me to see myself as a smart, perceptive, observant person. This self-definition—this **sense of self**—ends up imposing limits. It keeps me from recognizing and appreciating the fuller range of my human experience.*

An Awakened Capacity of Type Five: Unattachment

Being in real contact with your grounded body and sweet heart quiets the mental activity and allows you to begin trusting that what you need to know or understand will be available when it's needed. *There's great freedom in releasing your attachment to having all this knowledge* stored away. You are more able to live as a participant in the world, rather than simply an observer.

It's when you have forgotten and lost contact with this innate capacity that you start holding onto your inner resources and not sharing yourself with others.

Keeping an emotional distance and relying on your mental expertise reinforces your feeling of being all alone in the world. You forget that there's more to you than your head, and that developing a deep connection to your body is the first key to unlocking the door to a freer life.

The Type Five Iceberg Model reiterates some of this material in a visual format.

The model starts with some of the expansive qualities that are innate gifts of individuals dominant in this type. These qualities are naturally and increasingly experienced as we recognize and gradually release our attachment to our more limited definition of self. It also increases our understanding of the observable expressions found above the waterline in Type Five individuals, and fills out more of what goes on below the waterline, i.e., those inner dynamics that shape and motivate the behaviors that occur when the personality has its grip on us. (Refer to chapter 5 for more discussion on the Iceberg Model.)

Decoding the Personality Structure of Type Five

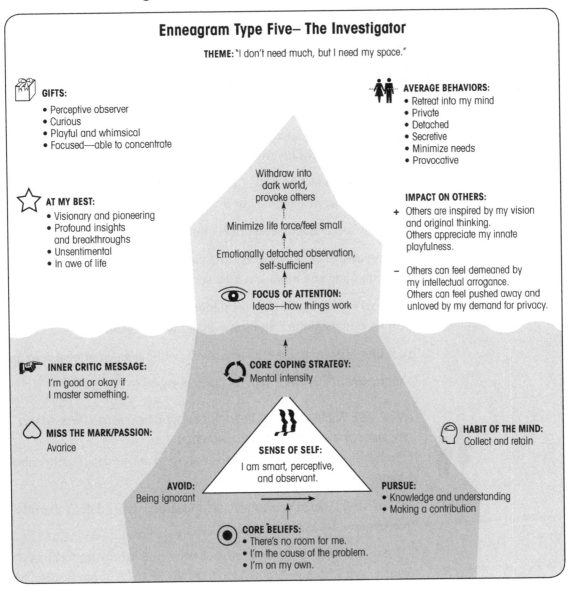

Figure 8-2: The Iceberg Model for Type Five

Type Five's THEME
"I don't need much, but I need my space" is the theme of this personality structure.

Above the Waterline

The Gifts, Daily Habits, and Challenges of Type Five

GIFTS and AT MY BEST
(When I'm expansive and at my healthiest)

I am perceptive. I observe with a clear, objective mind.

I am curious about many things. Learning new information and understanding how life works are fascinating to me.

I am playful and whimsical. I can be slightly mischievous and bring humor to otherwise difficult or threatening ideas.

I can stay focused and see a project through to the end.

I am capable of being visionary and pioneering. New ways of understanding and new ideas arise spontaneously.

My observations can lead to revolutionary breakthroughs, changes in people's understanding, and solving practical problems.

I am unsentimental. I see life objectively, without an emotional reaction.

I am in awe of life—its mysteries, its majesty, its workings.

AVERAGE BEHAVIORS *(Distinguishing characteristics when my personality has its grip on me)*

I am heady. I live in my mind and analyze whatever data I gather about a topic.

I am private. I like to work alone, behind closed doors. I don't like others to bother me.

I distance myself from external activities and from my feelings. I'm preoccupied with my ideas and am mentally intense. I become detached.

I keep my physical and emotional needs to a minimum. For example, I may not spend time on my appearance or physical care. To keep the demands on my physical or emotional energy to a minimum, I ask for little from others.

I am secretive, and I keep my thoughts and ideas to myself.

I can be provocative, especially when I am seeing the dark side of life and pushing other people to face it as well. I don't mind making others feel uncomfortable.

FOCUS OF ATTENTION, or FOA *(Where I put my attention when I'm attached to my personality)*

NOTE: This is a brief description of what happens as the FOA becomes narrower and narrower. It's important to note that the degree to which our FOA is activated is shaped by our degree of presence. With more presence, what we pay attention to expands, rather than narrows.

When I'm in the grip of the personality, I put my attention on the inner world of ideas and figuring out how things work. I want to know as much as possible about a particular subject matter so I can master it. Really, I feel safest when I know more than others about a topic.

As my mental intensity increases, I have less energy for engaging in life. I pay less attention to matters of the body and heart. I stand apart from others, preferring to observe rather than engage.

Because people's emotions, life situations, and needs can easily overwhelm me, I become more detached and self-sufficient. *When I pay little attention to the rest of me, my world can feel small. I can feel small in relationship to the world.*

My world can become dark, and I begin to see things that others don't have the competence to recognize. With a demeaning attitude, I prod and provoke others, and now I'm even more alone.

My IMPACT ON OTHERS

+ *Positive:*

- Others are inspired by my vision and ability to think originally, which creates new possibilities.
- Others appreciate my innate playfulness and my wonderment about life.

- *Negative:*

- Others can feel demeaned—and even as if I find them contemptible—by my intellectual arrogance.
- Others can feel pushed away and unloved by my demand for privacy.

Below the Waterline

To understand the inner dynamics for Type Five, we turn our attention to what lies under the surface of the water, starting at the bottom and working up.

Type Five's CORE BELIEFS

These core operating principles filter through many layers of life, in both seen and unseen ways.

I believe that there's no place for me in the external world. It seems to me that *all the seats are taken at the table.* I also believe that there's no support available to me, and that I'm on my own. My life is based on scarcity of resources. I believe that I cause problems, so others are therefore better off without my engagement.

The TRIANGLE OF IDENTITY

What I PURSUE

I *pursue* knowing more and being more knowledgeable in certain topics than anyone else. I do whatever it takes to compile as much information as needed to be smart. Sharing my knowledge is a way that I can create a place for myself in the world and make a contribution.

What I AVOID

I *avoid* experiences where I don't understand what's going on and where I feel ignorant. In those situations, the chaos of life would consume me. Having no knowledge to offer creates terror. Being actively involved with others when I don't feel prepared is definitely one of the hardest things in life to do.

My CORE COPING STRATEGY

I *cope* by being in my head so that I can figure things out and understand what's going on. Analyzing things helps me cope. I handle interactions by telling others what I know about things I studied. Those topics may seem idiosyncratic or rarefied to others. I'm self-sufficient, minimizing my emotional needs and not asking others for anything, because they may want something back from me. I don't feel that I can give much energy to others, because my own energy would be depleted.

SENSE OF SELF *("I am...")*

I see myself as smart, perceptive, and observant. I think of myself as having something unique and insightful to offer, and I rely on my head to get the insight or to prepare for as long as I think I need. I need to be mentally well-prepared before moving into action, so I don't like to be rushed into what I consider premature activity.

WHERE I MISS THE MARK
(The energetic drive of the passion)

I need to hold on to the few resources that I have, including my energy, since that seems limited. I don't know if I have enough energy to get through the demands of the day, so I need to keep from emptying myself by giving too much emotionally to others. Since I rely on my mind for creating a safe structure for me, I hang onto my own analysis and anticipated outcomes that result from my understanding. I guard against letting others know what my feelings are; I'm not even sure myself. Thus, I withhold myself emotionally and energetically from others. This passion is called *avarice*.

REMINDER: No matter what type you are dominant in, the passion is a part of the personality and is a motivator that drives your emotional life. The passion covers up a wound in your heart[1] and creates an emotional reaction to how you relate to life, which takes you away from what your soul loves. This is true for all personality types.

HABIT OF THE MIND *(Fixation of the personality)*

I live in my mind, and *retain* its activity.[2]

I observe rather than participate in life. In my mind, *thinking about* what's going on in the world *is the same as participating in* the world and in my life. I catalogue my knowledge so that I can mentally pull out whatever information I think I need. I can recite it with authority while the listeners fade into the background of my awareness.

REMINDER: No matter what type you are dominant in, the fixation is a part of the personality. It's a motivator in your fixed behaviors and thoughts about yourself and the world. It bolsters a false sense of reality, and as the ego's automatic, unquestioned way of solving problems with life, it takes you away from your true self. This is true for all personality types.

INNER CRITIC MESSAGE
(What my Inner Critic insists upon)

My inner critic insists that I must master knowledge—ideas, information, understanding a particular subject matter—in order for me to be *okay*.[3] It insists that my mastery is based upon my mind, and that I must know more than others about any given topic. As long as I'm caught in the web of my inner critic, I will continue substituting what's in my head for real life. Real life is grounded in the body, opens the heart, is curious, and includes engagement with others.

Each of the elements described above contributes to the whole experience of what we have come to think of as ourselves. The core belief, the emotional force of the passion, the mental habit (fixation), and the inner critic all unconsciously conspire to reinforce the Triangle of Identity.

Additional Information on Enneagram Type Five

What causes me *stress*

My stress is greatly increased when others make emotional demands on me or want more of my time and energy. I believe that I only have so much energy available, and if I give too much to others, I will be depleted.

When I'm most *constricted and inflexible*

Everything is meaningless to me.

I cut myself off from all.

I focus on the dark side of life and provoke others to do the same.

Other Personality Types Related to Type Five

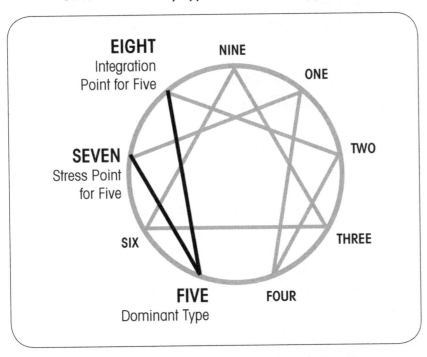

Figure 8-3: The Stress and Integration Points for Type Five

People dominant in Type Five experience characteristics of Type Seven under stress. Type Seven is the *Stress Point* for Type Five. For more information on this, see chapter 10. Pay particular attention to the sections on average-level behaviors and to the "Notice and Observe Patterns" section of that chapter.

Type Five's *Integration Point*, including the *Hidden Dimension of Self*, is found in Type Eight. See chapter 11 for more information on Type Eight. For Type Five's Integration Point, pay particular attention to the "Gifts" and "At My Best" sections in chapter 11. For Type Five's Hidden Dimension of Self, review the sections on average levels of behavior in that same chapter.

The Enneagram also works in reverse, which yields helpful information to everyone discovering their dominant type: Type Five is the Stress Point for Type Eight, and it's the Integration Point for Type Seven.

Recognizing Patterns That Pull You Off-Course

Notice and Observe Patterns

In this section you'll find some of the patterns that are associated with the Type Five personality structure. These patterns provide useful information. Rather than making you bad or wrong in some way, these patterns can be used as signposts on your path of awakening. They help you notice and get to the heart of your experience in a tangible, direct way. Eventually, you can relax the particular, habitual—and often troublesome—strategies, which will allow you to be more present, open, and free.

The pattern of focusing on your inner world of ideas
Notice the tendency to withdraw into your mind.

People dominant in Type Five can be tempted to disengage from having a direct experience of external situations or of themselves. They substitute analysis, comparison and evaluation, model-making, and mental commentary for participation and engagement in life. It's easy for them to mistake the model of a world that they've constructed inside their mind for the real, living one outside of their mind.

Notice if the inner world of ideas is taking more time and energy than you're giving to engaging with the external world and living your life.

The pattern of getting ready to be ready

You may notice that you have difficulty coming to the end of a project or task, as you're not sure that you've covered all of your bases. You may find yourself wanting to do more research or reading, even when others are asking (which may feel like *pressuring* to you) for a finished project.

You may find yourself wanting to practice, practice, practice, while being reluctant to give the final performance. Perhaps you find yourself continuing to touch up a painting or reworking an article that you've written. People dominant in Enneagram Five often find it hard to feel that they have prepared enough. If you're dominant in this type, a good question to ask yourself is, "When is enough, enough?"

The pattern of believing *minimal* is the best

Notice your tendency to minimize your needs.

Do you almost forget to eat? To sleep? To go to the bathroom? To take care of daily living activities? Notice when you get so engrossed in creating mental explanations for the workings of a particular topic that the external world is nearly forgotten. It's as if the body doesn't exist, or you see it as a burden.

You may notice that the more energy you expend by focusing on your mind, the more intense and anxious you feel.

If this is a prominent pattern for you, you may also find yourself:

- becoming more agitated with others, and/or attempting to provoke them
- being stingy with your time and energy; being unwilling to share them with others

The pattern of needing to be in the role of *expert*

Being the *expert* on any given topic is one of the ways that Fives compensate for their feeling of awkwardness in social situations. The *expert* becomes a social identity, and it's the basis for interaction.

Of course, people dominant in other Enneagram types can be experts as well. For a Five, however, it's valuable to notice when you feel *compelled* to know more than anyone else, and to let them know what you know. Showing your mastery of a topic may serve as a mask that protects your feeling of vulnerability.

In a meeting or social encounter, you might notice that you do most of the talking and explaining, and you pay little attention to the perspectives of others. You might argue with, dismiss, or denigrate what others have to say about the topic of your expertise.

> **NOTE:** *Type Fives, especially, need to be reminded that noticing is not a mental exercise. It's an embodied practice in increasing awareness: awareness of one's physicality, awareness of one's emotional experiences, awareness of one's patterns that are related to the use of the mind. A caution to you is to not think about observing, but to give yourself a little distance from your mental processes so that you might observe them with a new dimension of objectivity that includes compassion.*

Surprising and Effective Practices for Building Your Capacity

The following capacity-building practices will help you turn toward your true nature.

1. Use breathwork/meditation/mindfulness to quiet the mind.

Just notice the inner mental activity when it arises. When you notice this insistent and determined mental noise, return to your breath and experience the sensations created in your body by the movement of breath. Although this will initially feel foreign and perhaps even a little unnerving, returning time and time again to the direct sensations in your body provides a counterbalance to mental activity.

2. Find your body! Awaken it with movement.

Yoga, aikido, chi gung, and other forms of conscious movement will help you focus on the inherent connection between mind and body. It may feel awkward and even scary to come into contact with your body, as this will be new territory for you.

This is one of the most profound practices you can adopt. Developing a strong relationship to your body and being aware of your own physicality are keystones to your liberation.

Your body is a source of vast intelligence. As you learn to experience the language of the body via sensations, you add a brilliant dimension of intelligence to your repertoire.

3. Allow your "fair witness" to observe (nonjudgmentally, of course) the tendency to buy into the belief that you are separate from the rest of the world.

Allow your natural curiosity to question your beliefs.

Be willing to stay with the fair witness—the neutral observer—during the process of exploring your beliefs. Pay attention to the sensations that arise in your body and to the feelings that arise from your heart.

Your curiosity is an amazing gift on your journey of self-understanding.

Can you be willing to not know the answers to your self-inquiry and still be okay?

4. Notice what you ignore in life.

What areas of your life have you cut yourself off from? Friendships? Finances? Self-care? Taking care of your home environment?

Identify one area at a time, and focus your energy on taking small steps to develop that aspect of yourself.

Some of these areas may feel quite foreign to you. So consider taking another risk by researching what other sources of support are available. There are most likely professional resources available, but another big step would be asking a trusted person for some help.

You may discover that there's more support available for you than you ever thought possible.

5. Begin to enjoy the experience of *inner knowing* in contrast to having *mental knowledge.*

As you become more grounded and centered in your body, you will have increased access to different forms of knowing that transcend mental constructs. You will strengthen your trust that you are part of the larger human community, and you will increase your deep wisdom that comes from intuitive knowing.

Forging Your Healing and Evolutionary Path

A major theme of this book is that the primary reason for working with the Enneagram is to help us awaken to our true nature. It puts us on a path of healing and real transformation that, for most of us, takes place over time—with patience, trust, faith in our awakening journey—and by being as present as possible. Section III takes us into processes that support and are beneficial for everyone, regardless of type.

Not surprisingly, there are specific processes that are vital for individuals dominant in each type.

If you are dominant in Type Five, your healing and evolutionary path includes the following:

Having direct experiences of life and not just observing it. Begin making real contact with your body. Allow that intelligence to expand and inform you. Rather than diminishing your sense of knowing, you will begin to access more sources of intelligence.

Notice that you can become very demanding and rather pompous as the Type Eight personality has you in its grip. That's right. While you might see yourself as not taking up much space, you do have times when you intrude your will on others. It's hard to embrace this revelation—this discovery of the *Hidden Dimension of Self*—but as you do, it will help you recognize your inner strength. From this source of strength, you can be here in the world with more substance and authority.

REMINDER: The Hidden Dimension of Self is found at the average and lower levels of health in the Integration Point.

As you come into deeper contact with your body, you can begin to **trust the tenderness of your heart.** Your capacity for making true heart connections with others will sweeten your life and your relationships. As an unquestionable member of the human community, you will find others who honor and appreciate your heartful contributions.

Become more present to the moment and **realize that you don't have to figure things out.** As you connect with your intuitive knowing, you will discover that you have access to the knowledge you need, and when it's needed. Your trust in your intuitive nature and in your ability to connect to divine knowing will increase and support you.

Become more aware of the majesty and wonder of what's here and surrounding you.

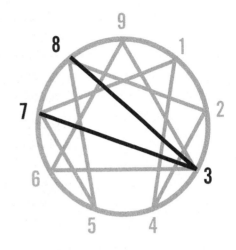

Social Style Cluster Two

The Assured, Confident Group—
Types Three, Seven, and Eight

Shared Themes

Asserting and inserting one's power and influence into a relationship, conversation, conflict or decision-making situation is one strategy that can be used to cope with stress that accompanies interpersonal relationships.

When in the grip of the personality, people dominant in these three Enneagram types share the common personality structure of being externally oriented and having expansive energies. People dominant in Types Three, Seven, and Eight typically communicate directly, and sometimes powerfully. They go after what they want, insistent that their wants get met. Other people typically recognize that an assured-type person is in the room: their voice and laughter is apt to be louder; they tend to move with confidence and decisiveness; and they exude an air of personal power.

NOTE: *In colloquial language, this sense of confidence is sometimes referred to as presence, but this is not what we mean by the word presence when we refer to being unattached to one's habitual patterns. Presenting oneself as assured and assertive can be an automatic pattern.*

If your dominant type is in this cluster, you appear to be comfortable being at the center of attention and yet keeping other people at an emotional distance. It is difficult to keep your heart open, as emotions seem far too messy and uncontrollable, and lead to a unwelcome sense of vulnerability. Assured types often secretly feel that important things happen when they are in the room, so you may feel responsible for *making things happen*.

Having the capacity to be direct, assertive, and communicate clearly are healthy attributes. However, when an *assertive strategy* is an automatic and habitual pattern, you may get what you want, but it comes at a high emotional cost. Not only does this strategy tend to distance people, but it distances you from yourself. The externally oriented focus leaves little room for recognizing one's inner life.

Energetically, people who are dominant in these type structures often are experienced by others as having *big* energy, being driven, and even pushy. Horney called this strategy *pushing against others*. The intensity of this energy is used to protect against hurt and to free a person to do what they want in the world.

If you are dominant in one of these types, you face a double-edged dilemma. In many cultures, this energy is rewarded with prestige, status, and financial gains. Thus, the assertive energy is both reinforced by the personality and by some cultures, making it seem counterintuitive to even question it.

An important part of the inner journey for people dominant in these three structures is moving *from* "going forward and going for it" *to* "opening their precious hearts."

The Human Condition and Consciousness of Type Three: The Achiever

A strong believer in personal development and continual learning, DeeAnn came to coaching to better understand how she could use the Enneagram in her own growth and apply it in her international consulting business. Her ceaseless work and high standards were rewarded with satisfied repeat clients and a high income that afforded her family a very comfortable lifestyle. At this point in her life, she was also starting to recognize the impact of her hard-pushing style, and that her children needed more attention than she could give them with her frequent travel.

During the course of the coaching relationship, DeeAnn saw the following:

- *how she competed in everything. She couldn't remember a time in her life when it felt okay to just be average at anything.*
- *how important it was to have others acknowledge her successes. She discovered that even when an achievement was celebrated and rewarded, the satisfaction quickly evaporated, and she soon needed another "hit" of recognition.*
- *her ability to adapt quickly into being whatever she thought others expected her to be—the best mom, the best consultant, the best client, the best yoga student.*
- *how hard she was on herself. She never gave herself a break.*

As she developed self-observational skills, she began to see how hard she'd worked to receive recognition for being at the top of her game. This is how she'd organized her whole life. Recognizing how this formerly unconscious need led to pushing herself so hard brought up a great deal of sadness.

One major theme of coaching focused on developing a new relationship with her heart. She was so accustomed to setting and reaching external goals, that, initially, she felt estranged from what would bring her joy and pleasure. Her first steps included slowing her pace of life to have more room for spontaneous and fun experiences with her children. Remembering how much she'd loved playing music as a child, she signed up for flute lessons to revive a long-lost pleasure. The caveat was that she not perform for anyone, and practice playing for her own enjoyment.

The Internal Coherence of the Type Three Experience

Your True Nature

If this is your dominant Enneagram point, your soul is naturally drawn to the preciousness of life—your life, and the life of everyone and everything else. You recognize the sparkling radiance that is inherent in the nature of everything, and you take joy in the radiance and glory of your true nature. Your heart resonates with sweetness, and you realize that your value is inherent in just being.

When not in touch with your true nature, what you might not recognize *yet* is that you don't have to do anything in order to experience the value and preciousness of your life. Your heart is magnificent, and it will guide you to your authentic self. You don't have to perform for others to receive their admiration and approval to be in touch with the delicious being that you are.

The Story of Your Life:
Relating to Your Inner and Outer World

Your inner sense of self and your place in the world were set in place early in life. How you internalized your experiences contributed to the characteristic way you relate to yourself and others, and to your very way of being. If this is your dominant type, the following brief story of your childhood inner experience will likely sound very familiar.

As a tiny child, you were tuned in to the feelings of others. Through your intuitive nature, you experienced the disappointment that came from the unfulfilled desires of parents, and especially those of the person who most nurtured you—your mother figure. You had a deep bond with that person and did whatever you could to adapt yourself so that you would please and stay connected to her.

Your parents convinced you that there wasn't anything you couldn't do. You often heard, "We're totally behind you. You'll do great," or "You're our star." You soon came to believe that anything you attempted, you had to succeed and achieve at a high level. In fact, you felt that you had to be the best. Perhaps you remember staying home from school or another public activity if you felt that you couldn't succeed or come out on top at a specific event.

Being loved felt like it was dependent upon fulfilling these expectations. You experienced that you were valued for being and doing things extremely well. However, something was missing. It was natural to believe that you were only valued for your successes, not for who you were.

You were the hero of the family and internalized the message that it was "not okay to not be okay." You would do whatever it took to look like you "had it all together" so that you wouldn't disappoint your family.

You haven't always been sure why you decided on a particular course of action. It was hard to know what you really wanted for yourself. In fact, that may still be a really hard question to ask.

You came to organize your life around the idea that you needed to adapt yourself to what you thought other people wanted you to do or be. It never felt okay to have deep feelings or follow the inklings of your heart. The pain behind this is that you never felt loved just for yourself.

What you didn't see is that your own heart yearns to know itself. What you couldn't see is that you have worth and value in just being, and that being the best isn't a criterion for being loved and valued. You have a sweet, tender, loving heart that longs for you.

Your Great Loss

As a little being, even before your conscious thought and language skills developed, you had experiences that left you feeling separated from these essential qualities that your soul loved—that it was in tune with. This pain was too much to bear, so the ego structure began to form, taking on the role of protecting you from the severity of this early loss.

We remember that the ego attempts to mimic our true nature, though it can never be successful in doing so. So, the Type Three personality structure has tried to recreate this capacity for brilliance and for creating value. The ego thinks that *it* is what's brilliant, and it takes on the job of trying to make your value increase through driving you to be constantly working to reach the top of whatever role or function you have in life. The ego's value is, of course, reinforced in many cultures, companies, and environments, magnifying the feeling that the ego is doing exactly the right thing. When the ego takes on this grand sense of importance, you lose contact with your authenticity, which emanates from your heart.

Here is the great loss—the pain—for Type Three: Lacking a sense of your own inherent worth and value. The resulting disconnect from your beautiful heart leads to feeling that there's nothing in your heart—that there's only emptiness there. You can easily feel like a fraud.

The Inner Logic and the Triangle of Identity for Type Three

Type Three's CORE BELIEF

We see that a core belief is set into place, providing an unconscious filter that accepts only information that supports the ego's belief. This filter, unfortunately, misses and dismisses data that would otherwise provide alternate perspectives. This belief acts as a core operating principle that shapes a person's relationship to life.

Each core belief is false but feels real until we can compassionately bring it into the light of awareness. It's particularly important to approach this with great kindness and truthfulness.

For the person dominant in the Type Three structure, there's a core belief that your worth and value come from achievements. You must be outstanding—not just in a few things, but in everything you do that is publically witnessed.

You believe that you are loved for your performance. Not thinking that you'll find satisfaction for just being yourself, you continue to drive toward achieving one goal after another.

Life feels like it is a contest, and the person with the most rewards and awards wins. You strive to come out on top.

How might this show up in your life? Here are some examples of what you might hear yourself think, say, or do/not do:

- What's my next goal? Without a goal, I'm a loser, lacking any real value.
- Okay, now just get it together. I can't let them see me sweat or not have it all together.
- I'll do what it takes to be named the captain of the team or be recognized as the best of my class (as a piano student, a swimmer, a salesperson, a vice-president). Whatever my role, there's just no excuse for not being the best.
- I'll collapse tonight, but tomorrow, I push on.

This core belief leads us to the **Triangle of Identity**, *which provides a shorthand illustration of how you "do" life.* I invite you to try on the following description to see how it fits with your experience.

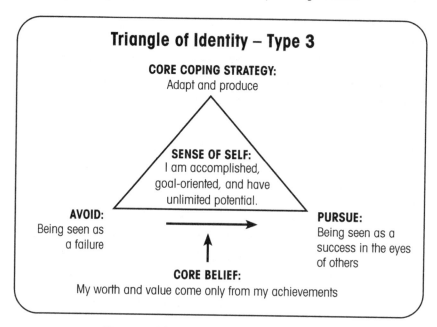

Triangle of Identity – Type 3

CORE COPING STRATEGY:
Adapt and produce

SENSE OF SELF:
I am accomplished,
goal-oriented, and have
unlimited potential.

AVOID:
Being seen as
a failure

PURSUE:
Being seen as a
success in the eyes
of others

CORE BELIEF:
My worth and value come only from my achievements

Figure 9-1: The Triangle of Identity for Type Three

Here is how a person with the Type Three personality structure might recognize this inner logic that is illustrated by the Triangle of Identity:

I pursue being successful in the eyes of others. I take on goals that I perceive as having a high value in the eyes of those whom I value. It seems that there's never an end to how many goals I need to successfully complete. No matter how many I achieve, there'll always be more goals to pursue. And even when I receive recognition, the impact is not felt long enough, and soon, I need more recognition to reinforce my sense of having worth.

I avoid what I perceive as failure: not reaching goals that are valued by others. To fail would be to experience and reinforce a deep belief that I don't have real value for who I am. I avoid putting myself in situations where there's a good chance that I won't succeed, whether that be participating in auditions for a school performance, engaging in an athletic competition, or applying for a job position that I would enjoy. Dealing with failure is the hardest thing in life for me.

I cope by adapting and producing results in whatever environment I'm in. I easily reinvent myself and can change quickly from being a high-producing member of my team to being the most flexible and accomplished yoga student to being a gracious and inspiring hostess.

As an extension of my coping, I can see that my life is or has been organized around creating conditions that would lead to recognition for my successes and avoiding circumstances where I could feel vulnerable. It seems that being recognized should make me happy, but it never lasts. I'm so used to setting goals for myself and doing whatever I can to reach those goals in a superior way, that, once reached, I create another goal. To get the right people to see me in a good light, I can stretch the truth.

If I can only be seen as competent and successful, then I'll feel valued, at least for the moment.

All of this leads me to see myself as accomplished and goal-oriented, with unlimited potential. This self-definition—this sense of self—ends up imposing limits. It keeps me from recognizing and appreciating the fuller range of my human experience.

While setting and accomplishing goals are positive qualities, when overused, they limit my ability to recognize the deeper desires of my heart and to feel part of a larger web of life. When my life energy is consistently focused on accomplishments, I miss out on having an authentically fulfilling life.

An Awakened Capacity of Type Three: The Authentic and Truthful Heart

Being in real contact with your heart allows you to experience tenderness, the sweetness of yourself and others, and your innate preciousness. Your direct experience of your own truth and authenticity comes when you slow your pace, allow your inner feelings to come to the surface, and tune into your heart's desires. Ongoing contact with your heart's energy will eventually lead you to recognize your inherent value. This discovery parallels another: having authentic contact with your heart doesn't diminish your capacity for being excellent in what you do. What's missing is the compulsion of constantly pushing yourself.

It's when you have forgotten and lost contact with this innate capacity that you get on the treadmill that drives you. You begin to claim credit for what's not yours to take credit for. You think your success is due to your ability to produce, ignoring the many other contributing factors. This external focus leads you to forget what your heart wants.

Be careful not to make this contact with your heart into another goal. Paradoxically, developing a deep and abiding connection to your heart is the first key to unlocking the door to a freer life.

The Iceberg Model for Type Three reiterates some of this material in a visual format.

The model starts with some of the expansive qualities that are innate gifts of individuals dominant in this type. These qualities are naturally and increasingly experienced as we recognize and gradually release our attachment to our more limited definition of self. The Iceberg Model also increases our understanding of the observable expressions found at the average level of behavior of Type Three individuals, and it fills out more of what goes on below the waterline, i.e., those inner dynamics that shape and motivate the behaviors that occur when the personality has its grip on us. (Refer to chapter 5 for more discussion on the Iceberg Model.)

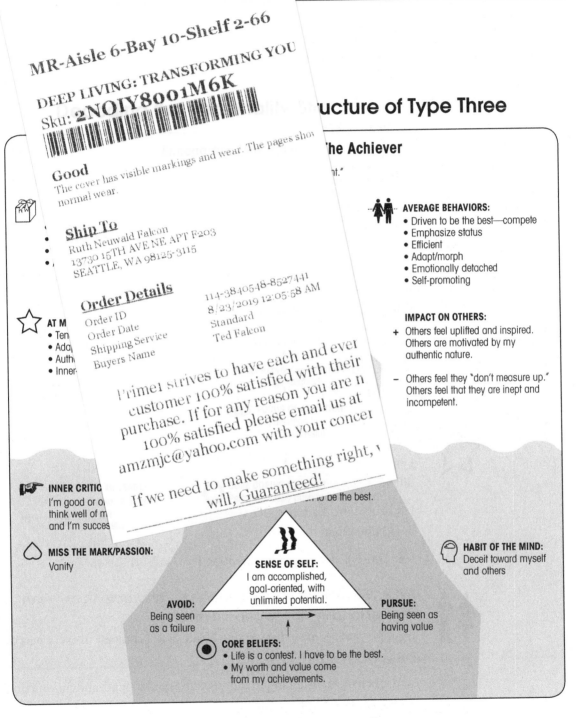

...ucture of Type Three

...he Achiever

..."..."

AVERAGE BEHAVIORS:
- Driven to be the best—compete
- Emphasize status
- Efficient
- Adapt/morph
- Emotionally detached
- Self-promoting

IMPACT ON OTHERS:

+ Others feel uplifted and inspired. Others are motivated by my authentic nature.

– Others feel they "don't measure up." Others feel that they are inept and incompetent.

AT M...
- Ten...
- Ada...
- Auth...
- Inner...

INNER CRITIC...
I'm good or o... think well of m... and I'm succes...

MISS THE MARK/PASSION:
Vanity

SENSE OF SELF:
I am accomplished, goal-oriented, with unlimited potential.

AVOID:
Being seen as a failure

PURSUE:
Being seen as having value

HABIT OF THE MIND:
Deceit toward myself and others

...to be the best.

CORE BELIEFS:
- Life is a contest. I have to be the best.
- My worth and value come from my achievements.

Figure 9-2: The Iceberg Model for Type Three

Type Three's THEMES

*"I can be anything I want" and/or "The little engine that could"[1]
are the themes of this personality structure.*

Above the Waterline

The Gifts, Daily Habits, and Challenges of Type Three

GIFTS and AT MY BEST
(When I'm expansive and at my healthiest)
I focus on developing myself and contributing my achievements to help the world.

I excel at motivating and inspiring others to do their best. I'm a good role model.

I believe in myself and in my abilities. I use this natural confidence to support my success.

I have the capacity to be my best without causing damage to myself or others.

I am tender toward myself and others.

I am adaptable and can easily adjust to changing situations or to different environments, while still remembering who I am.

I am authentic. I am in touch with my inner truth and make decisions based upon that.

I am inner-directed, paying attention to what has heart for me.

AVERAGE BEHAVIORS *(Distinguishing characteristics when my personality has its grip on me)*
It's important for me to look and to be the best. I compete in every part of my life to come out on top.

I am efficient, focusing my attention on the goal at hand, and minimizing my energy toward non-priorities.

Appearances matter. I am aware of the status of what I achieve, what I do, and what I own.

I cover up any sense of vulnerability and do what's needed to come across as having it all together.

I constantly adapt myself to meet what I perceive to be the expectations of others. I can be chameleon-like and project a particular image of myself to others.

I am emotionally detached. Feelings are too messy, and I'd rather emphasize getting ahead in life.

I overpromote myself to make myself look even better in the eyes of others and especially to those who have prestige and high status.

FOCUS OF ATTENTION, or FOA *(Where I put my attention when I'm attached to my personality)*

NOTE: *This is a brief description of what happens as the FOA becomes narrower and narrower. It's important to note that the degree to which the FOA is activated is shaped by our degree of presence. With more presence, what we pay attention to expands, rather than narrows.*

When my personality has its grip on me, I put my attention toward being at the top of my game and being seen as successful. This is what gives me a sense of having value and worth, and I have a lot of energy to put into this quest. I produce at the highest levels to gain recognition.

The more important to me the feedback from others becomes, the more I gauge their responses and adapt to fit the specific situation.

This keeps me turned away from myself. I lose my connection to my tender and sweet nature and become more superficial and self-promoting.

My IMPACT ON OTHERS

+ Positive:
- Others feel that they're uplifted and inspired to reach their higher potential.
- Others are deeply touched by my authentic nature.

– Negative:
- Others feel that they don't or can't measure up to the status I project or to my expectations.
- Others feel undervalued and unimportant.

Below the Waterline

To understand the inner dynamics for Type Three, we turn our attention to what lies under the surface of the water, starting at the bottom and working up.

Type Three's CORE BELIEFS

These core operating principles filter through many layers of life, in both seen and unseen ways.

I believe that my basic worth comes as a result of what I produce and achieve. I must be at the top—not just in a few things, but in everything I do.

I believe that I'm loved for my performance. I don't think I'll find worth from just being myself, so I drive myself by being focused on external goals to achieve.

The TRIANGLE OF IDENTITY

What I PURSUE

I *pursue* success, as this is what gives me a sense of value. For me, success is defined by achieving goals that have high status in the eyes of those who I want to recognize and value me. Setting goals, taking action to reach those goals, and having others recognize my accomplishments provide an important structure for my life. This keeps me busy, and I can't imagine how to live life without functioning in this way. I notice that even when I receive recognition, its effect is short-lived. Soon, I need more recognition to reinforce my sense of having worth, and so I go into overdrive to push myself to the top.

What I AVOID

I *avoid* what I perceive as failure: not reaching goals that are valued by others. To fail would be to experience and reinforce a deep belief that I don't have real value for whom I am. I avoid putting myself in situations where there's a good chance that I won't succeed, whether that be competing for a higher-status client than I've had before, auditioning for the lead in a theater production, or entering a running marathon.

My CORE COPING STRATEGY

I *cope* by working hard, performing for others, or reinventing myself to be successful in whatever environment I'm in. I can change quickly from being a sought-after motivational speaker to the best-read member of my book club, from being a first-rate parent to the most productive fundraiser on a nonprofit board. I expect those who I have a close association with, such as family members or staff, to be on top of their game, as well. They're a reflection of my worth—their status or level of achievement reflects on me.

SENSE OF SELF *("I am...")*

I see myself as being accomplished, goal-oriented, and having unlimited potential. While these are positive qualities, they limit me when I don't allow myself to be vulnerable or even to be average in some things.

WHERE I MISS THE MARK
(*The energetic drive of the passion*)

I (my personality) desperately want to be seen as the source of my accomplishments, my success, and whatever material wealth I have. I want to be recognized and acknowledged for rising to the top. I don't want to really experience my feelings or give my spiritual nature much attention. This passion is called *vanity*.

REMINDER: No matter what type you are dominant in, the passion is a part of the personality and is a motivator that drives your emotional life. The passion covers up a wound in your heart[2] and creates an emotional reaction to how you relate to life, which takes you away from what your soul loves. This is true for all personality types.

HABIT OF THE MIND (*Fixation of the personality*)

If I'm honest with myself right now, I realize that I'm not honest either with myself or others about who I am. I put on the mask of a certain persona, creating an identity that matches what I think others expect from me. Eventually, I begin to believe this false mask and forget about my authentic self. I can make myself be whatever I think others need me to be in order to receive their attention and recognition. This is called *deceit*.

REMINDER: No matter what type you are dominant in, the fixation is a part of the personality. It's a motivator in your fixed behaviors and thoughts about yourself and the world. It bolsters a false sense of reality, and as the ego's automatic, unquestioned way of solving problems with life, it takes you away from your true self. This is true for all personality types.

INNER CRITIC MESSAGE
(*What my Inner Critic insists upon*)

My only value lies in being successful and accomplished.[3] The rules of my inner critic insist that I must get attention from others for my successes, otherwise, I'm a loser and have no inherent value in just *being*. For example, if I don't receive external recognition for a certain endeavor, then I feel devalued and have to work harder at gaining recognition. As long as I'm caught in the web of the inner critic, I'll sacrifice my own heart's desires to the achievement of outer goals, which ultimately leads to inner emptiness.

Each of the elements described above contributes to the whole experience of what we have come to think of as ourselves. The core belief, the emotional force of the passion, the mental habit (fixation), and the inner critic all unconsciously conspire to reinforce the Triangle of Identity.

Additional Information on the Enneagram Type Three

What causes me *stress*

I experience stress when others want me to be emotionally close and intimate, as it is difficult to show them my heart. I experience stress when I expect myself to be accomplished in everything I do, and when I feel compelled to have all the symbols of status and success. To avoid this stress, I keep my guard up most of the time so that others won't see that I am feeling insecure, vulnerable, or lacking confidence.

When I'm most *constricted and inflexible*

I do whatever it takes to look good. This means that I'll deceive others about my accomplishments.

I will take the most expedient route, despite its impact on others.

I will use and exploit others so I look successful.

I am totally out of touch with the desires of my heart.

Other Personality Types Related to Type Three

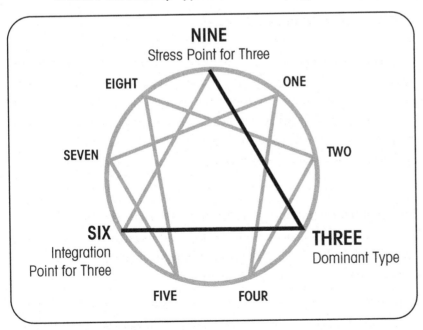

Figure 9-3: The Stress and Integration Points for Type Three

People dominant in Type Three experience characteristics of Type Nine under stress. Type Nine is the *Stress Point* for Type Three. For more information on this, see chapter 6. Pay particular attention to the sections on average-level behaviors and to the "Notice and Observe Patterns" section of that chapter.

Type Three's *Integration Point*, including the *Hidden Dimension of Self,* is found in Type Six. See chapter 14 for more information on Type Six. For Type Three's Integration Point, pay particular attention to the "Gifts" and "At My Best" sections in chapter 14. For Type Three's Hidden Dimension of Self, review the sections on average levels of behavior in that same chapter.

The Enneagram also works in reverse, which yields helpful information to everyone discovering their dominant type: Type Three is the Stress Point for Type Six, and it's the Integration Point for Type Nine.

Recognizing Patterns That Pull You Off-Course

Notice and Observe Patterns

In this section you'll find some of the patterns that are associated with the Type Three personality structure. These patterns provide useful information. Rather than making you bad or wrong in some way, these patterns can be used as signposts on your path of awakening. They help you notice and get to the heart of your experience in a tangible, direct way. Eventually, you can relax the particular, habitual—and often troublesome—strategies, which will allow you to be more present, open, and free.

The pattern of creating goals in every part of your life

Identify the consequences, both positive and negative, of living a goal-oriented life. What do you lose by continuously focusing your energy on creating goals and striving to achieve them?

Notice that it can be challenging to even imagine another way of living. A useful step at this point is being willing to recognize and discern the difference between the compulsive, have-to quality of being goal-driven, as opposed to keeping focused on what has heart and meaning for you.

Notice the tendency to feel that you need to be the best, and be outstanding. This can leave you experiencing the need to give yourself constant pep talks, affirmations, or talk yourself into taking on the next goal, much like the train engine that repeated, "I think I can, I think I can…"

You may notice that it feels like you're always metaphorically climbing a hill, or a even a mountain. You may find yourself pushing forward, always in motion. Giving yourself a break from your relentless inner drive can feel irrational and impossible. These experiences signal that it's time to change gears. Even gradually slowing the regular pace at which you walk can help you experience having a bit more internal space.

Remember that this goal orientation has helped protect you against feeling that early hurt from childhood.

The pattern of presenting a successful image is the source of great fatigue and stress

If this is a dominant pattern for you, you may notice:
- When you are successful, even extremely successful, you might occasionally feel sad, and a sense that something is still missing.
- Regardless of your level of success, you may feel restless or experience the need to push yourself even further, especially if someone else is being acknowledged. You might become aggressive and push the other person out of the picture.

The pattern of desiring to seek attention

The Type Three personality is the embodiment of the universal need for recognition and acknowledgement. People dominant in Three want others to "see me." When that focus takes most of your energy, however, you can lose your sense of self.

Taking this pattern to a deeper and more tender level, notice when the desire for attention is tied to your need to feel more valued and worthwhile. Being both honest and compassionate with yourself is necessary to support you in moving to an experience of greater self-awareness and liberation.

People with Type Three personalities tend to have a great capacity for adapting to different circumstances.

- This quality can be an enormous asset when it reflects one's ability to be flexible and responsive.
- It can be detrimental when one adapts in order to fit into an acceptable image. It takes enormous energy to reshape our image and identity into what we anticipate will help us look good to others.
- Notice your capacity for identifying your own values, needs, and feelings. What's important to you? Notice if taking steps to identify your own feelings leaves you feeling vulnerable, even slightly naked. This is likely to be a cue that your feelings need more attention.

The pattern of tending to stretch the truth:

Are there any places where you deceive others or where you deceive yourself? For example, perhaps you exaggerated your background to someone that you wanted to impress, such as a potential employer or a new dating partner, then found yourself telling more white lies in order to shore-up your initial story.

You might notice the tendency to tell little white lies when it's convenient or to create false stories that will shine the best light on you. Sometimes deceit shows itself by putting on a different persona for different people. The tendency towards *falseness* is one of the unconscious Type Three strategies that takes you away from your authentic self.

But even when you are both truthful and successful, you still might have an unfounded, but underlying, fear of being a fraud or being a disappointment to a person whom you respect. The resulting feeling of vulnerability is difficult to be with, so you find yourself trying harder to be what you think they want you to be.

Surprising and Effective Practices for Building Your Capacity

The following capacity-building practices will help you turn toward your true nature.

1. **Create time and space that is just for you—where you are not responding to any outside demands, and there's no need to perform.**

   This time and space is for exploring you. For example, you might want to begin with creating a collage that reflects what brings you joy. You may want to create an altar or sacred space that speaks to your deeper self. You may want to take a painting or writing class where the focus is on the process and on authentic expression, and not the product.

   This will be part of your practice in turning your attention inward.

2. **Practice sharing your real self with others.**

   You may want to begin by seeking safe people with whom you can share your feelings, doubts, and needs. This practice of being real with others may create a sense of vulnerability or of being exposed so be tender with yourself. You may be surprised to learn that others value your openness and more authentic nature.

3. **Be curious about your urge to succeed—at any price.**

   Notice your motivations behind the desire to succeed. Who and what defines success for you?

4. **Pay attention to your heart.**

   When you find you're driving yourself relentlessly, stop and ask yourself what you are feeling.

   Shift your attention from the outside world to the inner world. Become more familiar with the sensations around your heart; begin to open your heart to yourself. Allow yourself to relax around your heart; invite yourself into your own heart. Breathe.

If this feels like foreign territory, identify people who can support you in the practice of being in your own heart. This may be a spiritual teacher, coach, mentor, or a group that focuses on developing qualities of the heart.

As you develop a stronger relationship with your heart, notice the things that change in your life.

5. Practice asking yourself, "What is true about this situation?"

People with Type Three patterns can spin a situation to make it look good or acceptable. This can happen so quickly and automatically that you don't realize you are doing it. As you assess a situation that you are tempted to use to make you look good, ask yourself whose approval you are trying to get. Reflect on what deeper value there is for you in staying with what's true.

Forging Your Healing and Evolutionary Path

A major theme of this book is that the primary reason for working with the Enneagram is to help us awaken to our true nature. It puts us on a path of healing and real transformation that, for most of us, takes place over time—with patience, trust, faith in our awakening journey—and by being as present as possible. Section III takes us into processes that support and are beneficial for everyone, regardless of type.

Not surprisingly, there are specific processes that are vital for individuals dominant in each type.

If you are dominant in Type Three, your healing and evolutionary path includes the following:

Allow yourself to experience the underlying hurt and grief that lie just underneath the mask of having it all together. Your heart is yearning for your attention and your compassion for yourself.

Shift your center of gravity from outside to inside. Start paying attention to what touches you, what would nourish your heart. You don't have to know the answers in advance. Just take it a step at a time.

Despite all the confidence you display to the world, notice that, underneath, you can lack confidence and feel anxious and worried as you experience your Hidden Self (which is at Type Six). It's hard to accept this discovery of the *Hidden Dimension of Self*—but as you do, it will help you come into contact with your authentic confidence. From this confidence, you can also come to know that beyond your self-interest, there is joy and value in contributing to something bigger than yourself, such as a collaborative or team effort. You no longer need to be the star.

> **REMINDER:** The Hidden Dimension of Self is found at the average and lower levels of health in the Integration Point.

Experience how it is to be with yourself. Your authentic heart will give you glimpse after glimpse of what your true value is.

Doing and Being are no longer separate domains in your life. You experience yourself as a *Being* who functions effectively and with heart in the world.

The Human Condition and Consciousness of Type Seven: The Enthusiast

Stan is a talented, quick-witted, and outgoing man who was drawn to coaching because he was frustrated about where he was in his life. He had held sales and business development positions in the food and wine industries. His current position is in the restaurant world, where he has been able to put his love and expertise of food, cooking, and menu development into practice. While he loves his work, he feels like he's not as far along in his career as he had expected. He has changed residences frequently, built up very little in savings, and has had numerous challenges with managing his money.

He wanted to learn to be more accountable to himself.

When Stan discovered that he had a Type Seven personality, he began to recognize that his current circumstances were outcomes of several long-held patterns:

- *He saw that he was mostly on-the-go, full of anticipation about what was next, and seldom being where he actually was—he was seldom "present." His excitement about trying new experiences overshadowed his ability to focus on what his life actually needed.*

- *He saw how hard it was for him to commit. Interested in diverse activities, he found himself sampling a little of one thing, then, becoming quickly bored, he moved on to something else. He saw how this happened at work, in relationships, and with some friendships.*

- *He got antsy and anxious if he thought he might miss an opportunity.*
- *His forté was trying new things; what was difficult was letting himself experience the sadness associated with some recent and significant losses in his life.*

One major coaching theme for Stan focused on slowing down and paying attention to what he was feeling. Feelings felt foreign unless they were just happy ones. Stan found sadness, and other feelings he viewed as negative, not only hard to tolerate, but he also couldn't imagine why there would be any value in feeling them. Initially, he wanted to skip over these feelings as quickly as possible. With time, Stan came to realize that these feelings would remain under the surface if not addressed, but when felt, could lead to a greater depth within himself.

It's not unusual for individuals dominant in Type Seven to severely underestimate the amount of time tasks take. As difficult as it was, he practiced reducing the number of activities in his weekly schedule by 25 percent to have the experience of more space in his day. When he found that his calendar was still full, he reluctantly reduced the number of scheduled activities again. He experienced a habitual anxiety when there were moments of quiet, but as he learned that he could tolerate anxiety, some of its longtime control over him subsided. He could incorporate important moments of quiet into his day. Much to his surprise, these moments were ones he came to highly prize.

Stan also began to recognize the connection between the habitual pattern of anxiety and the difficulty he had with accountability. As he took his commitments to himself more seriously, and honed strategies for completing important tasks, he came into a new understanding and appreciation of life.

The Internal Coherence of the Type Seven Experience

Your True Nature

If this is your dominant Enneagram point, your soul is naturally drawn to the joy and freedom that is inherent in every moment. You love the limitless and infinite nature of all that is. You and everything in life are constantly evolving and expressing qualities of newness, freshness, and bountiful exuberance.

When not in touch with your true nature, what you might not recognize *yet* is that all of this joy and freedom that you love is here, only in this moment. You need not go anywhere or change what you are doing to experience the astonishment that is available here and now.

The Story of Your Life:
Relating to Your Inner and Outer World

Your inner sense of self and your place in the world were set in place early in life. How you internalized your experiences contributed to the characteristic way you relate to yourself and others, and to your very way of being. If this is your dominant type, the following brief story of your childhood inner experience will likely sound very familiar.

As a small child, you were filled with curiosity, a sense of adventure, and wanting to try everything you could. Life was an endless source of possibilities to be experienced.

You moved quickly between different activities, as nothing held your interest for very long.

At an early age, perhaps around the age of three, something happened in your family that left you feeling prematurely cut off from your mother (or other nurturing figure). Perhaps she went back to work, or got sick, or had another baby. All you knew is that your source of nurturing was no longer as available as she had been. The withdrawal of her constant care was a source of much pain—more pain than you felt you could tolerate.

At some point, you made an unconscious decision. You decided, "Well, I can't trust someone else to take care of me. I'm going to take care of myself. I'm not going to wait around, waste time, and feel sorry for myself. I'll just make sure I get what I want."

At another level, you made a decision not to feel pain. It felt like a waste of time.

Inside, you had a vague sense that you had never really been filled up, that your need for being nurtured had never been deeply satisfied. You started to look for things that would fill up this hole, this place of emptiness.

Even at this young age, you found endless toys, games, other playmates, and other distractions to help you not feel your feelings. You were a kid on the move. You got bored easily, and couldn't tolerate not being busy. Besides, there were so many interesting things in life to explore. You could be the center of attention, the life of the party, the initiator of all things fun. That was your mission—to have fun. You may have heard, "Would you just settle down and focus on one thing? Why do you always have to be going out?"

Underlying your attraction to all things interesting, you felt hurt, grief, and fear. You did your best to keep your mind active and you always looked to the next diversion. You found yourself looking ahead, anticipating what the next fun thing would be. And you protected yourself against really letting other people in—letting them see the whole you.

You came to orient your life around the idea that pain was not okay to experience, that it was unnecessary. Your life became formed around the idea that you needed to take care of yourself because no one else would really take care of you.

What you didn't know is that your pain will not overwhelm you, but is instead a pathway to your deep satisfaction. What you didn't know is that you have an amazing capacity for experiencing the depth, richness, and gratitude of your heart. What you couldn't know is that when you are in the present, life is vibrant, fulfilling, and a place of awe.

Your Great Loss

As a little being, even before your conscious thought and language skills developed, you had experiences that left you feeling separated from these essential qualities that your soul loved—that it was in tune with. This pain was too much to bear, so the ego structure began to form, taking on the role of protecting you from the severity of this early loss.

We remember that the ego attempts to mimic our true nature, though it can never be successful in doing so. So, the Seven personality structure has tried to recreate the experience of being free and joyful. Your attention moves quickly from one thing to another, so that you stay on the surface of your experiences. Not landing long enough to absorb what the situation, person, or environment has to offer, your thirst for fulfillment cannot be satisfied.

Here is the great loss—the pain—for Type Seven: It feels as if the real fulfillment that you are looking for doesn't exist. It will never truly be found. As you stay in a constant search mode, your heart aches because it is not being touched by this endless array of activity.

The Inner Logic and the Triangle of Identity for Type Seven

Type Seven's CORE BELIEF

We see that a core belief is set into place, providing an unconscious filter that accepts only information that supports the ego's belief. This filter, unfortunately, misses and dismisses data that would otherwise provide alternate perspectives. This belief acts as a core operating principle that shapes a person's relationship to life.

Each core belief is false but feels real until we can compassionately bring it into the light of awareness. It's particularly important to approach this with great kindness and truthfulness.

If you are dominant in Seven, you are needing to be satisfied, but that quality is elusive. It seems out of immediate reach. You believe that you need to go outward into the world, and perhaps there you will find your source of satisfaction.

Not trusting others to fulfill your needs or provide you real support, you believe that you are on your own for finding satisfaction. In the midst of all the activity, there is a sense of loneliness.

How might this show up in your life? Here are some examples of what you might hear yourself think, say, or do/not do:

- There are so many exciting opportunities. I want to try them all. What should I do next?
- Don't ask me to deal with the details. That can get boring fast. And I came up with the idea. Time for someone else to step in.
- I've *always* wanted to go to that destination (or own that car, or have that experience). I'm going to make plans for it right now.
- I get so frustrated when my spouse wants me to stay home and take care of chores. I helped over the weekend and have already made plans for something that I really want to do. Why can't he understand that?

This core belief leads us to the **Triangle of Identity**, *which provides a shorthand illustration of how you "do" life.* I invite you to try on the following description to see how it fits with your experience.

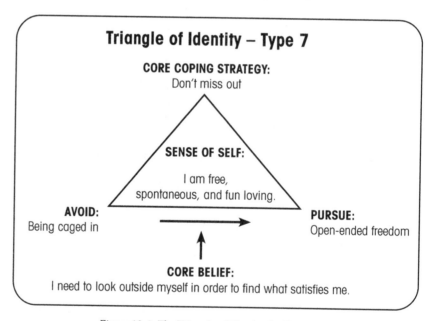

Figure 10-1: The Triangle of Identity for Type Seven

Here is how a person with the Type Seven personality structure might recognize this inner logic that is illustrated by the Triangle of Identity:

I **pursue** the freedom to do as I please. There are so many things that I want to try and my list keeps growing. I want to do it all. I put my attention on being spontaneous and want to be able to respond at a moment's notice. I have to get my needs met, and it's possible that any of these things could do that. If something feels like a downer, then I move on quickly.

I **avoid** anything that could cage me in—an uncomfortable or painful situation, for example. The sense of danger that comes with being trapped is terrifying, and it likely includes situations or people that could get boring. I can feel anxious and frustrated if I don't get to do what I want when I want. I use shortcuts to get around obstacles so I can get what I want faster. The sense of missing out on something is one of the hardest things in life for me to deal with.

I **cope** by making sure I don't miss out on the amazing opportunities that are available. I am on the go and don't make commitments easily, because something more interesting and fun could come along.

As an extension of my coping, I can see that I have organized my life around the idea that what matters most is being free to pursue my constant happiness. If I focus on what could make me happy, life is great. I get so excited about possibilities and think a lot about what is coming next. My mind spins quickly as I focus on planning ahead. By anticipating the future, I can avoid most sad or lingering, unhappy feelings. If only I can keep trying new experiences, then I'll feel free, at least for a moment.

All of this leads me to see myself as a free, spontaneous, fun-loving person. This self-definition—this **sense of self**—ends up imposing limits. It keeps me from recognizing and appreciating the fuller range of my human experience.

While being spontaneous and fun-loving are positive qualities, when overused, they limit my ability to experience a deeper sense of satisfaction, an inner quiet, and an ability to be with the unknown. When my life energy is consistently focused on being optimistic and fun-loving, I miss out on having a truly fulfilling life.

An Awakened Capacity of Type Seven: Wonderment through Sobriety and Presence

You have an enormous capacity for wonder and gratitude. You have a deep and open-hearted appreciation for whatever comes. You are able to settle in, and you enjoy the astonishing gifts available in every moment.

This capacity is expanded whenever you sink into the fullness of the moment and absorb your experience. Here, you know the depth of life, and you are affected by it all. This discovery parallels another: having authentic contact with your heart does not diminish your capacity for being joyful. In fact, it heightens it. What is missing is the unhelpful compulsion of moving constantly from one thing to the next.

It is when you have forgotten and lost contact with your innate capacity for the wonderment of life *in this moment* that you want more and more things or experiences. That's when it feels like you can never get enough.

You forget that being here to experience this moment will bring your greatest satisfaction, and that this is a key to unlocking the door to a freer life.

The Type Seven Iceberg Model reiterates some of this material in a visual format.

The model starts with some of the expansive qualities that are innate gifts of individuals dominant in this type. These qualities are naturally and increasingly experienced as we recognize and gradually release our attachment to our more limited definition of self. The Iceberg Model also increases our understanding of the observable expressions found at the average level of behavior of Type Seven individuals, and it fills out more of what goes on below the waterline, i.e., those inner dynamics that shape and motivate the behaviors that occur when the personality has its grip on us. (Refer to chapter 5 for more discussion on the Iceberg Model.)

Decoding the Personality Structure of Type Seven

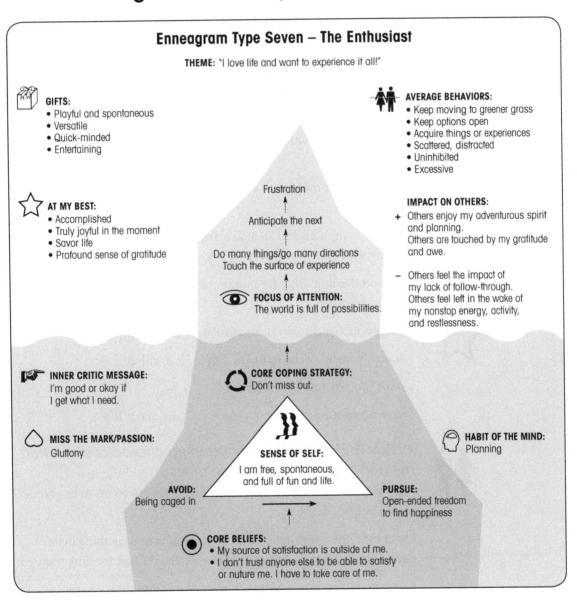

Enneagram Type Seven – The Enthusiast

THEME: "I love life and want to experience it all!"

GIFTS:
- Playful and spontaneous
- Versatile
- Quick-minded
- Entertaining

AT MY BEST:
- Accomplished
- Truly joyful in the moment
- Savor life
- Profound sense of gratitude

AVERAGE BEHAVIORS:
- Keep moving to greener grass
- Keep options open
- Acquire things or experiences
- Scattered, distracted
- Uninhibited
- Excessive

IMPACT ON OTHERS:

+ Others enjoy my adventurous spirit and planning.
  Others are touched by my gratitude and awe.

− Others feel the impact of my lack of follow-through.
  Others feel left in the wake of my nonstop energy, activity, and restlessness.

Frustration

Anticipate the next

Do many things/go many directions
Touch the surface of experience

FOCUS OF ATTENTION:
The world is full of possibilities.

INNER CRITIC MESSAGE:
I'm good or okay if I get what I need.

CORE COPING STRATEGY:
Don't miss out.

MISS THE MARK/PASSION:
Gluttony

SENSE OF SELF:
I am free, spontaneous, and full of fun and life.

HABIT OF THE MIND:
Planning

AVOID:
Being caged in

PURSUE:
Open-ended freedom to find happiness

CORE BELIEFS:
- My source of satisfaction is outside of me.
- I don't trust anyone else to be able to satisfy or nuture me. I have to take care of me.

Figure 10-2: The Iceberg Model for Type Seven

Type Seven's THEME
"I love life and want to experience it all!" is the theme of this personality structure.

Above the Waterline

The Gifts, Daily Habits, and Challenges of Type Seven

GIFTS and AT MY BEST
(When I'm expansive and at my healthiest)

I'm playful and spontaneous. I am energetic and can respond freely and in the moment.

I am versatile. I move with ease into a vast array of topics, tasks and activities.

I am quick-minded and an avid learner. I have fun *sparring* with others and my wit comes through naturally.

I am entertaining. My easy humor, happiness, and sense of fun are enjoyed by others.

I am productive, practical, and prolific. I am accomplished.

I am truly joyful in the moment. I'm in love with life.

I savor life, whatever it brings.

I have a profound sense of gratitude and awe about life.

AVERAGE BEHAVIORS *(Distinguishing characteristics when my personality has its grip on me)*

I move to where the grass is greener, and it always seems to be greener someplace besides here.

I wait until the last minute to make plans in case something better comes along. I like to keep my options open so I avoid feeling trapped.

I acquire and consume experiences and/or things. I may never use what I get, but at the time, it feels like I have to have it.

My energy is scattered, distracted, and unfocused. I move haphazardly without a sense of direction and have difficulty staying with or completing projects.

I am uninhibited. I dismiss or override any need to limit myself.

I excessively pursue pleasure or acquire far more than is necessary.

FOCUS OF ATTENTION, or FOA *(Where I put my attention when I'm attached to my personality)*

NOTE: *This is a brief description of what happens as the FOA becomes narrower and narrower. It's important to note that the degree to which our FOA is activated is shaped by our degree of presence. With more presence, what we pay attention to expands, rather than narrows.*

When my personality has its grip on me, I put my attention on the outer world of possibilities. I don't like the feeling of being limited in what I can do. With my attention split between what I'm doing now and what's next, I only skim the surface of my experiences.

As I start to fill my calendar with experiences that have the possibility of bringing satisfaction, I find it hard to decide between options. I often jump from one experience to another to get a taste of what it has to offer. And why not? Isn't this what is meant by having fun and being spontaneous?

As I go in more directions, it is more difficult to follow through with any of them. I get easily distracted, and both my anticipation and anxiety increase.

I become frustrated, because nothing is actually satisfying me or fulfilling. There is something off or wrong about all the options, and I get fearful that nothing will ever satisfy me.

My IMPACT ON OTHERS

+ *Positive:*
   • Others are invigorated and stimulated by my enthusiasm.
   • Others feel engaged by my optimism and love of life.

– Negative:
- Others feel frustrated by my lack of commitment and follow through.
- Others are irritated by my restlessness and need for *instant gratification.*

Below the Waterline

To understand the inner dynamics for Type Seven, we turn our attention to what lies under the surface of the water, starting at the bottom and working up.

Type Seven's CORE BELIEF

These core operating principles filter through many layers of life, in both seen and unseen ways.

No one can be trusted to satisfy or nurture me. Others won't give me what I'm looking for. I am on my own.

I believe that my source of true satisfaction is *out there* somewhere. Something exists that is even better than what I have now. I just need to keep searching for it. I believe, on the one hand, that *it* must lie just around the corner. On the other hand, I despair of ever finding *it.*

The TRIANGLE OF IDENTITY

What I PURSUE

I *pursue* the freedom to do as I please. There are so many things that I want to try, and even while I'm participating in one event, I'm already thinking about the next. I'm proud of my spontaneity and flexibility, which allow me to respond in the moment to new opportunities. Even though I sometimes secretly feel fatigued, I am on the go—meeting new people, or finding the newest fun gadgets, or signing up for one new adventure after another. If there's a hint of possible boredom or of someone being a downer, I make a quick exit to something I anticipate will bring me greater pleasure.

What I AVOID

I *avoid* anything that could potentially cage me in an uncomfortable or painful situation. The sense of danger that comes with being trapped feels like a sense of death. With too much downtime, or quiet, or when people are talking too slowly, or when events are not moving quickly enough for me, I can feel anxious and impatient. I easily get frustrated if I don't get to do what I want when I want.

I take shortcuts to get around obstacles so I can get what I want faster.

My CORE COPING STRATEGY

I *cope* by making sure that I don't miss out on the amazing opportunities that are available. I am on the go, and I don't make commitments easily because something more interesting could come along. For example, as much as I might enjoy having dinner at a just-opened restaurant with friends, an even more tempting invitation could come my way.

I am always searching for interesting new activities and experiences. New opportunities seem to constantly appear on my radar screen, and I respond enthusiastically. I tend not to stay with anything (or sometimes anyone) for an extended length of time. And I have a backup plan. My coping strategy keeps me in the mode of activity, of doing.

SENSE OF SELF ("I am...")

I see myself as fun and spontaneous. I am stimulating and stimulated. While these are positive qualities, they limit me when I don't allow myself to take the time needed to experience the full range of life's emotions, including the inevitable sadness that comes with loss.

WHERE I MISS THE MARK
(*The energetic drive of the passion*)

I miss the mark by trying to fill up my inner emptiness with things and experiences—now. In other words, my habit is to jump over uncomfortable feelings as quickly as they arise. By thinking that my satisfaction is going to come from finding *it* in the external world, I move farther and farther away from myself. My insatiability ultimately leaves me feeling more empty. I feel anxious that I may make the wrong choice and thus miss the one true source of happiness. So rather than selecting one choice, I will try to have as many experiences as possible. This passion is called *gluttony*.

> **REMINDER**: No matter what type you are dominant in, the passion is a part of the personality and is a motivator that drives your emotional life. The passion covers up a wound in your heart[1] and creates an emotional reaction to how you relate to life, which takes you away from what your soul loves. This is true for all personality types.

HABIT OF THE MIND *(Fixation of the personality)*

I anticipate that something better than what is here, is out there. And if the next thing isn't better, then what comes after might be what I'm looking for. The anticipation keeps me focused on planning what's next, rather than experiencing what is right here. Thus, I miss what is available to me in the present.

> **REMINDER**: No matter what type you are dominant in, the fixation is a part of the personality. It's a motivator in your fixed behaviors and thoughts about yourself and the world. It bolsters a false sense of reality, and as the ego's automatic, unquestioned way of solving problems with life, it takes you away from your true self. This is true for all personality types.

INNER CRITIC MESSAGE
(What my Inner Critic insists upon)

My inner critic rewards me when *I get what I need*.[2] It rewards my continual search for a new experience or more material goods. It tries to convince me that being on the lookout will ultimately be fulfilling. As long as I'm caught in the inner critic's web, I remain focused on looking for the next thing, without hope of real satisfaction *now*.

Each of the elements described above contributes to the whole experience of what we have come to think of as ourselves. The core belief, the emotional force of the passion, the mental habit (fixation), and the inner critic all unconsciously conspire to reinforce the Triangle of Identity.

Additional Information on the Enneagram Type Seven

What causes me *stress*

My stress increases when I feel stuck with a commitment that keeps me from doing other things that I want to do. Conversely, my stress is increased when I feel overwhelmed by all the activities that I have gotten involved in. When I have too many balls in the air, I can be frantic.

When I'm most *constricted and inflexible*

I escape from pain at all costs.

I'm impulsive and irresponsible.

I can be reckless and out of control.

I can become overwhelmed and paralyzed.

Other Personality Types Related to Type Seven

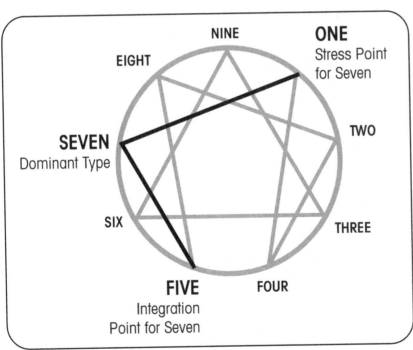

Figure 10-3: The Stress and Integration Points for Type Seven

People dominant in Type Seven experience characteristics of Type One under stress. Type One is the *Stress Point* for Type Seven. For more information on this, see chapter 12. Pay particular attention to the sections on average-level behaviors and to the "Notice and Observe Patterns" section of that chapter.

Type Seven's *Integration Point*, including the *Hidden Dimension of Self*, is found in Type Five. See chapter 8 for more information on Type Five. For Type Seven's Integration Point, pay particular attention to the "Gifts" and "At My Best" sections in chapter 8. For Type Seven's Hidden Dimension of Self, review the sections on average levels of behavior in that same chapter.

The Enneagram also works in reverse, which yields helpful information to everyone discovering their dominant type: Type Seven is the Stress Point for Type Five, and it's the Integration Point for Type One.

Recognizing Patterns That Pull You Off-Course

Notice and Observe Patterns

In this section you'll find some of the patterns that are associated with the Type Seven personality structure. These patterns provide useful information. Rather than making you bad or wrong in some way, these patterns can be used as signposts on your path of awakening. They help you notice and get to the heart of your experience in a tangible, direct way. Eventually, you can relax the particular, habitual—and often troublesome—strategies, which will allow you to be more present, open, and free.

The pattern of your high energy

The high energy of Type Seven can show up in different ways.

Notice your tendency to *push* your energy out into the world. This might show up as talking fast and sometimes forgetting to inhale.

It might show up as often overbooking yourself and trying to be in a lot of different places at almost the same time. One challenge for Sevens is that there doesn't seem to be a limit to things to do and places to go. Notice when you put off making a decision to be with a particular friend in anticipation of something even more fun, such as getting last-minute tickets to a sold-out concert.

Do you have a difficult time saying no to all the wonderful opportunities that come your way? Perhaps you notice that it feels that this is a *once-in-a-lifetime* situation, or that you'll *miss out on something important* if you pass on this opportunity.

Observe if you are trying to avoid something, such as a sense of boredom or another feeling that you have defined as negative.

This high, outward-moving energy is fed by adrenaline and can be quite intoxicating. Living with an adrenal rush can feel quite normal for a Seven. While it may be fun to have this enthusiasm for all the possibilities in life, you might also notice that you're often exhausted or stressed. Remember that this intensity has helped protect you against feeling that early hurt from your childhood.

The pattern of being the entertainer and being *on*

Type Sevens often find themselves in the role of entertaining others and revving up the excitement. They sometimes find that *they have trained others* to expect them to be *"up"* and energized.

What does being up do for you? How does it impact your experience of yourself? Notice your own expectations of yourself as the *center of a gathering*. Notice how being *up* impacts the quality of your relationships.

The pattern of how you deal with pain and grief

When you take a moment to slow down, what do you experience?

Notice if you have a sense of sadness or anxiety. Notice if it feels acceptable to experience something other than being *upbeat and positive.*

People dominant in Seven often try to avoid any sense of inner pain because it feels like it will consume them, and they'll always be in pain. There is a tendency to shortcut grief or other painful inner feelings and to *just get on with it.*

Interrupting the grief process only serves to bury feelings, which will surface at another, equally inconvenient time, and with perhaps more intensity. Notice what you tell yourself about having feelings other than those associated with being *on*.

The pattern of feeling frustrated and impatient

Notice when you get impatient or frustrated. Stop and take a few deep breaths. What does impatience feel like? Notice what you tend to do to discharge or alleviate the discomfort of impatience.

What does frustration feel like? What is your tendency when you experience frustration? How do you react? How does it impact your life? Notice how frequently you say that you are frustrated and how frequently you feel frustrated.

The pattern of always anticipating what's around the corner

Type Sevens tend to use much of their energy to anticipate what is next.

How do you experience anticipation? Notice when you are focusing on *what's next?* rather than being fully attentive to what is happening now. Notice what the experience of anticipation feels like for you—where do you experience it in your body? In what types of situations? What are the consequences for you of living in *anticipation mode?* What do you miss out on when your attention is enmeshed with anticipation?

Surprising and Effective Practices for Building Your Capacity

The following capacity-building practices will help you turn toward your true nature.

1. Quiet the mind.

People dominant in Type Seven tend to have busy minds filled with anticipation and mental chatter. Developing a meditation practice that supports you in coming back to your body and your physical sensations will help you to refocus your attention and take the pressure off your mind.

This practice requires patience. It is not meant to be *figured out* and completed in a few sittings. Quieting the internal mental messages is a lifelong commitment.

You may also discover that taking quiet walks in nature will support you in quieting yourself.

2. Practice a new way to schedule.

Those dominant in Seven often find that they are rushed and frequently late for appointments. You might notice that you have not given yourself enough *buffer time* between appointments or that you have allocated too little time for any one task or appointment.

Take a look at your calendar. Cut the number of appointments and activities by at least twenty-five percent each day for a week and see what happens. You may actually need to cut the number of activities you schedule by fifty percent to enjoy being where you are. Cutting your appointments by this percentage may feel impossible; however, give it time to work. Compassionately notice the internal pressure to fill every moment, and notice what is under this pressure.

3. Experience and stay with feelings.

Those dominant in Seven tend to interrupt a complete processing of their feelings, both the positive and the painful ones. Allow yourself to have a direct experience of having your feelings. For example, when you have just had a difficult conversation with a friend, notice what you are feeling during the conversation. What happens when you simply *stay with* those feelings as they arise? What does *the particular* feeling that is arising now feel like in your body?

You might notice that you need to slow down—way down—in order to have a fuller experience of your feelings. When fully experienced, a feeling tends to change into something different—a different feeling. Typically, something within you opens, and you have a freer experience of yourself, often accompanied by a deep sense of relief.

4. Enjoy what is here now.

Take time to be aware of the gifts you have in your life at this time and to *take in* the wondrousness of life. Experiment with what it feels like to simply *take in.* You'll notice that this is a very different energy than *pushing out,* which is what you typically do when your personality has its grip on you.

What would support you in creating space to experience more of what is available to you in this moment? What is different for you when you do create space in which you can just *be* rather than focus on *doing*?

5. Give yourself a chance.

People who most identify with the Type Seven personality tend to be both multi-talented and impatient with slow-moving processes, thus they tend to avoid staying with activities that require developmental knowledge or skill-building. When you do this, you short-change yourself and often do not know what you are fully capable of. For example, you may wait until the deadline for a project is near before starting on it. The result is that you don't have time to dig into the more intricate aspects of the project. You end up with an adequate or even a good product, but one that is not fully satisfying to you. So take the time to develop yourself, experience the deeper dimensions of your efforts, and bring your abilities to fruition.

You put pressure on yourself when you expect to be an *instant expert.* Of course, you're bright and can generally pull off new challenges with your charm. But there are other ways to share your talents. For example, experiment with slowing down your timeline between learning something new and delivering a workshop on it.

Stay focused on seeing tasks through to completion. Notice what you experience when you bring closure to a task. How does this feel?

Forging Your Healing and Evolutionary Path

A major theme of this book is that the primary reason for working with the Enneagram is to help us awaken to our true nature. It puts us on a path of healing and real transformation that, for most of us, takes place over time—with patience, trust, faith in our awakening journey—and by being as present as possible. Section III takes us into processes that support and are beneficial for everyone, regardless of type.

Not surprisingly, there are specific processes that are vital for individuals dominant in each type.

If you are dominant in Type Seven, your healing and evolutionary path includes the following:

Refocus your attention *from* getting fulfillment outside of yourself *to* experiencing the present moment. Consciously noticing your breathing will help you come into contact with the present and make contact with your body.

Let go of the conditions and rules (which include being up, being on the go) you place on your own happiness. These conditions keep you locked in a box that can never be satisfied. Be amazed by what you discover when the false conditions are released.

Your inner critic holds substantial power when it is unrecognized or uninterrupted. As much as you pursue things you enjoy, you can be extremely hard on yourself. Learning to minimize the impact of the inner critic will go a long distance in creating a true sense of inner freedom. Chapter 17 offers many strategies for working with the inner critic.

Notice times when you withdraw into a dark place in your mind (moving to your Hidden Self in your Integration Point, which is at the point for Type Five). It's really hard to see this in yourself, because it's so far outside of the way that you think of yourself. Yet, you can be lost in your head, become detached and provoke discomfort in others. As you slowly acknowledge and embrace these characteristics—this discovery of the *Hidden Dimension of Self*—you will recognize your capacity for quietness from within. From this source of inner quiet, you can naturally begin to experience more focus, clarity, and the ability to be with yourself.

> **REMINDER:** The Hidden Dimension of Self is found at the average and lower levels of health in the Integration Point.

Your heart is a source of limitless intelligence. Through it, you will come into contact with feelings that require your attention. And through it, you will realize deep gratitude for the awe and beauty of life.

11

The Human Condition and Consciousness of Type Eight: The Challenger

Lucas came to coaching at the urging of his wife. Exuding confidence and intensity, he went straight to his bottom line. He said that he'd been riding his teenage boys pretty hard because he wanted them to learn to stand up for themselves and show their strength so that others wouldn't take advantage of them. He felt that they were being irresponsible and goofing off too much, so he'd insisted on instilling a good work ethic in them.

It hadn't been effective. The sons were good kids and didn't really get into trouble, but they were both pushing back against him, and he got a little rougher with them than he'd intended.

Ultimately, he wanted to be a good role model for them, and so he came for coaching on how to be a more effective parent.

Lucas took an introductory workshop on the Enneagram and learned that he was dominant in Type Eight. In the coaching relationship, he further learned:

- *He had not been aware of how big his energy was, nor the impact that it could have on others. He'd always thought it was a sign of confidence and and of knowing where he was going. He'd struggled with his sons, who did not exude the same level of toughness, but he came to realize that they experienced the world in ways very different than he did. Because he'd struggled as a kid to be respected, he was concerned that his sons would get beaten up by life.*

- *He was always ready to pick a good fight, even with his kids. He felt energized by letting others know exactly where he stood. Now he could see that he had experienced and, no doubt initiated, a considerable amount of discord with a lot of people.*

- *As much as he truly loved his family, it was really hard to tell his kids that. Rather, he gave them substantial gifts and special privileges, then expected that they'd mind him.*

- *He had a special relationship with a few people who were honestly accepting and kind to him. He discovered that this is where he experienced being more open and even vulnerable, which was a welcome relief from feeling he always needed to have his armor on.*

Initially, Lucas just appreciated having someone hear him out. He'd long felt that most others looked to him to deal with difficult issues and protect them, so not having to be the strong one in the coaching conversation was a totally unfamiliar experience.

A major theme of his coaching centered on ways he could begin to express his real concerns that he carried in his big heart. He experimented with new ways of communicating and "being real" with his sons—without being tough. He began to recognize that each son had his own specific needs.

With help from his wife, he worked with the new idea that others were not against him. Over time, he practiced giving at least some people the benefit of the doubt. As he experienced his own heart opening more, he was greeted with surprising feedback that reaffirmed others' affection for him.

The Internal Coherence of the Type Eight Experience

Your True Nature

If this is your dominant Enneagram point, your soul is naturally drawn to its aliveness and the grounded quality of inner strength. You experience that aliveness in yourself and in every part of life without needing to force it. You thrive on the profound immediacy of life that is right here, right now.

When not in touch with your true nature, what you might not recognize *yet* is that your open-heartedness and willingness to let others in are vital dimensions of your strength. The groundedness and strength you experience in your body provide you with the support to allow your heart to register your deep caring for others. Rather than pushing people away, they are naturally drawn to you. Life feels real, full, and immediate.

The Story of Your Life:
Relating to Your Inner and Outer World

Your inner sense of self and your place in the world were set in place early in life. How you internalized your experiences contributed to the characteristic way you relate to yourself and others, and to your very way of being. If this is your dominant type, the following brief story of your childhood inner experience will likely sound very familiar.

> As far back as you can remember, you were adventurous, active, had a lot of energy, and went after what you wanted—whether it was a toy, attention, jumping in the water, or playing hard. Why did adults often tell you to be quiet, or slow down, or not be so rough with others? You got in trouble a lot and may have heard, "Stop it! You're being bad." You felt so small and couldn't really protect yourself from these hurtful experiences.
>
> At some early time, you became aware of who had power—and it wasn't you. You experienced this power sometimes being used against you, which made you feel unsafe. You learned to hide your feelings, believing that to survive in the inhospitable world, you had to show that you were tough. The more chaotic your family life, the tougher you became.
>
> When you were young, there were times that you showed your very human need for love but felt rebuffed, betrayed, and rejected. At an unconscious level, you became determined to not allow yourself to be betrayed again. Showing your need for love led to pain. The experience of betrayal felt like a turning point, when you were forced to grow up fast.

You've spent a lot of energy trying to protect yourself against feeling hurt, and denying that you need the approval and affection of others. You lived with the message that you need to be strong and independent.

You came to organize your life around the idea that it's not okay to be vulnerable or to truly trust others. The very idea of being vulnerable brings up discomfort and feels to you like it would be a sign of weakness.

What you didn't see in yourself was the amazing strength that you have in your heart. What you couldn't see is that you will always be a person of strength, even when your heart is open.

Your Great Loss

As a little being, even before your conscious thought and language skills developed, you had experiences that left you feeling separated from these essential qualities that your soul loved—that it was in tune with. This pain was too much to bear, so the ego structure began to form, taking on the role of protecting you from the severity of this early loss.

We remember that the ego attempts to mimic our true nature, though it can never be successful in doing so. So, the Eight personality structure has tried to create this experience of aliveness and strength. It *pushes your energy* out into the world. You put more energy into your actions than might be required for the task at hand, creating a substitute for your natural aliveness. You meet challenges head on and even look for new things to challenge you. No hill is too high to climb. Others experience you as a force to contend with. Your ego operates by magnifying, pumping up, and exerting a lot of energy.

Here is the great loss—the pain—for Type Eight: At a deep, cellular level, there's a sense that "somebody out there" betrayed you, causing deep, nearly unbearable pain. This led you to make an unconscious decision to steel yourself against the possibility of ever being betrayed again. This deep inner hurt is something you have carried with you for your entire life. Thus, you have pushed away precisely what your soul most yearns for—the aliveness of the full-hearted contact with yourself, with others, and with life.

The Inner Logic and the Triangle of Identity for Type Eight

Type Eight's CORE BELIEF

We see that a core belief is set into place, providing an unconscious filter that accepts only information that supports the ego's belief. This filter, unfortunately, misses and dismisses data that would otherwise provide alternate perspectives. This belief acts as a core operating principle that shapes a person's relationship to life.

Each core belief is false but feels real until we can compassionately bring it into the light of awareness. It's particularly important to approach this with great kindness and truthfulness.

If you are dominant in Type Eight, you believe the world is unjust. You need to protect yourself and those less powerful from the unfairness and injustice of others. You can't show your vulnerability because others will take unfair advantage of you. Therefore, you must show your strength and power.

How might this show up in your life? Here are some examples of what you hear yourself think, say, or do/not do:

- Decisive action is needed to meet this threatening situation. I'll take charge because I can make things happen now.
- Hell, yes, I take risks. I enjoy testing my mettle against the odds.
- I like a good fight. Who cares if I argue loudly and sometimes get forceful? Somebody here has to show others what it takes.
- I'm not apologizing for saying it like it is. It angers me when others aren't honest.

This core belief leads us to the **Triangle of Identity**, *which provides a shorthand illustration of how you "do" life.* I invite you to try on the following description to see how it fits with your experience.

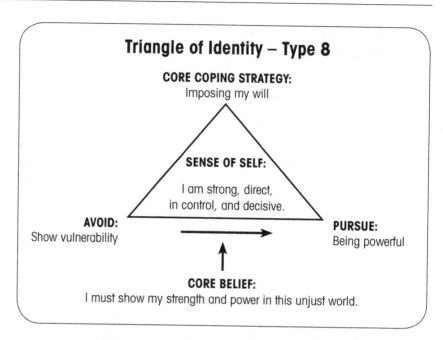

Figure 11-1: The Triangle of Identity for Type Eight

Here is how a person with the Type Eight personality structure might recognize this inner logic that is illustrated by the Triangle of Identity:

> I **pursue** being in control and expressing my power. I want to be in charge of my own circumstances and of my future. I live life with gusto, putting out a lot of energy, and challenge those who would get in my way.

> I **avoid** anything that I think makes me look weak, soft, or vulnerable. To show my tender side feels like the riskiest thing I could do, as my weakness could easily be used against me. Thus, it's important to stay in control at all costs, and show that I'm tough.

> I **cope** by imposing my will. I direct—and eventually dominate—a situation, expanding my control over other people and over things. The more expansive my energy, the more protected and less vulnerable I feel. When I impose my will, I expect that others will fall in line.

> As an extension of my coping style, I can see that I have organized my life around the idea that I need to be strong and in control of life. If I am in control, then life works great. I can keep the upper hand so that others cannot take advantage of me. Keeping others at a distance lessens my sensitivity to them. Because I'm not in contact with my

own heart or that of others, it is easy to demand that I get my way. If I can keep any sense of vulnerability hidden, even from myself, then I'll feel outwardly powerful, at least in the short term.

*All of this leads me to see myself as a strong, in-control, and self-reliant person. This self-definition—this **sense of self**—ends up imposing limits. It keeps me from recognizing and appreciating the fuller range of my human experience.*

While being strong and direct are positive qualities, when overused, they limit my ability to connect with and express my more sensitive and caring nature that allows other people into my heart. When my life energy is consistently focused on pushing myself to the limit, I miss out on having a truly meaningful and fulfilling life.

An Awakened Capacity of Type Eight: Heartful Strength

You have a deep capacity to care for others. This can be expressed through direct communication and through your ability to mobilize action for the good of others. As you stay connected to the inherent strength of your body and the openness of your heart, you're a force for good in the world. This discovery parallels another: being open-hearted does not diminish your capacity for strength. What is missing is the compulsion to use more energy than is needed for the situation.

It's when you have forgotten and lost contact with your innate capacity for sensitivity for yourself and for the humanity of others that you become demanding, pushy, and intense. You keep an emotional distance from yourself and others, becoming identified with a very limited version of yourself.

You forget that your love of connection and willingness to let others in is a part of your strength. It's a key to unlocking the door to a freer life.

The Iceberg Model for Type Eight reiterates some of this material in a visual format.

The model starts with some of the expansive qualities that are innate gifts of individuals dominant in this type. These qualities are naturally and increasingly experienced as we recognize and gradually release our attachment to our more limited definition of self. The Iceberg Model also increases our understanding of the observable expressions found at the average level of behavior of Type Eight individuals, and it fills out more of what goes on below the waterline, i.e., those inner dynamics that shape and motivate the behaviors that occur when the personality has its grip on us. (Refer to chapter 5 for more discussion on the Iceberg Model.)

Decoding the Personality Structure of Type Eight

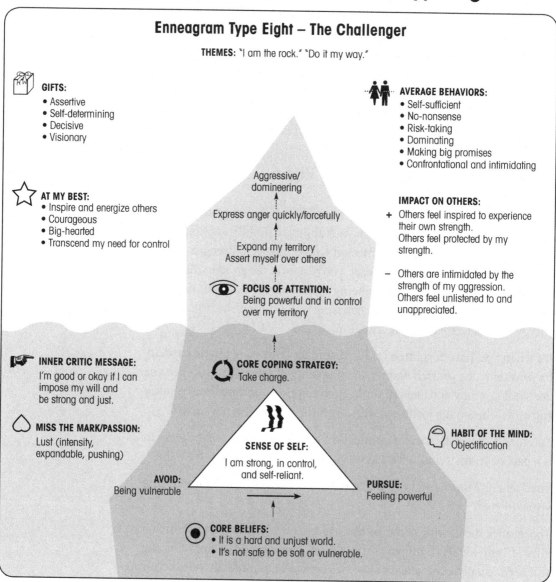

Enneagram Type Eight – The Challenger

THEMES: "I am the rock." "Do it my way."

GIFTS:
- Assertive
- Self-determining
- Decisive
- Visionary

AT MY BEST:
- Inspire and energize others
- Courageous
- Big-hearted
- Transcend my need for control

AVERAGE BEHAVIORS:
- Self-sufficient
- No-nonsense
- Risk-taking
- Dominating
- Making big promises
- Confrontational and intimidating

Aggressive/domineering

Express anger quickly/forcefully

Expand my territory
Assert myself over others

FOCUS OF ATTENTION:
Being powerful and in control over my territory

IMPACT ON OTHERS:
+ Others feel inspired to experience their own strength.
  Others feel protected by my strength.

– Others are intimidated by the strength of my aggression.
  Others feel unlistened to and unappreciated.

INNER CRITIC MESSAGE:
I'm good or okay if I can impose my will and be strong and just.

CORE COPING STRATEGY:
Take charge.

MISS THE MARK/PASSION:
Lust (intensity, expandable, pushing)

SENSE OF SELF:
I am strong, in control, and self-reliant.

HABIT OF THE MIND:
Objectification

AVOID:
Being vulnerable

PURSUE:
Feeling powerful

CORE BELIEFS:
- It is a hard and unjust world.
- It's not safe to be soft or vulnerable.

Figure 11-2: The Iceberg Model for Type Eight

Type Eight's THEMES

"I am a rock," and/or "Do it my way!" are the themes of this personality structure.

Above the Waterline

The Gifts, Daily Habits, and Challenges of Type Eight

GIFTS and AT MY BEST
(When I'm expansive and at my healthiest)

I can be assertive. I have the capacity and confidence to meet and overcome obstacles.

I am self-determining. I make decisions for myself and follow through with action.

I am decisive. I quickly respond to problems by advancing appropriate solutions.

I am visionary, seeing new scenarios that others often do not see.

I inspire and energize others to act with confidence and courage.

I am courageous, protecting others who are in the underdog position. I can challenge those in positions of power when I think they are acting unjustly.

I am magnanimous, having a gentle and big heart.

With my focus on the well-being of others, I transcend my need to be in control.

AVERAGE BEHAVIORS *(Distinguishing characteristics when my personality has its grip on me)*

I am self-sufficient. I think that I don't need anyone.

I am a no-nonsense person. I am direct, saying it like I see it, which seems perfectly obvious to me.

I take risks, often unnecessary ones, as I like the intensity of playing for high stakes.

I am dominating and refuse to compromise. I like to exert my power over others and have them capitulate to doing it my way.

I make big promises. I think it gives me currency with others and increases my stature, influence, and power.

I am confrontational and intimidating, which overwhelms others with the force of my intense energy and anger.

FOCUS OF ATTENTION, or FOA *(Where I put my attention when I'm attached to my personality)*

NOTE: This is a brief description of what happens as the FOA becomes narrower and narrower. It's important to note that the degree to which our FOA is activated is shaped by our degree of presence. With more presence, what we pay attention to expands, rather than narrows.

When my personality has its grip on me, I put my attention on experiencing my strength, power, and control over my territory, which might include my family, property and wealth, decisions at work, and brief interactions with those whom I conduct my personal business. The more I control, the more I can protect myself and others who are important to me from the injustices of life.

As the need expands to provide protection from the threat of hostility or harm from others, I enlarge my sphere of influence and ownership. I assert myself, often quite forcefully, and make it clear that others shouldn't impinge on my territory. I express my anger quickly, and it can dissipate quickly, as well. I don't understand why that should overwhelm others, but it does.

To provide even more protection from threats, I become aggressive, domineering, and intimidating. I energetically push people, and I may physically push people away. My sensitivity to others becomes increasingly diminished.

My IMPACT ON OTHERS

+ *Positive:*
- Others feel my strength, support, and protection when it's needed.
- Others feel inspired by the generosity of my spirit and my capacity to take a stand.

– *Negative:*
- Others can feel intimidated by my forcefulness.
- Others feel unheard, unseen, and unappreciated.

Below the Waterline

To understand the inner dynamics for Type Eight, we turn our attention to what lies under the surface of the water, starting at the bottom and working up.

Type Eight's CORE BELIEFS

These core operating principles filter through many layers of life, in both seen and unseen ways.

I believe that it's an unjust world. I need to protect myself from the unfairness and injustice of others. I cannot show my vulnerability, because others will take unfair advantage of me. Therefore, I must show my strength and power.

The TRIANGLE OF IDENTITY

What I PURSUE

I *pursue* being in control and expressing my power. I like the aliveness I feel when I'm up against a challenge, as my ability to make things happen the way I want shows how in charge I am of my own circumstances. In work and in play, I live life with gusto, putting out a lot of energy, and I expect the same from others. I like to push my limits. That makes life worth living.

What I AVOID

I *avoid* anything that I think makes me look weak, soft, or vulnerable. I dare not ask for help or show dependence upon others, as that would be taken as a sign of weakness. Showing what I think of as weakness sets me up for being taken advantage of. I made an agreement with myself that I wouldn't put myself in a situation where I could ever be betrayed or hurt again.

My CORE COPING STRATEGIES

I take charge. I mobilize whatever resources are needed to make things happen. I can direct—and eventually dominate—a situation, expanding my control over other people and over things. The more I force my energy outward, the more protected and less vulnerable I feel. Then, others are less likely to oppose me, and if they do, I will impose my will. I expect that others will fall in line.

SENSE OF SELF ("I am...")

I see myself as a strong, in-control, and self-reliant person. I am strong-willed and get things done. While these qualities are positive, my over-reliance on them means I have great difficulty in experiencing the full range of my humanity, including hurt feelings and vulnerability. I don't recognize that vulnerability contributes to my real source of strength.

WHERE I MISS THE MARK
(*The energetic drive of the passion*)

I live life with intensity, and sometimes excessive intensity. I use more energy than I need for most activities and interactions. The more I push outward and the more energy I expend, the more real I feel. My intense energy pushes other people away from me, and, simultaneously, feels like it protects me. Ultimately, however, that creates the exact opposite of what I really want. This passion is called *lust*.

REMINDER: No matter what type you are dominant in, the passion is a part of the personality and is a motivator that drives your emotional life. The passion covers up a wound in your heart[1] and creates an emotional reaction to how you relate to life, which takes you away from what your soul loves. This is true for all personality types.

HABIT OF THE MIND *(Fixation of the personality)*

I *objectify* others[2] so that they don't seem real or special to me. The *others* in my life just become objects that could get in the way. This makes it easy to see the other person as a threat to my control, and I make the other person my enemy. Doing so allows me to express my anger and rage.

> **REMINDER**: No matter what type you are dominant in, the fixation is a part of the personality. It's a motivator in your fixed behaviors and thoughts about yourself and the world. It bolsters a false sense of reality, and as the ego's automatic, unquestioned way of solving problems with life, it takes you away from your true self. This is true for all personality types.

INNER CRITIC MESSAGE
(What my Inner Critic insists upon)

I am good or okay if I am strong and in control of a situation.[3] My inner critic doesn't allow me to discern between situations in which I could relax and those in which taking charge would be appropriate. As long as I'm caught in the inner critic's web, I try to impose my control and truth over other people. I carry a huge burden of feeling responsible for others.

Each of the elements described above contributes to the whole experience of what we have come to think of as ourselves. The core belief, the emotional force of the passion, the mental habit (fixation), and the inner critic all unconsciously conspire to reinforce the Triangle of Identity.

Additional Information on the Enneagram Type Eight

What causes me *stress*

My over-reliance on my bodily strength is a cause of stress and eventually contributes to significant physical problems. When I become overly self-sufficient, demanding, and controlling, my stress spirals upward. It increases when I avoid showing tenderness.

When I'm most *constricted and inflexible*

I am dictatorial and can be violent.

I am filled with uncontrollable rage.

I am above the law.

Other Personality Types Related to Type Eight

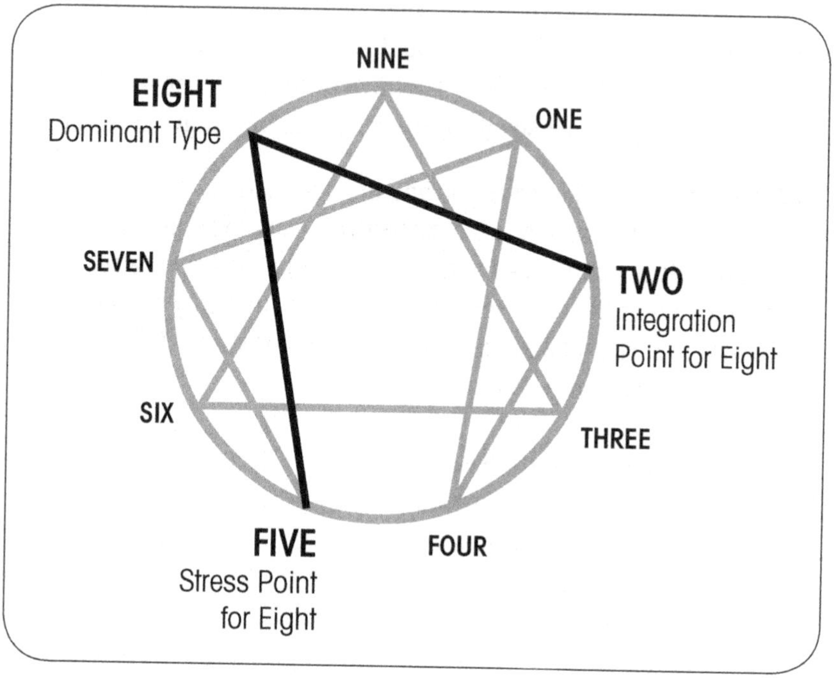

Figure 11-3: The Stress and Integration Points for Type Eight

People dominant in Type Eight experience characteristics of Type Five under stress. Type Five is the *Stress Point* for Type Eight. For more information on this, see chapter 8. Pay particular attention to the sections on average-level behaviors and to the "Notice and Observe Patterns" section of that chapter.

Type Eight's *Integration Point*, including the *Hidden Dimension of Self*, is found in Type Two. See chapter 13 for more information on Type Two. For Type Eight's Integration Point, pay particular attention to the "Gifts" and "At My Best" sections in chapter 13. For Type Eight's Hidden Dimension of Self, review the sections on average levels of behavior in that same chapter.

The Enneagram also works in reverse, which yields helpful information to everyone discovering their dominant type: Type Eight is the Stress Point for Type Two, and it's the Integration Point for Type Five.

Recognizing Patterns
That Pull You Off-Course

Notice and Observe Patterns

In this section you'll find some of the patterns that are associated with the Type Eight personality structure. These patterns provide useful information. Rather than making you bad or wrong in some way, these patterns can be used as signposts on your path of awakening. They help you notice and get to the heart of your experience in a tangible, direct way. Eventually, you can relax the particular, habitual—and often troublesome—strategies, which will allow you to be more present, open, and free.

The pattern of intensifying your energy

One of the challenges that people dominant in Eight face is the intensity with which they live life. Remember that this intensity has helped protect you against feeling that early hurt from your childhood.

- Notice what your energy *feels like* to you. Can you sense it in your body?
- Notice how you *push your energy* into others. You might experience that you are energetically pushing against others with the force of your energy. Notice the volume of your voice and physically pushing out your chest.
- What are you looking for from the person you are interacting with when you're using your intensity? What happens inside you when the other person is also intense?
- What happens when the other person backs away from you? What happens when you relax your energy, even just a little? What difference does that make in an interaction?
- Notice how people interact with you. Do they tend to move toward you or away from you? Do others tend to keep a *respectful distance* from you, or do they back away because they're overwhelmed by your energy?

- Notice if you feel more alive when your energy is big and is pushing against others. What are some of the consequences of your intensity on your mental, physical, and emotional health; on your relationships; and on other aspects of your life?
- You might also notice that you want to own and control more things or people, scooping them under your sphere of influence. What urge is satisfied when you expand your territory of control? What motivation lies underneath this urge?

The pattern of being the rock

People dominant in Type Eight feel that they need to be strong not only for themselves but for others. And they define strength as not expressing their more tender feelings, and not being vulnerable.

- Notice what being strong feels like for you. What physical sensations tell you that you are strong? What's underneath the compulsion to be strong?
- How does being the rock contribute to your *sense of self*?
- Notice how it is for you when you take a stand. How hard is it for you to have a change of heart or perspective? If you feel that, once you've taken a stand, you can't change, what do you tell yourself about changing? What do you sense you're risking?
- How satisfying are your relationships? Whose needs are being met when you take the stand of being the strong, in-control person in the relationship?

The pattern of protecting your tender side

Eights think that they have to be tough, and they equate bold, big energy and directness with strength.

- What is your experience of your heart when you define this intense energy with strength?
- Are there people with whom you can share your true feelings, your doubts, your sorrows? How do others get to know your softer side? What requirements do you have for letting another person in?
- How do you show your tenderness and deep caring towards those who are important to you? Try to identify what words you use or what actions you take. What have you noticed about how these people respond to your actions and words?

- When you allow yourself to experience more of your tenderness, what difference does it make for you? What difference does it appear to make in your relationships?

The pattern of believing it's you against the world

When in the grip of the personality, people dominant in Eight have a hidden sense that others are against them, and will treat them unfairly or take advantage of them in some way. To protect themselves or those they are protecting, they can put up a ready-made defense system that dares people to defy them. Others feel that you're rejecting them from the outset, and therefore keep you at a distance.

If you have a sense that you or the territory that you control is threatened, notice if you are quick to anger. Sometimes your anger explodes when you're not expecting it to, leading to aggressive behavior that you may later regret or have to explain away to others.

Seldom do any of us encounter real dangers or threats. What if others weren't really against you? What difference would that make in your interactions? In your anger level?

Surprising and Effective Practices for Building Your Capacity

The following capacity-building practices will help you turn toward your true nature.

1. Become acquainted with a quieter dimension of your life.

It may be surprising to you to realize that anger does not necessarily need to be expressed outwardly. Sometimes, it's more than sufficient to just allow yourself to feel the pulse of anger moving through you, without taking action or voicing it.

Get to know the circumstances under which you become most reactive, most angry. Are there certain things that are more apt to set you off? You might also notice if you're more reactive when you drink alcohol or use other drugs.

Once you begin to identify these circumstances, experiment with allowing yourself to have a direct experience of your anger. Wait and listen. Quietly observe how it rises up within you, then courses through your body without your having to do anything else. Notice what your anger wants you to do or to say. Take long, deep breaths into your belly, and just observe the nature of this pattern without following through on your urges.

2. Experiment with your energy.

How do you know how much energy or force is required to complete a certain task or to have a successful negotiation? People dominant in Eight use an excessive amount of energy, regardless of the amount that's actually required for the task. Experiment with decreasing the amount of force or energy that you're using for a particular task or interaction. It'll feel unfamiliar and initially may lead to an undesired experience of vulnerability. Stay with it, and see what the actual outcome is. Likely, you'll find that you do not need to expend nearly the amount of energy that you typically use, but still get satisfying results, perhaps even better ones than you were getting before.

Practice relaxing your energy, and not holding on to something so tightly (both literally and figuratively). What does it feel like to *let go*?

You also can explore the level of energy expressed in your willfulness, that experience of "it will be done my way!" What do you tell yourself will happen if something is not done your way?

What do you know about simply *allowing* rather than pushing? You have the capacity to use different amounts of energy in different circumstances. Practice discerning how much energy is needed. When is enough, enough?

3. What if others are really not against you?

You have a natural inclination to believe that others are a potential threat or that they could be in a position to take advantage of you. It can feel like they're on the other team, or on the other side of the encroaching battle. But what if that isn't true? What if you're really on the same side, wanting the same thing, even if you have a difference of opinion about strategies?

How would that impact you? How would that change your orientation to the other person?

You may be surprised to experience that you have a natural tenderness for others. When you keep your heart open and allow yourself to be touched by another human, you come into contact with a powerful, magnetic quality. Your own heartfulness offers a source of surprising intelligence and strength. Many people dominant in Type Eight report that as their own hearts open, people they care about are more open-hearted and want to be closer to them.

An effective practice in letting others in is to slow your pace, quiet your energy, and truly listen to another person's perspective with an intention of understanding them more fully. You can also share your perspective, not from a place of having to get your way, but from an intention of mutual understanding and creating a solution where both of you feel good about the outcome.

4. Enjoy without controlling.

What do you do to simply enjoy, without the need for owning or controlling?

Taking time in nature to quiet yourself and *to be*, without a focus on outcomes, is naturally restorative.

Learn to ground yourself in the moment and find your inner sense of center. Here, within your belly, you can develop access to a natural source of embodied and natural strength without effort.

Practice meditation and conscious-breathing techniques to help you reduce your inner tension and stress. Walk more consciously, using a slower pace and taking in some of the neutral, external world. Notice the aliveness that's available to you without overexerting yourself.

What do you notice when you quiet and calm yourself? What is it like to let yourself into your own heart? You might discover your extraordinary capacity for being a force for genuine, real love.

5. Take care of your body.

As a by-product of using a lot of physical energy, it's easy to override the needs and signals that your body communicates.

Living with such gusto pushes the limits of your body, and, over time, this can lead to serious health consequences.

Pay attention to your health habits. Have you had a recent physical exam? Do you eat regular meals or tend to have one really large meal? Do you get a full night's sleep or try to get by with as little sleep as possible? Are you constantly on the go, or is there a balance between your outgoing activities and slowing down? Depending on your current health habits, it may serve you to consult with a health practitioner who can help evaluate your health status and work with you to determine the need for any adjustments in your health-related activities.

Become more attuned to what is good and not so good for your body—your body will tell you which is which—to help you make wise decisions.

Forging Your Healing and Evolutionary Path

A major theme of this book is that the primary reason for working with the Enneagram is to help us awaken to our true nature. It puts us on a path of healing and real transformation that, for most of us, takes place over time—with patience, trust, faith in our awakening journey—and by being as present as possible. Section III takes us into processes that support and are beneficial for everyone, regardless of type.

Not surprisingly, there are specific processes that are vital for individuals dominant in each type.

If you are dominant in Type Eight, your healing and evolutionary path includes the following:

Discover the innate strength that is an integral part of letting other people be close to you. As you open your heart to yourself and to others, bit by bit, you'll discover a strength that you haven't known before.

Let go of the role of constantly being the rock for others. Let others know that you, too, value and need support. The mutual expression of support is a part of important, healthy relationships.

Notice that you have needs. This is so hard to see in yourself, as it's not been a part of your self-image. But you're human, and all humans need others and need to be cared for. When you don't recognize this within yourself, you can unconsciously look needy as you move to the Hidden Self in the Direction of Integration at Point Two. It's hard to accept this discovery of the *Hidden Dimension of Self*—but as you allow yourself to recognize your desire to be shown love and are able to identify how you have unconsciously expressed this desire in a way that looks needy, it surprisingly will lead you to come into contact with your true inner strength. From this source of real strength, you are a natural catalyst for creating a positive impact in the world.

> **REMINDER:** The Hidden Dimension of Self is found at the average and lower levels of health in the Integration Point.

Allow your deep caring of others to be expressed. You have an amazing capacity to connect with and uplift people. Your authentic caring and love of others are your most naturally powerful and influential gifts.

Surrender to the simple joys of just being alive. You have a natural capacity to savor the fullness and delight of even the seemingly small things in life. Your senses come alive as you take in the smile of another, of a cloudless or cloud-filled sky, of the sun-drenched fragrances of a warm fall day, of a child at play. There's no end to the possibilities available to you for experiencing the richness of the simple pleasures that enliven your soul.

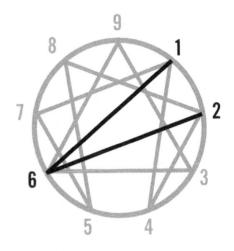

Social Style Cluster Three

The Service-Oriented, Responsible Group— Types One, Two, and Six

Shared Themes

Figuring out the *rules of engagement* and *what needs to be done* are two strategies that can be used to cope with the stress that accompanies interpersonal relationships for people dominant in Types One, Two, and Six.

When in the grip of the personality, people dominant in these three Enneagram types share the common personality structure of having a strong inner sense of obligation. They can be called the *service-oriented types*.

If your dominant type is in this cluster, you may notice the premise that you have to take care of what you see as your responsibilities before taking care of your own needs. You are probably vigilant and often scan the environment to ensure that you follow deeply embedded inner rules that tell you what you need to do. Thus, your *sense of self* revolves being responsible and dutiful. Your own mental rules and inner guideposts are subject to the mind's ever-changing nature.

Each of these types has difficulty in quieting their minds. Service-oriented types often secretly feel that they are better than others because of what they feel are their *superior* ways of making things work right or of taking care of others. They can be counted on to fulfill their responsibilities.

Being of service to others is a healthy attribute. However, when the *dutiful* strategy is an automatic and habitual pattern, the resulting stress—and the eventual burnout—that is heightened by the never-ending list of things that need to be fixed will take their toll. Since the list of responsibilities continues to expand, there is never adequate time to take care of personal needs, and a sense of being unappreciated grows. Ultimately, people dominant in these types can sacrifice their own lives by continually trying to *make things right,* insisting that others' needs come before their own, or being overly responsible to a host of external commitments.

Energetically, people dominant in these three type structures often display what Horney called *moving toward others*, as they monitor the environment for cues that they need to *do something*. They may convey a sense of urgency, or express an imperative to keep busy, becoming quite anxious when they don't know what to do next. They may seem overly ready to help out or to take on additional responsibilities, even at their own expense. They may also appear fidgety or tense, especially in quieter moments.

An important part of the inner journey for people dominant in these three structures is moving *from* "being busy and dutiful" *to* "contacting the still mind."

The Human Condition and Consciousness of Type One: The Reformer

A professional in midlife transition, Veronica was drawn to coaching by a desire that is shared among many people at this stage of life. She wanted to live with purpose, and she wanted to experience more balance and inner peace.

A longtime executive director for a large, non-profit organization, she felt spent by over twenty years of shouldering the responsibilities that go with leading a mission-oriented enterprise. She planned to retire from her position and wanted to approach her final year with the organization differently.

She loved her work and devoted long hours to it, often working far into the night for the good of the cause. She also wanted things done a certain way, and she took on tasks herself if she wasn't happy with how her staff handled things.

Veronica had been introduced to the Enneagram years earlier but was just now returning to it, as she realized that it held some answers for her. Dominant in the Type One personality structure, she began to recognize the following longheld patterns:

- *the high expectations she had for herself, and for everyone who worked for her. She could be both critical and resentful when her staff did not live up to the standards that should have seemed obvious to them. She judged herself heavily when she didn't live up to her own standards, as well.*

- *the belief that she was personally responsible for almost everything that involved her. The more stressed she was, the greater the sense that she was responsible for making things right. "If I don't fix it, who will?"*
- *making a mission out of most things that she did. She saw that most tasks and projects took on an exaggerated significance in an attempt to reach some ideal.*
- *the familiar feeling of being frustrated with whatever was going on, and not able to celebrate the fruits of the amazing contributions of her organization.*

One major theme of the coaching relationship focused on practicing kindness to herself. She came to see how hard she was on herself, being highly self-critical and hearing mostly negative messages that came from an insistent and stern inner voice. She worked with a gentle yoga teacher who helped her soften the tightness in her body. She spent more time with a couple of important friends who loved her and provided another source of kindness. She practiced letting people be gentle with her, even though she found that to be extremely difficult.

Over time, she became kinder to herself and found that her attitude toward her staff also softened. While listening to their perspectives with less need to defend her ideas, she came to discover that they were on the same side of most issues as she, even if they expressed themselves in a different way.

Structuring her life to work less hours, she registered for a photography class, a secret desire that she'd never allowed herself to try before. Her new, ongoing practice was to disengage from the inner critic and refocus on her breath, her belly, and her heart.

The more present Veronica became, the more grateful she was for even the little joys and blessings in life, and the more she accepted herself.

The Internal Coherence of the Type One Experience

Your True Nature

If this is your dominant Enneagram point, your soul is naturally drawn to the integral goodness of life. You resonate with the integrity and alignment of your body, heart, and mind with the Light above and the ground below. Everything has its place. Your expanded perception includes seeing the perfection of life's unfolding, even when there's trouble in the world. You open to and respect your own goodness.

When not in touch with your true nature, what you might not recognize *yet* is that there is nothing you need to make happen or fix in order to experience the sweet nature of goodness. There's momentous relief in realizing that there's a greater intelligence at work, and that you're an integral part of this.

The Story of Your Life: Relating to Your Inner and Outer World

Your inner sense of self and your place in the world were set in place early in life. How you internalized your experiences contributed to the characteristic way you relate to yourself and others, and to your very way of being. If this is your dominant type, the following brief story of your childhood inner experience will likely sound very familiar.

From your earliest childhood years, you tried so hard to be good, but it often felt like you couldn't be as good as you needed to be. As you grew, you sensed that you were expected to assume a great deal of responsibility, and that you needed to live up to a certain standard. You may have heard a message similar to "You can do better than that" or "That's not right and you know it. Get it right."

You internalized these expectations and took it on yourself to see what needed to be fixed and to fix it. Even when you were young, you followed certain procedures or internal rules to lessen the possibility of error. It was hard to meet your own standards, and you got frustrated when others didn't look like they were trying as hard as you.

You looked to your father or father figure for guidance, however, that person might have been very strict or too lax for you. With the guidance that you were looking for absent, you started to set your own boundaries, and in effect, starting policing yourself. You were hard on yourself, and punished yourself before anyone else could punish you or tell you that you were doing something wrong. You put enormous energy into trying to be beyond error itself, and you became very critical of yourself. It was very painful if someone else reprimanded you.

In attempts to be helpful to others, you could also be hard on others. Even now, you may sometimes feel like you're the only one who can do it right, and that you're the only adult in the room.

Your life became organized around the concept or the necessity of being right, because it's simply intolerable to make a mistake or, worse, to be criticized, as this only reinforced your sense of being wrong or bad. This has created a lot of constraints and tenseness in your body. You have spent much of your life trying to be good, because it was hard to see yourself as a good person.

What you didn't see in yourself was your inherent goodness. You didn't realize that being human includes making human mistakes. You didn't know that what may seem like imperfection is not a reflection of some deep-rooted flaw but a part of the natural flow of life. Your heart longs for you to be kind to yourself. You can trust your strong inner compass to guide you in following your higher purpose and savoring the joys of life.

Your Great Loss

As a little being, even before your conscious thought and language skills developed, you had experiences that left you feeling separated from these essential qualities that your soul loved—that it was in tune with. This pain was too much to bear, so the ego structure began to form, taking on the role of protecting you from the severity of this early loss.

We remember that the ego attempts to mimic our true nature, though it can never be successful in doing so. So, the One personality structure has tried to recreate the experience of perfection and a sense of rightness in life. It's a lot of work to create perfection when there are so many aspects of life that seem poorly structured or faulty in their functioning. There's always a sense of obligation, and there's never an end to the things that need fixing.

Here is the great loss—the pain—for Type One: There's a sense of having fallen out of grace, and that there's something essentially wrong, even bad, about you. It feels like you have to constantly work hard to overcome whatever it is that feels wrong, shouldering an enormous sense of responsibility. When your inherent goodness isn't recognized, your sense of something being wrong in you is further magnified.

The Inner Logic and the Triangle of Identity for Type One

Type One's CORE BELIEF

We see that a core belief is set into place, providing an unconscious filter that accepts only information that supports the ego's belief. This filter, unfortunately, misses and dismisses data that would otherwise provide alternate perspectives. This belief acts as a core operating principle that shapes a person's relationship to life.

Each core belief is false but feels real. The more it can be brought into the light of awareness with great compassion and truthfulness over time, the less hold it will have.

For the One structure, the core belief is that, "Something is wrong with me. I can't trust myself to be good, therefore, I have to guard against my own potential wrongdoing. I have to create my own rules and police myself so that I will be good."

How might this show up in your life? Here are some examples of what you might hear yourself think, say, or do/not do:

- It's my responsibility for making and doing things right. I'll work as hard as I need to get things done. Who else would do this?
- If I'm not hard on myself and keep correcting myself, then

something ugly could pop up.

- Sure I have a lot of opinions. I can see very clearly what's right and what's wrong.
- What's wrong with these people that they can't figure this out?

This core belief leads us to the **Triangle of Identity**, *which provides a shorthand illustration of how you "do" life.* I invite you to try on the following description to see how it fits with your experience.

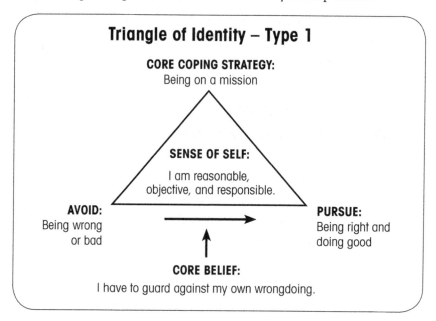

Figure 12-1: The Triangle of Identity for Type One

Here is how a person with the Type One personality structure might recognize this inner logic that is illustrated by the Triangle of Identity:

*I **pursue** doing what is right and that will result in me being a good person. I see what needs to be improved, and I put a lot of energy into making it right.*

*I **avoid** being wrong or being criticized, which makes me feel like a bad person. I keep myself in check, correcting myself and others to avoid the internal experience that I'm at fault, and thereby guilty of being bad.*

*I **cope** by being on a mission. The mission is supported by having high standards and opinions about how things could be improved, and* *being responsible for making things better.*

As an extension of my coping strategy, I can see how my life is or was organized around the importance of fixing things, including myself. The resentment that comes from dissatisfaction with how things are fuels the engine to get things done. If only I can fix the situation, then I can feel like I am good, at least for the moment. Having spent much of my life trying to be good, I can be very critical of myself first, which spills onto others.

All of this leads me to see myself as a reasonable, responsible, and objective person. This self-definition—this **sense of self**—*ends up imposing limits. It keeps me from recognizing and appreciating the fuller range of my human experience.*

While these are positive qualities, when they're overused, they limit my ability to acknowledge and express my emotional or spiritual dimensions. Any experience that I interpret as being nonrational is suppressed, creating a buildup of explosive energy. This self-concept obstructs my ability to recognize that my perspective is one of many possibilities.

An Awakened Capacity of Type One: Joyful Serenity

You have an amazing capacity for accepting the fullness of the moment with a quiet joy and serenity. With a mind that's calm and accepting of what's here, you heart is filled with awe. When you look out at the world from this orientation, you know that all is well and right.

When you have forgotten and lost contact with your innate capacity for serenity with the way things are, you can become resentful because of the mistaken sense of having so much to do and the belief that others aren't pulling their own weight. It feels as if there's a never-ending list of things that need your responsible attention, and you increasingly become insistent that yours is the right way. You become identified with a very limited definition of yourself.

You forget that you're not responsible for fixing the world. You forget that there are other valid viewpoints, and that there's a bigger intelligence than what you can see through your own eyes. Accepting the moment is a key to unlocking the door to a freer life. Practicing acceptance does not diminish your capacity for contributing to the higher good. What's missing is the compulsion to be responsible for it all.

The Iceberg Model for Type One reiterates some of this material in a visual format.

The model starts with some of the expansive qualities that are innate gifts of individuals dominant in this type. These qualities are naturally and increasingly experienced as we recognize and gradually release our attachment to our more limited definition of self. The Iceberg Model also increases our understanding of the observable expressions found at the average level of behavior of Type One individuals, and it fills out more of what goes on below the waterline, i.e., those inner dynamics that shape and motivate the behaviors that occur when the personality has its grip on us. (Refer to chapter 5 for more discussion on the Iceberg Model.)

Decoding the Personality Structure of Type One

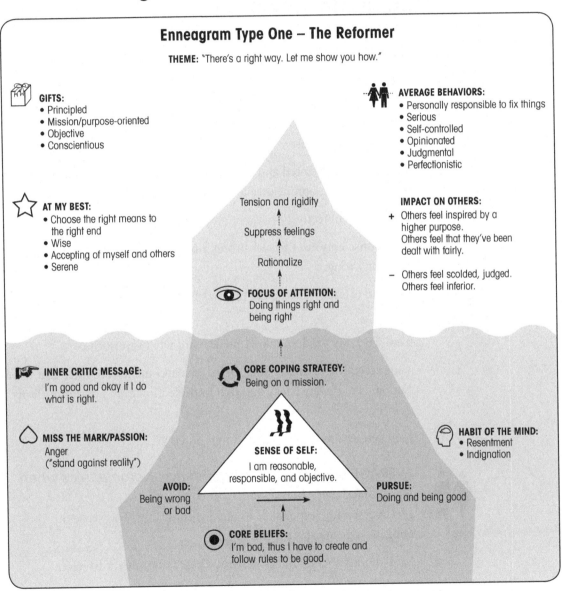

Enneagram Type One – The Reformer

THEME: "There's a right way. Let me show you how."

GIFTS:
- Principled
- Mission/purpose-oriented
- Objective
- Conscientious

AT MY BEST:
- Choose the right means to the right end
- Wise
- Accepting of myself and others
- Serene

AVERAGE BEHAVIORS:
- Personally responsible to fix things
- Serious
- Self-controlled
- Opinionated
- Judgmental
- Perfectionistic

IMPACT ON OTHERS:
+ Others feel inspired by a higher purpose.
  Others feel that they've been dealt with fairly.

– Others feel scolded, judged.
  Others feel inferior.

Tension and rigidity

↑

Suppress feelings

↑

Rationalize

↑

FOCUS OF ATTENTION:
Doing things right and being right

INNER CRITIC MESSAGE:
I'm good and okay if I do what is right.

CORE COPING STRATEGY:
Being on a mission.

MISS THE MARK/PASSION:
Anger
("stand against reality")

HABIT OF THE MIND:
- Resentment
- Indignation

SENSE OF SELF:
I am reasonable, responsible, and objective.

AVOID:
Being wrong or bad

PURSUE:
Doing and being good

CORE BELIEFS:
I'm bad, thus I have to create and follow rules to be good.

Figure 12-2: The Iceberg Model for Type One

Type One's THEME:

"There's a right way; let me show you how" is the theme of this personality structure.

Above the Waterline

The Gifts, Daily Habits, and Challenges of Type One

GIFTS and AT MY BEST
(When I'm expansive and at my healthiest)

I am principled and hold high ideals. My principles guide my daily living and decisions.

I am mission-oriented and have a higher purpose. I am involved in issues that have significance for the larger good.

I see things objectively, without emotional overtones or judgment.

I am conscientious. I have a strong inner compass of what is morally right or wrong.

The end is important. So are the means. I do not sacrifice one for the other.

I am wise. My wisdom takes into account what is possible.

I am accepting of myself and others. I have come to recognize that to be human is to be imperfect, and that imperfection does not diminish my goodness.

I am serene and experience an inner quiet.

AVERAGE BEHAVIORS *(Distinguishing characteristics when my personality has its grip on me)*

I feel personally responsible to make things right. This sense of obligation permeates my thinking.

I am serious and see life as *weighty*. There's no time for frivolous pursuits.

I control myself and push away my inner impulses.

I have and often voice opinions on just about everything. I think and talk in terms of what *should* be done.

I am quick to judge others. I constantly judge myself, and my every thought and action are under critical scrutiny.

I spend a lot of energy in trying not to make mistakes. I seek perfection and am often disappointed in myself for not achieving it. So I try even harder.

FOCUS OF ATTENTION, or FOA *(Where I put my attention when I'm attached to my personality)*

NOTE: *This is a brief description of what happens as the FOA becomes narrower and narrower. It's important to note that the degree to which our FOA is activated is shaped by our degree of presence. With more presence, what we pay attention to expands, rather than narrows.*

When my personality has its grip on me, I put my attention on getting things right, even if I'm the only one defining what is right. What gets my attention are things that need to be improved, changed, or fixed. This entails monitoring verbal and written communications to make sure that I get things *right*. It entails scanning for cues from the environment to determine if comments that are made during a conversation mean that I need to make a change.

It feels deadly for me to be wrong, so I can come up with rationales for my decisions, leaving little room for questioning or uncertainty. *Because* is one of my frequently used words.

I don't trust my body or my feelings. Both feel irrational and messy, so I try to suppress them.

The more I suppress my inner experiences, the tighter and more tense and rigid I become. My body often aches, and it becomes increasingly difficult to enjoy any aspect of life.

+ My IMPACT ON OTHERS

+ Positive:

- Others can be inspired by my integrity, conscientiousness, and willingness to take a stand for the higher good.
- Others appreciate my concern and fairness.

– Negative:

- Others can feel judged, criticized, and inferior.
- Others may feel the need to monitor or restrain themselves so that they're not scolded.

Below the Waterline

To understand the inner dynamics for Type One, we turn our attention to what lies under the surface of the water, starting at the bottom and working up.

Type One's CORE BELIEF

This core operating principle filters through many layers of life, in both seen and unseen ways.

My core belief is that I am inherently bad. I have to create my own rules, and I police myself so that I'll make myself good.

The TRIANGLE OF IDENTITY

What I PURSUE

I *pursue* doing things that I think are good and will result in me being a good person. When aspects of my environment, including tasks, people, systems, or situations are not dealt with correctly, I naturally take it on myself to remedy them. There is an order that makes perfect sense to me, and if it's not in place, I create the order.

What I AVOID

I *avoid* being wrong or criticized, which makes me feel like a bad person. I monitor and regulate myself and whatever is in my environment to guard against the possibility that my emotions or instincts would overtake my logical mind, as that would likely lead to making mistakes. Dealing with imperfection is the hardest thing in life for me.

My CORE COPING STRATEGY

I *cope* by turning tasks into a mission that will result in improvements. I hold high standards and expectations for myself and others, and I'm quick to voice my opinions about how things could be better. I easily shoulder responsibility for fixing whatever doesn't look right to me.

SENSE OF SELF *("I am...")*

I see myself as reasonable, objective, and responsible. I keep my emotions in check, as they only make things messy. As a rational person, I see things rightly and know the best course of action.

WHERE I MISS THE MARK
(The energetic drive of the passion)

I have a simmering anger toward many things that go on around me and in the world. I don't express this anger directly because it could get out of control. But I certainly feel exasperated and experience an internal stewing.

This simmering anger can be an expression of my righteousness or an expression of my ego's belief that it really does know what is best. In reality, this happens when I resist *what is.*

> **REMINDER:** No matter what type you are dominant in, the passion is a part of the personality and is a motivator that drives your emotional life. The passion covers up a wound in your heart[1] and creates an emotional reaction to how you relate to life, which takes you away from what your soul loves. This is true for all personality types.

HABIT OF THE MIND *(Fixation of the personality)*

I experience a great amount of resentment, which is fueled by my judging mind.

I can have a strong sense of indignation and irritation when others don't act in accordance with what I think is best or when life doesn't unfold the way I think is right.

REMINDER: No matter what type you are dominant in, the fixation is a part of the personality. It's a motivator in your fixed behaviors and thoughts about yourself and the world. It bolsters a false sense of reality, and as the ego's automatic, unquestioned way of solving problems with life, it takes you away from your true self. This is true for all personality types.

INNER CRITIC MESSAGE
(What my Inner Critic insists upon)

I have a strong inner critic, which is quick to judge myself and others, and it has a litany of "shoulds" and obligations.[2] This inner critic insists that I *do what is right*. That is, I must follow my inner critic's assessment of what it deems to be right if I am to see myself as being okay. As long as I'm caught in the web of my inner critic, I'll be highly critical of myself and others, which creates enormous inner pain.

Each of the elements described above contributes to the whole experience of what we have come to think of as ourselves. The core belief, the emotional force of the passion, the mental habit (fixation), and the inner critic all unconsciously conspire to reinforce the Triangle of Identity.

Additional Information on the Enneagram Type One

What causes me *stress*

My stress increases when I try to control everything so that I do things perfectly. I become overwhelmed when I try to fix too many things at once. And I become fatigued by constantly adhering to impossibly high standards. My constant vigilance causes stress and, often, physical pain.

I become stressed when others don't understand how hard I'm working to do things well.

When I'm most *constricted and inflexible*

I am constantly resentful.

I am unreasonable and closed to any compromise.

I am unethical and act in contradiction to stated principles.

I am brutal in my criticism and self-reproach.

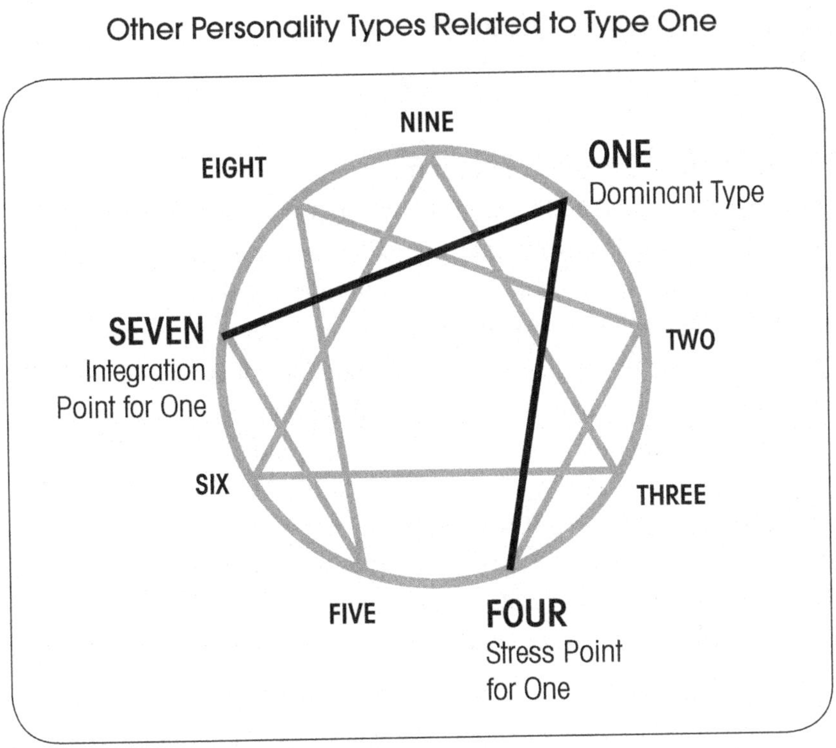

Other Personality Types Related to Type One

Figure 12-3: The Stress and Integration Points for Type One

People dominant in Type One experience characteristics of Type Four under stress. Type Four is the *Stress Point* for Type One. For more information on this, see chapter 7. Pay particular attention to the sections on average-level behaviors and to the "Notice and Observe Patterns" section of that chapter.

Type One's *Integration Point*, including the *Hidden Dimension of Self*, is found in Type Seven. See chapter 10 for more information on Type Seven. For Type One's Integration Point, pay particular attention to the "Gifts" and "At My Best" sections in chapter 10. For Type One's Hidden Dimension of Self, review the sections on average levels of behavior in that same chapter.

The Enneagram also works in reverse, which yields helpful information to everyone discovering their dominant type: Type One is the Stress Point for Type Seven, and it's the Integration Point for Type Four.

Recognizing Patterns That Pull You Off-Course

Notice and Observe Patterns

In this section you'll find some of the patterns that are associated with the Type One personality structure. These patterns provide useful information. Rather than making you bad or wrong in some way, these patterns can be used as signposts on your path of awakening. They help you notice and get to the heart of your experience in a tangible, direct way. Eventually, you can relax the particular, habitual—and often troublesome—strategies, which will allow you to be more present, open, and free.

The pattern of being the judge

When in the grip of the personality, people dominant in Type One feel the heavy weight of an inner critic, also known as *the judge*, that's relentless in its negative commentary on others and on one's self. The critic has an endless number of *rules* and expectations for perfection.

The work of the judge is sometimes loud, and sometimes quiet, and is so persistent that it seems to have a life of its own. It also can feel like the voice of God.

What are the messages of your inner critic? Notice its persistence. What do you notice about the impact of the inner critic's messages to you? How does the inner critic affect how you relate to others? Detect the critic's expectations as you go through your day.

Notice how the standards or rules that the inner critic uses to evaluate your behavior change from situation to situation. Observe what you do to comply with the inner critic.

Remember that being the judge has helped protect you against feeling that early hurt from your childhood.

The pattern of resentment and anger

Notice how often you experience either anger or resentment. Keep track of this for a few days. Is it okay for you to be angry, or do you try to suppress your anger? Notice how you express or suppress your anger.

Even if it's unacceptable to be angry, how does it leak out? Listen to the sound and intonation of your voice.

What does your resentment feel like? How do you know when you're resentful? What do you tell yourself? What physical sensations do you experience?

How do you behave?

The pattern of having a tense body

People dominant in Type One tend to hold a significant amount of tension in their bodies. Tension is a way of suppressing unacceptable emotions and attempting to restrict unacceptable behaviors. Tension can be thought of as a physical manifestation of the inner critic.

Notice where you tend to hold your tension. Your shoulders? Your back? Your jaw? Where do you experience pain? Do you have frequent headaches or migraines? Other physical ailments?

How does bodily tension influence your ability to be flexible and to move with ease?

The pattern of shouldering responsibility

When the personality is in the driver's seat, people dominant in Type One feel obligated to *do the right thing* and *to fix* whatever they deem needs fixing. They shoulder responsibility as a way to compensate for what they perceive others aren't doing or aren't doing well.

They may be quick to point out to others what needs to be done differently, and take it on themselves to make sure it gets done in accordance with their perception of what's *right*. One of their challenges is to discern between their responsibility and the responsibility of others. They have a tendency to constantly monitor the environment, and it's hard for them to draw the line between what *is and is not* theirs because it seems so obvious as to what needs to be done.

What responsibilities do you take on that truly are not yours? Notice what lies beneath the urge to take on additional responsibility. What is your inner critic's role in taking on responsibility that's not yours?

The pattern of talking down to others

Notice when you try to educate others. You might find yourself talking down so that they can *see the errors of their ways.* This is sometimes referred to as parent-to-child communication. Notice the tone of your voice. What's the underlying message that is being conveyed?

Notice what you do to try and convince others of the correctness of your perspective. Do you ever feel like you're scolding others?

How effective are you when you use this communication style? How influential are you?

The pattern of secret behaviors

The inner critic is a tough taskmaster. It's impossible to constantly control and restrict every aspect of our lives. The more people dominant in One try to repress their emotional or instinctual nature, the more likely they are to have some form of escape hatch[4] as an outlet or release from these restrictions. These indulgences might include bingeing on so-called forbidden food, smoking, illicit sex, the use of illegal drugs, or other behaviors that they would typically condemn but find a way to rationalize. These become part of the secret life of the individual.

Do you have secret behaviors? What are they? How could they be a reaction to the heavy restrictions of your inner critic?

How have you explained these behaviors to yourself? How do you feel when you use them?

Surprising and Effective Practices for Building Your Capacity

The following capacity-building practices will help you turn toward your true nature.

1. Get to know your inner critic.

The inner critic has cast itself as the central and most important figure of your inner psyche. It's important to learn as much about its workings as you can, without becoming attached to or identified with its messages. Create some distance between yourself and the critic and its messages. You can become more familiar with the inner critic by writing down the messages that you have carried around in your head. Consider carrying around a pad of paper for jotting down all the messages that you hear. Up to now, these may have sounded akin to God's words. Now it's time to see them for what they are and their impact. (Chapter 17 addresses the inner critic in some detail.)

Remember that these messages keep you from your own knowing and from your inner wisdom. The inner critic isn't interested in your well-being or in helping you *be better*. It's only interested in its own survival and in keeping things the same. As you create distance between yourself and these messages, they'll carry less weight and you'll have greater access to your heart and to a quieter mind.

2. Go beyond the ego's perfection.

The ego will seldom, if ever, reach a sense of satisfaction with the way things are, and with the perfection that exists beyond our limited human way of seeing life.

Allowing yourself the gift of imperfection is humbling and freeing. Put down the burden of trying to make life perfect—it'll always be imperfect from our human eyes, and after all, you (and we) are human. Your worth isn't based on being perfect.

Experiment with being consciously imperfect. Practice *making mistakes*.

3. Give yourself and others a break.

People express themselves differently than you do. Consider this: What if they aren't *wrong* but simply see the situation from a different perspective than you do? How has being certain served you? How has it limited you?

What would you need to let go of in order to allow for this possibility and to accept this as a valid alternative?

How might it support you to accept the viewpoints of others, even if those are different from yours?

What do you appreciate about others? Practice putting your attention on what's working well and on giving sincere compliments.

As for giving yourself a break, what brings joy to your life? What do you do for play? What brings laughter? What do you love?

If you don't know the answers to these questions, give yourself time to explore. Then, schedule time just for you every week that's for enjoying and appreciating yourself and your life.

4. Take care of yourself *(but not as a "should")*.

- Therapeutic massage or energy work can help you release the tension in your body.
- Incorporate yoga or simple stretching exercises to focus your attention on taking care of your body. It will support your mental and emotional well-being, too.
- Develop a meditative practice to support you in seeing your busy mind at work, and to support the development of a quieter, clearer mind.
- Drop your trying. Adopt enjoyment. See what's worthwhile and a source of grace, joy, or blessing right now.

5. Accept tenderness and caring.

- Remember moments in which you were touched by others' kindnesses toward you. Spend time tapping into any experience of receiving this kindness you might've had.
- What would allow you to receive kindness, caring, generosity, and love from others now?
- Practice staying available and open to receiving.

Forging Your Healing and Evolutionary Path

A major theme of this book is that the primary reason for working with the Enneagram is to help us awaken to our true nature. It puts us on a path of healing and real transformation that, for most of us, takes place over time—with patience, trust, faith in our awakening journey—and by being as present as possible. Section III takes us into processes that support and are beneficial for everyone, regardless of type.

Not surprisingly, there are specific processes that are vital for individuals dominant in each type.

If you are dominant in Type One, your healing and evolutionary path includes the following:

Become accepting of all of yourself. Habitual beliefs, ideas, and opinions have kept you contained and tense. There's much more of you to experience.

Quiet the mind and let go of constantly monitoring yourself and your environments to determine what needs to be fixed.

Make contact with your heart, and notice what you're feeling. You may experience a lot of sadness and other emotions that are initially difficult to bear. Yet much of your desire to make the world a better place comes from your deep caring.

Notice when you become scattered, distracted, self-centered, and have a hard time following through. It's so hard to see these qualities in yourself, as they are far outside the scope of your self-identity. Yet in your natural movement into the *Hidden Dimension of Self* found in Type Seven, you will experience these characteristics. You probably never had permission to express them, so they seem like the antithesis of what is acceptable to you. Yet as you recognize and begin to accept these qualities in yourself, they will lead you to experience and integrate the higher levels of Seven—your natural joy and love of life.

> **REMINDER:** The Hidden Dimension of Self is found at the average and lower levels of health in the Integration Point.

Accept the nature of the human experience with its strengths, its limitations, and its majesty. Look up and notice what you see. There's so much in life that calls for your gratitude and awe. This is the gift of your Integration Point.

13

The Human Condition and Consciousness of Type Two: The Helper

Christina had been experiencing an inner urge for some time that she couldn't quite name. A highly regarded expert in her field, she could no longer continue with her long work hours, anxious nights, and the financial strain created by undercharging for her services. While she wanted to change her life, she didn't know what that meant and was reluctant to find out. Still, she sought coaching to support her through this time of internal and external transition.

When she discovered that she identified with the Type Two personality, she began to recognize the following patterns that had shaped her life:

- *the habit of overgiving and overextending herself to others. She realized how much of the time she thought about her clients, her friends, and her family members, wondering how they were coping with life's challenges and if there was something else she could do for them.*
- *how hard she worked to make sure other people's needs were met, and her secret resentment when she felt unacknowledged or unappreciated. It was difficult to acknowledge the resentment, as she always tried to be upbeat and positive.*

- *how much attention she paid to how other people responded to her. She interpreted certain behaviors to mean that others liked or disliked her, and her interpretation could affect how she felt for several days.*
- *the difficulty in pursuing what she wanted from life. While there were things she enjoyed, she often was reluctant to engage in them as feelings of guilt would arise.*

As Christina's self-observational skills developed, she began to see both the obvious and the very nuanced ways in which she created situations that were designed to extend herself to others and, in turn, have people like her. Even when she received positive feedback, the impact on her was fleeting. She was amazed at how hard it was not to get hooked by what she thought other people needed from her.

Developing the skill and the capacity to say no to the frequent requests for her time and expertise yielded positive results. This allowed her to say yes when she actually meant it. She was amazed that, most of the time, others respected her decisions. She worked on recognizing when guilt got ignited. With time, with compassion for herself, its control in her life diminished.

One major coaching theme focused on identifying what would truly nourish her heart as an alternative to focusing on other people. She found that taking care of herself required that she have downtime— and alone time—to explore what had meaning for her. *She learned to write herself into her own calendar in order to reinforce this commitment. She eventually recalled how much she had loved poetry as a girl and young woman, and as she began reading and writing her own, her creative energies opened. This quiet space supported her tuning into that inner urging, which was slowly leading her toward a life where she more consciously could acknowledge and integrate her spiritual nature.*

The more present Christina became, the more she came to experience and accept her authentic loving nature.

The Internal Coherence of the Type Two Experience

Your True Nature

If this is your dominant Enneagram point, your soul is naturally drawn to having a deep connection to others. You experience the pure bliss and sweetness of this heart connection without any need to create it. It is just there. Through the heart connection, you're experiencing the delicious quality that is called love.

When not in touch with your true nature, what you might not recognize *yet* is that you don't have to work to create love. You're absolutely lovable and your loving nature is part of your true gift. When you're truly present, and not grasping to make a connection, you have more contact with your own heart. This helps you realize your own needs for balance and self-care. As you focus on this unfamiliar territory, you learn about your own worth and lovability, without needing to earn it.

The Story of Your Life: Relating to Your Inner and Outer World

Your inner sense of self and your place in the world were set in place early in life. How you internalized your experiences contributed to the characteristic way you relate to yourself and others, and to your very way of being. If this is your dominant type, the following brief story of your childhood inner experience will likely sound very familiar.

> From your earliest years, you were a caring, helpful child. Even as a tiny being, you somehow intuited what other people needed and reached out to help others. Perhaps you had younger siblings and felt responsible for taking care of them, even though you were still a toddler or young child yourself.
>
> You soon became to believe that others' needs, particularly the needs of significant others, were more important than any needs you might have. There were times you may have sensed that you were parenting your parents.

You came to believe that love was something that you had to get, and to get it, you first needed to give. As you gave to others, you secretly hoped that they would show you how much they approved of you. If they didn't show love and appreciation in the way that resonated for you, a feeling of being rejected arose.

As you continued to work hard to earn the love of others, it felt that you carried the weight of your family on your shoulders. You were so good at being helpful that others came to see you as being able to shoulder responsibility. Your childhood passed you over.

With the focus on others, you forgot about having your own needs, doubts, and hurts. You learned to feel guilty if you expressed or even experienced your own needs.

You may have heard, "Oh, don't be so selfish. Come take care of your sister," or "Quit whining. Don't you know how much worse off other people are than you?"

Even when you were sick, you may have felt that you couldn't inconvenience others. Perhaps even now it is difficult to recognize that, as a human being, you have needs.

The harder you tried to take care of others, the more you looked for signs of affection—a warm smile, a tight hug, a warmly felt appreciation. It secretly made you angry that others didn't appreciate your efforts more, but you couldn't openly show your anger.

You came to organize your life around the idea that you had to sacrifice yourself in order to receive whatever love looked like in your home. You didn't feel that you were loved or lovable for yourself.

What you didn't see is that you're indeed loved and lovable. What you didn't see is that love is always available to you, just by your being present. What you couldn't see is that you're naturally a source of warmth and caring, even when you recognize and address your own needs.

Your Great Loss

As a little being, even before your conscious thought and language skills developed, you had experiences that left you feeling separated from these essential qualities that your soul loved—that it was in tune with. This pain was too much to bear, so the ego structure began to form, taking on the role of protecting you from the severity of this early loss.

We remember that the ego attempts to mimic our true nature, though it can never be successful in doing so. So, the Two personality structure has tried to recreate the experience of real love through "doing" love, through trying to make love happen. In this way, love becomes an action, a behavior, rather than a true connection with your own and another's heart. The ego takes on a huge project that can never be satisfied or satisfying. Trying to make this connection over and over is exhausting, and at best, only results in a momentary relief.

Staying connected with yourself and with your own heart is required to experience a deep connection with others.

Here is the great loss, the pain for Type Two: Feeling separated from real love conveys a false sense that you're not inherently lovable, and that you have to work hard to create the experience of love. You feel you have to prove your lovability to others, so enormous energy is spent on finding ways to be helpful, caring, and generous.

The Inner Logic and the Triangle of Identity for Type Two

Type Two's CORE BELIEF

We see that a core belief is set into place, providing an unconscious filter that accepts only information that supports the ego's belief. This filter, unfortunately, misses and dismisses data that would otherwise provide alternate perspectives. This belief acts as a core operating principle that shapes a person's relationship to life.

Each core belief is false, but feels real until we can bring it into the light. It is particularly important to approach this with great compassion and truthfulness.

The Two is a heart-oriented type, so as we explore it, we are in very tender territory. Here we see that there are intertwined beliefs, all based on the false presumption that love is not available unless you do something for others first. The fundamental belief is that you have to take care of others before you earn the right to be loved and accepted. Thus, the needs of others come first. You must attend to them before being allowed to have your own needs. It is selfish to have needs of your own.

If you're dominant in Type Two, how might this show up in your life? Here are some examples of what you might hear yourself think, say or do/not do:

- I really don't know how to say no to others. It feels like they know what will push my guilt buttons to get me to agree to take on more responsibilities. But everyone has a lot to do, so why shouldn't I take on the task? If I say no, I will look selfish.
- I often tell people how great they are, make positive comments on something specific about them that I think they would like and tell them how proud they should be of themselves. Doesn't that put me in a good light with them?
- I frequently give gifts to others or extend my help to others. Secretly I hope others will show their appreciation of my generosity.
- How will I ever have time to do everything that I've promised other people? I'm a little tired, but I'll find the energy and figure out a way.

This core belief leads us to the **Triangle of Identity**, *which provides a shorthand illustration of how you "do" life.* I invite you to try on the following description to see how it fits with your experience.

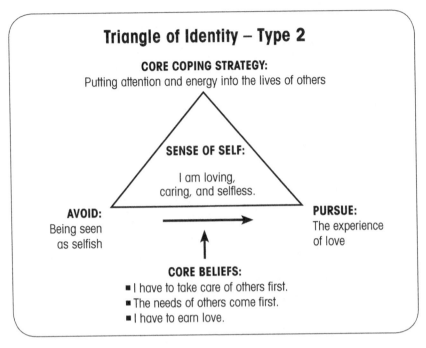

Figure 13-1: The Triangle of Identity for Type Two

Here is how a person with the Type Two personality structure might recognize this inner logic that is illustrated by the Triangle of Identity:

> I **pursue** situations that help create a physical or energetic relationship with others in order to experience a loving connection, and to affirm my loving nature. I define love as reaching out to someone else or doing something for them, to feel a connection with them.

> I **avoid** any experience that would leave me feeling selfish, which would mean that I'm not a loving person. To acknowledge or put attention on my own needs feels threatening. I avoid being seen as even having needs. Putting direct attention on me and asking for what I need, and receiving from others, are the most difficult things in life to do.

> I **cope** by attending to and putting my energy into other people. The lives and needs of others feel far more important, interesting, or urgent than what is happening in my own life. With my attention focused outside of myself, it is easy to think that I don't have needs or that they

are less important than those of others.

As an extension of my coping strategy, I can see how my life has been organized around getting people to like me and, really, to accept me. When I can get positive recognition from them, then I can feel lovable, at least for the moment. Having put so much of my life energy into having people find me worthy of love, I can easily feel rejected and hurt if people back away from me or give me feedback that feels critical, as they sometimes do.

*All of this leads me to see myself as a loving, caring, and selfless person. This self-definition—this **sense of self**—ends up imposing limits. It keeps me from recognizing and appreciating the fuller range of my human experience.*

While being interested in and caring for others are positive qualities, they limit my ability to acknowledge my own needs and express my creative nature when those positive qualities are overused. When my life energy is consistently focused on what I think others need, I miss out on having my own fulfilling life.

An Awakened Capacity of Type Two: Creativity through Humility

The quality of humility signals a particular kind of relationship within oneself and with others. When you recognize that everyone has needs, you include yourself in that awareness. The distinction between the needs of others and your needs melts away, and the needs of others are neither more or less important than yours. When you open your heart to yourself—to all of you, including your interests, joys, and hurts, and take care of yourself in the same meaningful way that you would try to do for others—your capacity for experiencing love is like no other. This gives space for your creative voice to shine through, which fills you up and helps you feel whole.

When you have forgotten or lost contact with your innate capacity for humbly recognizing your own needs, your focus is on what you mistakenly see as the more important needs of others. Guilt rises up when you even begin to consider yourself.

Humbly accepting yourself and your needs are keys to unlocking the door to a freer life. Being generous to yourself doesn't diminish your capacity to be generous with others. What is missing is the compulsion to overdo your attention on others.

The Iceberg Model for Type Two reiterates some of this material in a visual format.

The model starts with some of the expansive qualities that are innate gifts of individuals dominant in this type. These qualities are naturally and increasingly experienced as we recognize and gradually release our attachment to our more limited definition of self. The Iceberg Model also increases our understanding of the observable expressions found at the average level of behavior of Type Two individuals, and it fills out more of what goes on below the waterline, i.e., those inner dynamics that shape and motivate the behaviors that occur when the personality has its grip on us. (Refer to chapter 5 for more discussion on the Iceberg Model.)

Decoding the Personality Structure of Type Two

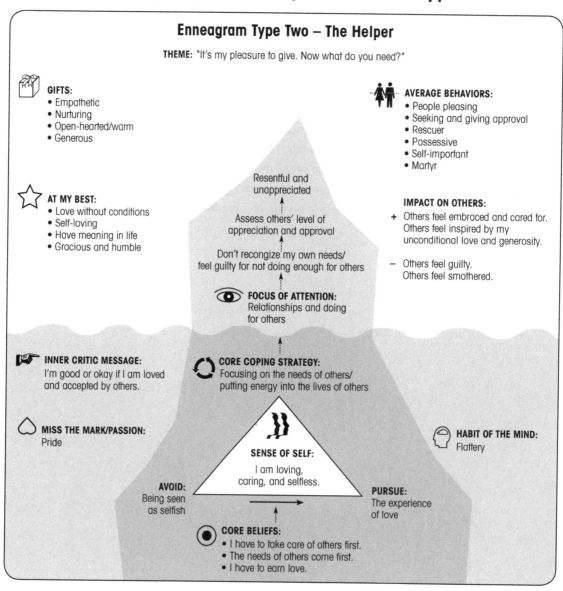

Enneagram Type Two – The Helper

THEME: "It's my pleasure to give. Now what do you need?"

GIFTS:
- Empathetic
- Nurturing
- Open-hearted/warm
- Generous

AT MY BEST:
- Love without conditions
- Self-loving
- Have meaning in life
- Gracious and humble

AVERAGE BEHAVIORS:
- People pleasing
- Seeking and giving approval
- Rescuer
- Possessive
- Self-important
- Martyr

IMPACT ON OTHERS:

+ Others feel embraced and cared for. Others feel inspired by my unconditional love and generosity.

− Others feel guilty. Others feel smothered.

Resentful and unappreciated

Assess others' level of appreciation and approval

Don't recognize my own needs/ feel guilty for not doing enough for others

FOCUS OF ATTENTION: Relationships and doing for others

INNER CRITIC MESSAGE: I'm good or okay if I am loved and accepted by others.

CORE COPING STRATEGY: Focusing on the needs of others/ putting energy into the lives of others

MISS THE MARK/PASSION: Pride

HABIT OF THE MIND: Flattery

SENSE OF SELF: I am loving, caring, and selfless.

AVOID: Being seen as selfish

PURSUE: The experience of love

CORE BELIEFS:
- I have to take care of others first.
- The needs of others come first.
- I have to earn love.

Figure 13-2: The Iceberg Model for Type Two

Type Two's THEME:

"It's my pleasure to give. Now, what do you need?" is the theme of this personality structure.

Above the Waterline

The Gifts, Daily Habits, and Challenges of Type Two

GIFTS and AT MY BEST
(When I'm expansive and at my healthiest)

I am empathetic. I can step into other's shoes and extend myself to them.

I am nurturing. I have an innate sense of what others need. I have the capacity to nourish others.

I am open-hearted and warm. My emotional warmth has an embracing quality, and allows others to feel cared for.

I am generous in doing sincere good works. I can be selfless in giving to others.

I have unconditional love for others. I give without expecting anything back. There are no *strings* attached.

I extend the same generosity and love to myself as I extend to others.

I find meaning in my own life. I find joy in being alive and paying attention to my own needs.

I am gracious and humble. I recognize that life incorporates graciousness in both giving and receiving.

AVERAGE BEHAVIORS (Distinguishing characteristics when my personality has its grip on me)

I am a people-pleaser. I try to get people to like me through my giving behavior.

Approval is important for me to receive and to give. I look to others for their approval.

Others may see me as a rescuer. I tend to attract people into my life who, from my perspective, need rescuing. This is also known as *co-dependency*.

I can be possessive of others, wanting their attention and closeness. Other people may see me as being intrusive and trying too hard to get physically or emotionally *close and personal* with them.

I like to feel that I'm important in other people's lives and am able to see what their needs are before they do. I sometimes think, "Where would they be without me?" I like being a special or privileged friend.

I can be a martyr for others. I sacrifice myself to meet what I think are the ever-present needs of others.

FOCUS OF ATTENTION, or FOA *(Where I put my attention when I'm attached to my personality)*

NOTE: *This is a brief description of what happens as the FOA becomes narrower and narrower. It's important to note that the degree to which our FOA is activated is shaped by our degree of presence. With more presence, what we pay attention to expands, rather than narrows.*

When my personality has its grip on me, I put my attention on relationships with others. I feel that I can easily see the needs of others, and quickly move into action to help them out or just by extending myself to them. There are so many people who can use my help. I lose contact with myself, and forget to attend to my own needs.

As I increase the amount of attention I put on others, the possibility of having needs of my own doesn't exist. I feel guilty attending to myself, and doing so makes me look needy. It's my job to give, and it's not okay to accept help from others.

The more I give, the more my own resources run dry and I'm stretched beyond what I can sanely do. I avoid taking care of important parts of my life. I increasingly look for signs that what I'm offering is appreciated. I assess the behavior of others to determine the sincerity of their gratitude and approval. If their level of appreciation doesn't measure up to the amount that I feel I've given, then my resentment builds.

My IMPACT ON OTHERS

+ *Positive:*
- Others feel embraced and honored by my genuine warmth and caring.
- Others are inspired by my authentic and unconditional love.

- *Negative:*
- Others feel guilty and unable to *keep up* with my degree of giving.
- Others feel smothered and irritated by my over-solicitousness and emotional stickiness.

Below the Waterline

To understand the inner dynamics for Type Two, we turn our attention to what lies under the surface of the water, starting at the bottom and working up.

Type Two's CORE BELIEF

These core operating principles filter through many layers of life, in both seen and unseen ways.

I believe that I have to take care of others first, before I can be loved and accepted.

The needs of others come first. I must attend to them before I'm allowed to have my own needs. It is selfish to have my own needs.

I have to earn love.

The TRIANGLE OF IDENTITY

What I PURSUE

I *pursue* situations that help create a physical or energetic relationship with others in order to experience a loving connection, and to affirm my loving nature.

Not recognizing that love is core to my very *being*, and that I only experience it when I'm simply present, I put effort into *trying to make*

277

love happen. I interpret love as extending (or overextending) myself to create a connection, with the presumption that my action of reaching out to people will show them how thoughtful and generous I am. It is hard to recognize that I want them to mirror back their love for me.

What I AVOID

I *avoid* any experience which could be interpreted to mean that I'm not a warm, generous person.

To first be clear with myself on my needs and then to directly communicate them makes me feel selfish and even guilty, both of which are painful experiences. When I put others first and put my own well-being aside, I avoid recognizing my own unique and inner desires. Asking for what I need, accepting help, and, paradoxically, even receiving real expressions of love from others are the most difficult things in life to do.

My CORE COPING STRATEGY

I *cope* by attending to and putting my energy into other people. I *leave myself*, metaphorically, and sometimes literally, to jump into the lives of others. For example, I may think about all the tasks that they have on their plates, and then I take responsibility for addressing those tasks. Or I might spend a lot of time cooking for an ill friend or cleaning her home over an extended period of time, without consideration for my own health. With my attention focused outside of myself, it is easy to think that I don't have needs or that they are less important than those of others.

SENSE OF SELF *("I am...")*

I see myself as loving, caring, and selfless. These are positive characteristics; however, they become limiting when I feel obligated or compelled to be this way. There are many other characteristics that I don't allow myself to experience or express.

Always feeling that I must help others leads me to feeling deprived and resentful of others, though this is difficult for me to recognize in myself.

Since it isn't okay for me to have needs, I feel I cannot directly ask others for help. I do try to provide indirect hints, but I really think other people should know what I am looking for.

WHERE I MISS THE MARK
(The energetic drive of the passion)

I feel that I am in a better position to help others than they are to help themselves. I sometimes think that I know more than they do about what will make them feel better. Since I don't recognize my own needs easily, I don't put my attention on what I'm truly feeling or what is behind my actions. Feeling that I'm *exempt from* having the very human needs that others have or believing that I know what's best for others are characteristics of the passion of pride.

> **REMINDER**: No matter what type you are dominant in, the passion is a part of the personality and is a motivator that drives your emotional life. The passion covers up a wound in your heart[1] and creates an emotional reaction to how you relate to life, which takes you away from what your soul loves. This is true for all personality types.

HABIT OF THE MIND *(Fixation of the personality)*

I give a lot of what I consider positive attention to others. I unconsciously think that by praising others, they will see me in a positive light, so I am on the outlook for something to praise. For example, I might comment on another presenter's slideshow or on her jewelry. Or I might make repeated comments about how generally wonderful another person is. Often, these comments are not authentic. This is called *flattery*.

> **REMINDER**: No matter what type you are dominant in, the fixation is a part of the personality. It's a motivator in your fixed behaviors and thoughts about yourself and the world. It bolsters a false sense of reality, and as the ego's automatic, unquestioned way of solving problems with life, it takes you away from your true self. This is true for all personality types.

INNER CRITIC MESSAGE
(What my Inner Critic insists upon)

I'm not valued or loved if I don't put others' needs ahead of my own.[2]

My inner critic has rules upon which to evaluate how others treat me. For example, if someone doesn't give me a big enough smile, it is the inner critic's evidence that I'm not loved, and that I haven't done enough to be loved. As long as I'm caught in the inner critic's web, I will continue to sacrifice my own needs and general well-being to others, maintaining a cycle of resentment and avoiding living my own life.

Each of the elements described above contributes to the whole experience of what we have come to think of as ourselves. The core belief, the emotional force of the passion, the mental habit (fixation), and the inner critic all unconsciously conspire to reinforce the Triangle of Identity.

Additional Information on the Enneagram Type Two

What causes me *stress*

I feel stressed when people ask more and more of me. My stress builds when I feel obligated to take care of too many people, and, simultaneously, I resent them for not appreciating me enough. When I try my best to put the focus on others and they don't, in turn, reach out to me with the same degree of attention, I can feel rejected and abandoned. I don't understand why they pull away from me.

I can also feel stressed when people tell me to *take care of myself.* I don't quite know what they mean, nor how to do any better than I am.

When I'm most *constricted and inflexible*

I manipulate others to think they can't do without me.

My tendency for worry becomes exaggerated and turns into overbearing self-importance.

I have a condescending, patronizing attitude toward others and instill guilt in them for not doing enough for others or for me.

I wear myself out because I don't take care of my own health needs.

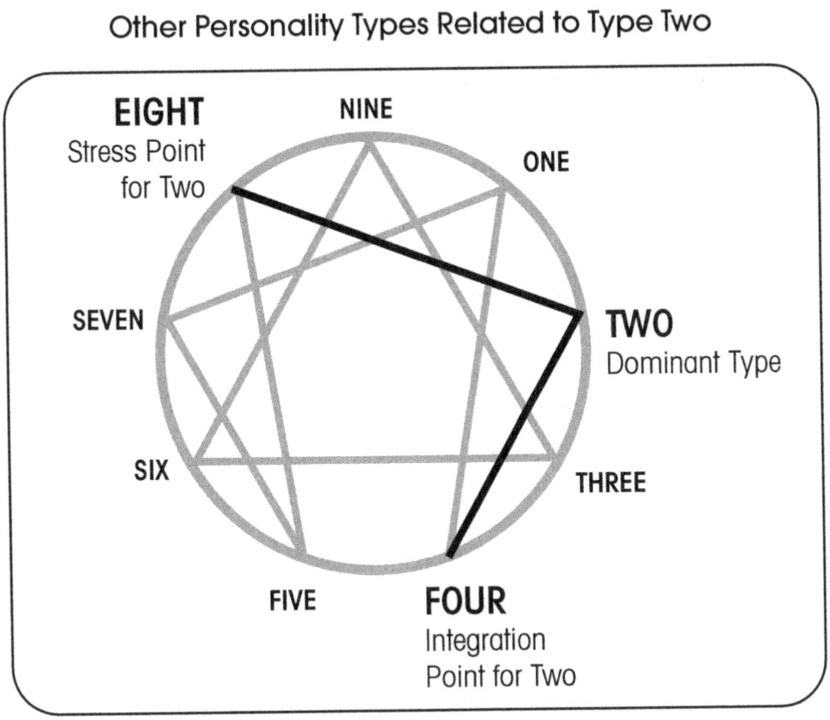

Other Personality Types Related to Type Two

Figure 13-3: The Stress and Integration Points for Type Two

People dominant in Type Two experience characteristics of Type Eight under stress. Type Eight is the *Stress Point* for Type Two. For more information on this, see chapter 11. Pay particular attention to the sections on average-level behaviors and to the "Notice and Observe Patterns" section of that chapter.

Type Two's *Integration Point*, including the *Hidden Dimension of Self*, is found in Type Four. See chapter 7 for more information on Type Four. For Type Two's Integration Point, pay particular attention to the "Gifts" and "At My Best" sections in chapter 7. For Type Two's Hidden Dimension of Self, review the sections on average levels of behavior in that same chapter.

The Enneagram also works in reverse, which yields helpful information to everyone discovering their dominant type: Type Two is the Stress Point for Type Four, and it's the Integration Point for Type Eight.

Recognizing Patterns
That Pull You Off-Course

Notice and Observe Patterns

In this section you'll find some of the patterns that are associated with the Type Two personality structure. These patterns provide useful information. Rather than making you bad or wrong in some way, these patterns can be used as signposts on your path of awakening. They help you notice and get to the heart of your experience in a tangible, direct way. Eventually, you can relax the particular, habitual—and often troublesome—strategies, which will allow you to be more present, open, and free.

The pattern of communicating indirectly

Notice the tendency to *go around* an issue and not directly ask for what you need.

You may think that others should be able to read your mind about what you want or need. However, that generally is not the case.

Notice if you have a tendency to act as if you're just fine and have no needs or wants. It is likely that this is what others will think.

They won't have a clue unless you communicate more directly.

Remember that this pattern of not being clear about—and not directly communicating—your needs has helped protect you against feeling that early hurt from your childhood.

The pattern of self-sacrifice

Notice when you feel that you have to reach out to others, or jump in to help them out, or say yes to requests even when you want to say no. Do others always come first? This is a sign of *people-pleasing*.

People dominant in Type Two often feel that they have to sacrifice themselves by forgetting about their own needs. If this is a strong pattern for you, you may notice some related patterns:

- You have a lot of people in your life who depend on you. Some of those people might seem like they need a lot from you. You're likely seen as a *rescuer*. This is immensely draining. And this pattern tends to act as a magnet to attract people who are needy.

- Some people distance themselves from you. They might be experiencing you as quite needy or intrusive. This may come as quite a surprise for you.
- There is something nagging you. It's likely that it's your needs that are nagging, because whatever is denied us gets bigger in our lives. To keep from experiencing these deeper needs or the sense that you've been denied, you may give yourself some type of superficial treat that you feel you deserve, such as a pedicure, a new outfit, or an electronic gadget. This type of reward is often a substitute for what would really nurture and nourish you. See if you're choosing goodies that truly support you or ones that sabotage you.
- This is the time to be both observant of and compassionate with yourself.

The pattern of the centrality of relationships

Notice if you feel that your life is *suspended* if you're not currently in an intimate relationship.

How much of your attention and energy is focused on being with others, and creating closeness and special relationships with them?

The Type Two personality is the embodiment of having warm relationships, which is a crucial dimension of being in the human family. When that focus takes most of one's energy, however, the individual can lose a sense of self.

How often do you sense that you really do know best what another person needs, even if they haven't asked for it? The propensity to sense that you have special insights into another's needs can lead you to doing things for that person that are not particularly necessary or even wanted.

Notice the tendency to *flatter* others. Observe what you're trying to achieve through praising another. The initial response is to believe that flattery is an expression of your generosity. In-depth exploration may identify your desire to receive positive attention from the other person. This can be difficult to acknowledge, so both honesty and compassion for yourself is vital.

Because flattery is an exaggerated expression of complimenting another, it will feel false to the person whom you're trying to please. You may achieve the opposite of what you really want in the relationship.

Notice your relationship to yourself, to your heart. How would you characterize it? What keeps you from developing a deeper relationship to your heart? What supports this relationship?

Surprising and Effective Practices for Building Your Capacity

The following capacity-building practices will help you turn toward your true nature.

1. What are your needs?

What is it that you need? Who do you need it from?

As hard as it is to recognize your needs, they're an undeniable part of being human. Denying your needs keeps you in an illusion. If it feels *selfish* to have needs of your own, recognize this as a pattern of the Two's personality structure. In reality, acknowledging the feelings in your heart and honoring your need for self-nurturing will eventually create more balance and ease in your life.

As you recognize your needs, and voice them, your communication with others will become clearer. The strings and conditions that are an aspect of habitual giving will diminish. If you're unclear as to what you need, slow down, go look in a mirror, and sincerely ask yourself, "What do I need?" Allow your needs to be known to yourself and to others.

Consciously work with bringing your attention back into your own life. Allow it to return back home. While it will feel very awkward to experiment with this, you'll come to see just how much energy you make available for everyone else. It's your turn.

2. Experiment with nourishing yourself.

What would it look like to focus on self-care to nourish yourself? Let go of any reasons for not doing so at the moment, and give time to reflect on what would most replenish and honor your soul.

This is one of the hardest things for people with a Type Two personality to learn because it feels so counterintuitive. But here goes: As you nourish and allow yourself into your own heart, the more you'll experience your genuine gifts of unconditional love, and the more your authentic relationships with others will be based on a true connection of your heart to the hearts of others. Others are far more likely to be deeply touched by who you are and to warmly embrace you.

With a greater degree of self-nourishing comes the capacity to savor and enjoy what you really love. You can more easily and confidently say no to those activities that are not right for you, and to say a resounding yes with honesty when you're called to do so.

3. Create a practice for developing a clear, quiet mind.

The pattern of the Two personality structure is to express caring for others through action.

Your mind is usually very active, and having a clear, quiet mind can seem impossible, so creating a practice for quieting the mind can feel daunting. It is easy to keep busy or have a lot of noise, such as TV or radio constantly on in the background as a way to distract you from this inner noise, but neither are effective nor sustainable in actually quieting the mind. It usually helps to work with a teacher or a coach to support you in developing a practice for building your capacity to experience more inner quiet.

A quieter mind allows you to develop an awareness of your mental chatter or anxiety without feeling compelled to act on all this inner activity. With practice, you can experience important shifts toward greater liberation, health, and emotional intelligence.

4. Find support for opening your heart to yourself.

Your natural gift is your beautiful and loving heart. If you don't allow yourself into your own heart, and fully receive the real gift of love from others, however, you'll not experience the depth of connection you so deeply desire. Identify people who can support you in the practice of being in your own heart. This may be a spiritual teacher, coach, or mentor, or a group that focuses on developing qualities of the heart.

Reading heart-centered books or other healing literature can also support your practice.

5. Practice showing your love for others by simply **being with** them.

If you're likely to show your love for others by *doing* something for them, try something new—just *showing up.*

What most people really want from others is someone to listen deeply, to appreciate them for who they are. *Loving by doing* can get in the way of having a real relationship.

When you can just be available to the people you care about without moving physically toward them into their personal field, you'll likely experience that they meet you and don't move away from you. This is what you have really wanted at a deep level.

Forging Your Healing and Evolutionary Path

A major theme of this book is that the primary reason for working with the Enneagram is to help us awaken to our true nature. It puts us on a path of healing and real transformation that, for most of us, takes place over time—with patience, trust, faith in our awakening journey—and by being as present as possible. Section III takes us into processes that support and are beneficial for everyone, regardless of type.

Not surprisingly, there are specific processes that are vital for individuals dominant in each type.

If you are dominant in Type Two, your healing and evolutionary path includes the following:

Stay with your own experience, even while noticing that you may want to jump into someone else's life. To stay with your own experience, it's important to learn to *feel into* your energetic field. Being in contact with your belly and the sensations in your body will help you learn to sense into and contain your energy so it doesn't unconsciously spill over into other people's lives. The material in Section III of this book offers more guidance in developing a conscious relationship to your own energetic field.

Come into real contact with your own heart. You've learned to keep a distance from your own heart, but now it's time to allow it in. Spend time in quiet, paying attention to your heart, and what it is trying to tell you. Many people find it helps to write about the experiences that they are having and perhaps recognizing as being quite old or familiar.

Your inner work involves learning to accept yourself and your needs, to accept the depth of who you are, and to fall in love with yourself. As an outgrowth of this, the connections you consciously develop with others will take on an authentic mutuality.

This is big work. It can be supported by working with a skillful Enneagram-based coach, spiritual guide, or therapist, or by engaging in a specific group of people that supports your work.

Notice that you can become emotionally needy, hypersensitive, jealous, and live in fantasy. This is hard to discover this in yourself—this *Hidden Dimension of Self*—as you think of yourself as the one who is selfless and generous with others. But there are times when you become self-absorbed and feel that you're exempt from the expectations and norms that others follow. You can despise those who you think are causing you pain. You probably never had permission to express any of these qualities, but they are part of your inner experience of growth. As you recognize and embrace them without acting them out, you'll begin to recognize your individuality and the source of your authentic and creative nature.

> **REMINDER**: The Hidden Dimension of Self is found at the average and lower levels of health in the Integration Point.

Let go of the need to only have positive feelings. Having a full range of feelings is part of being fully human. Recognizing and experiencing feelings that you have considered negative do not mean that you act them out, but that you realize that they exist and don't push them away. As you learn to be with all of your feelings, you naturally begin to have a deep sense of integration and wholeness that will strengthen over time.

Experience the presence of the love that just *is*. The nature of reality is love. By being present to yourself and to others—by *being in* and *with your heart*—you experience the realness of love with its nourishing, expansive, and truly indescribable qualities. In contrast, any effort to make love happen is a pale and unsatisfying experience. Being an expression of this beautiful love is your true gift.

The Human Condition and Consciousness of Type Six: The Loyalist

Sandra is a warm, intelligent, and likable woman who had spent the last few years focusing on the needs of her growing family and helping her elderly parents. She had been the steadfast sibling who always made herself available for doctor visits and coordinating the myriad of services her parents came to need.

With her dad still living nearby, she felt it was time to begin preparing herself for the next stage of life, which included meaningful work. But she was having a difficult time moving forward. She came to coaching wanting to get beyond the frequent feelings of frustration, of disappointment, of being overwhelmed, because then, she thought, she could move forward.

She poured herself into the Enneagram, discovered that she related to the Enneagram Six, and came to recognize the following familiar patterns:

- *the feeling of being pulled in so many directions, not knowing what to do next, then feeling swamped by having so much to do. She had taken on many commitments.*
- *being paralyzed around moving into new territory. She got stopped in her tracks when she faced taking action in unfamiliar situations She realized that she got overwhelmed with fear.*

- *the unending desire to know exactly what was coming next, and what was expected of her. She saw how she predicted outcomes of conversations or activities before they occurred.*
- *constant worrying about what could happen in the future.*

With her overactive mind, one major theme of coaching focused on helping her get into her body. Sandra learned that she didn't have much of a direct relationship with it, despite working out most days. With practice, she began making contact with her body, and discovered that this helped her mind relax. She began to see that she was intuitive but had almost always dismissed this internal guidance.

With the development of a stronger sense of being grounded, she began taking small but important action steps that were guided by her own inner knowing. It was challenging for her to remember that she had access to this guidance, and she usually was surprised and empowered by it. Regular practice in stepping back from her frequent internal dialogue and instead to breathe and land in her body have helped her make better decisions around commitments, and are helping her to clarify a work path that can call upon her best gifts.

The more present Sandra becomes, the more freedom, self-confidence, and sense of well-being she experiences.

The Internal Coherence of the Type Six Experience

Your True Nature

If this is your dominant Enneagram point, your soul is naturally drawn to experiencing true guidance. There is an inherent trust in the ground of *being* which guides you each step of the way. You have no need to focus on figuring out everything in advance. Each moment unfolds with new insights and awareness. You feel so at home in yourself, and you have unshakeable faith that you'll be shown the way.

When not in touch with your true nature, what you might not recognize *yet* is that you don't have to work so hard at experiencing support and solidity. When you're truly present—that is, when you have taken up residence within yourself—you have more contact with the actual support that is available to you. With sustained attention toward the aliveness of your inner body and toward maintaining a soft and open heart, you recognize that support doesn't come from mental activity but arises from this inner experience. You find yourself feeling more and more at ease.

The Story of Your Life:
Relating to Your Inner and Outer World

Your inner sense of self and your place in the world were set in place early in life. How you internalized your experiences contributed to the characteristic way you relate to yourself and others, and to your very way of being. If this is your dominant type, the following brief story of your childhood inner experience will likely sound very familiar.

As a very young child, you were particularly attuned to what would help you know how to navigate the world. You naturally wanted to feel secure and safe, because the world outside felt big and unknown.

You looked to your father (or another protective figure) to provide the guidance and structure that would give you courage to be independent and safe in the world. But you were often disappointed, or you experienced anxiety. That guidance didn't feel consistent, or it was either too strong or not strong enough.

From the beginning, it seems like you felt a pull between different people in your life, a pull between different parts of your life. You experienced wanting to be supported and knowing you could depend on others, and, at the same time, you wanted independence. You looked for the right amount of closeness—close, but not so close as to be overwhelmed. Either extreme felt threatening.

The pull between two opposites appeared everywhere in your life. Sometimes you were supportive to others; sometimes you felt like a bull in a china shop. Often indecisive, you vacillated, not knowing what direction to take. Many internal voices kept you off balance and looking for home base. You may have heard, "Would you make up your mind?!" Or "Just get a plan and stay with it. Quit wavering."

With so little internal stability, it was easy to feel pessimistic about life.

You could easily spot where problems would occur, and so you tried to avoid them. Not knowing your next step or what was expected of you could be paralyzing.

As you grew, you looked to others for guidance and safety—perhaps looking to a trusted adult, an idea to believe in, or a group that adhered to a set of principles you could trust. On the other hand, you might have rebelled against any form of authority.

You came to orient your life around trying to know what would happen. This led you to trying to find and experience support and guidance, and to avoid the unknown. Not trusting the answers that you found, you kept looking outside of yourself.

What you didn't know is that you can trust yourself, and you can trust being. What you didn't know is that you have your own inner guidance and authority. You couldn't have known that, by not trying to create it, the support is always here, in the present. You couldn't have known that the ground of being will always support you—that is your true nature.

Your Great Loss

As a little being, even before your conscious thought and language skills developed, you had experiences that left you feeling separated from these essential qualities that your soul loved—that it was in tune with. This pain was too much to bear, so the ego structure began to form, taking on the role of protecting you from the severity of this early loss.

We remember that the ego attempts to mimic our true nature, though it can never be successful in doing so. So, the Six personality structure has tried to use the mind to create the experience of support and real guidance, and mentally tried to prepare for all contingencies, by looking at all angles, and noticing and conjuring up what could go wrong—all of which leads to much worry and confusion.

Here is the great loss—the pain—for Type Six: There's a sense that there is no support for you and your world. It feels as if the ground below you has dropped away. You alone have to figure things out in this scary, unpredictable world. How can you be safe? It's very lonely and confusing without some type of trustworthy guidance.

The Inner Logic and the Triangle of Identity for Type Six

Type Six's CORE BELIEF

We see that a core belief is set into place, providing an unconscious filter that accepts only information that supports the ego's belief. This filter, unfortunately, misses and dismisses data that would otherwise provide alternate perspectives. This belief acts as a core operating principle that shapes a person's relationship to life.

Each core belief is false but feels real until we can compassionately bring it into the light of awareness. It is particularly important to approach this with great kindness and truthfulness.

For those dominant in Type Six, your core belief is that the world is unsafe. It's full of threats, and you can't trust the world, others, and even yourself to make the right decisions and do the right things. You need to be prepared to protect yourself and loved ones from many threats.

How might this show up in your life? Here are some examples of what you might hear yourself think, say, or do/not do:

- I don't know what to do next. It's so hard to make a decision. I want to decide, but then I doubt and second-guess myself.
- Who will listen to me? You say I need *more* self-confidence? *What* self-confidence? I have little or none.
- I'm worried sick that those I care about won't be okay. They could be at risk.
- Sometimes, when I rely too much on the suggestions of others, I get disappointed in the outcomes and start questioning if I can trust them.

This core belief leads us to the **Triangle of Identity**, *which provides a shorthand illustration of how you "do" life. I invite you to try on the following description to see how it fits with your experience.*

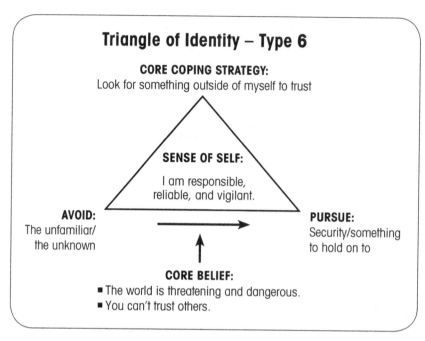

Figure 14-1: The Triangle of Identity for Type Six

Here is how a person with the Type Six personality structure might recognize this inner logic that is illustrated by the Triangle of Identity:

I pursue experiences where there is something secure to hold on to, so that I feel supported and safe. I look for something solid that gives me a sense of guidance and direction. I want to know that I have covered all the bases.

I avoid unfamiliar and unknown situations, because then any sense of safety or support is at risk. I don't want any surprises.

I cope by looking for something outside of myself to trust. I might find this source of trust in a strong belief system; a group oriented to a particular social cause; a civic, political or religious group; a job; a spiritual teacher; or a strong partner, for example.

As an extension of my coping strategy, I can see how my life has been organized around finding and experiencing safety and security, and avoiding the unknown. If I can feel that I am in safe territory, then I will find the guidance I need and life will support me. Doubting the answers that come from within, I look outside of myself to my family, work, religion, or other external source of support.

All of this leads me to see myself as a reliable, responsible, vigilant, and likeable person. This self-definition—this sense of self—ends up imposing limits. It keeps me from recognizing and appreciating the fuller range of my human experience.

While these are positive qualities, when they're overused, they limit my ability to acknowledge and express my emotional or spiritual dimensions. If I see myself only as being likeable or reliable, my sense of self is dependent on what responsibilities I take on and how well I fulfill my obligations. This undermines my own authority for my life. In addition, there are many other characteristics that I don't allow myself to experience or express. Always feeling that I must be responsible leads me to eventually feel resentful and blame others for the multiple and conflicting responsibilities that are on my plate. And then I don't allow myself to experience the power of my own presence.

An Awakened Capacity of Type Six: Courage

Courage comes from trusting that I am supported in taking on whatever challenge is mine to meet. I am grounded in my belly. Courage also means to "stand by my heart." As I listen to what my heart knows, I can take appropriate action, or take no action at all, depending upon what is most needed in the moment. My mind is still and quiet, supporting the experience of sturdiness and courage. These are the precious qualities of the Spiritual Warrior.

It's when you have forgotten and lost contact with your innate capacity for courage, you deal with the anxiety and fear that are just underneath the surface by getting busy. You can barrel forward or feel paralyzed around what is most important, but either way, you generally keep a number of balls in the air. You forget that the real ground of safety and knowing resides within. Learning to listen to the quiet inner guidance does not diminish your capacity to act. What is missing is the compulsion to have to stay busy.

When you forget your true nature, you become identified with a narrow version of yourself, based upon wanting to create support and guidance. Identifying with limited version reduces your capacity to be at home in yourself.

The Iceberg Model for Type Six reiterates some of this material in a visual format.

The model starts with some of the expansive qualities that are innate gifts of individuals dominant in this type. These qualities are naturally and increasingly experienced as we recognize and gradually release our attachment to our more limited definition of self. The Iceberg Model also increases our understanding of the observable expressions found at the average level of behavior of Type Six individuals, and it fills out more of what goes on below the waterline, i.e., those inner dynamics that shape and motivate the behaviors that occur when the personality has its grip on us. (Refer to chapter 5 for more discussion on the Iceberg Model.)

Decoding the Personality Structure of Type Six

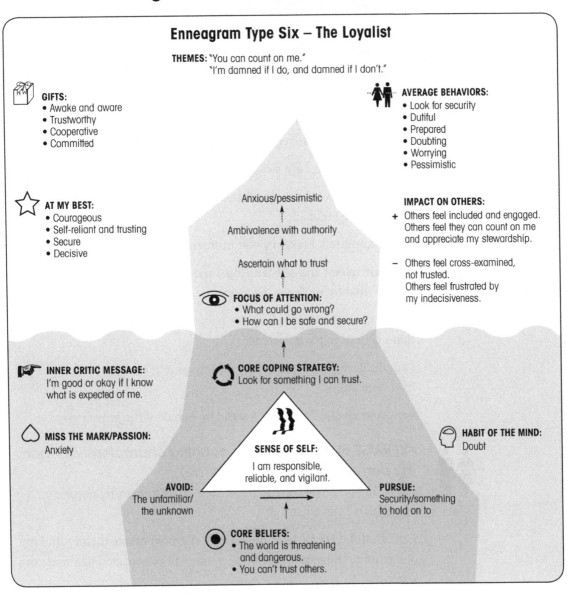

Enneagram Type Six – The Loyalist

THEMES: "You can count on me."
"I'm damned if I do, and damned if I don't."

GIFTS:
- Awake and aware
- Trustworthy
- Cooperative
- Committed

AVERAGE BEHAVIORS:
- Look for security
- Dutiful
- Prepared
- Doubting
- Worrying
- Pessimistic

AT MY BEST:
- Courageous
- Self-reliant and trusting
- Secure
- Decisive

Anxious/pessimistic
↑
Ambivalence with authority
↑
Ascertain what to trust
↑

IMPACT ON OTHERS:

+ Others feel included and engaged.
Others feel they can count on me
and appreciate my stewardship.

− Others feel cross-examined,
not trusted.
Others feel frustrated by
my indecisiveness.

FOCUS OF ATTENTION:
- What could go wrong?
- How can I be safe and secure?

INNER CRITIC MESSAGE:
I'm good or okay if I know
what is expected of me.

CORE COPING STRATEGY:
Look for something I can trust.

HABIT OF THE MIND:
Doubt

MISS THE MARK/PASSION:
Anxiety

SENSE OF SELF:
I am responsible,
reliable, and vigilant.

AVOID:
The unfamiliar/
the unknown

PURSUE:
Security/something
to hold on to

CORE BELIEFS:
- The world is threatening
and dangerous.
- You can't trust others.

Figure 14-2: The Iceberg Model for Type Six

297

Type Six's THEMES

"You can count on me" and/or "I'm damned if I do, and damned if I don't" are the themes of this personality structure.

Above the Waterline

The Gifts, Daily Habits, and Challenges of Type Six

GIFTS and AT MY BEST
(When I'm expansive and at my healthiest)

I am awake to what is happening in the external environment—both positively and negatively.

I am trustworthy. I am steadfast, responsible, and can be counted on.

I am cooperative. I see others and myself as being equal contributors to efforts that benefit all.

I am committed. I take my commitments seriously and follow through.

I am self-reliant and self-trusting. I pay attention to my inner knowing and use that to guide my decisions.

I am secure within myself and as part of the groups and organizations that I choose to participate in.

I am decisive. I take different perspectives into account, then make a firm decision.

I am courageous. I can take a stand on behalf of the greater good.

AVERAGE BEHAVIORS *(Distinguishing characteristics when my personality has its grip on me)*

I look for security. I want to make sure I find something outside of myself that I can trust.

I am dutiful. I try to determine what's expected of me, then I fulfill my obligations. Obligations seem to be internally connected to a sense of security.

I always try to be prepared for whatever may come my way. I try to cover all the bases as a way of being safe.

I doubt myself and ask, "What if?" I vacillate between choices, often second-guessing myself. On the other hand, I can be pushy and take action without a second thought. Then I don't feel the doubt.

I anticipate all the things that can go wrong, and these become impossible obstacles to overcome, even before I take any action. I worry.

I can be pessimistic and can move into seeing things as catastrophic. I focus on what is not working, and I magnify the negative possibilities and outcomes. I can be very agitated.

FOCUS OF ATTENTION, or FOA *(Where I put my attention when I'm attached to my personality)*

NOTE: This is a brief description of what happens as the FOA becomes narrower and narrower. It's important to note that the degree to which our FOA is activated is shaped by our degree of presence. With more presence, what we pay attention to expands, rather than narrows.

When my personality has its grip on me, I put my attention on what could go wrong. To prevent problems or, even worse, catastrophes, I put a lot of energy into developing plans and systems that create safety and security. But doubt overshadows my confidence. I get caught up in my commitments and forget to check with my inner guidance.

I can be hypervigilant about my environment and look for cues regarding whether I can trust myself or others. While I want to believe some source of authority outside myself, I may become suspicious of authority. I've been disappointed before. Wanting to trust, and not knowing who or what I can trust, creates a sense of ambivalence.

With less to trust, my anxiety grows ever-present and overwhelming. I become pessimistic and emotionally provoked.

+   My IMPACT ON OTHERS

—   **+ *Positive:***

- Others appreciate my loyalty and my stewardship toward issues that I care about.
- Others feel included, engaged, and valued.

– *Negative:*

- Others can feel confused or frustrated by my indecisiveness.
- Others can feel hurt or angered by the doubt and suspicion toward them that I express.

Below the Waterline

To understand the inner dynamics for Type Six, we turn our attention to what lies under the surface of the water, starting at the bottom and working up.

Type Six's CORE BELIEFS

These core operating principles filter through many layers of life, in both seen and unseen ways.

I believe that the world is full of threats. I can't trust the world or other people, and I don't trust myself to make the right decisions or do the right things. I need to be prepared to protect myself, family, or others in the community from these threats.

The TRIANGLE OF IDENTITY

What I PURSUE

I *pursue* having a sense of safety and solidity that I can count on. With so much shakiness in life, what or who will be there for me and for those I love? Before I can make good decisions, I look for a trustworthy source of guidance and direction. But before I can make a move, I want to know that I have covered all the bases and that I won't have to deal with any surprises that could threaten those I have responsibility for.

What I AVOID

I *avoid* unfamiliar and unknown situations, as they create a deep sense of anxiety for me. It's difficult to make decisions without knowing in advance what the outcome will be. The unknown is more threatening to me than staying with familiar circumstances, even if those circumstances no longer serve me. Putting myself into unknown territory is the hardest thing in life for me to do. The resulting anxiety can feel unbearable.

My CORE COPING STRATEGY

I *cope* by looking for something to believe in, something that will provide support. For example, I might try to find a work or intimate partner who will provide a reliable source of security. A stable work organization, or a social, civic, or religious group with a strong belief system could also provide a sense of familiarity and constancy that I can fall back on. Or I might try to push through my anxiety by overcommitting to others and being on the go—which feels safer than experiencing my inner discomfort.

SENSE OF SELF *("I am...")*

I see myself as being responsible, reliable, and vigilant. I'm loyal to others to a fault. While these are positive attributes, they become limiting when I feel obligated or compelled to be this way. They can create restrictions in experiencing the full range of my humanity, which includes trying new things and being loyal to my own inner guidance.

WHERE I MISS THE MARK
(The energetic drive of the passion)

I feel and identify with enormous fear and free-floating anxiety. I either become paralyzed by my anxiety and fail to take the necessary steps to move in the direction that I want to go, or I try to blast my way through the discomfort of the anxiety, and can end up pushing my way through uncomfortable situations.

> **REMINDER:** No matter what type you are dominant in, the passion is a part of the personality and is a motivator that drives your emotional life. The passion covers up a wound in your heart[1] and creates an emotional reaction to how you relate to life, which takes you away from what your soul loves. This is true for all personality types.

HABIT OF THE MIND *(Fixation of the personality)*

I'm filled with doubt and worry; I just don't know what to do next. I often feel pulled between polar opposite responses to situations that arise in my life. I put experiences into mental categories that create an experience of "this or that?" This inner duality keeps me off-balance.

I look for ways to create stability from external sources, but I end up changing my mind about how to move forward. I don't trust my own thinking, and I worry that I'm making the wrong decisions.

> **REMINDER**: No matter what type you are dominant in, the fixation is a part of the personality. It's a motivator in your fixed behaviors and thoughts about yourself and the world. It bolsters a false sense of reality, and as the ego's automatic, unquestioned way of solving problems with life, it takes you away from your true self. This is true for all personality types.

INNER CRITIC MESSAGE
(What my Inner Critic insists upon)

My inner critic insists that I do what is expected of me,[2] which seems to require an immediate response from me. When I let my inner critic have free reign, I am constantly trying to identify what is expected of me and to fulfill those expectations as a way of creating a sense of security. It is exhausting to be so vigilant, to figure out what I think the expectations of others are, and to try so hard to fulfill them.

The inner critic always points my attention to the outside world. When I follow this course and get caught in the inner critic's web, I forget what it is that I want in my own life, and I lack trust in my inner knowing.

Each of the elements described above contributes to the whole experience of what we have come to think of as ourselves. The core belief, the emotional force of the passion, the mental habit (fixation), and the inner critic all unconsciously conspire to reinforce the Triangle of Identity.

Additional Information on the Enneagram Type Six

What causes me *stress*

I feel stress when I have made commitments to more people than I can deliver. My stress increases when I am forced to make a decision, and I feel unprepared. I may feel that I haven't collected enough information to make a good decision or that I am being rushed.

When I'm most *constricted and inflexible*

I trust no one. I am deeply suspicious of the motives of others.

I hang out with people or groups that are *bad* for me.

I am unreliable and put blame on everyone else for things gone wrong.

I am emotionally all over the map, lacking stability.

I am paranoid, feeling that others are out to get me.

Other Personality Types Related to Type Six

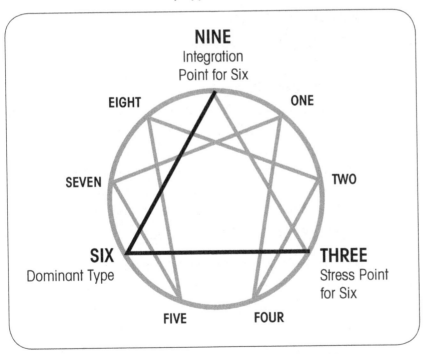

Figure 14-3: The Stress and Integration Points for Type Six

People dominant in Type Six experience characteristics of Type Three under stress. Type Three is the *Stress Point* for Type Six. For more information on this, see chapter 9. Pay particular attention to the sections on average-level behaviors and to the "Notice and Observe Patterns" section of that chapter.

Type Six's *Integration Point*, including the *Hidden Dimension of Self*, is found in Type Nine. See chapter 6 for more information on Type Nine. For Type Six's Integration Point, pay particular attention to the "Gifts" and "At My Best" sections in chapter 6. For Type Six's Hidden Dimension of Self, review the sections on average levels of behavior in that same chapter.

The Enneagram also works in reverse, which yields helpful information to everyone discovering their dominant type: Type Six is the Stress Point for Type Nine, and it's the Integration Point for Type Three.

Recognizing Patterns That Pull You Off-Course

Notice and Observe Patterns

In this section you'll find some of the patterns that are associated with the Type Six personality structure. These patterns provide useful information. Rather than making you bad or wrong in some way, these patterns can be used as signposts on your path of awakening. They help you notice and get to the heart of your experience in a tangible, direct way. Eventually, you can relax the particular, habitual—and often troublesome—strategies, which will allow you to be more present, open, and free.

The pattern of diminished self-confidence

People dominant in Type Six are challenged by a lack of self-confidence when in the grip of the personality. It may show up in some of the following ways:

People dominant in this type are apt to diminish their accomplishments or, more likely, forget them altogether. What accomplishments have you had in life? What are you forgetting?

Go back through the different phases or decades of your life and write down whatever you can remember.

Do you ask others for advice on what to do? Notice how many people you ask for advice about any one situation. What are your inner rules for accepting or ruling out the advice of others? Do some people carry more weight with you?

Does a certain percentage of these external resources have to agree on a course of action?

What are you looking for when you ask for advice?

Do you have a tendency to change your mind frequently? Do you notice that you sometimes feel pulled between diametrically opposed answers, such as yes and no?

If you notice this tendency, be an observer the next time it happens. What part of you tends toward the affirmative? What part of you tends toward the negative?

What roles do fear and doubt play in your decision/indecision?

What leads you to your final answer?

Remember that the lack of trust in your inner knowing has helped protect you against feeling that early hurt from your childhood.

The pattern of fear and anxiety

People dominant in Six can experience a great deal of fear and anxiety. There is a distinction between these experiences: Fear is a response to an actual threat. Anxiety is pervasive experience of distress or dis-ease that exists in the absence of an actual harm, and in anticipation of potential danger. Both are common experiences in the Type Six personality structure.

What conditions or situations tend to ignite fear for you? What are the common themes among those situations that are fear-producing? What is actually threatening you?

Get to know anxiety. It is agitated in a busy mind. What is your experience of anxiety as a mental condition?

What does anxiety feel like in your body? How do you know that you are experiencing it? Where is your breath when you are anxious? Do you remember having a breath? Having a body of substance?

Try breathing when you are experiencing anxiety, and notice if that changes your sensations. Is there another word for your sensations other than anxious or fearful?

What is underneath your fear? You may not know the answer right away, but it is a question worth investigating.

The pattern of the reign of the inner committee

The *inner committee* is a source of confusing mental chatter and indecision. It is composed of any number of members, each of whom *thinks* he/she has something to contribute to your decision. Each committee member typically represents a particular viewpoint; some of these you learned as a child. For example, you may have an unruly uncle, a prissy cousin, a boss, a mother, a scholar who expects perfection, and a younger version of yourself as a counter-culture teen all sitting on your inner committee.

Who sits on your inner committee? Can you recognize who or what each member represents? You can give these members names to help you identify them more clearly.

In what way does the committee serve you? In what ways does it undermine you? What are the costs and benefits of investing time and energy in listening to these different voices?

Where is the voice of real authority on this committee?

The pattern of being prepared for all contingencies

Reflect on a recent experience in which you prepared for anything that could happen, including worst-case scenarios. As you bring awareness to this situation, can you identify what story you were telling yourself about what could happen if you didn't prepare?

What did you actually do to prepare?

Are you aware of what was going on inside of you during your preparations? If so, how familiar is this experience for you?

How did this focus on being prepared provide real support for you? How did it serve you? How did it not serve you?

What did you trust or not trust about yourself in this situation?

The pattern of overcommitment

It is easy for people dominant in Six to overcommit themselves, thus jamming up their lives and creating stress.

When is the last time you overcommitted yourself? What was the impact created by this overcommitment? What were the consequences of saying yes to more things than you realistically can do? What did this do to your stress level?

How did it impact your relationships? How did you get out of the bind?

Compassionately notice what is underneath this pattern of overcommitment. What problem are you trying to resolve?

The pattern of worry and pessimism:

In the throes of the personality, people who identify most with Type Six can be consumed with worry about what *might happen* in the future, with a bias for a worst-case scenario.

Notice the circumstances that capture your energy in worry and pessimism about the future. Do you notice that both of these mental activities are pointed toward something that hasn't happened?

How pervasive are these mental activities? How often do the things you worry about come to fruition? Can you notice these as patterns, and not as the truth about life?

Surprising and Effective Practices for Building Your Capacity

The following capacity-building practices will help you turn toward your true nature.

1. Quiet your mind.

You may have noticed how many of your type's patterns are connected to unrelenting mental activity. There are a number of strategies to allow your mind to quiet.

Find your way back into your body. Become attuned to having a direct experience of sensations in your body. It can be helpful to begin your awareness with your feet and toes, as these are the farthest from your head. Experiencing the life in your body, and settling into all the cells and your physical structure, can shift your energy downward. Remember that this isn't *thinking about* your body, but experiencing sensations that are available to you in the here and now.

Commit to a mind-quieting practice. A practice that can be very helpful is a seated meditation with your eyes slightly open and focused on one point in front of you. Some people find that this helps them to stay connected to their bodies while consciously breathing and quieting their energy.

2. Acknowledge anxiety, befriend courage.

Fear, anxiety, and insecurity exist. Fear is a natural response to the presence of objective threats to one's physical well-being. Anxiety is a pattern that is particularly acute when we are moving into unknown territory.

Get to know anxiety through your expanding capacity for observation. Recognize it as a pattern and not an objective truth.

It often helps to take one step at a time when moving into new territory. Allow in and celebrate your successes along the journey, even if they seem small.

Experiment with feeling your anxiety and taking steps anyway.

Honor the courage that you already have. Your courage and strength ultimately are required for exploring your own self-development. Find a Deep Coaching professional, a class, or a group that can provide the kind of support you need.

Reclaim faith in yourself and in the universe.

Look for what is working in your life. Express gratitude for the many gifts you have in your life. Acknowledge every time that you trust yourself.

Look for signs that the universe works. They abound.

Spend time in nature and appreciate the serenity and the natural cycles of seasons and of life, using nature as a great teacher.

3. Acknowledge your inner authority.

Catch yourself wanting to figure out how things will be in the future. Come back to the present. Come back to experiencing your breath and sensations in your body. When you experience yourself in your body, you can ask yourself, "What do I know to be true in this moment?" Wait for your body to answer. Listen to what arises. Repeat the question, "What else do I know to be true in this moment?" You may find you know more than you thought.

4. Acknowledge the insight that has been made available to you.

If this information guides you to some action, take it.

Listen to your inner knowing and follow through with whatever step is asked of you. Often, it will not be a big outer step, but an inner letting go or recognition.

Over time, you will come to experience more and more of your precious inner authority.

5. Look for the positive aspects of a situation.

People who have Type Six patterns are easily attuned to the negative dimensions, skewing their perceptions. Remember to notice what is working, what is possible, what is inspiring, what is uplifting.

Forging Your Healing and Evolutionary Path

A major theme of this book is that the primary reason for working with the Enneagram is to help us awaken to our true nature. It puts us on a path of healing and real transformation that, for most of us, takes place over time—with patience, trust, faith in our awakening journey—and by being as present as possible. Section III takes us into processes that support and are beneficial for everyone, regardless of type.

Not surprisingly, there are specific processes that are vital for individuals dominant in each type.

If you are dominant in Type Six, your healing and evolutionary path includes the following:

See through your fears and fearful thinking, and use these as cues to come back into contact with your body.

Take steps to trust your inner knowing. Pay attention to the cues that serve as subtle communications, giving you some direction on a decision of little importance. Build your capacity for listening and following through on this guidance. It will become a stronger sense of knowing over time.

Experience the courage of following through on your convictions. Notice how it feels when you stand by your heart.

Notice when you just want to get comfy, go along with others, and sink your head into the sand. These are hard to see in yourself, as they are far outside your self-definition. You probably didn't get to indulge in these behaviors much in your young life, but they do show up in your life now as you experience your Hidden Self (in the Direction of Integration at Point Nine). The more you can acknowledge and own these experiences without taking action on them, the more you free yourself to enjoy real presence.

> **REMINDER:** The Hidden Dimension of Self is found at the average and lower levels of health in the Integration Point.

Discover your own inner authority and begin to recognize that the support you have been seeking is everywhere and is always available. Your experience of being grounded and present will astound you with the guidance that is provided.

Section III

CHANGE FOR LIFE

15

What Does It Mean to Change?
A Doorway to Expansiveness

After learning about the limitations and pain created through being identified with the patterns of our personality, and then awakening to the specific, higher dimensions of our nature that lie beyond the engaged personality, it's logical to ask, "Now what? How can I use this material to have a more fulfilled life, to feel more inner peace, and to be at home in myself?"

This question brings into focus the process of being engaged in the change process, our assumptions about change, and how we approach it.

Conscious Change and Changing Consciousness

What has been your experience of change? How have you undertaken change in your own life?

I've discovered that most people who are interested in self-development have a deeply embedded—and erroneous—belief that there's something about them that needs to be changed, fixed, or improved. This belief is widespread and generally unquestioned. Why else would there be a multi-billion-dollar industry selling "self-improvement"? Why else would anyone have dozens of books on self-help, psychology, and spirituality filling their shelves and stacked on the floor?

Most people who are interested in self-development have a deeply embedded—and erroneous—belief that there's something about them that needs to be changed, fixed, or improved.

313

With further questioning into these beliefs, we can recognize an even deeper and more painful belief: that we're inherently faulty or inadequate.

Thus, the basis of much personal growth work is based on the fundamental assumption that something is wrong. From this perspective, people often treat themselves in a machine-like way: trying to fix, ignore, or get rid of whatever aspect of being human that doesn't work or doesn't seem acceptable. Sometimes that approach can have positive results. But my response to this is *Ouch!* As pervasive as this assumption is, it comes with considerable costs.

I've found three common approaches to change—both in the self-improvement field and in individual lives—based upon the belief that "there's something wrong with me." See if any of these approaches feel familiar to you.

1. **The *add-to approach*, that is, adding something to yourself to make you okay.**

   Often, this involves creating goals to achieve a desired outcome that will solve some problem. Most of us have had experiences around setting goals, such as losing weight, becoming a millionaire, running marathons, having a dream property or dream partner, receiving a longed-for career promotion or recognition, or simply gaining new tools or strategies to be more effective or successful in achieving the intended goal.

   I'm not saying that setting goals or learning new skills aren't useful. They make an important contribution to realizing outcomes that have value in different contexts. They're the basis of performance evaluations and accountability in most organizational environments. They help create momentum, and they give shape to direction and focus. Creating and reaching goals is especially important in the first half of life as we build careers, grow families, and strengthen a sense of our own capacity and confidence. But, as with all useful strategies, if they're *overused* as a strategy to make up for what's considered an internal deficiency or to make life shiny on the outside, then they actually work against the authentic development you're no doubt seeking.

Because goals are such a big part of Western culture, it's tempting to think that life functions best when you're focused on achieving outcomes, but that doesn't leave much room for life's preciousness to be experienced or to have a real encounter with exactly what's needed for your own growth.

It's also tempting to try translating a goal-setting process to our inner lives, such as getting through a difficult emotional experience or a loss in a prescribed amount of time because we think that's how it should work. This generally proves ineffective over the long term because the internal rhythm of life operates with its own intelligence and at its own tempo. It doesn't have the sense of urgency or obligations that are easily imposed by the ego.

In the process of coming into greater contact with our inner rhythm, listening to the call of the soul, and honoring the unfolding of our lives, we learn to trust that what's best in our lives has little to do with the ego's goals.

In the process of coming into greater contact with our inner rhythm, listening to the call of the soul, and honoring the unfolding of our lives, we learn to trust that what's best in our lives has little to do with the ego's goals.

2. The getting-rid-of-something approach, which is founded on the idea that something within oneself has to be removed.

This is accompanied by attempts to overcome, extinguish, cover over, or repress an unacceptable feeling, sensation, or quality that doesn't align with one's self-image. Have you ever tried to stamp out, push away, push down, or distract yourself from some experience you considered unacceptable?

This approach is accompanied by self-criticism and a hardening toward yourself. This judgment often gets catalyzed when you are not living up to the inner critic's message, such as those identified in Section II for each type. Those messages from the critic carry a very limited breadth of experience that is acceptable from the ego's perspective. For example, you might judge yourself for having certain emotions, for repeating a behavior that you know doesn't align with your sense of self, or for not being able to gain some momentum behind an important priority.

315

The soul has its own rhythm and its own intelligence. It knows what it needs to heal and to thrive.

One unintended impact of this approach is that it basically serves to keep your attention on what you consider "bad," further keeping you entrenched in an unwinnable situation.

I have seen this experience in many of my clients who were in an early stage of making a major change as they entered midlife. Here's an example:

Jessica had decided to leave the profession in which she'd excelled throughout her adult life. Now in her mid-50s, it was time for a change to something else, though she wasn't sure exactly what that would look like.

Initially, she came to coaching thinking that she needed to "get past" the not knowing and the fear of moving into something new. She carried a belief that she should know what to do and be able to let go quickly of the loss associated with leaving her previous, high-status profession. She thought something was wrong with her for not being able to make things happen, and fast. The harder she pushed herself to make decisions, the less energy she had, and the more self-judgment and lethargy she felt.

To her initial dismay, she found that the inner life does not operate at the same speed or in the same way as the external world. Similar to the add-on strategy, trying to rid oneself of an experience, too much forcing, or trying to make something happen before its time, generally backfires. Here, the ego is trying to control both the process and the outcome of the inner life, which it's not equipped to do.

The soul has its own rhythm and its own intelligence. It knows what it needs to heal and to thrive. In the process of gaining more understanding and insight into ourselves, our main role is to develop a deeper ability to listen to the cues of the soul and to follow its lead.

3. Trying to *transcend* what's happening in the here and now.

In this third common approach to change involved with self-development, we attempt to rise above whatever isn't working and hang out in what feels like a more ideal state. Transcendent experiences do occur under various circumstances. Transcendent experiences can be exquisite and help us recognize that, most of the time, we experience only a limited aspect of reality. They can contribute to creating new neurological pathways, which can help build capacity for higher levels of awareness.

But, it's easy to confuse transcendent experiences with "checking out" and simply denying what needs attention on this plane. When used as an escape from life, it will most certainly sabotage you.

Using this approach, you'll likely feel that the stuff of daily life is undesirable or even below you. You may be drawn to spiritual experiences that take you to an exquisite and magical place, and with closer examination, realize that nothing has changed in your day-to-day life.

To ignore the reality that comes in daily life has consequences. For example, relationships, finances, social bonds, and a work or love life can get messy and chaotic. If these are further dismissed, it's easy to overlook the important lessons of life that are available in every moment, and to miss the richness and vast possibilities that show up right here. In truth, the ordinary details of life are a source of insight, change, and transformation.

Can you see how little room there is for kindness toward the human experience from these dominant, change-oriented perspectives? Can you see how you might find yourself pushing away from or against life, holding back, straining, constantly efforting, or simply leaving contact with your life? Each of these approaches, in its own way, reflects a struggle with the natural flow and great intelligence of life itself. Each one takes us out of a direct experience with what's available in the present moment.

The experience of needing to change what we think is inherently wrong with ourselves is deeply rooted in the personality structure. The experience of the *great loss* identified in earlier chapters leads to the embedded experience of being inadequate. And there's some truth to the feeling of inadequacy. Remember that the personality structure is trying to replicate our awakened qualities, which it doesn't have the capacity to accomplish. So, it's true that the personality structure—or the ego itself—

> *There's nothing inadequate about your authentic nature. It will always be a source of truth, nourishment, and astonishment.*

is inadequate in creating the authentic experience of true nature. It can't give you what you're looking for. It will always leave you hungering for something different, something more.

This is one of the great paradoxes of our lives.

However, there's nothing inadequate about your authentic nature. It will always be a source of truth, nourishment, and astonishment.

Another Approach to Change, and a Breath of Fresh Air

What would it be like to allow in the full experience of your life, to accept yourself and to accept life? Most people find this to be a totally foreign concept, and at odds with how they have long related to themselves.

When you relate to life with a compassionate acceptance of yourself, and allow yourself to have the internal and very human experience that you're having, without necessarily taking action on those experiences, something powerful happens. Inner constrictions unexpectedly start to soften and a seemingly miraculous new internal quality rises to the surface. The quality is often accompanied by more internal spaciousness and a sense of your own substance. You come in contact with more of your authentic depth, along with the gradual realization that there's more to you and that you have more choice than ever anticipated. Your sense of self changes through this experience of being present to yourself.

This approach invites you to turn your attention back toward your moment-to-moment experience, using the orientation and tools we discussed in chapter 4:

- Being curious
- Practicing compassion
- Embracing radical honesty
- Trusting the process

Turning *Toward* Yourself

Revisiting the Vital Role of Self-Observation

Most of us haven't been accustomed over the course of our personal history to allow the rich experience of life to actually *be*. We have a lot of ways of interfering with our actual experiences. As a result, life can feel disappointing—that it doesn't measure up to our ideas of what a rich life is. We have a lot of concepts and feelings about ourselves and about others, and those ideas and feelings are generally not rooted in the actual experience that's happening here and now, but are instead based upon some early interactions or experiences in our childhood. The ideas of who you are, who others are, and how life works become substitutes for what's here, now, and a deep awareness of who you are.

There are many misconceptions about what it means to turn toward yourself and to allow life to be. Here are two of them.

Misconception #1:

Not surprisingly, turning toward oneself is sometimes confused with "navel-gazing," or being consumed with every nuance of an experience, which makes it overly meaningful and extremely personal. But there are important distinctions. Navel-gazing might best be understood as a way in which we can withdraw into our own life and become identified with whatever feelings or ideas are coming up. However, when we're identified with our own experiences *at the expense of being aware of what's going on around us,* life becomes distorted. When we're consumed with images, feelings, ideas, and pains, that exaggerated Focus of Attention generally ends up in magnifying the false sense of self. And it can be difficult to move into action under these circumstances.

In contrast, what I'm calling *turning toward yourself* brings a rapt focus of objective attention toward the inner experience. The inner observer is engaged to increase awareness of what's showing up in thoughts, feelings, and sensations, however, these do not define you. They are human experiences that are showing up *through you,* but *are not you.* When we use this orientation to change, we don't take these experiences so personally, yet we still acknowledge their presence when they show up.

You stay with yourself rather than leave yourself.

Turning toward yourself allows you to be in contact with the intelligence of your body and, through being very kind to yourself—regardless of your current state—to heal. You stay *with* yourself rather than leave yourself.

The neutrality of the observer is key to its effectiveness. The inner critic can try to replicate the observer, however, the critic always carries a judgment that compares what you're doing to what it expects of you or against some yardstick that is often below your level of awareness. The resulting evaluation can be positive or negative, but either way, there is a judgment.

The neutrality of the observer means there's *awareness without evaluation*. For example, as you're reading this book, your observer can notice how you're holding the book, where tightness or tension is in your body, the rhythm and pace of your breath, the thoughts that are floating through your mind, and any judgments you might have. These are simply experiences to be recognized without engaging and getting Velcroed to them.

But pay attention to that which is observing your experience right now. You might recognize that it's not a mental or conceptual activity. It's bigger than that. It has a different dimensionality than your usual experience. Your perceptual field has more depth and breadth, and it's not crowded with opinions.

Here's a metaphor that may help you distinguish between your regular state of mind and this more expanded and neutral capacity of your observer: Let's say that you're in the midst of the hustle and bustle at an airport. Your tension rises as you approach the security screening point. Your attention is focused on how you can get through this process as quickly as possible as you begin to remove your shoes and other items that will set off buzzers if you take them with you through the screening apparatus. You just don't want to be here, doing all this, going through this hassle. Does this feel familiar?

With your inner observer engaged, you could actually notice that some people in line seem to be tense and recognize that this felt tension is amplifying the racing of your own heart. You take a few deep breaths.

While you still do what's needed to progress through the security point, you don't get caught in the content of the experience with opinions and evaluations.

Why does this have value? Because your expanded field of awareness allows you to be in the midst of this experience without it negatively impacting you. You might even find humor in it.

Yes, it takes a lot of practice and awareness, but even in an environment filled with activity and distraction, the neutral, inner observer is available. It's a vibrant key to developing a new relationship with yourself that's characterized by more ease and freedom.

The inner observer is a capacity that you have access to, but you may not have yet developed. It takes practice to turn your attention toward it, rather than being engaged with the content of a busy mind or reactive feelings. Of course, various forms of meditation support the development of this capacity. But this capacity isn't just for meditation or other times outside of your usual life activities. You can build and strengthen this observation muscle in day-to-day life by remembering to take a step back, breathe, and notice what's happening in your experience at the very moment.

Misconception #2:

A second misconception that many people have is that turning toward their experience and allowing it in will give power to the very aspect of themselves that they judge and/or fear. The story behind this misconception is that turning toward one's experiences increases the likelihood that this dimension of life will grow, take over, and possibly take control.

In contrast, and paradoxically, when we allow the many dimensions of life to be, even those that we've harshly judged, and we bring the observer's awareness and compassion to them, rather than taking over, they diminish, and take up less internal space. Most people say that they feel freer, more spacious, and more at ease when they've allowed their inner experiences to surface.

Just the opposite of what causes most people to tremble is what actually happens. Allowing your inner experience, and accepting it as part of your human nature, is completely counterintuitive for most of us.

EXERCISE: Let's take some time to reflect on this.

Just today, in what ways did you push away your experience? There are so many strategies that we have for doing this, and it's such a common reaction, that most of us don't recognize the frequency nor the degree to which we turn away from our life's experiences, and truthfully, away from ourselves.

We find that these turning-away-from-experience strategies are found in the personality structure itself, so it's no wonder that may feel familiar. From the list below, see which ones you recognize in your own life.

Common Strategies for Turning Away from Life:

Deny: Denial is a process in which we don't recognize the existence of a behavior or feeling. It's not on the radar screen. One way of denying a feeling is by overriding it. For example, some people find it especially difficult to allow a sad feeling, so they "turn on" their upbeat energy. For others, it's difficult to accept a feeling of happiness or serenity, so the personality's solution focuses on what could go wrong. Others deny having feelings of anger, and so they numb themselves to those experiences.

Dismiss: When one dismisses, there's a quick recognition that a feeling (or situation) exists, but it's quickly pushed to the side. One way to dismiss is to think that your experience isn't important and quickly move onto something else. Sometimes, we might dismiss a feeling because it feels that it could be too overwhelming. When we don't give our inner experiences a chance to even be felt before we override them, they accumulate and weigh us down.

Judge: When one judges, there's a process of making something right or wrong. When it comes to our internal lives, it's easy to make any given feeling or sensation wrong. When we judge an experience, we end up sitting in judgment of ourselves, which is a source of considerable suffering. This is such a familiar and shared experience among all human beings that I've devoted all of chapter 17 to sharing how to develop a deeper understanding of the inner critic and how we can change our relationship to it.

Act too quickly: A good example of this strategy is an uncomfortable, internal feeling of unrest, anxiety, or being stirred up. Rather than experience the sensations as temporary, it's easy to jump into action as a way of resolving the discomfort of the sensations. Often, these sensations get interpreted as meaning, "you're supposed to do something now." But this is a misunderstanding. Acting too quickly is only a short-term solution, as the sensations are sure to reappear. Most of the time, the experiences are so unwelcome that we don't realize that they are unconsciously driving our behavior.

In fact, "acting out" is really acting out the patterns of our type. It feels incredibly natural—it's how most of us have known ourselves and others for much of our lives.

Here are additional, specific strategies that we unintentionally use to turn away from life. Each correlates to one of the nine Enneagram personality structures:

Type One: Trying hard to make yourself, situations, people, or things be perfect.

Type Two: Trying too hard to have a connection with others.

Type Three: Being overly focused on creating and achieving goals.

Type Four: Being overly sensitive to how others respond to you.

Type Five: Retreating too often into the world of ideas and concepts.

Type Six: Being overly prepared for anything that could go wrong.

Type Seven: Being overly busy with anticipating and lining up more experiences or getting more goodies.

Type Eight: Being overly demanding.

Type Nine: Repeatedly numbing out to anything that could disrupt your comfort.

Rather than fully allowing in the expansive sense of being seen, heard, or met with acceptance, it's not unusual to try to get back to normal.

Inhabiting Your Life

Turning *toward* your life involves another active ingredient: allowing yourself into your own life.

What would it be like to move into your own life right now? To take up residence within yourself?

Allowing the experiences that you have is one of the great paradoxes of the Enneagram, and it's one of its most profound teachings and practices. A very important distinction exists here: allowing yourself to experience whatever is arising as a feeling or bodily sensation isn't the same as acting on it.

Acting on a thought or feeling is one way we discharge the energy around an experience that is uncomfortable. It's what happens when we "act out." A lot of times this discharge of energy comes out as reacting to something or someone that's in your environment. In fact, "acting out" is really acting out the patterns of our type. It feels incredibly natural—it's how most of us have known ourselves and others for much of our lives.

Paradoxically, it's just as easy to discharge energy by giggling, laughing uncontrollably, or cutting off our experiences in other ways when we're spiritually or emotionally filled. Rather than fully allowing in the expansive sense of being seen, heard, or met with acceptance, it's not unusual to try to get back to *normal*.

Allowing, or *being with* your inner experience is an entirely different matter, and for most of us, a radical re-orientation. It's probably not something that you've been taught how to do or had modeled by others. But to allow your inner experience by simply recognizing it and not having an opinion about it, and not acting on it, is powerful. It creates an inner shift in your sense of self. What freedom there is!

The Enneagram points to our strengths and gifts, to patterns that cause trouble or unnecessary conflict in our lives, and to everything in between. **When we deny or judge any part of ourselves, we create a war within. We become divided against ourselves, and that creates an obstacle to our growth and development.** When you feel lost or not whole, it's likely because there's some part of yourself that you have cut off. These parts are known in psychological and spiritual literature as *the shadow*.

The Activated Shadow

We unsuspectingly give energy to those areas of our lives that we don't acknowledge. When issues, feelings, or experiences that come up repeatedly are unacknowledged, they tend to become magnified and pop out when least expected. When you avoid an issue or topic in your life, it consumes precious life energy and creates unneeded tension. It leads to *constriction*.

Much is being asked of you at this time, and, if you're like many others, you've set high intentions to be more compassionate, open-hearted, grateful, authentic, and awake—qualities that reflect the higher dimensions of your true nature. Interestingly, the desire to express your higher nature often comes with a strong temptation to leave yourself, to be outside of your own experience.

One way we unconsciously block this natural flow of energy is by having an opinion or judgment about our current state or feeling, which results in making it more concrete.

Every one of us was conditioned not to allow in whatever experiences we might be having. This conditioning has come at a great cost. If you consider it, there are many prohibitions against having human experiences. For example, you might think it's not okay to have anger, resentment, or to be anxious or needy, or even to be open and vulnerable. The result is to try to extinguish what you consider unacceptable feelings or sensations. There are many states that you've been told are not okay or that, by virtue of your particular Enneagram structure, you believe aren't okay. They are totally outside of your self-concept. But the truth is, these are part of being alive. You actually have access to the entire gamut of feelings or energies, but many are hidden to you.

That begs the following question:

If the Enneagram helps us express the higher aspects of life, why would we want to allow in these so-called lower experiences?

Let's take the experience of anger as a way to look at the real issue. Having an experience of anger does not mean that you are an angry person, or that you need to act out your anger. You're human, and anger is part of the human experience. It's easy to get confused between *having an internal experience and taking that experience on as a part of you or as something that has to be expressed to others.* It's easy to become identified

Allowing your experience reflects your capacity for saying yes to yourself, and to the infinite that is within you.

with the experience of anger, and to think that it is says something about you, personally.

States, feelings, sensations, thoughts—the whole human experience is naturally in constant motion because we are energy. Every possible state of feeling will eventually arise and fall away, if we let it. **One way we unconsciously block this natural flow of energy is by having an opinion or judgment about our current state or feeling, which results in making it more concrete.** Or we try to block it, deny it, avoid it, or make it mean something. There are so many ways that we unconsciously try to control the natural flow of life—not wanting what is here.

Allowing Your Life's Flow

So, it's a very big deal to practice allowing life to flow, to allow yourself to have your experience. And why would you want to? Because then you're developing your capacity to accept yourself. You are inviting yourself to be at home with yourself. Then, you're not divided against yourself. You're not struggling against the world. It's a very big deal.

When we are in the process of real growth and change, we experience the paradoxes of life over and over. The more you allow yourself to have a full, inner experience without judging it, without acting it out, and without becoming identified with it, the lighter and more fluid you will find yourself. Your old ideas about who you are begin to dissolve. Allowing your experience reflects your capacity for saying yes to yourself, and to the infinite that is within you.

Allowing yourself into your own life is central to your fulfillment and authenticity in every dimension of life.

Even as you read this, you are building new muscles for dipping into your life. New neural pathways are being created, and, with experience after experience, you'll find yourself more at home within.

This is the organic, evolving nature of change.

16

Presence as the Basis for Real Change

Turning toward your life, and inhabiting it, provide strong support for your growth and development. It's also a practice in being present.

Presence is such a frequently used word that it's lost its true meaning and significance. There are books, teachings, and poems that speak of it. Entire spiritual traditions are based on it. It's a fundamental principle in the Enneagram and for our approach to change. Sometimes I hear it referred to as if it's a given, as if everyone knows what it means and how to "do" it.

If it's so much a part of today's language, at least in certain circles, why isn't there more evidence of presence in day-to-day life? Could we be misinterpreting what presence really means? Could we be looking in the wrong place?

Presence: It's Not What You Think

In my own history, there have been many times when I *thought* I was present, especially in circumstances when life was going well. As I've come to further recognize, understand, and more deeply experience the state of presence, it has been humbling for me to see that, in retrospect, what I had thought was presence was really the activity of an automatic pattern. I misinterpreted a nice feeling as presence, but in truth, it was a habitual pattern of my personality. A perfect example comes from one of the things that I most love—being in nature. How often did I hike the most beautiful of trails, only to realize later that I was totally lost in reverie or thought? Yes, it felt good, but no, it was not presence. I was not present.

Presence is often confused with the familiar experiences associated with our particular personality structure. Since those habitual patterns are how we came to know ourselves, it makes perfect sense to mistakenly associate an experience of a pattern with presence. For example, if you're trying to be the best meditator the teacher has ever had, that is not presence. That is the Type Three structure at work. If you're enjoying the process of creating a grand, conceptual map while ignoring the needs of your body, that is not presence. That's a familiar and automatic Type Five pattern operating.

Enneagram pioneer Hudson has often noted, "We don't have any idea of how not present we are."

That jaw-dropping statement naturally leads to important questions:

> *What does this mean?*
>
> *What haven't I yet experienced?*
>
> *What am I confusing with the true experience of presence?*
>
> *What am I hanging onto instead of being present?*
>
> *What is blocking the experience of presence?*

Myths and Beliefs

Here are three myths that I come across frequently in my conversations with clients and students. Which of the following could be blocking a deeper experience of presence for you?

Myth #1: Presence always feels good.

One assumption is that we are present in our happiest, most upbeat moments. We're not supposed to have difficult experiences when we're present.

In reality, we come into contact with all of life's experience in presence. Some of those moments are sublimely beautiful. Sometimes we experience our natural strength, or brilliance, among other possible precious qualities. But we sometimes experience difficult and hard-to-be-with memories or sensations from the past, or challenging current life circumstances. When we "show up" to allow in these experiences, we receive great support and are almost always brought into a new relationship with ourselves and with our circumstances.

> *After being employed in public education for many years, Stephanie decided to embark on a career in consulting. Well-qualified in education and expertise, a main hurdle for her was deciding how much to charge and learning how to communicate that to potential clients. She had developed a habit of substantially under-charging for her services, then feeling depressed and, sometimes, taken advantage of.*
>
> *She came to realize that she was aware of—but not really present to—the discomfort she experienced around money. By giving her clients a rate that did not reflect her value, she reacted to the discomfort by trying to override and avoid the pain that lived underneath her ambivalence. When she learned a process for having the direct experience of her discomfort without trying to get rid of it or change it, she felt more spacious within herself as the level of discomfort changed. That internal space allowed her to practice quoting and billing her services at higher levels while being able to tolerate some level of discomfort.*
>
> *Staying present to her experience, the spaciousness continued to expand as the discomfort decreased so that bidding her services and, subsequently, billing appropriately were no longer such big deals for her. The previous unease associated with money no longer had such an energetic charge.*

Presence does not decide what it likes and doesn't like. Our minds do that, leading to an idea of what is acceptable and isn't acceptable to experience.

Presence does not decide what it likes and doesn't like. Our minds do that, leading to an idea of what is acceptable and isn't acceptable to experience. Being aware of a problem or issue that shows up in life is not the same as presence, either. We can be aware of, yet still try to negate, an issue's energetic hold on us. With practice, we learn that those issues have more staying power when we do not allow ourselves to experience the invisible sensations that accompany the issue. Their power decreases when we do

We increasingly connect with the life-affirming qualities that provide fuel for clarifying and living our deeper purpose.

allow ourselves to make direct, felt contact with them—to be present to them. Then, we have less need to react to the difficult experience. It's our unaccepting reaction that creates more pain.

Myth #2: Presence isn't practical.

Another assumption is that presence is separate from functioning in real life. This gets translated into the personal belief that *I can't do what I need to do if I'm focusing on presence.* All the really important aspects of life require that I jump back into my usual way of living. Presence just gets in the way and makes me ineffective.

This myth may play out in this way:

> *I'll schedule some time to meditate, or breathe, or go to a workshop. It will feel good. Then, I'll get back to my real life.*

In reality, presence is not dualistic. There are no different boxes or compartments. Real presence informs and supports daily living, and it's profoundly practical. Being present as we interact with loved ones, co-workers, and strangers, or while we're driving or buying groceries, for example, offers a totally different relationship to ourselves and to others than does following the dictates of the personality structure.

Myth #3: Presence means "going somewhere else."

Sometimes presence mistakenly gets translated into entering into a trance-like state. This may show up as visualizing a beautiful place, or becoming ungrounded and leaving contact with *here.* While visualizing can have powerful benefits, it's not the same as presence.

In reality, the specific patterns associated with each Enneagram type gives us precise information on our unconscious strategies for leaving presence. These patterns make up the inner stories of our lives that turn us away from being here. To reiterate, because these patterns are so familiar, we can easily confuse them with being present.

True presence is orienting ourselves to the truth and the reality that's available to us in the moment. Entering deeply into the experience of reality creates a shift within, and we experience ourselves and our relationship to the environment differently. Here, we increasingly connect with the life-affirming qualities that provide fuel for clarifying and living our deeper purpose.

Building Your Magnificent Capacity for Presence: Accessing the Three Centers of Intelligence

You are wired for presence—for groundedness, for open heartedness and for clarity and trust. You have the resources for developing profound moments of presence. In Enneagram language, these resources come in the form of Three Centers of Intelligence: the Belly/Instinctual Center; the Heart/Feeling Center; and the Head/Thinking Center. These correspond to particular locations in your physical body.

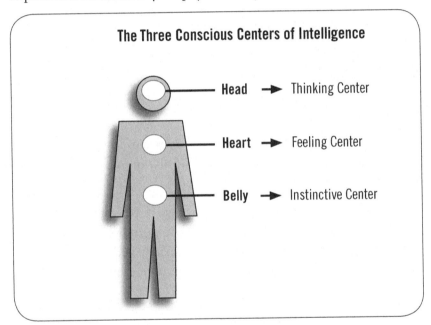

The Three Conscious Centers of Intelligence

Head ➤ Thinking Center

Heart ➤ Feeling Center

Belly ➤ Instinctive Center

Figure 16-1: The Three Centers of Intelligence

Having sensate, direct, lived-in contact with each of the centers offers intelligence that is far more extraordinary than the busy mind can conjure. The Centers of Intelligence, contacted through sensations, allow you to be in real contact with what is actually here. Then you can respond with what is needed in the moment—a gift of enormous practicality. The Centers give you something real around which to center yourself. This is the foundation of presence.[1] Once again, most of us are not taught to know, access, or use the wisdom of these centers in life, yet they are central to experiencing yourself as a whole human being; to experiencing your true aliveness. *Deepening your contact with each Center of Intelligence is a vital key to inner change and transformational shifts.*

Let's turn our attention toward each of the centers, with the intention of building your capacity for increasing contact with the real strengths of each center.

The Belly Center: Grounded and Alive

This center is a place of "gut knowing," of inner strength and aliveness, of substance, and of inner authority. No doubt, you have had a gut reaction; a time you intuitively knew that something was right—or not—for you.

What did you do with that knowing? Dismiss or override it with seemingly apparent logic or reasonableness? Or with a sense of what you *should* do, or some other mental activity? Or were you swayed by the input of others?

When you have not followed your gut's knowing, what was the usual outcome? How many times have you said to yourself, "I should have listened to my gut"?

The belly's intelligence speaks in the language of sensations throughout the entire body and sparks the urge to move in a certain way. It takes time and intentional practice to develop some fluency with this language so that you have a deeper sense of what's being communicated.

During a long walk, I inquired inwardly as to how I might convey a sense of what it is like to "live in the belly center." It's been a long journey for me to find my way into my belly. When I started, it was a totally foreign undertaking, and it remains a capacity that I continue to build. As I walked, all kinds of kinesthetic information came to me, some of which I'll try to share here. In a sense, my body is talking to your body.

What I've found to be most helpful is to not think about the body, but to let your energy drop, so that the sensations that are always in your body begin to come into awareness. A helpful mantra is "where do I experience sensations now?" You might want to start by standing in place and using the following statements to help guide you into a more direct experience with your own precious body. More useful than *thinking about* each of the following steps is to take the time needed with each statement until you *experience* some new sensation in yourself. Allow yourself to take in the sensation. You may find this fun, strange, or perhaps a little scary. I invite you to be curious and see what you learn.

I breathe…and sense into how the breath moves
in and out of my body…
I allow the breath to move more deeply within me…
perhaps I experience it all the way into my belly.

I experience the sensations in my body associated
with the in-breath…and the out-breath.
While still in contact with the movement of my breath in and out,
I bring attention to my feet.

I experience sensations in my feet. I feel the weight of my body
in my feet as they contact the ground.
I experience the sensations of my body's length.
I experience the sensations of having my back and my backbone.

My body takes up space. When I walk, I am aware that I
take up space. I notice the sensations in my body as I move through
space. I experience that my belly guides my movement.
I move from my belly.

As I experience whatever sensations arise now
in my body, I can look and see what is
around me, in my environment.

I see things from a fresh perspective.

I have substance.

I am landing in my body.

I reside here…in my body.

You can use this process for orienting toward your body as a regular practice for moving into deeper contact with your sensations and, thus, with your instinctive center.

If you are not in contact with your body's intelligence, then it is very easy for habitual thought—or emotional or behavioral patterns—to determine the course of your life.

One other recommendation here is to *relax*. It's a revelation to recognize that by relaxing tensions in the body, you come into contact with sensation.

Some people experience discomfort when coming into contact with the body's sensations. The body holds significant moments in your history, even if they didn't seem that significant to you at the time. And some people have had traumatic experiences in their childhood that continue to signal caution and sensitivity in coming into contact with the body. If it feels difficult to do this on your own, it will be important for you to work with a Deep Coaching practitioner or a specially trained somatic practitioner (or bodyworker) who can support you in gradually coming into a deeper and more trusting relationship with your body. Remember that coming into contact with this intelligence takes time, so practice with patience.

Learning to listen to this internal intelligence is a trust walk. Your body is what is here on this earth now. If you are not in contact with your body's intelligence, then it is very easy for habitual thought—or emotional or behavioral patterns—to determine the course of your life. Having the direct experience of the body's sensation *refocuses* attention from the personality's Focus of Attention (referring back to each type's propensity for narrowing the field of awareness to a particular object), as well as providing a foundation for real choice.

Here are some additional activities for developing contact with this center:

- many forms of conscious movement, such as yoga, chi gung, and akido
- horseback riding
- massage that strengthens awareness of body
- giving a voice to the body
- getting in touch with the natural energy of anger
- free-form dancing

Having contact with the body is always available to us, twenty-four hours a day, every day. You can use any and every activity or any moment of stillness in your day to practice developing this contact. For example, you might experience being conscious of sensations as you place your hands on your steering wheel, or allowing in sensations of the water while washing your hands, or paying close attention to the flavors and textures of food as you're eating. Anytime we consciously allow in these sensations, we discover that there's a vast amount of information available that's typically ignored when we are less conscious.

Most people discover that they don't take in or recognize these sensations if they don't slow their pace. Thus, it's tempting to read about the body's intelligence—even imagining or anticipating what it might be like to experience it—then think we know what it's like. What we call *thinking* is the easier route because of habit and conditioning. Without actually sinking into the sensations that arise in our bodies, we lose contact with a profound source of wisdom that's only available through the body. Without this connection to the body, we also lose contact with a source of deep guidance that's within ourselves. When we skip the body, it's no wonder it feels like something profound is missing within. It's no wonder that the sense of aloneness and the inner struggle continue unabated.

The Heart Center: Receptive and Authentic

As we enter the second Center of Intelligence, we do not leave behind our connection with the Belly Center. It provides an essential foundation for coming into contact with the Heart Center.

This Center of Intelligence is key to entering into a fuller experience of presence, more deeply inhabiting this precious gift of life, and to expressing our authentic self in the world. My intention is that my heart is speaking to your heart as you read.

The heart is the center through which you experience your compassion, openheartedness, tenderness, receptivity, authenticity, and love without conditions. When you want to know your inner truth, your heart will guide you if you will listen deeply and with honesty. These expansive qualities are the very ones that are so needed in our lives and world.

I used to think that I was really openhearted because I had a lot of sensitivity and feelings around most everything. I was shocked to discover that this did not mean that I was in touch with my Heart Center. Instead,

One of the greatest heartbreaks is to see how frequently and how far we've become distanced from our true nature.

I was reacting to life (which, by the way, felt very normal) rather than fully letting life in. There are many ways of reacting to life. For example, some of us guard our hearts because we're convinced that we will be hurt, rejected, or abandoned once again and will not be able to cope. Some of us are emotionally volatile and think we're not authentic if we don't fully express those emotions. Most of us keep so busy that we have no idea what our Heart Center actually feels like. Some of us fear that if we show up with our hearts, there'll be nothing there—we fear being empty. Sometimes it just feels as if our heart is so burdened with sadness from an unknown source that it doesn't feel safe to experience it. It would be too overwhelming. Sentimentality is another distortion of real contact with the heart. These leaky feelings serve as a cover or a substitute for what the heart is actually experiencing.

You can see that there are a lot of ideas about and reactions to actually being in contact with our hearts. A lot of fear comes to the surface. Reading and having a real conversation about the heart can bring up a lot of tenderness and a sense of protectiveness. In truth, every one of us has had our heart broken too many times to count. When we were young, our heartbreaks seemed way too big to bear, so we found a way to cope that protected us from the seemingly unbearable.

Truthfully, many adults continue to use the protective coping mechanisms from their childhood because they haven't yet learned to develop and trust their capacity for being with the heart's tenderness, sometimes rawness and exquisiteness. So, these coping mechanisms remain among the obstacles that create distance from the center of each individual's inner truth and authentic nature. That's an exorbitant price to pay.

Opening to the heart does not mean that we will not again experience heartbreak. In fact, we will. But now, knowing ourselves to be different than who we originally thought, we can tolerate more sadness, more tenderness, and, yes, more receptivity, spaciousness, and love. Our hearts can tolerate being broken because this is a necessary and organic part of the emotional and spiritual maturation process. And one of the greatest heartbreaks is to see how frequently and how far we've become distanced from our true nature.

If you are no longer willing to pay the price of keeping a painful distance from your heart, I invite you to slowly and respectfully enter into this delicate yet powerful space.

> *Do you recognize how deeply your heart wants to be fully inhabited? Do you recognize how lonely you are when you are not residing in your own heart?*

Without developing your capacity to be in direct contact with your own heart, it is easy to feel lost, lonely, or fearful that you'll be discovered as a fraud and inherently lacking real value. Being grounded in your physical body allows the Heart Center to be contacted. Here, your experience of your true and sacred nature expands. It is your birthright.

Here are two simple suggestions for expanding your capacity to be in contact with your own heart:

1. First, come into contact with your breath and the sensations in your body. Remember that this can take time, but it is an important step in helping you experience your physical ground, your solidity and substance. It helps create a foundation of real safety.

2. As you continue breathing, move the focus of your attention to the center of your heart space, located behind your sternum. What sensations do you notice? Just breathe into it and notice what is there. Perhaps you will feel very little, or you might feel a lot. Whatever is there, just breathe into it with no judgment and no rush. Do your best to stay with it, without trying to change anything. That's what your heart really wants. It wants your presence.

It wants to know that you are on its side.

If you use this practice on a regular basis, you will begin to develop more of a conscious relationship with your heart energy. It is only through real contact with the heart—with its sensations—that you come to experience your true nature. Thomas Merton called the heart the *point vierge*, the place where the human and the Divine meet.[2] It's here, in the deep heart, that you eventually come into contact with the mystery and the sacredness that is hidden in your soul.

Just as it is vital to come into contact with the body's intelligence, experiencing real contact with the Heart Center is central to your transformational work. But it is tender work. Even if you know yourself as a heartful person, be especially kind and gentle with yourself. If it feels too overwhelming to do this work on your own, find a practitioner that you can work with to support you on this important journey.

Once again, I recommend that you focus on relaxing. It's a revelation to recognize that by relaxing tensions in the body, you come into contact with sensation. And by coming into contact with the sensations in the heart, you begin to realize that there is a tender, caring being here.

Some additional strategies for paying attention to your heart include:

- participating with a group of people who are compassionate and accepting, and who practice these same qualities for themselves
- engaging in somatic work, in which you put conscious attention on your emotional state
- *staying with* the experience of receiving and *allowing* in whatever arises
- yoga or other body-oriented techniques with a specific focus on physically and energetically opening the heart
- giving a voice to the heart through singing, writing, speaking
- writing, painting, or any conscious personal expression that is not focused on outcome or product

The Head Center: Quiet and Spacious

As we continue this journey of psychological and spiritual development, we come into direct contact with the third Center of Intelligence, the Quiet, Spacious Mind. Here, we experience mental clarity and an inner, divine knowing, sometimes called gnosis—a knowing that is a kind of consciousness beyond what is available to our more familiar senses or reason. As this center quiets, we have *access to a greater level of trust in ourselves and trust in the unfolding of life.*

This is in stark contrast to the usual habits of the busy mind, which only offers a well-rehearsed and automatic way of living, and is dominated by unconscious beliefs, fears, and doubts, and by the self-imposed "authority" of the inner critic and constrictive inner stories. These powerful forces that unconsciously shape our lives until they are brought into acute awareness abound in mass consciousness. Look objectively at just one newspaper or listen to one newscast today, and you'll see that blame, judgment, fear, and so-called rationales given for many decisions all pass for news.

Since the busy mind is a well-rehearsed and automatic way of living, it represents the *path of least resistance* and what most people resort to under most life circumstances. Yet, have you noticed the relief associated with the quieting of constant mental chatter?

The great teachings from Buddhism remind us that it is our constructs and ideas that keep us mentally busy, and separate us from what is real and from our deeper nature. From our study of the Enneagram, we see that there are type-related, fixed ideas about everything—about what is right or wrong, about how to avoid hurt, about what we suppose are our inadequacies, about who other people are, about how the world works. These ideas take up enormous mental space and shape our orientation to life itself. The tighter we hold onto these constructs, the more separate we feel, and the greater our delusion becomes. The spiral continues: the more separate we feel, the more fearful we become, and then we do what we can to control the uncontrollable. Our Focus of Attention becomes more distorted and narrower. Here, it is difficult to see the choices that we actually have.

But we do have choice! And an important choice is to ask, "Where am I putting my attention?" Just posing that question can support us in getting some perspective.

Some people are concerned that a *quiet mind* is fine for meditating or other set-aside times, but impractical for life. In reality, these practices do not diminish one's intelligence or ability to function but provide increased clarity and perspective. Having a little more time between habitual ideas

What you are doing is changing your relationship to the mind from the center of all that is, to its proper place in your life.

gives a higher source of intelligence—often experienced as intuition—to download insights, understandings, and new information that otherwise would be lost to us.

How is the capacity for a quiet mind developed? Just as we've been paying attention to the sensations coming from the other centers, you can notice the sensations in and around your head. If there is a lot of tightness or agitation, it can help to gently massage your forehead, around your eyes, and around your entire scalp. Gently pulling on your hair can also release tension.

Some people find that acupuncture and other forms of working with their energy, or chi, relieves mental pressure and allows for increased mental clarity and spaciousness.

Another way of supporting the quieting of the mind is to work with an awareness of all three centers. Imagine hearing, "just quiet your mind." What is the result? Your mind is in no position to quiet itself, for the very act of mentally trying to become quiet activates it. However, focus on dropping your attention into direct contact with the sensations of your body and connecting with the belly in the moment. What do you notice? You may recognize that the mind is not the center of your attention. And as you bring your attention to the quality of your Heart Center in the moment, over time you will further notice that your relationship to each of the centers begins the process of shifting into a re-alignment. What you are doing is changing your relationship to the mind *from* the center of all that is, *to* its proper place in your life. By not taking the incessant mental activity as truth, you dis-identify with it. You are building your capacity for all of your centers to work together to support your development.

One of my clients used the term *spiritual chiropractic* as a metaphor for the unmistakable and palpable inner alignment that occurs when we engage all three centers. Over time, you experience more of your wholeness and integrity that the aligned centers support. You'll feel more at home and more centered in yourself.

You might notice feeling more in love with yourself. You are in the process of becoming more present, more grounded, more able to experience an inner peace, even when the outer world is frantic. And through your presence, you naturally become a catalyst for the positive change, an agent for authentic love that is so needed in your family, your community. *Now, how might your loving presence impact the world?*

Here are a few other suggestions for practicing quieting the mind:

- mindfulness meditation
- present-moment awareness—paying attention to the information coming through all of your senses
- listening to/being curious about yourself with *neutral acceptance/ non-judgment*
- becoming fully engaged in a creative/artistic experience or in improvisational speaking/improvisational theater in the presence of nonjudgmental individuals

I still have a picture of a fallen leaf given to me by a wise friend many years ago to remind me to look at my feet. The wisdom (below) from early naturalist John Burroughs suggests looking *under*foot as a lovely metaphor for coming back to here.

> *The lesson which life constantly repeats is to "look under your feet."*
> *You are always nearer to the divine and the true sources*
> *of your power than you think.*
> *The lure of the distant and the difficult is deceptive.*
> *The great opportunity is where you are.*
> *Do not despise your own place and hour.*
> *Every place is under the stars.*
> *Every place is the center of the world.*

—John Burroughs (1817-1862)
Studies in Nature and Literature

When all three centers are engaged in what they were designed to do, we are more open, receptive, flexible, healthy, and expansive. We are more present and awake. This is a rare experience in daily life, and it's part of the life journey to spiritual awakening.

It is simple, but it is not easy. It is never automatic. It always requires consciousness. And it will always deliver surprises. This is the trust walk of a lifetime.

Deepening Your Presence

As you learn to put more of your Focus of Attention on your centers, you are already interrupting, or softening, some of your personality type's patterns. But there are times when some patterns insistently repeat themselves. As Stephanie's experience exemplified (found under *Myth #1* earlier in this chapter), you can bring more presence to your experience to find out what is underneath the patterns.

What follows is a description of this more advanced work with presence that can be applied to daily life. I include it because it supports our innate capacity for healing and growth. If you are feeling particularly vulnerable or at all uncomfortable with this process, I would suggest you find a professional trained in the Deep Living work to guide you in practicing this process.

I recommend that you first read through this full description of this process, then return to it for a step-by-step guide when you are ready to allow presence to support you in experiencing a transformational shift. You'll discover here a radically different, compassionate, and loving approach to change.

The Deep Living Transformation Process (DLTP)[3]: Healing Troubling Patterns

1. Detect a Pattern That Is Active in Your Life.

To apply this work in a meaningful way into your life, it is important, first, to be able to recognize personality patterns that no longer support you, and, in fact, may be causing trouble. The descriptions and observations of the personality types in Section II of this book delineate many patterns.

How do you know when a particular pattern has been activated? What is it about your experience that tells you, "It's here!" Remember that these patterns can feel like your second nature, and they can be tricky to notice. So, we become pattern detectives.

Each pattern offers specific cues, or signals, that can serve as flags to get your attention and bring awareness to the pattern. For example, you might notice that you have a certain recurring thought, or an emotional experience that's associated with a pattern of one of the types. Or you might notice a faint but familiar body sensation, or recognize that you just behaved in a troublesome but familiar way. For example, you might find that you're snarly with someone and then recognize that there is a band of tightness around your head. Or you might feel really small and recognize a thought, such as, "I'm going to get emotionally hurt if I say something."

So, cues that a pattern has been activated can be found in a number of experiential channels, such as specific thoughts, emotional experiences, attitudes, bodily sensations, or behaviors. One or two of these channels might be easier for you to recognize.

Another way to recognize that a troublesome pattern is at work is when regular feedback at home or work points to a behavior that's not effective.

Generally, there is a particular attachment to the pattern—it's hard to imagine not having it. Sometimes it feels as if an alien has taken you over, and you realize that you have had this experience before, probably many times. Now, you are just more aware of it.

You might notice that you feel absolutely justified in reacting to a situation the way you did. This attitude is not at all unusual when we recognize a pattern: "Yeah, but he deserved that from me," or "I deserve to do that or have that because I've worked so hard."

The process of *recognition* is a major step in beginning to release and relax around your pattern. Remember that most of us go through our lives with little recognition that certain patterns or coping strategies are shaping our self-identity and stealing from our real freedom. Remember that these strategies developed for good reason. Unfortunately, they can easily become unconscious, habitual patterns that we over-utilize, even when they're costly to us.

Another good way to recognize a pattern is to notice when you feel tense, irritated, constricted, inflexible, angry, or even when you feel nothing—an emotional flatness. At first, you may not notice the pattern until after you've had a recent experience of it. You see it in the rearview mirror, so to speak. After you've become more familiar with this pattern, you may notice when you are in it. Consider this real progress! Eventually you'll come to a point where you can notice the pattern just *before* it takes hold and choose to do something different. This is true choice.

After a pattern is identified and named, it can be astonishing to see how many ways—in a wide range of circumstances and with people from different parts of life—that the pattern is expressed. It can be hard to be honest with yourself about this, yet it is necessary if you want to be free. When you tell the truth at least to yourself, you take a step in the direction of liberation. Patterns have a strong addictive quality. Some patterns are very destructive and others less destructive. But they are all a type of addiction. Riso often called these patterns *the basic addictions* of life.

Another cue that a pattern has been activated is that you feel down about life or about yourself, or you're pumping yourself up. Patterns do not lead to genuinely positive feelings.

2. Normalize the Pattern.

It's easy to become self-judgmental about the pattern that you're noticing.

Remember, having automatic patterns is completely normal. Unfortunately, most people in the world spend a great deal of energy expressing themselves through their patterns. You are among those waking up to the effect and the pain of patterns that do not yield beneficial outcomes. You are on a courageous journey. Recognizing patterns is an important step in both allowing yourself to be human and awakening to what lies beyond those patterns.

Recognizing and normalizing a pattern will help you take additional steps to bring more presence into your inner work. Honor yourself for this.

The following process will support you in going *underneath* the content of your experience, into deeper contact with yourself. Invite in the balm of presence to help you heal and release some of the compulsive power of a troublesome pattern.

You are shifting from identifying with the pattern to inquiring about it.

3. Conscious Cooking—Learning to Be with Your Experience.

Once you have identified a pattern that you'd like to focus on and have recognized that you're on an important journey, there are steps to help you gain more emotional health and an increased sense of inner peace. I call this "conscious cooking."

Notice and Observe

When you recognize that a pattern is showing up, see if you can just notice that it's here. If you judge yourself for having the pattern, that will only serve to reinforce it. Rather, the noticing can help you see it more clearly for what it is—a pattern. It's not the real you; it is how you've learned to cope with being in the world.

It helps to bring the following orientation to this process of noticing. You'll see here an application of the four tools that we discussed in chapter 4:

Approach it with an open mind. Be curious about it. This will feel quite strange, since you've probably been used to avoiding, denying, or judging your experience of this pattern, even if unconsciously, for a long time.

Here's a way of being curious: Try saying, "Isn't that interesting? There it goes again. Hmmm…I'm experiencing this again." You might be able to find the humor in this noticing process. Clients and workshop participants often say that this tool is so helpful because it *lightens the load* and keeps them from taking their patterns too seriously.

You are shifting from **identifying** *with the pattern to* **inquiring** *about it.*

Consciously breathe, and stay in contact with your breath.
There is much more to you than the existence of this pattern, though it can feel like it's taking up your whole life while you are experiencing

345

it. If you keep breathing and feeling your feet on the ground and your body in the chair, for example, you will notice that there is something here to support you.

Your contact with your body and its sensations offers a source of strength. You're using your body's intelligence to support you.

Be kind and compassionate with yourself. This pattern has existed for some very good reasons, even if it no longer serves you well. Remember that you did not actively choose this pattern, but that it comes with the territory of your particular Enneagram configuration. It is part of the larger human condition.

Here, you're using your heart's intelligence to support you.

You've probably had a lot of practice in being judgmental toward yourself. It's fundamental to a lot of suffering in people's lives, and it is one of the most damaging aspects of the personality's structure. Please remember, this judging, critical voice has little value for adults. Invite your "fair witness,"—that aspect of yourself that is simultaneously observant and non-judgmental—to be your ally. This practice will support you in experiencing *another degree of freedom* in your life.

As you stay with your experience and let go of the judgment, the intelligence of a quieting mind supports you.

Allow Your Experience—Be with It

For the process to work, it is important to allow yourself to *be with* and stay in the full experience of the inner sensations that arise from under the patterns. This means breathing *into* the sensations and keeping your attention focused on the sensations themselves. This is a foreign experience for many people. Nevertheless, it has great value.

While staying with the felt inner sensations, you may feel emotional or physical pain that you don't understand in some part of your torso. For example, you may feel a tight knot that extends from your stomach up to your ribcage. Or you may feel a constriction in your throat. Just keep breathing and staying with these sensations. You don't need to understand why you're having these sensations at this point.

You may notice that your attention wanders. Bring it back to the uncomfortable sensations.

Your nonjudgmental attention will "cook" the patterns so that something different is experienced, in its own time and pace.

This is a new and challenging approach. It's natural to:
- Push away the sensations to repress their existence; however, this leads to an exaggerated internal tension.
- Numb yourself so that you don't feel.
- Act out the hurt that you may be feeling.
- Short-circuit the experience—just touching into it, then determining that you've done enough with it. The ego might say, "I'm done."

Being with the uncomfortable experience is learning how to contain and have the full experience and range of the pattern within yourself—regardless of how long it takes—which allows the inner experience itself to heal and change. This process can take from a few minutes on only one occasion to needing longer periods that need to be repeated many times.

Just by the very act of noticing this pattern, it is likely that something about it will actually shift, *especially if you don't try to make anything happen.* Just let it be. This is not an invitation to act out from this pattern. Be aware of any internal justification to act it out. This is just another layer of pattern.

Through noticing, you are actually creating a little distance between yourself and the pattern. You're not taking it as personally and may begin to see it as separate from yourself. You're de-Velcroing some aspect of the pattern from whom you really are.

As you continue breathing and keeping your attention on the active sensations, you'll eventually notice that something happens. Generally, it's a feeling of something opening up inside, gaining a little more space, a little more ease. You may actually feel tired but quite rejuvenated.

You're supported by presence, the great field of inexplicable spaciousness and Being that holds us all.

If you're trying to make a good decision, initiate an important project that you've been having trouble with, or any number of other life circumstances, you may well find that, having fully allowed your very human experience to exist without judging it, you can move forward from a new place—one filled with more clarity, ease, and energy.

Acknowledge the Process

This process, though simple, is anything but easy. It calls upon several things from you: A great and conscious commitment to becoming freed from the compulsion of personality patterns, a radical orientation toward compassion, and a level of courage that you may not know you had. You're discovering something important about yourself. With every use of this approach, you are changed.

It's valuable to acknowledge and honor your inner work.

The Nature of the Process

There are numerous ways to explain what happens in this process. Fundamentally, its effectiveness is possible due to factors that include our willingness to go beyond our conscious choice and willfulness.

On one level, our patterns are associated with our particular neurological system. Our neurology and brain structure are changed when we bring this much consciousness to our inner work. Old neural connections are shaken up and new neural pathways are set in place.

Many people feel that through being so connected to their inner experience and the internal shifts that occur, they have been touched by grace, by an invisible and beneficial force. In other words, they didn't have to fix themselves or make something happen. Rather, when they showed up, the Universe extended a helping hand.

From a spiritual perspective, at the core of this process is *the power of presence.*

You're not all alone when you're coming into contact with the sensate experiences that result from your hurts, disappointments, and wounds. You're supported by presence, the great field of inexplicable spaciousness and Being that holds us all. As many early spiritual mystics knew, the constancy of curious attention, loving compassion, and breathing toward those difficult interior places have the effect of changing the heavy weight of lead into precious gold.

4. Releasing the Pain in and of Patterns.

This transformative process points to the existence of a level of pain that has become trapped internally, and that provides at least some of the fuel for the troubling patterns to continue. One of the great gifts of going through this experience of coming into direct contact with this level of pain is that you can see that there is a deeper reason—a previously hidden source of energy—for the pattern that you couldn't have known about before.

Pain does not get resolved by judging or denying or avoiding ourselves. Nor does it get resolved by identifying with and reinforcing it. **It's our reactions to the unconscious pain that provides the basis of our personality's patterns. And those patterns are what lead many to think that there's something wrong with them.** It's my intention that this exploration and inquiry will lead you to experience greater compassion for yourself and for others who also have troubling patterns that neither you nor they may be able to understand from a purely cognitive level.

It's important to reiterate that this is a challenging process to do on your own, especially the first few times. If you're trying to work through an especially persistent and troublesome pattern of the personality, it will be helpful to work with a professional who is knowledgeable about this process. In time, you'll find that you can use it more easily on your own.

The use of this presence-based process highlights the integration of breath and attention with nonjudgment and curiosity as a powerful vehicle for transformation and, truly, for life. Each of us carries within us the alchemical capacities for turning the lead of our psychic suffering into gold, which translates to a greater sense of ease and lightness. This is indeed cause for celebration.

Change Your Relationship with the Inner Critic and Change Your Relationship to Your Life

Ahh, the inner critic. Here's one thing that everyone in the world has in common! You see it in every opinion and judgment you have. There is no question—how you experience yourself is intimately related to the amount of internal life space your inner critic takes up! It can't help but affect your relationship to yourself and others, the decisions that shape your life, and how you *do* life. Left to operate on its own, it exhorts a heavy price that's ultimately paid by a scarred and deadened soul.

The inner critic is one of the most powerful influences that keeps you from being present.

When it takes a turn outward, the critic is reflected in the often *secret* judgments held toward loved ones and friends and even toward strangers. Evidence of its prevalence at a more global level is demonstrated through unresolved race relations, in the lens through which different secular or religious sects and communities relate to each other, and in international relations.

The inner critic is a primary cause of enormous suffering in the world.

If you ask, "What can I do to make a positive difference in my experience of life?," one of the most tangible and potent places where you can put your energy is in changing your relationship to the inner critic. This

The Enneagram offers us enormous insight into the inner critic and its relationship to your own inner authority.

chapter will help you unravel the inner critic narrative and address how you can take steps immediately to shift how you relate to this aspect of the personality's structure.

As a review, we remember that one of the most powerful ways of working with the Enneagram—once you've learned about your dominant personality patterns and core type—is to begin to see how those patterns operate on a day-to-day basis. As clarity sharpens the idea that these habits are part of a personality structure and not just an inevitable or unacceptable part of yourself, it's possible to gain a little distance from them. Eventually, you recognize the pattern in action, along with its unintended impact, and you eventually unhook from the power of the patterns. Identifying them as part of who you are no longer seems so attractive. In relaxing your identification with them, you orient to your more awakened nature with its inherent spaciousness and ease. You're less at the effect of the pattern, and you have more choice.

One of the major patterns that is an element of every personality is that of superego, also called the inner critic, or the IC. It can play a dominant role in your life if it is operating without your awareness. Not surprisingly, the Enneagram offers us enormous insight into the inner critic and its relationship to your own *inner authority*.

The Functions and Purpose of the Inner Critic

Having an inner critic is not a choice you get to make. It's part of every personality structure. It exists. It takes up some portion of your psychic energy, whether you obey it, try to ignore it, or try to fight it off.

Here are three ways of understanding that inner critic and what it sees as its role:

1. It's *the voice that evaluates*
2. It's *the voice of external authority, internalized*
3. It's *the police force for your ego's agenda*

We'll expand on each of these roles below.

The Voice that Evaluates

With increased awareness of the IC, you will notice that it communicates many messages about you, to you. The messages are all evaluative, all opinionated—and they can focus on every part of life:

- about your body; its weight; its size and shape; its capacity to perform in every arena, from physical tasks to sexual activity
- about your finances and earnings; how much it thinks you should be earning; what you have to show for your efforts
- about your role in your family as a parent, sibling, adult child, grandparent, or other role
- about how "together" you think you are or aren't; how you think others might evaluate you based on you having your act together
- about how you relate to others
- about your decisions in every and any part of life
- about your intelligence, skills, and life know-how
- about the value of your life and work
- about who and what you are, and who and what you should be

The inner scale of adequacy plays a substantial role in the activity of the inner critic.

Truthfully, it can and generally does comment on anything and everything that you think, say and do, and measures all that on its scale of right and wrong, or on its self-created scale of adequacy. The inner scale of adequacy plays a substantial role in the activity of the inner critic. For example, some people resist starting a project that could have value and meaning because of an inner message that they don't have what it takes or that they in some way do not deserve to take on a project of this nature. This inner voice may ask, "Who do you think you are, anyway?" Potentially meaningful projects that are sabotaged can span an entire range of human activity, from asking a person out for coffee, to inviting neighbors over for dinner, attending a pottery-making course, applying for a new position, changing careers, or mobilizing resources to provide clean water in an impoverished community.

EXERCISE: Think about your answers to the following questions as a way to start looking at how this scale functions in your own life.

What is your scale based on?

One way you can begin identifying the scale that your inner critic uses is by recognizing and naming what you feel you don't have enough of.

For example, do you feel that you don't have enough intelligence, enough talent, enough capacity, enough credentials, enough good looks, enough money, enough energy, enough power, or enough influence?

What are you not doing because of a message that there is something lacking in you?

Who created the criteria for this scale? Where did these criteria come from?

Likely, your scale is based upon the interaction of prominent messages from your emotional and social environment and from your particular personality structure.

Perhaps you've been influenced by messages from your dominant culture or subculture about the importance of having certain qualities or experiences.

For example, much of the abundance/manifestation work that is plentiful on the Internet, bookshelves, and workshops inadvertently gets into the realm of the inner critic. While many of the ideas taught or suggested in this literature are healthy and very useful, some of it is not and leads to an underlying feeling that something must be wrong with you or you must be doing something wrong if you aren't manifesting your dream life.

For those who consciously follow a particular spiritual path, there can be a sense that they need to be more conscious, more enlightened, more evolved. Thus, they condemn themselves when a very human emotion, such as anger or shame or depression, shows up. If this sounds familiar, it's because a dimension of the inner critic, called the spiritual superego, moves into action, judging you against some elevated state of being that you aren't actually experiencing.

Whose idea—or what idea—of how life is supposed to look is the basis for your internal yardstick?

These measurements can come from a wide range of sources, some of which we will explore further in this chapter.

Your inner critic has a long history, so it helps to recognize how and where it got its start.

The Externalized Voice of Authority, Internalized

Your IC has a long history, so it helps to recognize how and where it got its start.

Embedded in the ego structure is the capacity for learning how to be a human being. Since the moment you were born, you were mirrored by important others. Fortunate children were oohed and aahed over and cuddled by adoring family members and friends. Yet, no matter how loved you were, you naturally were also an unwitting source of tension, stress, and discomfort for parents or caregivers who were trying to figure out how to be parents or just get through life themselves.

You have your own life experience, and you may or may not remember your earliest years. No doubt, you actually received a lot of different messages about what was good and bad from the earliest days, months, and years of your life. And whatever these messages were, they were filtered by your personality structure (as discussed in chapter 2). For example, twins with different personality structures receiving the very same messages (which, in itself, is open to question) from their parents would have *received* the messages in different ways.

But let's get back to you. It's likely that there was a discrepancy between what your caretakers intended to convey and how you interpreted their communications. Once again, it's important to take into account the interaction between your early environment and your temperament and personality structure.

As you became a toddler and young child, it was expected that you would learn how to live with others. You received instructions (clear and distinct or vague and hazy; strictly enforced or not enforced) on how to become a member of the larger human family. All that training created a container called *social conditioning*. You needed to learn what your boundaries were. Your instructions included how to know the difference between right and wrong. This helped you develop a conscience to guide your choices. When you were little, it focused on how to share toys, how to behave in church or at school, how to be nice to your little sister or to be loving to your grandmother. Maybe you were taught how to be polite to different authority figures and to your elderly great-aunt that you saw once a year. Maybe you were raised by others outside of your birth family and got confusing messages about how you were supposed to act. You may or may not have acquiesced to your social conditioning, but, either way, you got messages, sometimes confusing ones, about how you were supposed to behave. If you rebelled against authority, perhaps you thought you escaped the effects of this training, but that is not possible.

Was early guidance important? Absolutely. We are social beings. We all need some direction in learning how to be a part of the social world. But most often, the training didn't stop there.

You may have been compared to others, either favorably or unfavorably. Did you have an older brother or sister who excelled in subjects favored by your parents or caretakers? Or maybe you had a younger sibling who couldn't measure up to you? Did you receive a message that your success in life depended on how well you did in certain sports, in the arts, in the classroom, or in business? Or that your worth depended on making sure other people's needs were met?

You have a unique historical experience regarding what was encouraged/ not encouraged, expected/not expected, rewarded/punished, and valued/not valued in your social and emotional milieu that formed your early life.

And there were different sources of these messages: mainly from parents or guardians, but also from other important adults, such as grandparents and extended family members, church or school authorities, or informal group and organizational leaders.

EXERCISE: The Discovery Process— Your History with the Inner Critic

You may have explored the inner critic before. Try approaching this discovery process as if you're attempting to understand it for the first time. What is your history with the inner critic experience? I encourage you to write your answers.

What are the messages that you have historically heard from your inner critic?

What was encouraged/not encouraged, expected/not expected in your family of origin? What was rewarded/punished, valued/not valued in the social and emotional milieu that formed your early life?

What person or group do you associate with these messages?

Go back through your list of inner critic messages and see if they sound like anyone's voice. (For example, the voice of a parent, grandparent, or sibling? A teacher or other guiding figure? The media? A church leader? A teenage version of yourself?)

How have you historically dealt with this voice?

We have many ways in which we cope with these messages.

Select three of the most important messages you've written down during this exercise and examine how you've dealt with them. For example, do you tend to resist or fight the messages? Do you tend to believe the messages and follow what they have to tell you?

NOTE: Recognizing the messages of the inner critic historically or in current time can be a challenge because they often seem like a given—a truth that is not open to exploration and curiosity. It may be necessary to revisit this material and the exercises several times to clearly identify these messages.

What has been the impact of the inner critic on the quality of your life and on how you've expressed yourself up to now? This may be a difficult question to answer, but I encourage you to spend time on it. For example, how has the inner critic influenced how you feel about yourself? Are you aware of any limits it has placed on what you do or would like to do?

What is your dream for your life? Do you have any long-held hopes for your life?

- What dream(s) have you put on the back burner, dismissed, or forgotten?
- Did you allow yourself to have a dream for your life?
- What personal qualities or gifts have you wanted to share, or what contributions have you wanted to make, that have been shelved or postponed?

NOTE: Many people experience that they have edited their life dreams. That is, they culled them back, thinking that they were impractical or impossible to reach.

The Voices of Today

Let's fast forward and look at today, instead of your past. So, here you are, at whatever age you are, probably somewhere between eighteen and ninety-eight.

To what degree do the messages that you remember receiving still linger within you? Maybe it doesn't feel so much like lingering, but rather that they show up as the commander-in-chief!

Are you trying to determine what your current or past friends will think of you? Are you concerned about what a parent or sibling will say to you if you follow your dream? It doesn't matter if your parents are alive or have passed—it's not at all unusual to be concerned with what they would think of you now, as if they were still living.

Are there internal messages that are insistent forces in how you're living your life?

What do you hear yourself say back to yourself? Do these messages feel eerily familiar?

That inner mechanism that we've been referring to as the inner critic has the amazing capacity to internalize the external messages that you received when you were very small and to make them your inner police force.

Digging deeper, you can ask again: "Whose voices are these, really?"

The internal messages that you hear are primarily now, from your own internal system. If that is the case, how do you know which ones you really need and give you good guidance, and which ones are no longer useful and no longer serve you?

The Police Force for Your Ego's Agenda

How do you distinguish between your authentic conscience and the messages of your inner critic?

This is where the Enneagram offers valuable insight into the workings of the IC, as it points to the different ways that each of nine personality/ego structures experiences this authoritative, evaluative energy.

You remember that the ego structure is designed to approximate the qualities that delight the soul. As we have noted throughout the book, the ego structure can only create a faux, or false, experience of the real awakened qualities. The ego, not realizing this, is set up with a big agenda to try to do the very thing it cannot do. The inner critic might be considered, at best, a project coordinator, and, at a more severe level, a police force that marshals all its efforts to insure that the ego is staying on target to accomplish its big project. In a sense, it's a staunch defender for the status quo of the ego.

Are You Doing Enough for the Ego's Big Job?

What is the project that your ego is trying to accomplish? If you've been able to identify your dominant type, you may want to review the section on the chapter of this type that discuses the Inner Logic and Triangle of Identity. You'll remember that each personality structure is attuned to a particular way of being in the world that feels right. Each ego structure has a built-in defense to maintain its way of being, and it insists that individuals dominant in that type adhere to certain rules. There's an internal logic that the IC is monitoring, along with a warning about being in some kind of danger if you don't listen up and follow its rules.

The inner critic is monitoring for the following:

Type One: Are you being good enough? Are you doing things right? If you let up on taking responsibility, you're in danger, so listen to me and I'll make things better. I'll straighten you out!

Type Two: Are you being caring and helpful enough? Are you being generous and loving? If you're selfish, you're in danger, so I'll straighten you out!

Type Three: Are you being recognized enough for your successes? Are you staying on top of your game? If you get lax and don't show that you have it all together, you're in danger, so I'll straighten you out!

Type Four: Are you being authentic enough? Are you being true to your feelings? If you aren't unique and responsive to your feelings, you're in danger, so I'll straighten you out!

Type Five: Are you smart enough? Are you competent enough? Are you figuring out how things work? If you don't have enough expertise, you're in danger, so I'll straighten you out!

Type Six: Are you keeping yourself safe enough? Are you fulfilling the expectations of others? If you're not fulfilling those expectations, you're in danger, so I'll straighten you out!

Type Seven: Are you free enough? Are you being spontaneous and having fun? If you show your sadness, you're in danger, so I'll straighten you out!

Type Eight: Are you strong enough? Are you in control? If you show any vulnerability, you're in danger, so I'll straighten you out!

Type Nine: Are you calm and peaceful enough? Are you keeping the harmony in the environment and staying above conflict? If not, you're in danger, so I'll straighten you out!

***NOTE**: If you take a look at the blueprint for each type again, you'll see that the IC message reinforces every other aspect of that particular type's architecture.*

There is a particular way of overdoing some behavior for each egoic structure that reflects the message of its particular inner critic. You can see how hard each person works to make sure that he or she follows the internal logic and rules of that structure.

I'm not implying that, as individuals, you only receive the messages associated with your type. However, seeing the IC through the lens of each type provides more information on what might not be so obvious as you're trying to understand how the IC works.

When you remember that the ego structure does not represent who you truly are, it can be easier to step back and say, "Wait, this voice is just a pattern. It's not the real deal!" That's a very liberating stance to take!

It's easy to see why it's difficult to discern between the inner critic and your own guidance. The inner critic takes on so many roles--the evaluating voice, the externalized voice of authority that has become internalized, and the internal police force—that its influence comes from many directions. It's likely that the critic has hijacked the role of your guidance so that it feels like the real thing. In order to begin to sort through what's real and what's coming from this imposter, you need to know how to spot the IC when it's operating.

> *There is a particular way of overdoing some behavior for each egoic structure that reflects the message of its particular inner critic.*

How Can the Inner Critic Be Identified?

How can you know when the inner critic is activated? Here are three of its trickier characteristics:

1. The inner critic operates on all volumes.

Sometimes the strength of the IC is loud and in your face. You can't miss it and it's easy to spot how insistent it seems. But it's very tricky. It can also operate quietly, just under the radar. It's akin to the volume dial on a radio. It can blare so loudly that the neighbors call and demand that you turn it down, or it can be at the lowest volume with a barely audible zzzzzz. Yet, it's there, and its impact is no less pervasive or deadly.

Because it's often the loudest of the interior voices, it's easy to assume that it's right. But that's not so.

2. The inner critic operates on automatic.

The IC is always, always operating on automatic. When you're not questioning, recognizing, and naming it, it does as it pleases. It's only when it comes into more awareness that you can change your relationship to it, gain some distance from it, and broaden your repertoire of responses. It's simply another personality pattern, albeit, a strict one.

3. The inner critic multiplies itself.

One of the trickier aspects of the IC is to "judge the judge." That is, even when you notice that you're judging yourself, the IC can jump right in and take that seat next to you, and judge you for judging it. It has a multiplier effect. In that sense, it can feel like you'll never be able to work with it skillfully.

Let's dig deeper into your personal experience of the inner critic to help you detect its activity.

The Mental Experience

I've heard many of my clients and students say that they're aware of an inner dialogue with a voice that acts like it gives you a truth that dare not be questioned. (No, you're not talking about people who are crazy—we're all a little crazy. This voice exists for everyone.) The force of this voice is such that to dare to question it can seem like great peril will come to you. This, by the way, is a form of *psychological blackmail!*

For some people, this voice sounds like the very voice of God and carries so much authority that it can seem impenetrable. But the voice of God, it is not.

There are so many inner noises, how can you be certain that you have come into contact with the IC? Here are some of the general flags to let you know that it's switched on.

A Deflated Ego

One of the phrases I often hear from clients is, "This is what I'm struggling with." If you know about struggling, then take a closer look at the role of the inner critic.

Whenever you feel bad about yourself, you can suspect the IC is at work. People often recognize the IC operating because they have low opinions of themselves, experience low-level depression, or are angry at or disapproving of themselves for any number of reasons. This also shows up as not believing in yourself, your capacities, or what's possible for you.

It shows up when you're negatively evaluating yourself against someone else or against some internal measure.

This is at the root of feeling hopeless and resigned about your situation. When the deflation is especially active, there's a negativity about yourself, your life, and/or your future that colors your whole experience, although other people may have no idea of your internal struggle.

It's common for people dominant in certain personality types to have a frequent experience of a deflated ego. It's not your true nature to feel bad about yourself, but it's how many of us have been conditioned. I've heard clients say that if they don't feel bad about themselves, then something must be wrong. I find it saddening that it can be more acceptable and natural to feel bad about oneself than to be self-accepting.

I find it saddening that it can be more acceptable and natural to feel bad about oneself than to be self-accepting.

Evaluating Others

When you feel bad about yourself, it often shows up in what you think about others. If you noticing that you're comparing yourself to others, or that you have a critical attitude toward certain people, that can be a cue that you have a hidden, negative evaluation of yourself that's reflected back to you by these individuals. In psychological terms, this is called *projection*. Negative self-evaluation can easily be pointed toward the outside world.

An Inflated Ego

Surprised? Yes, whenever the critic is trying to manipulate the ego into acting in a certain way, it's still the IC at work. Here, the experience is one where the inner critic poses as a cheerleader, pumping you up to be the latest and greatest in whatever way the IC directs. There is a certain inner—if not outer—swagger, and an arrogance that accompanies this stance. In other words, there's a pumped-up attitude of confidence that you *really have done a great job.* It may be true that you performed well. But the IC can then exaggerate it, telling you that you not only knocked it out of the ballpark, but you also do it so much better than others. You might notice that you're patting myself on the back or telling others how well you did, or you're just feeling very self-pleased.

Truthfully, when the inner critic is active, a lot of energy is going into convincing yourself and others about your greatness. If you investigate what you're feeling underneath the self-aggrandizement, you'll likely discover that you feel that you have to go out and do it *at least that good the next day.* Maybe you need to do even better. So, the IC is still perceivable, if a little more tricky.

Just as the inner critic can offer a deflating message that sounds like the voice of God, the inflating voice can sound divinely inspired, as well. If you have a consistent message that you need to *push yourself* to the next level, that's much more likely to be the inner critic talking than anything your divine source would say. Certain personality structures are more oriented to this inflationary activity. It can be very difficult to challenge that hyped-up voice because it can feel that, without that constant reminder of how awesome you are, the balloon could deflate, and you could fall into no-man's-land.

It's important to make a distinction here between an authentic feeling of goodwill toward and confidence in yourself *and* the need for constantly reminding yourself of a pumped-up image that you have to prove to yourself and others. Of course, everyone needs to be able to acknowledge his or her gifts, recognizing something that they feel good about. It's important to check out the difference between these states for yourself, because a consistent need to prime the pump of confidence means that the inner critic is having its way with you.

Every personality structure has a way of inflating the ego, priding itself on being the best in certain attributes. Even if it isn't true that the individual is really expressing those assets, there's a secret (or not-so-secret) arrogance that, "I am better at this than anyone else."

It's not your awakened nature to pump yourself up in order to feel good about you. You don't need to manipulate yourself in order to be deserving of real love, respect, and acceptance, and you'll never be able to manipulate yourself enough to experience the wonder and preciousness that you are. These authentic, uplifting qualities disappear in the face of being pressed, of being manufactured. When you can relax into your true nature, the real qualities arise.

The inner critic becomes particularly activated and accelerated when you are on a path of change and growth.

It's All About the Ego!

Have you noticed that when the IC is either inflating or deflating your ego, the Focus of Attention is entirely on you! Just take a look. It puts you in the center of attention, even if the voice insists that you're nobody! It compares you to some visible or invisible, or tangible or intangible, yardstick. So, while it might seem that it's about someone else ("Those people have got what it takes"), it always comes back to you. More specifically, the egoic version of you ("You don't have what it takes, and you'll never get it." Or, "Baby, you really have it. Just keep it up!").

The Loud, Anti-Growth Force

While it can show up under any and all circumstances in life, the IC becomes *particularly activated and accelerated when you are on a path of change and growth.* Perhaps you're considering a career change or being more engaged with a spiritual community. Perhaps you want to write a novel, compose music, create a new product line, or work in a developing country for a year. Maybe you just feel in your bones that it's time for you to go deeper to learn more about yourself. You might hear messages like:

"Who do you think you are? Who is going to listen to you, anyway?"

"What a waste of time. Get back to what's important!"

"You've got to be kidding! How will you survive? Stop dreaming."

"See? You tried it, and it didn't work. Forget it!"

"What about your friends and family? You are *so* selfish!"

The inner critic becomes more important than your dreams, more important than your growth, more important than evolving into the person that you really are!

"Forget about following that silly idea of yours. Just accept your lot in life and be happy with what you have."

"Get real. Just look around you. Are all these other people changing their lives? What would happen if everyone did this?"

"Look, you know your partner will never go for it. If you move forward, you're going to be left all alone."

When you listen to and believe the voice(s) of the inner critic, the inner critic becomes more important than your dreams, more important than your growth, more important than evolving into the person that you really are!

Some people find that the inner critic offers an unconscious excuse for not following their passion, heart, or priorities. One way this occurs is by getting distracted by other things that "should be" taken care of first. In fact, *should* is one of the critic's favorite words.

When you get distracted or use an excuse not to move forward, you deprive yourself of a deeper, richer expression of yourself that's aligned with what has meaning and value for you. And it deprives others of your gifts that you will and can only share when you've grown into a fuller, more integrated self. Following the change-averse messages of the inner critic leads to two major losses.

As part of how it functions, realize that the IC creates amnesia around many of your experiences, around many of your gifts and talents, and around what's really important for you. By time and time again diminishing you and belittling what's really important to you, it serves to distract and dismiss what you have to offer through simply showing up as the real you!

The inner critic is a centerpiece of the architecture of the personality. It helps keep the ego in power by undermining the individual's trust in self and in the divine. When believed, it takes the individual away from his or her true nature. Through listening to and believing in and identifying with the inner critic, a person loses connection with his or her soul.

Tracking the Body's Experience

Have you noticed how your body responds to these mental voices? There are any number of somatic (kinesthetic/bodily) sensations that can arise. Neuroscience research connects many chronic physical diseases and pain to various mental patterns. Here are a few:

- tightening of muscles in any part of your body—your jaw, shoulders, neck, throat and face, for example, or a big knot in your belly
- a sense of weakness, as if you can barely hold yourself up
- chronic pain in any part of your body
- a palpable heaviness in the center of your chest
- a somatic sense of mental fogginess
- teeth-gnashing
- a chronically upset stomach
- a paralysis or heaviness that makes it hard to move
- heart palpitations

The inner critic creates amnesia around many of your experiences, around many of your gifts and talents, and around what's really important for you.

To track the sensations in your body, frequently spend time paying attention to specific areas in your core and in your extremities. Be curious about whether sensations that arise have a sense of familiarity, even if you haven't previously been so aware of them. If there's a sense of familiarity, it's worthwhile spending more time with this area.

You may be surprised to discover that what feels so familiar and normal somatically is connected to the uninterrupted internal evaluator. Its effect is often to shut down your energy, distract you, or to build intensity so that you take up fights that have little to do with what's really going on. Without awareness, it's easy to succumb to familiar somatic experiences as being inevitable.

What are your familiar somatic sensations? Taking your exploration another step, can you trace these sensations to the inner critic messages that are associated with them?

The Emotional Experience

With increased awareness of the inner critic, you may notice that, just under the mental activity, there is emotion. Often, the emotion that the inner critic is covering is hard to identify or allow. Here are some of the main emotions that bubble under the surface (or on the top, as the case may be).

Fear

Fear shows up as an anticipation of all the things that could possibly go wrong if you don't do what the critic requires, or if you listen to and follow the thread that runs truer and deeper within you. This emotion is associated with a sense of lacking the capacity or resourcefulness to take the appropriate action. It has two possible effects: One effect is paralysis, of not being able to move forward on what you really want. The second effect looks like the opposite—and that is to push your way through with a lot of energy, not allowing yourself to feel the fear. Perhaps you knock some heads along the way.

A related emotional experience that is also felt by the body is anxiety. This can be a deeply uncomfortable energy to experience, as it comes with an internal buzz, such as wanting to get out of your skin, and a strong urge to do something now!

Apathy, or Resignation

Apathy and resignation show up when you are convinced by the IC that there's nothing you can do about your situation, that the air has been taken out of your sails, and that you or what you desire doesn't really matter much anyway. The emotional flatness of resignation and the deadening experience of depression deflate and drain one's energy.

Anger

The inner critic can use anger to make itself bigger and more powerful and to show a sense of righteousness. Overly expressed anger can generate a lot of energy, and the inner critic will provide a sense of justification for every expression of anger, including explosiveness.

Shame

A sense of shame arises—often—and it's one of the hardest emotions to allow. Much deeper than embarrassment, shame brings a fundamental sense of unworthiness, or a deep inadequacy, or a sense that you are fraudulent and it's been discovered. You don't want people to see who you think you are, because it would be too painful. You may have the experience of having no inherent value. Any of these feelings are difficult to allow, yet they, too, are part of the larger inner-critic pattern. It's no wonder you want to avoid that experience. *It's easier to beat yourself up with the inner critic's voice than to feel the pain of shame.* But this emotion is the parallel to the inner critic: They both have a lot of energy, both are based upon a false sense of inadequacy, and both can be painful to recognize within yourself.

It's not you that is inadequate—it's the ego, which has an inherent inadequacy because it's based upon a false sense of yourself.

Did you catch that? It's not you that is inadequate—it's the ego, which has an inherent inadequacy because it's based upon a false sense of yourself. This is an example of how the ego builds a parallel (and false) life to your true nature. (As a reminder, this is the *parallel living* that we discussed at the end of chapter 1.)

Everyone feels shame at times, if they allow themselves to. What's most dangerous about shame is not that we have it, but that we try to avoid it at all costs. Addictions of all kinds are one of the primary ways we mask the experience of shame. These addictions come in the form of alcohol and drugs, or too much of anything, such as too much television, too much exercise, too much food, too much medication, too much sex, or too much Internet, to name a few from among a long list of possibilities. When we engage in some activity too much, it's because it's the easiest thing for us to do. It's the path of least resistance. Yet these too-much activities all come with high costs.

The unacknowledged inner critic and its partner, unacknowledged shame, both live in the roots of our addicted lifestyles and in our culture. We are called to bring these internal dynamics into the light so that they might lose some of their energy and power in our lives.

I encourage you to be gentle with yourself as you explore this. At the same time, whenever you can accept what is arising, and stay with and breathe into the experience, something shifts. Your capacity for living more fully and more at home in your skin expands.

Guilt

Another emotion associated with the inner critic is guilt. If you don't do something that your inner critic insists on, then guilt can easily arise. If you review the statements under "Are You Doing Enough for the Ego's Big Job?" section earlier in this chapter, you will again see how insistent the inner critic can be. For example, are you being helpful or smart or peaceful or responsible enough, according to the given directive? If not, you may experience big doses of guilt. And it can feel like there's nothing you can do about it. Of course, that isn't true.

Let's take a look at another dimension of how this guilt process works internally. For many people, guilt is experienced as a necessary ingredient required to move into action. Without the pressure of guilt building up, there's a fear that maybe you wouldn't do what you are supposed to do. On the other hand, guilt is accompanied by enormous internal pressure that can feel paralyzing, which creates a huge inner conundrum. The more paralysis, the less you can move into action, and the more magnified the guilt is, and the louder the inner critic is, the more paralysis. In the midst of all this, it's easy to feel resentment toward whatever you're feeling guilty about! This creates a closed and repeating system that feels horrible.

On the next page is a graphic that exposes how this system works. And every part of this system feels true. Once again, it feels like how life is.

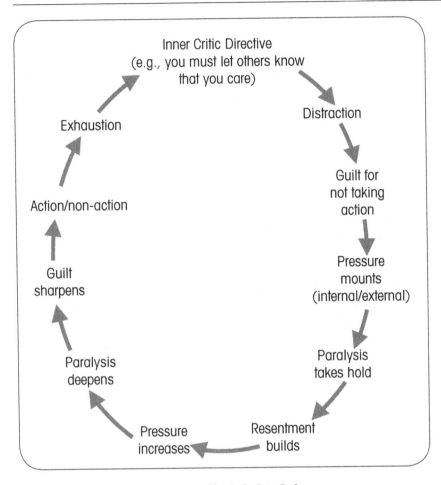

Figure 17-1: The Guilt-Grip Cycle

Here's an example of how this works in our lives:

Sandy has agreed to be responsible for an annual fundraiser for a nonprofit, where she is in her second year on the board. (The Directive from her inner critic: Be the chairperson for the annual fundraiser.)

She realizes that the task is a huge undertaking. It feels overwhelming and she feels unsupported by the larger board. Her daughter, a junior in high school, is also active as the president of the student council and in theater. She's also getting ready to look at colleges. Sandy has been an involved mom and easily focuses on her daughter's needs at this important time. In addition to time spent with her daughter, she finds *a lot of other things that she feels need her attention. Consequently, she puts the fundraiser on the back burner for several months. (The **Distraction** from the inner critic's demand.)*

She is almost constantly aware of feeling Guilty for not staying in contact with the committee members who have agreed to take on specific roles, and for not providing direction to the fundraising initiative itself. At the same time, she feels the Pressure mounting. It gets to the point where she feels nearly Paralyzed, but she manages to pull enough energy together to have committee meetings to coordinate the multiple tasks. Even as she does so, she can feel the Resentment building within herself, and she realizes that she doesn't want this responsibility.

*As the date of the fundraiser approaches, the **Pressure** mounts. More **Paralysis** sets in, and she is filled with **Guilt**. She gets into **Action** with her committee in the last few weeks before the event. Even though the fundraiser has a good outcome, she's **Exhausted** and feels like a wreck.*

The energy that is eaten up by the *guilt-paralysis-pressure-resentment cycle* overshadows and steals from the energy that was required for the task. In fact, this cycle can take far more energy than the task itself. Yet, in the midst of the cycle, Sandy couldn't see alternatives.

Perhaps you can see this repetitious cycle in your own life, around personal and public activities. When you become aware of how it's actually working in your life, and as this awareness grows, it's possible to interrupt the cycle.

For example, when you can notice that you're feeling guilty, ask yourself, "What am I telling myself that I'm supposed to be doing? What are the shoulds? How is this undermining the task at hand? Where am I putting unnecessary energy? Am I feeling resentful? If so, who or what am I feeling resentful toward?"

Taking a few breaths can not only help you gain perspective but pull you out of the cycle.

Recognizing the Ultimate Impact of the Inner Critic

All of this activity does not take place without having an impact on you and, very likely, on those around you. As you begin to recognize the life history of your inner critic, and the internal messages that you've been listening to and giving some degree of authority and importance to, it may become quite clear that there've been significant consequences in your life.

Let's look at how this relates to you.

When have you not tried something you really wanted to do?

How have you felt about yourself in the wake of an IC attack?

How has the ego-deflating or -inflating tendencies in your own life impacted other people who are important to you?

Can you remember feeling shame or guilt about something you did or did not do?

Can you name some specific and unintended consequences of the IC as the dominant or most influential voice in some of your decisions?

It's not unusual to feel a sense of grief, loss, and remorse when you reflect on these questions. In just trying to do your best, you find that you've been listening to a substitute for your real guidance, and you've lost some precious moments in your life.

The inner critic, when uninterrupted and *believed*, ultimately is the voice of self-rejection. Time and time again, the fundamental message is that you are not living up to your end of it's requirements. You're not staying within the confines of its restrictive and evaluative authority.

As we noted earlier, the inner critic doesn't like it when we are changing, growing, maturing, so it's vital to your well-being to bring its activity and its impact into awareness.

In this process of self-discovery and making your way back home to yourself, let me once again offer a gentle reminder that it's important to let yourself be with whatever feelings are coming up rather than trying to change them. There is no doubt that it is heartbreaking to recognize the degree of suffering that has been imposed by our identification with the inner critic, and other aspects of our personality structure.

Letting our hearts break allows us to be more discerning and honest with ourselves. It opens the door to softening the grasp of the personality and healing some of the inner pain that we've carried around. Letting our hearts break invites us into a renewed and loving relationship with ourselves.

This journey is worth the heartbreak.

Now, let's look at one more important element as we begin to unravel the power of the inner critic.

The Internal Power-Victim Dynamic

Earlier I discussed the inner critic as the internalized voice of authority. The word *authority* can be laden with images and meanings. If you look up the word in the dictionary, you'll see synonyms like "control, rule, directs thoughts or actions, issues commands and punishments." The underlying experience is that an *authority has control over something else.* And what is the quality of that voice? Powerful!

Thus, authority doesn't exist on its own, but rather in relationship to something else. What is the something else that the inner critic is locked into a relationship with?

Of course, it's the part of us that feels like it lacks power. It's the inner child, the part that feels victimized. It's perfectly normal to not want to acknowledge this part of life as an adult, but as long as it stays in the shadows of one's life, *the critic-victim dynamic* will have more food to sustain it.

The inner critic doesn't have much basis for existence if there's not an internal, powerless one. As you identify and begin to question or interrupt the critic's activity, the more you're responding to it from the stance of being an adult. The strategies discussed on the following pages support you in doing that.

Strategies for Unhooking from the Inner Critic's Noise

In order to unhook from the IC, it's necessary to recognize and accept it as a knowable part of life. Lately, you've been identifying some of the messages of your inner critic, learning how it works, and recognizing some of the ways it can show up in your life. It can be a further revelation to learn that it's possible to quiet its inner activity. With awareness, practice, and a commitment to well-being (yours and that of others), its impact can be decreased. While the IC may not go away completely, it can be rendered quite ancillary and even impotent.

Here are some specific steps for unhooking from the IC that I have found useful both in my own life and for my students and clients.

1. Recognize the inner critic

With your increasing awareness, see what you notice about your own experience when the IC is active. This will increase your capacity for observing it!

2. Name it

Call it out. "Oh, you're the inner critic. I see what you're up to." When you do so, it actually helps create a little distance between you and it. It's no longer you being the inner critic (it has you), but now you have it! In other words, you begin to take it less personally, and, eventually, less seriously. This is a vital step in becoming freer.

3. Confront it

Now that you've called it out, it's time to stand your ground. (It just takes practice.) Here are some examples:

"I guess you didn't like that I did that. Oh, well. Thanks for the information, but honestly, I'm doing just fine."

"You were certainly loud about that. I heard you, and I don't need any more of your advice about it."

"Stop."

Can you see how you are taking on responsibility for yourself as an adult? The inner critic had its say, treating you like a errant child. Tell it "Enough!" The inner critic has probably had its own way for a long time, so confronting it is going to take practice—lots of practice. I tell my students that they may need to confront the critic hundreds of times—sometimes in the same day! Remember that you are building a new muscle and creating new neurological pathways.

Another strategy is to interact with the inner critic through written dialogue. Many people find that writing helps them gain clarity on what all this internal activity is. One approach is to write with two colored pens; one which will write out the voice of you as a curious person who is the focus of the inner critic messages. and the other which will write out the voice of the inner critic. Or you could write with both hands, each one representing one of these voices.

Write the dialogue that is going on inside, but do so from a place of being curious about what the inner critic is trying to accomplish, and being willing to offer it some other strategies.

Next-Step Strategies

Keep it busy with some other activity

Your inner critic has been a very active part of your psyche for a very long time. It seems to need a job, so, repurpose it!

One of my very favorite strategies is to send it outside on a big clean-up mission. I tell mine to wipe off every leaf on the tree out my window or to clear the dust off the road. Give it something to do that takes a lot of time. If the critic returns, send it back out.

Exaggerate it

Another useful technique is to agree with it and, more importantly, to exaggerate it. If you're hearing, "You are such a jerk!" meet that with, "You're right. I'm a complete and total jerk. No one is a bigger jerk than me. I have hurt more people than anyone else in the world. I'm thousands of times worse than anyone else!"

It won't be long before you find yourself laughing at the absurdity of this, and that's the point. This is an aikido move—going with the energy, make it bigger and bigger until it's completely ludicrous. It puts the initial statement into a whole different framework.

> **REMINDER:** The more you can actually play with the inner critic voice, the less seriously you take it, and the less negative impact it will have.

Agree with it

Here's one more strategy that I just love. This often shows up when you're moving into totally new territory. This could be moving toward a new career; beginning a long trip; starting your book. The voice says, "You have no idea what you're doing. You're insane." You know what? The voice is completely on track! The only thing off is its *evaluative* nature. But the truth is, you don't know what you are doing. Why should you? You don't know how it will turn out. You're on a trust walk.

Now you can face the voice, and say, "You're absolutely right. I have no friggin' idea what I'm doing, but it sure is fun and scary at the same time. I'm choosing this because this is what I must do."

There are dozens more ideas about what you can do to work with this inner activity. Do be careful not to judge the inner critic! It's just another way that the IC takes over. So, it's not about making your inner critic bad, but rather realizing that the IC just no longer serves you in the way that it may have at one time, and you have earned the right to tell it so.

Learning to interrupt the inner critic changes your relationship with you. This task is pivotal to evolve into a healthy, mature relationship with yourself.

Is There Any Other Truth to It?

You have seen that the IC is an outgrowth of your social conditioning and the interiorized authorities from childhood. It's also a distorted aspect of your true guidance—that sense of inner knowing about what is truly the better choice in any given situation. In a sense, the IC does not trust your

Look at your inner critic as a mechanism that almost forces you to become more conscious, particularly if you want to mature into your real self, your true adulthood.

authentic inner guide, nor does it trust you to follow it. As an element of the egoic structure, it tries to take charge.

It can inhibit and even freeze attempts to follow the internal urge and spiritual inclination that encourages you to grow. That is, the ego tries to substitute for and bypass a more trustworthy internal guidance system.

Does the IC have any value in adulthood? If so, what? My response is that about 98.5 percent of the IC's existence is simply as a pattern of needlessly evaluating and assessing you against some intangible criteria. It has no value in adulthood, except for the following caveat: You can look at it as a mechanism that almost forces you to become more conscious, particularly if you want to mature into your real self, your true adulthood. So, from that perspective, it can help you wake up to your true, awakened nature.

Beyond that, the 98.5 percent of the inner critic has no value.

Identifying the Kernel of Truth

But what about the other 1.5 percent of the IC?

Ahh, this is what can hold a kernel of truth. The IC is trying to act like a guidance system, no matter how distorted it gets. It's so noisy that it can take some skill in teasing out that kernel of truth that can actually have considerable value. This is not theoretical. It is practical, though it requires practice, practice, practice, as does anything of value.

Here's an example of a typical approach to responding to the inner critic:

Behavior: You've just scolded your child in front of his friends before letting him off for school.

Your Response: The IC judges you harshly for berating your child. You believe it, feel terrible, and because you feel so bad about how you treated your child, and the mental and emotional aftermath is so painful, you try to push away the voice, turn on some soothing music in the car, and think about the day ahead.

Result: Nothing changes. It's likely that some version of that scenario is repeated in the future.

The judgmental nature of the inner critic shuts down the possibility of learning and growing from the experience.

Here is the same example, showing the process of coming into contact with the kernel of truth:

Behavior: You've just scolded your child in front of his friends before letting him off for school.

Inner Critic: Almost immediately, you experience the effects of the IC hammering you for being such a disastrous parent. "Look at how you screamed at him? That was terrible. You should never have had children! He's never going to forgive you."

Your Response: "Oh, there it is—that's the inner critic. Okay, I'm going to breathe and get curious. Hmmm—is there something for me to learn here?" You could stay with the uncomfortable experience long enough to ask, "What about this message is true? Well, it is true that I yelled at my child. Yes, it's true that it was unnecessary. Ouch. That doesn't feel good." (Perhaps shame or guilt show up here. Allow yourself to notice this and be with the inner experience to the degree possible.) "Okay, here's an opportunity. Perhaps I can take a look at what caused my behavior and identify some alternative strategies."

With this recognition, there is no judgment, just a recognition of the naked truth. It's not loaded down with pejoratives of the inner critic. So, now, you have something to work with. You actually have an opportunity for learning and for growth.

Your Curiosity Continues: This is still a difficult experience for you, but you stay with it and recognize that your child really pushed a button for you.

Here's another truth. He didn't listen to you, and you are furious. Still no judgment. Can you be curious about why you are so furious?

As you pay attention to your own experience, you can look at what's beneath the story of why you're so angry at your son. Perhaps you get a glimpse that you often experience anger when you don't feel listened to. In fact, there's a lot of energy around this issue.

The judgmental nature of the inner critic shuts down the possibility of learning and growing from the experience.

Now, you have contacted a painful place in yourself that has fueled anger and led to a behavior that has left you feeling bad.

Follow-up: What can you do now? You could start noticing your inner experience when you don't feel listened to. You might notice that this experience is familiar, and perhaps you've responded much the same way in the past. It might occur to you that if you just took a few breaths when this type of situation arises in the future, you could respond differently. Or you could work with the Deep Living Transformation Process described in chapter 16 to begin healing this painful place.

I would bet that you'll be more aware in the future when your child—for the umpteenth time—doesn't obey you. I would guess that even if you feel the anger, you might stop before yelling at him. And you might take a different approach in talking with him.

This shows just one example of how you can **tease out the kernel of truth** and let the noise of the inner critic take a backseat. From this kernel of truth, you learn something about the situation, and because you're present to the inner experience, your response will be modified.

This change was able to happen because judgment didn't interrupt the feedback process. That's a big deal! Judgment almost always gets in the way of real growth, which just keeps a person stuck in a repeating cycle.

Discerning between the Inner Critic and the Voice of Inner Authority

Here are three key ways to discern between the kernel of truth and the IC noise.

1. Become familiar with your inner experience associated with both the inner critic and inner authority, and name these experiences.

What is your mental experience? What is the quality of the voice that you hear? What is its volume? How familiar is this voice? What is its message? What are your body's sensations? What are you noticing about your emotions?

The voice of the inner critic sounds very familiar to most of us. And the familiar can feel like the safest voice, if not the most satisfying. It tends to be the loudest and most threatening voice. The voice of inner authority is often quieter, more subtle. It may be insistent, returning to you in your quieter moments over and over again, but you may not have learned to trust it. It's a voice that is easy to ignore or to get drowned out in the cacophony of a life. This voice often calls us to something that is new and unknown in life, and it can feel scary to deeply listen to it.

The IC noise, on the other hand, is loaded. You feel its weight on you. The kernel of truth is just that—it's clean, it's clear, and though there may be sadness or anguish in coming into contact with that truth, there is a certain neutrality and relief with it. There is no judgment.

2. Notice your level of curiosity and openness to new information.

If it's difficult to be curious, to explore new information, then the inner critic is probably at work. Its most prominent feature is its propensity toward being certain about its ability to evaluate the object of its attention against some scale of adequacy.

Inner authority allows for the unknown and, in fact, seeks an experience of deeper truth. When it hears truth, there is a inner alignment and sense of knowing that resonates deeply within the heart and belly. You feel as if you're standing in a new place within yourself when the inner authority is guiding you. When you speak it, you feel courageous.

3. Notice where you are on the continuum between harshness and compassion.

The inner critic voice most often carries a harshness or hardness to it. After all, its job is to keep you in line and keep the status quo. It does not allow for much deviation from its approved and narrow list of what's acceptable. This quality of its activity is why many people experience being so hard on themselves.

The inner critic is a source of great and universal suffering in the human condition. The quality that provides a healing salve in the face of this suffering is that of authentic compassion. This quality calls upon the kindness of the heart to meet the one who is suffering, and to recognize, soften, and soothe the edges of the pain.

The energy and compassion of the heart has no match.

Being a human is no easy task. Sometimes our highest nature comes through; most often, we fall surprisingly short of those idealized states. Compassion allows us to meet ourselves and others in our full humanity. Rather than casting off some part of ourselves that we considered unacceptable into the abyss, we discover another very human element within that will help make us whole.

In those moments when we can sink into the depth of our hearts, the truth and grief of our existence can be both expressed and healed.

Compassion heals, and that's what's needed in our individual and communal lives. It's the great antidote for the unconscious activity of the critic.

Gaining more frequent contact with your inner authority and its guidance will help you to build a grounded, authentic sense of confidence and keep you oriented toward your more wakeful presence. What is the quieter, truer message that is trying to get your attention? What is the inner urge that you've been avoiding? What would break your heart if you didn't move forward on it? What's being asked of your precious life that's far more important than any shoulds?

Now's the time to turn your attention to the quieter yearnings of your authentic heart to support you in your life, and to help you disengage from the inner critic. The energy and compassion of the heart has no match. It just needs the focus of your attention turned toward it.

18

Shifting Attention to Your Expansive Nature

A Brief Review

We've been exploring a deep and personal inner journey in this book. Recognizing the quest for authentic connection and fulfillment that I see so many people seeking, I have emphasized the value of focusing inward in order to become more familiar with the many dimensions of yourself and of your soul. The Enneagram has been explained as a map to help you illuminate and recognize a full range of specific experiences that you might have at various stages of your human and spiritual journey.

Many writers and inspirational speakers address the opportunities available for moving beyond the limitations of one's automatic way of living. Yet it can be difficult to know what those specific limitations are if you're closely identified with the patterns of your personality type, as most people are. I hope that *Deep Living* has given you a new lens for understanding the nature of the personality and its relationship to your truer nature, and that you are gaining more insight around why you may have been dissatisfied, felt stuck, or were disappointed in the past.

We've seen that our personality patterns have been used easily and unconsciously to cope with some of the fundamental sources of discomfort and pain that we human beings have. You've been encouraged to hold attitudes of kindness, acceptance, and the neutrality of the inner observer toward your experiences as an antidote to self-judgment and devaluation. Your historic patterns have served an important purpose of protecting you. To reiterate a statement from an earlier chapter, *your capacity as a psychological and spiritual being is maturing, and you are out-distancing your need for all that protection.*

You are so much more than your familiar patterns. Expansive, alive, courageous, and authentic qualities are part of your birthright and are an intricate dimension of your awakened nature. You may or may not recognize these qualities in yourself at this time, but they are available under the layers of the automatic conditioning. The authentic expression of these qualities emerge when you're in the state of presence. This is when you have the experience of being deeply aware of the sensations that show up in your body in the moment, and your identification with thoughts and emotional reactions diminishes.

The *counter-intuitive, acceptance-based model of change* supports you in allowing these qualities to arise. Rather than engaging in a struggle against some previously unacceptable aspects of yourself, we have explored a more spacious way of *being with yourself.* Maybe you have already discovered that this radically different orientation to change can create a powerful shift. Many related, presence-based strategies and practices have been shared throughout the book to support your journey back to yourself, to the moments when your attention is focused on having a direct experience of your groundedness, heartfulness, and clarity.

Shifting Your Attention

Another way of understanding the journey that we are taking here focuses on a theme running through this book: *Where are you putting your attention, in this moment?*

Becoming more conscious and more awake requires noticing where you're putting your attention and, when necessary, creating an intentional, conscious shift so that your attention is focused on that which supports you in having more contact with yourself, rather than on what takes you away from yourself.

Do you remember this graphic from chapter 3?

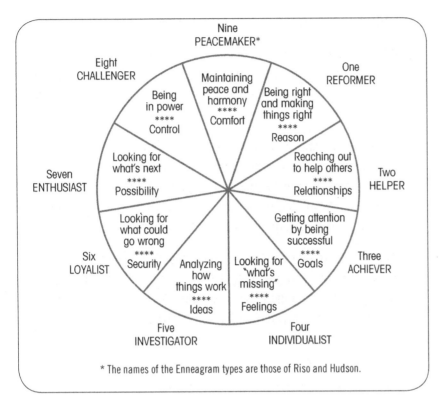

Figure 18-1: The Focus of Attention

We again see that each of the nine different Enneagram types has an automatic, conditioned way of pointing one's attention toward a particular object of interest. Regardless of the specific object of automatic attention (for example, helping other people; looking for what could go wrong; having a peaceful, comfortable environment; being in control), for each type, this very familiar and comfortable experience takes the individual away from what is actually here, in this moment.

You may have heard that "Where attention goes, energy follows." It's true. Conditioned responses act in many ways like a trained dog. These responses are a form of our energy that follow on the heels of the master— Attention. So, where you put your attention is very important.

Conditioned responses act in many ways like a trained dog. These responses are a form of our energy that follow on the heels of the master— Attention. So, where you put your attention is very important.

EXERCISE: Let's stop for a moment and check in.

1. Where has your automatic Focus of Attention gone historically? What do you pay the most attention to on a habitual basis? What feels like an absolutely right, familiar, and normal place for you to put your attention?

   To help you refine your awareness of the automatic recycling of patterns, feel free to return to the Iceberg Model for the type or types that you most relate to. Pay particular attention to the section on "What You Pursue" and the longer description of the activity created through the "Focus of Attention."

2. What happens with your thinking, your feelings, and your behavior once this habit of attention is engaged? What does it look like when your life's energy willingly follows your Focus of Attention? What are you actually doing? What are you saying? What are you thinking?

The next section of this chapter provides two more approaches to bringing more awareness to where you put your attention, and to helping you create more intentional shifts. Every time you turn toward a fresh, unconditioned experience that supports your development, you are counteracting the incessant activity of your personality. No need to worry about doing something "perfectly," that is, whatever your mind says would be perfect. There is no perfection, only practice. In this practice, the insistence of the personality becomes clearer, allowing you to see the force behind it.

But before talking about these two practices, I invite you to recognize that there's another urge within you that's also insistent. It's why you are reading this book, it's why you're on a quest for a real alternative to the life patterns that are no longer serving you. This urge is what informs the deepest part of you and encourages you toward what's possible in your more expansive nature. You may feel this urge as a calling to your true purpose, or to a truly liberated and awakened life, or as a yearning for deep connection with the Divine or higher consciousness, or as an undefined, but ever-present sense that you want to be fully at home with yourself.

You are wired for your awakened nature. You're neurologically and divinely designed to experience expansiveness, inner peace, at-homeness, and ease. That this insistent urge will not leave you alone is an expression of this wiring. You probably have an innate sense that you're at least on the right track, even if you don't know where you're going. While not knowing where you are going can be unnerving to the egoic self, it's a sure sign that the urge for your spiritual development and maturation is actively supporting your journey.

The strategies below are available anytime you need them. They are always within your reach. When you realize that you have forgotten all about being conscious and have been smack in the middle of your personality, you can just notice that fact, then take a breath, and practice coming back.

Shifting Your Attention and Realigning with Your Awakened Qualities

Strategy #1: Conscious Breathing

From my perspective, being conscious of your breathing is the most fundamental practice an individual who wants deeper satisfaction and fulfilment can use.

It's amazing how easy it is to forget that we are alive because we're breathing. This amazing capacity is taken for granted.

Fortunately, conscious breathing is always available to you, and it's always just one moment of awareness away. What makes breathing conscious is noticing that the breath is moving within and out of your body, that the movement of the breath changes your bodily sensations that can be both obvious and subtle, and that you are somehow affected through the felt experience of breathing.

There are many reasons why conscious breathing is a mainstay in presence work. Here's a partial list of those reasons.

1. Breathing is a powerful tool which begins to change awareness.

If you are focusing on your breathing, then you are training your attention to do something quite unfamiliar. This practice opens doors to much more expanded awareness.

2. Conscious breathing interrupts the automatic activity of the personality.

If you are intentionally refocusing your attention, it will interrupt the automatic activity of the personality. You'll notice that the automatic patterns are insistent about reasserting their dominance. Being gentle, yet strong, in your commitment can help you bring attention back to your breathing.

3. Breathing calms the sympathetic nervous system and activates the parasympathetic system.

Conscious breathing is incompatible with the stress response. Have you ever noticed that when you begin to focus on your breathing when you're feeling stressed, that the breathing itself changes? People often report that the pace of breathing slows, and that the breath lengthens and moves more deeply inside. That simple movement counteracts stress and helps you to change your felt state. The parasympathetic system helps "cook" and digest your experiences and restores equilibrium.

4. Conscious breathing brings attention to the body. It also:
- brings attention to sensation, the language of the Body Center
- allows you to feel grounded
- helps you to settle into yourself
- allows tensions to be more easily recognized and released
- connects you with the center of physicality when focusing on your belly
- attunes to the flow of energy through you, and invigorates your system

5. **Conscious breathing quiets the mind/mental activity.**

With conscious breathing, your mind has an object of attention or concentration. While the mind will do its best to recapture your attention (and will be successful doing so more times than you can count), when you remember to come back to breathing, your mind has less fuel that it needs to stay overly active.

6. **Conscious breathing reduces emotional reactivity.**

When you focus on breathing, you can notice the emotional reaction you might be having. Then, you can use this reaction as a cue to continue breathing and to get curious as to what the reaction is about. Rather than being completely taken over by the emotional reaction, you create some distance between you and it.

7. **Conscious breathing enhances your awareness of what and who is around you.**

When you are focused on breathing, you become more sensitive to the presence of others, to the environment, to the energy around you. All of this helps you to know that you are not alone but are connected to an expansive field than more limited perceptions would lead you to believe.

8. **Conscious breathing helps you have a stronger sense of substance and presence.**

When you are aware of your breathing, and thus in tune with your body, there is more of *you* actually available.

You can tune into information coming through your senses more clearly, taking in sight, sound, and sensation. Thus, you can be more responsive, and your presence can be more easily felt.

9. **Conscious breathing gives you access to more real choice.**

When you breathe consciously and your nervous system slows down, you're able to gain perspective. With perspective comes a greater range of options and choices. Rather than making a decision based on an emotional reaction, for example, you're more likely to make a decision that feels clean and clear and, undoubtedly, will be a more effective choice for you.

As your relationship to yourself changes, so does your relationship to everything.

10. Conscious breathing changes your relationship to yourself.

It is a key to changing the rhythm and patterns of automatic living. You come to know yourself differently. During those moments, you're not as subjected to the dictates of your personality.

11. Conscious breathing changes your perspective of you in relationship to the consciousness itself, to *beingness, to all that is.*

As your relationship to yourself changes, so does your relationship to everything. You'll experience moments when you do not feel separate or disconnected from your environment but are intrinsically aware that you are supported by the much greater presence, by the ground of *being* itself.

Learning to remember and tune into breathing as a daily practice takes time. As simple as it is, it's not easy to do, or everyone would be doing it more. However, over time you will develop your capacity for remembering your breathing more frequently, and you'll begin to experience your own benefits. This is the most important action you can take.

Strategy #2: The 70 Percent Rule

In tai-chi philosophy, there is something known as the 70 percent rule. It is this:

> *Estimate your greatest ability to perform any given exercise, then practice at only 70 percent of that maximum level.*

This simple and elegant principle is meant to translate to an inquiry around how much energy is actually needed to produce an outcome. It points to the importance of tuning into how much energy you habitually put into an endeavor.

You might feel like you have to give 110 or 125 percent or more to achieve a goal, and the next goal, and the following goal. What is the impact of that constant upsurge in energy?

Or you might find that you hold back on the amount of energy you put into most activities. You may be waiting for some magical solution to come your way or for all the external noise to quiet down before moving into action. What is the impact of putting so much energy into withdrawing?

Given the nature of the personality structure, we all have some place in life where we overdo and find ourselves out of balance. You may want to refer back to chapter 16, where there's a list of particular behaviors overdone by people dominant in each of the Enneagram types.

Here are additional ways of overdoing, based upon the three Social Style Clusters we've discussed

- Too much demanding or asserting yourself
  (Types Three, Seven, Eight)
- Too much isolating or withdrawing (Types Four, Five, Nine)
- Too much taking responsibility (Types One, Two, Six)

After you have identified where you habitually overdo, ask yourself these questions:

- How do you know when you've done too much of a particular endeavor?
- What signals or cues would tell you that you are in overdo mode? Notice any thought patterns, emotional experiences, or sensations in your body, for example, that would signal you to recognize that you're overdoing.
- What has been the impact of overdoing this quality or activity in your life?
- How much energy is actually needed?

Using the 70 percent rule, you can practice dialing back your energy.

EXERCISE: Without actually taking any outer action, see if you can sense into what it would feel like inside yourself to modify the amount of energy you exert in the particular areas where you overdo.

Imagine that you have one of those old-fashioned radios that has a round knob that adjusts the volume. Can you imagine turning the knob up so that it's at 100 percent volume of a particular energy that you use and that feels needed for a current task?

How does 100 percent feel to you?

What if you turned the knob all the way to the greatest volume? You might find yourself at 125 percent, or even more. How does that feel?

Turn the knob back to 100 percent and see how that feels inside.

Now, slowly turn the knob back down even more, to 90 percent, then 80 percent, then 70 percent. With each incremental change, notice how that affects your body. How does it affect you emotionally?

Here's an example of how this has worked in one person's life:

Justine was frustrated with herself because she was exhausted and burned-out from doing so much at work and at home. She tried to excel at every project and felt that excellence was expected of her. Over time, she realized that she really wanted to do well so that she would get approval from her family and from coworkers. Like many coaching clients of mine, she identified having an internal on-off switch: she was either all the way on, or collapsed in off. Neither of those polarities served her any longer.

We practiced working with the 70 percent rule. She could easily identify that she put at least 125 percent and generally more into her activities. She practiced feeling what it would be like to dial back to 100 percent. Even at that level, she felt like she was slacking off. But she so badly wanted to experience some relief that she was willing to reduce the increments until she got to 70 percent.

Then, I had her identify what she specifically would be doing less of and to write this information down.

Remember, when we do less of something that we've been doing habitually, that change creates a vacuum, so it's important to explore the next step. Justine did just that. She looked at what would help *her balance out her life, that is, what was missing from her life. She identified that she wanted to spend more time working in her garden, enjoying down time with her husband, and writing. She decided to start by spending more time outdoors and, specifically, being in her garden.*

In subsequent coaching sessions, she frequently reported that she loved this principle of 70 percent and found it to be immensely helpful. It helped her recognize how easily she could get out of balance. We returned to this principle time and time again to help her apply it to new situations, until she began to internalize it as a principle of her life.

Once you identify what you overdo, you can take the following steps:

1. Experiment with dialing down where you overdo. It can help to first let yourself experience this somatically. It can feel odd, but don't give up. Then, write down a very specific description of what your life will be like when you're putting your 70 percent into a habitually ramped-up experience. What specifically are you doing less of?

2. Explore what's missing in your life. What would you like more of? What do you need that you haven't yet addressed?

Start by selecting just one activity or one experience, and chunk it into small bites so that you can practice enjoying some aspect of this activity, rather than having to take it on, once again, at 125 percent. For example, if you want to have more gardening in life, perhaps you could start with planting three or four pots of flowers, herbs, or vegetables.

The Paradox and the Mystery

Clients and students often report that, most of their lives, they have followed beliefs and principles that seemed perfectly reasonable, natural, and familiar. They learned how life worked. Even when there was hard evidence that life really wasn't working so well, those tenets weren't brought into question, because, at a unconscious level, they provided a foundation for life. Then, something in life becomes so unsatisfactory or

The inner journey illuminates one deeply held belief after another, and it turns out those beliefs are taking us in exactly the opposite direction of what we really want.

painful, or there is such an urge for becoming more whole or alive, that the person had to start asking questions.

The Enneagram provides a brilliant map for identifying and questioning the very tenets that have provided a kind of psychic glue for the ego's self-identity, of how you have thought about yourself. Those tenets served a lot of purposes, and even if they were unstated, they contained what felt known.

Now, as some of these tenets have been brought to the light of awareness, they don't hold up so well. In fact, you may have begun to see that the way you thought life worked is actually the opposite of the way it really works. We find the Enneagram filled with these stunning paradoxes. The inner journey illuminates one deeply held belief after another, and it turns out those beliefs are taking us in exactly the opposite direction of what we really want. Going in the opposite direction of what we most deeply want in our lives—but that feels right to the personality—is the most familiar thing in the world to us. It constitutes the known. And the known pulls us along in the realm of what seems comfortable, reasonable, valued, and affirmed.

The U-Turn

Turning to move in the opposite direction of your habitual self means that you go against the grain of your automatic mode of living. It can feel, at the minimum, unfamiliar and very awkward, and on the most difficult end of the scale, very threatening and dangerous. Of course, what's threatened is our egoic nature. In reality, we're moving toward our soul's longing.

I call this move *making a U-turn*. Literally, it's what you do in traffic when you realize you're going in a direction that doesn't take you to your desired location. Sometimes life may ask that of you: To turn around and go in another—even the opposite—direction so that you can find and inhabit your own precious life.

There is not one U-turn in your journey, but many. Below are some examples of what a U-turn might look like based on a person's type. If you come to a U-turn that feels unfathomable or undoable, it may well be a cue to something that, paradoxically, will free you from long-standing limitations.

I'm not suggesting that you take action on a U-turn right now. It may not be time for you to do that. However, the time will come when you feel as ready as you'll ever be, and you challenge your ego structure's status quo. Because using this approach is incredibly counterintuitive, trying it on your own may feel too difficult. If that's the case, I recommend working with a qualified coaching professional to support your process.

Each time you take a counterintuitive step in the direction of the U-turn, something will change. Often, you will experience a new opening or lightness within. Once you realize that you didn't die when you took the U-turn, you may feel exhilarated over having experienced a measure of inner freedom. You may be tempted to ask, "Could it really be that easy?" The answer is both yes and no.

What feels nearly impossible before you practice it becomes quite doable over time. The initial, internal experience of "No way!" feels very real for a good reason, and it can put up all kinds of roadblocks. Many people experience how exaggerated the roadblocks can feel. And, then, you find that there is a way.

The other difficulty is that it's easy to forget all about the U-turns you have made in the past, leading to an amnesia of success. It's useful to make notes about your experiences to support you in taking the "road less traveled" again.

Taking a U-turn is not a one-time action. Building reminders about taking appropriate U-turn actions eventually helps the new approach become more real, conscious, and sustainable.

Taking a conscious U-turn is reason to celebrate.

Examples of Substantial U-Turns for Individuals, Based on Type

Personality Type	A Characteristic Pattern	Example of Making a Substantial U-Turn
One	Continuously trying to fix things	Leave something to be fixed alone and enjoy it as it is or enjoy another experience, even if it feels that there is something wrong
Two	Overextending yourself in trying to help others	Recognize, acknowledge, and attend to your own needs first, even when you perceive the needs of others as being more important than yours
Three	Competing in every part of life, and needing people to recognize how well you've done	Engage in an experience for its own sake with no outcome/product necessary; not telling anyone, except perhaps your coach or closest loved one, about your experience
Four	Living in a dream world of how the ideal life could be if only you were truly understood	Take specific steps toward tangible, desired outcomes, regardless of how ordinary those steps feel and even if you feel misunderstood
Five	Withdrawing into mental preparation mode	Get into/have direct contact with your body and engage with life, even if you feel unprepared
Six	Looking for information from numerous external sources to make a decision	Listen to your quiet inner voice and follow this inner guidance, even when you hear the inner cacophony of voices pulling you in different directions
Seven	Trying to have it all or do it all	Slow your level of activity, and fully focus on the inner experience of being with yourself, even when there are so many other things that interest you
Eight	Being overly self-reliant and strong	Allow, experience, and express your caring, vulnerable feelings, even when it feels like you are supposed to be the strong one
Nine	Avoiding conflict by trying to figure things out in your own mind	Stay engaged in conversations, including difficult ones, even when there is no predetermined solution, and you want to seek comfort

Figure 18-2: Examples of Substantial U-Turns for Individuals, Based on Type

Part of the paradox is that when you take this turn, you are moving away, at least temporarily, from the familiar, from the known. And you are moving toward the unknown. You can't know how this will look, feel, or be for you, because it probably hasn't been in the realm of possibility for you before. Moving into the unknown is the trust walk. It takes you into closer proximity to the mystery of life, into the mystery of who you truly are, into experiences that you didn't know were personally possible.

Your Great Work

This journey does not take you "out there," but instead centers on your own personal and directly lived experience. Focusing on your inner experience in the way I've talked about in this book is inherently practical. The inner shifts that you experience become translated into changes in your external life. You may not even know how the change has happened, but it has. You may have heard that "when engaged in deep work, nothing changes (in life) and yet everything changes (about life)." It's a great and delightful paradox that generally leaves people shaking their heads and laughing.

When a core Enneagram pattern is recognized for what it is—a deeply ingrained pattern that has been a basis for one's self-identity, but not one's real nature—it lifts a veil of untruth. You may experience this new awareness with amazement and shock, with a sense of having crossed over a deep ravine into entirely new territory, and/or with a sense of liberation. You may notice how much fatigue has been created by trying to live from the old, false self-identity and thus begin to feel lighter. One client noted what many others have said: that her shifts were redirecting the course of her inner life, and while little changed on the outside, it felt entirely different because so much had changed on the inside.

On one level, the Enneagram is a map of the truth of life. At some time in inner work, the underlying truths of a person's dominant Enneagram point become apparent. Below is a brief statement of truth that *transcends the patterns* of each type. When the ego is activated, these statements sound absurd. When read with presence, the statement associated with your type may resonate, or it may send a chill up your spine. Each of

Moving into the unknown is the trust walk. It takes you into closer proximity to the mystery of life, into the mystery of who you truly are, into experiences that you didn't know were personally possible.

When engaged in deep work, nothing changes (in life) and yet everything changes (about life).

these grand statements challenges a core rule of that Enneagram type's personality.

Type One: Recognizing that it is not my responsibility to fix everything, I relish the abundant joys in life.

Type Two: I ask myself, "What do I need?" and I willingly receive help.

Type Three: How other people see me is none of my business.

Type Four: The beautiful quality of my life is based on the small, ordinary moments.

Type Five: It is safe to be in the world.

Type Six: My security lies within me.

Type Seven: My fulfillment exists in experiencing the exquisiteness of the here and now.

Type Eight: Being vulnerable is the source of my true strength.

Type Nine: "My presence matters."[1]

To experience this truth requires trust, courage, acceptance, and love.

Love in Action

Why would you engage in this work if you did not have a deep urge within toward the fullness, the wholeness, the preciousness of life? While you may have picked up this book because you want to focus on your own well-being, any positive change in your relationship to yourself will have an impact on others. There is nothing more powerful, more healing, in the entire world than loving presence. Through your *being*, you're a vehicle for loving presence.

Circling back to the beginning of our exploration in chapter 1, the Enneagram *is* a map of love in action.

It teaches us all how to love ourselves enough to take the journey toward higher and healthier levels in our own life.

My great wish for all who read this book is that you'll continue to experience increasingly expansive love and presence in your life. The world needs it, and the world needs you.

Acknowledgments

While this book has been in development for five years, it is an outgrowth of many influences both recent and from earlier times. I have enormous gratitude for the many angels whose contributions have helped shape my life and encouraged me to stay true to this work. With their generous spirits, the book has taken flight.

I want to acknowledge and thank my personal spiritual teachers whose influence is incalculable in my development. In my early adulthood, Zen teacher Cheri Huber stirred my soul through her wise teaching and counseling. Her clarity and courageous honesty opened my eyes. Stephen Levine's "just this much" teaching ushered me into deeper levels of presence and helped me connect with my heart. While I had read about the Enneagram, the late Don Richard Riso and his colleague Russ Hudson offered divine wisdom through their stunningly compassionate, precise, and pioneering teachings. Their rich and profound body of work pointed me in the direction of my own. I've been further blessed by the privilege of working with them and teaching their workshops. Sandra Maitri is also an exceptional teacher. Her clear and wise presence is an inspiration for continuing on my own spiritual path. The loving presence of Sandy Marcus, teacher and guide, always opens me to what is astonishing within. Each of these transformational teachers has reflected the many facets of Being, and I will be forever grateful.

In addition to my formal teachers, my gratitude runs deep for the endless number of people who became informal teachers along this path. Among these, my fellow members of the International Retreat Group community have become models of the strength and love that arise from commitment, courage, and transparency.

Collaboration has been an important theme in my professional journey, and I want to acknowledge my Enneagram collaborator-companions. Thank you to Wendy Appel, Pam Fox Rollin, and Samantha Schoenfeld for our early work together. I especially thank Wendy, who was instrumental as the codeveloper of the early stages of the Iceberg Model found in this book. Dr. Vicky Cruz helped me recognize the reflection of the Enneagram in the body's emotional realm, and for her personal and professional kinship and love, I am deeply grateful. Dr. Ronna Phifer-Ritchie, my longtime Riso-Hudson teaching partner, deepened my understanding and appreciation of the relational aspects of the Enneagram. Her loving partnership over many years has been a privilege and a joy.

Further, members of the Deep Coaching Institute (DCI) community have been a source of enormous strength, support, love, and encouragement. Senior DCI faculty member Dr. Belinda Gore served as the midwife for the Deep Coaching Institute, and her continued sisterhood and guidance have value beyond words. In taking the reigns as DCI director, Diana Redmond has both provided excellent leadership and become a treasured friend and colleague. Faculty member Elizabeth Carrington-House's longtime professional and personal friendship is a gem, and her heartful support means the world to me. Over the years, the students, graduates, and mentors that have gone through the Deep Coaching Institute's Certification Program have read, given feedback, and offered insight on deep living. I feel great gratitude for the contributions and enthusiasm of each.

Along with my many clients and students over the years whose courageous explorations have helped me refine the work of deep living, I want to especially acknowledge my longtime coastside women's group of "Elegant Enneagrammers" who will always have a special place in my heart. Together, we experimented with early stages of the work in our monthly gatherings. The core group—Susan Bishop, Dr. Vicky Cruz, Bernadette McAllister, Jeannene Minnix Kingston, Kristy Koberna, Mary Knippel, Pat Muller, Audrey Poppers, Rosie Picchi, and Irma Velasquez—

all so generously contributed to this book through their curiosity, willingness, honesty, and precious vulnerability.

Thank you to the friends and colleagues who took the time to read the early versions of the manuscript and give me much-needed feedback. To Dee Doyle, Katie Gay, Mary Kay Holbrook, Paul Jaffe, Jan King, Melissa Neisser, and David Pinkston, thank you.

Undertaking a publishing project of this magnitude and complexity requires the tireless dedication and expertise of many saints! Jan King offered substantial guidance through the early stages of the book, and her sincere enthusiasm and understanding of the publishing industry urged me to continue when I wavered. Without Janica Smith managing crucial aspects of the book project and keeping the publishing process in perspective, I may never have finished. I'm grateful for her dedication, advice, and equanimity. Offering her excellent editing skills, her eye for precise detail, and her appreciation for this work, copy editor Lori Zue made me sound like a much better writer than I am. Cathy and Jack Davis valiantly tackled the intricacies of the complex interior design with professionalism, flexibility, and dedication—which was a godsend. Their commitment to excellence can be felt throughout the book. Thank you to Alan Hebel; he and his team added their creative expertise to the cover design. Heartfelt thanks to Amy Logan and Sue Kirtland for offering important feedback on several critical facets of the book's production. I deeply appreciate the guidance of Elizabeth Marshall in book promotion, and the wise and committed expertise of Mary Neighbour in being my trusted author's representative. She is a miracle worker.

Many personal friends and colleagues have been a source of generous love and frequent encouragement. Wild Women, Fab Co-labs, and many others: I know who you are and hold you dearly in my heart.

Both of my parents passed during the development of this book. In their final months and through their deaths, I learned a great deal about deeper living. Thank you to my sister, Mary Jo Ogden, for her love and caring, and to Mark and Kathy Ogden for their willingness to explore new territory and for keeping our family ties strong. I am forever grateful to the Rowan family, which includes our young grandchildren, for the joy you have brought to my heart.

My most influential, committed, and loving companion and supporter is my husband, Dr. Jim Murphy. I cannot conceive of how this book would ever have been written or published had it not been for all the ways Jim expressed his love, encouragement, devotion, and patience! No words suffice for how grateful I am for his being at my side—my partner in this amazing life journey—and for his extraordinary and wise spirit.

Resources

FOR MORE INFORMATION

The Deep Living Institute

At home in yourself. At ease in the world.

Founded by Dr. Roxanne Howe-Murphy, the Deep Living Institute offers a radically compassionate approach for true Self-recognition, deepening, and a profound relationship to the inner truth.

Grounded in the wisdom of the Enneagram and the power of presence, our experienced faculty, facilitators and coaches offer dynamic coaching, courses, retreats, products, and community engagement for integrating increased consciousness into daily living.

For more information and to stay apprised of new Deep Living events and offerings, visit us at www.deeplivinginstitute.com.

For support in the typing process, the DLI coaching staff offers individual typing interviews which can help point you in the direction of your dominant type. We also offer recommendations for online typing assessments. Visit www.deeplivinginstitute.com/coaching/.

The Deep Coaching Institute

Where the profound and practical meet.

The Deep Coaching Institute, founded by Dr. Roxanne Howe-Murphy, is an accredited school for growth oriented professionals who want to integrate and embody the art, science, and spiritual consciousness of the Enneagram into their business and personal lives.

For information on our core certification program, on-site trainings, workshops, retreats, and special events, visit us at www.deepcoachinginstitute.com.

Notes

INTRODUCTION

1. Richard Rohr, *Falling Upward: A Spirituality for the Two Halves of Life* (San Francisco: Jossey-Bass, 2011), xiii.

2. Laura A. Pratt, Debra J. Brody, and Qiuping Gu, *Antidepressant Use in Persons Aged 12 and Over: United States, 2005–2008*, NCHS [National Center for Health Statistics] Data Brief, no 76, (Hyattsville, MD: National Center for Health Statistics, 2011).

3. Substance Abuse and Mental Health Services Administration, *Results from the 2011 National Survey on Drug Use and Health: Summary of National Findings*, NSDUH Series H-44, HHS Publication no. (SMA) 12-4713, (Rockville, MD: Substance Abuse and Mental Health Services Administration, 2012).

CHAPTER ONE

1. P. D. Oupensky, *In Search of the Miraculous* (New York: Harcourt, Brace & World, 1949), provides additional information on the work of Georges I. Gurdjieff, a Greek-Armenian born in the 1870s, who brought the Enneagram symbol to the West. He didn't create the symbol, but uncovered it in his travels. He believed that a science of human transformation existed in ancient times but had been lost. After years of seeking and learning from spiritual teachers of ancient wisdom, he developed a system of psychology, spirituality, and cosmology to help students awaken to a more objective reality and their place in it. (Before the beginning of World War I, for example, he admonished his students that if humankind did not awaken, people would be killing each other by the millions.) The Enneagram was central to Gurdjieff's system.

2. The author wishes to acknowledge the many contributions of Wendy Appel, MA, to the development of the original version of the Iceberg Model. Together, she and the author used the iceberg to illustrate the "above the waterline" characteristics of each personality type and to identify some of the "below the waterline" dynamics that drive the personality.

3. The concept of parallel living—although it was not typically referred to as such—is a simplistic explanation of the very complex idea along the same lines proposed by Gurdjieff (see note 1, chapter 1, above). *One of his primary teachings focused on the operation of three Centers of Intelligence through which humans experience themselves. He taught that these centers do not function properly or equally in ordinary consciousness, creating various versions of a false sense of reality. See also P.D. Ouspensky, Psychology of Man's Possible Evolution (New York: Random House, 1974). For a further and helpful elaboration on this topic, see Don Richard Riso and Russ Hudson, Understanding the Enneagram: The Practical Guide to Personality Types (Boston: Houghton Mifflin Co., 2000), 251-283.*

CHAPTER TWO

1. Don Richard Riso with Russ Hudson, *Personality Types: Using the Enneagram for Self-Discovery* (Boston: Houghton Mifflin Co., 1996), 45–47.

2. Riso and Hudson, *The Wisdom of the Enneagram: The Complete Guide to Psychological and Spiritual Growth for the Nine Types* (New York: Bantam Books, 1999), 77–80.

3. G.I. Gurdjieff, *Beelzebub's Tales for His Grandson* (New York: Viking Arcana, 1992). See also Gurdjieff, *Views from the Real World* (New York: Dutton, 1975).

4. H. Almaas, *The Unfolding Now: Realizing Your True Nature through the Practice of Presence* (Boston: Shambala Publications, Inc., 2008). Almaas is the pen name of A-Hameed Ali, who has written extensively on the centrality of direct experience to transformation. He is the founder of the Diamond Approach, an integration of depth psychology and traditional spiritual inquiry.

CHAPTER THREE

1. Don Richard Riso and Russ Hudson have used the term *primal catastrophe* in teaching what is also called *the fall from grace*, the individual experience of separation from Essential Nature. This author is aware of their use of this term in their teaching dating back to at least 2001.

2. Sandra Maitri, *The Spiritual Dimension of the Enneagram: Nine Faces of the Soul* (New York: Jeremy P. Tarcher, 2000), 32.

3. Thomas Moore, *Original Self: Living with Paradox and Originality* (New York: Harper Collins, 2000), 3.

4. Karen Horney, *Self-Analysis* (New York: Norton, 1942).

5. Riso and Hudson, *Wisdom of the Enneagram: The Complete Guide to Psychological and Spiritual Growth for the Nine Personality Types* (New York: Bantam Books, 1999), 60-62.

CHAPTER FOUR

1. A.H. Almaas, *Facets of Unity: The Enneagram of Holy Ideas* (Berkeley, CA: Diamond Books, 1998), 21-32. In the chapter "Basic Trust," Almaas describes the importance of this particular type of trust to the soul's orientation toward its higher qualities and to Being.

CHAPTER FIVE

1. John Chryssavgis, *In the Heart of the Desert, Revised: The Spirituality of the Desert Fathers and Mothers* (Bloomington, IN: World Wisdom, 2008), 53-62. In his exploration of the lives of the early Christian desert elders, Chryssavgis offers insights on the connection between passions and the role of wounding and vulnerability in the healing journey.

2. Don Richard Riso and Russ Hudson, *Wisdom of the Enneagram: The Complete Guide to Psychological and Spiritual Growth for the Nine Personality Types* (New York: Bantam Books, 1999), 353. Riso and Hudson

discuss the inner critic messages, or what they call the *marching orders* for each of the nine types.

3. Riso and Hudson, *Wisdom of the Enneagram,* 91-93.

4. Maitri, *Spiritual Dimension of the Enneagram,* 245-262.

CHAPTER SIX

1. Chryssavgis, *Heart of the Desert,* 53-62.

2. Riso and Hudson, *Wisdom of the Enneagram,* 353.

CHAPTER SEVEN

1. Chryssavgis, *Heart of the Desert,* 53-62.

2. Riso and Hudson, *Wisdom of the Enneagram,* 353.

CHAPTER EIGHT

1. Chryssavgis, *Heart of the Desert,* 53-62.

2. Don Richard Riso and Russ Hudson use the phrases *mental retention* and *retain the material in the mind* to identify the fixation of Type Five.

3. Riso and Hudson, *Wisdom of the Enneagram,* 353.

CHAPTER NINE

1. Watty Piper, *The Little Engine that Could* (NY: Platt and Munk Publishers [an imprint of Grosset & Dunlap], 1930).

2. Chryssavgis, *Heart of the Desert*, 53-62.

3. Riso and Hudson, *Wisdom of the Enneagram*, 353.

CHAPTER TEN

1. Chryssavgis, *Heart of the Desert*, 53-62.

2. Riso and Hudson, *Wisdom of the Enneagram*, 353.

CHAPTER ELEVEN

1. Chryssavgis, *Heart of the Desert*, 53-62.

2. Don Richard Riso and Russ Hudson use the term *objectify* to identify the fixation of Type Eight.

3. Riso and Hudson, *Wisdom of the Enneagram*, 353.

CHAPTER TWELVE

1. Chryssavgis, *Heart of the Desert*, 53-62.

2. Riso and Hudson, *Wisdom of the Enneagram*, 353.

3. Ibid., 114.

CHAPTER THIRTEEN

1. Chryssavgis, *Heart of the Desert*, 53-62.

2. Riso and Hudson, *Wisdom of the Enneagram*, 353.

CHAPTER FOURTEEN

1. Chryssavgis, *Heart of the Desert*, 53-62.

2. Riso and Hudson, *Wisdom of the Enneagram*, 353.

CHAPTER SIXTEEN

1. As discussed in note 3 of chapter 1, teachings on the Centers of Intelligence were at the core of Gurdjieff's body of work and have informed this current writing.

2. Patrick Hart and Jonathan Montaldo, eds., *The Intimate Merton: His Life from His Journals* (San Francisco: Harper Collins, 2001), 124.

3. The DLTP is informed by ancient spiritual wisdom that used the power of attention and breath as a basis for inner healing and the more contemporary teaching of direct experience found in the Diamond Approach. See note 4 in chp 2 on p. 406.

CHAPTER EIGHTEEN

1. Riso and Hudson, *Wisdom of the Enneagram*, p. 34.

Selected Bibliography

Addison, Rabbi Howard A. *The Enneagram and Kabbalah: Reading Your Soul*. 2nd ed. Woodstock, VT: Jewish Lights Publishing, 2006.

Almaas, A. H. *Facets of Unity: The Enneagram of Holy Ideas*. Berkeley, CA: Diamond Books, 1998.

———. *The Pearl Beyond Price: Integration of Personality into Being; An Object Relations Approach*. Boston: Shambhala, 2001.

———. *The Unfolding Now: Realizing Your True Nature through the Practice of Presence*. Boston: Shambhala, 2008.

Arrien, Angeles, PhD. *The Four-Fold Way: Walking the Paths of the Warrior, Teacher, Healer and Visionary*. San Francisco: HarperSanFrancisco, 1993.

———. *Second Half of Life: Opening the Eight Gates of Wisdom*. Boulder, CO: Sounds True, 2007.

Brown, Byron. *Soul Without Shame: A Guide to Liberating Yourself from the Judge Within*. Boston: Shambhala, 1999.

Bryner, Andy and Dawna Markova, PhD. *An Unused Intelligence: Physical Thinking for 21st Century Leadership*. Berkeley, CA: Conari Press, 1996.

Cannon, Marcia, PhD. *The Gift of Anger: 7 Steps to Uncover the Meaning of Anger and Gain Awareness, True Strength, and Peace*. Oakland, CA: New Harbinger Publications, 2011.

Chryssavgis, John. *In the Heart of the Desert, Revised: The Spirituality of the Desert Fathers and Mothers*. Bloomington, IN: World Wisdom, 2008.

Chodron, Pema. *Start Where You Are: A Guide to Compassionate Living.* Boston: Shambhala, 1994.

———. *When Things Fall Apart: Heart Advice for Difficult Times.* Boston: Shambhala, 1997.

Cutsinger, James S., ed. *Paths to the Heart: Sufism and the Christian East.* Bloomington, IN: World Wisdom, 2002.

Dalai Lama and Howard C. Cutler, MD. *The Art of Happiness: A Handbook for Living.* New York: Riverhead Books, 1998.

De Salzmann, Jeanne. *The Reality of Being: The Fourth Way of Gurdjieff.* Boston: Shambhala, 2010.

Eden, Donna. *Energy Medicine for Women: Align Your Body's Energies to Boost Your Health and Vitality.* With David Feinstein, PhD. New York: Jeremy P. Tarcher, 2008.

Ford, Debbie. *The Dark Side of the Light Chasers: Reclaiming Your Power, Creativity, Brilliance, and Dreams.* New York: Riverhead Books, 1998.

Hart, Patrick and Jonathan Montaldo, eds. *The Intimate Merton: His Life from His Journals.* San Francisco: Harper Collins, 2001.

Horney, Karen. *Self-Analysis.* New York: Norton, 1942.

Howe-Murphy, Roxanne. *Deep Coaching: Using the Enneagram as a Catalyst for Profound Change.* El Granada, CA: Enneagram Press, 2007.

Huber, Cheri. *Suffering Is Optional: Three Keys to Freedom and Joy.* Murphys, CA: Keep It Simple Books, 2000.

———. *There Is Nothing Wrong With You: Going Beyond Self-Hate, A Compassionate Profess for Learning to Accept Yourself Exactly as You Are.* Murphys, CA: Keep It Simple Books, 1993.

Levine, Stephen. *A Gradual Awakening.* Garden City, NY: Anchor Books, 1979.

Lind-Kyle, Patt. *Heal Your Mind, Rewire Your Brain: Applying the Exciting New Science of Brain Synchrony for Creativity, Peace and Presence.* Santa Rosa, CA: Energy Psychology Press, 2010.

Maitri, Sandra. *The Spiritual Dimension of the Enneagram: Nine Faces of the Soul*. New York: Jeremy P. Tarcher, 2000.

McIntosh, Steve. *Integral Consciousness and the Future of Evolution: How the Integral Worldview is Transforming Politics, Culture and Spirituality*. St. Paul, MN: Paragon House, 2007.

Moore, Thomas. *Original Self: Living with Paradox and Originality*. New York: Harper Collins, 2000.

———. *Dark Nights of the Soul: A Guide to Finding Your Way Through Life's Ordeals*. New York: Gotham Books, 2004.

Naranjo, Claudio. *Healing Civilization*. Oakland, CA: Rose Press, 2009.

Oupensky, P. D. *In Search of the Miraculous*. New York: Harcourt, Brace & World, 1949.

Palmer, Parker. *A Hidden Wholeness: The Journey Toward an Undivided Life*. San Francisco: Jossey-Bass, 2004.

———. *The Promise of Paradox: A Celebration of Contradictions in Christian Life*. San Francisco: Jossey-Bass, 2008.

Pearce, Joseph Chilton. *The Biology of Transcendence: A Blueprint of the Human Spirit*. Rochester, VT: Park Street Press, 2002.

Riso, Don Richard. *Personality Types: Using the Enneagram for Self-Discovery*. With Russ Hudson. Boston: Houghton Mifflin, 1996.

———. *Understanding the Enneagram: The Practical Guide to Personality Types*, rev. ed. Boston: Houghton Mifflin, 2000.

———. *The Wisdom of the Enneagram: The Complete Guide to Psychological and Spiritual Growth for the Nine Types*. New York: Bantam Books, 1999.

Rohr, Richard. *Falling Upward: A Spirituality for the Two Halves of Life*. San Francisco: Jossey-Bass, 2011.

Salzberg, Sharon. *Lovingkindness: The Revolutionary Art of Happiness*. Boston: Shambhala, 1997.

Shirley, John. *Gurdjieff: An Introduction to His Life and Ideas*. New York: Jeremy P. Tarcher, 2000.

411

Shimoff, Marci. *Happy for No Reason: 7 Steps to Being Happy from the Inside Out*. With Carol Kline. New York: Free Press, 2008.

Tarrant, John. *The Light Inside the Dark*. New York: Harper Perennial, 1998.

Tolle, Eckhart. *A New Earth: Awakening to Your Life's Purpose*. New York: Penguin, 2005.

———. *The Power of Now: A Guide to Spiritual Enlightenment*. Novato, CA: New World Library, 1997.

Zweig, Connie and Jeremiah Abrams. ed. *Meeting the Shadow: The Hidden Power of the Dark Side of Human Nature*. Los Angeles: Jeremy P. Tarcher, 1991.

Zweig, Connie, PhD and Steve Wolf, PhD. *Romancing the Shadow: Illuminating the Dark Side of the Soul*. New York: Ballantine Books, 1997.

Index

Page locators in *italics* indicate figures.

About Roxanne Howe-Murphy

Dr. Roxanne Howe-Murphy integrates her education and the depth of her own personal work during four decades of professional experience in diverse fields—including rehabilitation, higher education, consulting, and coaching—in her most recent book, *Deep Living: Transforming Your Relationship to Everything that Matters through the Enneagram.*

A pioneer and global expert in integrating the Enneagram with executive and life coaching, Roxanne authored the internationally acclaimed book, *Deep Coaching: Using the Enneagram as a Catalyst for Profound Change*, which has provided guidance to thousands of coaches around the world. She founded the Deep Coaching Institute (www.deepcoachinginstitute.com), which offers accredited training programs internationally to growth-oriented professionals wanting to embody the practical intricacies and the profound art, science, and spiritual consciousness of the Enneagram into their businesses' professional practices.

Roxanne's personal style, her breakthrough methods for sustainable transformation, and her deep honoring of the soul's journey have inspired laypeople and professionals around the world.

Through the Deep Living Institute (www.deeplivinginstitute.com), Roxanne and her associates now offer the same expert guidance and a compassionate, presence-based approach for true Self-deepening for the lay public through courses, workshops, retreats, and coaching.

After living near the ocean for most of her adult life, Roxanne and her husband followed their heart's dream and moved to beautiful Santa Fe, New Mexico. Amid the beauty of the high-desert landscape, they enjoy hiking in the mountains and soaking in a vast array of distinctive artistic, multicultural, and educational activities. Roxanne has recently become an enthusiastic student of the cello.

For More Information

The Deep Living Institute

At home in yourself. At ease in the world.

www.DeepLivingInstitute.com

The Deep Coaching Institute

Where the profound and the practical meet.

www.DeepCoachingInstitute.com

CPSIA information can be obtained
at www.ICGtesting.com
Printed in the USA
FSOW03n2326260415
6741FS